Cisco OSPF Command and Configuration Handbook

William R. Parkhurst, Ph.D., CCIE #2969

Cisco Press
201 W 103rd Street
Indianapolis, IN 46290 USA

Cisco OSPF Command and Configuration Handbook

William R. Parkhurst

Published by:
Cisco Press
201 West 103rd Street
Indianapolis, IN 46290 USA

Printed in the United States of America 1 2 3 4 5 6 7 8 9 0

First Printing April 2002

Library of Congress Cataloging-in-Publication Number: 2001094058

ISBN: 1-58705-071-4

Warning and Disclaimer

This book is designed to provide information about Cisco IOS Software OSPF commands. Every effort has been made to make this book as complete and as accurate as possible, but no warranty or fitness is implied.

The information is provided on an "as is" basis. The authors, Cisco Press, and Cisco Systems, Inc., shall have neither liability nor responsibility to any person or entity with respect to any loss or damages arising from the information contained in this book or from the use of the discs or programs that may accompany it.

The opinions expressed in this book belong to the author and are not necessarily those of Cisco Systems, Inc.

Trademark Acknowledgments

All terms mentioned in this book that are known to be trademarks or service marks have been appropriately capitalized. Cisco Press or Cisco Systems, Inc., cannot attest to the accuracy of this information. Use of a term in this book should not be regarded as affecting the validity of any trademark or service mark.

Feedback Information

At Cisco Press, our goal is to create in-depth technical books of the highest quality and value. Each book is crafted with care and precision, undergoing rigorous development that involves the unique expertise of members from the professional technical community.

Readers' feedback is a natural continuation of this process. If you have any comments regarding how we could improve the quality of this book, or otherwise alter it to better suit your needs, you can contact us through e-mail at feedback@ciscopress.com. Please make sure to include the book title and ISBN in your message.

We greatly appreciate your assistance.

Publisher	**John Wait**
Editor-In-Chief	**John Kane**
Cisco Systems Program Manager	**Michael Hackert**
Managing Editor	**Patrick Kanouse**
Development Editor	**Christopher Cleveland**
Project Editor	**Marc Fowler**
Copy Editor	**Doug Lloyd**
Technical Editors	**Mike Bass**
	Brian Morgan
	Bill Wagner
	Robert White
Team Coordinator	**Tammi Ross**
Book Designer	**Gina Rexrode**
Cover Designer	**Louisa Klucznik**
Production Team	**Argosy**
Indexer	**Tim Wright**

Corporate Headquarters
Cisco Systems, Inc.
170 West Tasman Drive
San Jose, CA 95134-1706
USA
http://www.cisco.com
Tel: 408 526-4000
800 553-NETS (6387)
Fax: 408 526-4100

European Headquarters
Cisco Systems Europe
11 Rue Camille Desmoulins
92782 Issy-les-Moulineaux
Cedex 9
France
http://www-europe.cisco.com
Tel: 33 1 58 04 60 00
Fax: 33 1 58 04 61 00

Americas Headquarters
Cisco Systems, Inc.
170 West Tasman Drive
San Jose, CA 95134-1706
USA
http://www.cisco.com
Tel: 408 526-7660
Fax: 408 527-0883

Asia Pacific Headquarters
Cisco Systems Australia, Pty., Ltd
Level 17, 99 Walker Street
North Sydney
NSW 2059 Australia
http://www.cisco.com
Tel: +61 2 8448 7100
Fax: +61 2 9957 4350

Cisco Systems has more than 200 offices in the following countries. Addresses, phone numbers, and fax numbers are listed on the Cisco Web site at www.cisco.com/go/offices

Argentina • Australia • Austria • Belgium • Brazil • Bulgaria • Canada • Chile • China • Colombia • Costa Rica • Croatia • Czech Republic • Denmark • Dubai, UAE • Finland • France • Germany • Greece • Hong Kong • Hungary • India • Indonesia • Ireland • Israel • Italy • Japan • Korea • Luxembourg • Malaysia • Mexico • The Netherlands • New Zealand • Norway • Peru • Philippines • Poland • Portugal • Puerto Rico • Romania • Russia • Saudi Arabia • Scotland • Singapore • Slovakia • Slovenia • South Africa • Spain Sweden • Switzerland • Taiwan • Thailand • Turkey • Ukraine • United Kingdom • United States • Venezuela • Vietnam • Zimbabwe

About the Author

William R. Parkhurst, Ph.D., CCIE #2969, is a program manager with the CCIE group at Cisco Systems. Bill is responsible for the CCIE Communications and Services exams. Prior to joining the CCIE team, Bill was a Consulting Systems Engineer supporting Sprint. Bill first became associated with Cisco Systems while he was a Professor of Electrical and Computer Engineering at Wichita State University (WSU). In conjunction with Cisco Systems, WSU established the first CCIE Preparation Laboratory.

About the Technical Reviewers

Mike Bass has worked for 22 years in computer networking, the last 17 years at Sprint. Mike's networking experience began with mini-computer and mainframe networks and now consists of planning and design for distributed and peer-to-peer systems supporting voice, video, and data services. Mike is currently responsible for the introduction of new networking technologies to support Sprint internal associates.

Brian Morgan, CCIE #4865, CCSI, is the Director of Data Network Engineering at Allegiance Telecom, Inc. He's been in the networking industry for over 12 years. Prior to going to Allegiance, Brian was an instructor/consultant teaching ICND, BSCN, BSCI, CATM, CVOICE, and BCRAN. Brian is a co-author of the *Cisco Press Remote Access Exam Certification Guide* and technical editor of numerous other Cisco Press titles.

Bill Wagner works as a Cisco Certified System Instructor for Mentor Technologies. He has 23 years of computer programming and data communications experience. He has worked for corporations and companies such as Independent Computer Consultants, Numerax, Mc Graw-Hill/Numerax, and Standard and Poor. His teaching experience started with the Chubb Institute, Protocol Interface Inc, Geotrain, Mentor Technologies. He is currently teaching at Skyline Computers Corporation.

Robert L. White is an IP Network Design Engineer with Sprint's Long Distance Division internal data network. Robert's design expertise focuses on routing protocols, external gateway connectivity, and IP address administration on a large multi-protocol network.

Dedications

To my family and friends. In the final analysis, what else is there?

Acknowledgments

I would like to acknowledge the superb effort of all those involved with the development of this handbook. The reviewers of this book, Mike Bass, Brian Morgan, Bill Wagner, and Robert White, not only found the errors in the book but also contributed suggestions on how to improve the content and clarity of this handbook. Their efforts are greatly appreciated. I would also like to thank John Kane and Chris Cleveland of Cisco Press for their guidance and help in bringing this project to a successful completion. Finally, I want to thank my wife, Debbie, for her encouragement and support during the many evenings and weekends while I was spending more time with routers than with her. She was also the initial reviewer of this book and found misspellings, grammatical errors, and things that just didn't make sense. Once again she made me look good in the eyes of my editor.

Contents at a Glance

Contents

Introduction

I have been involved with the world of networking from many directions. My experiences in education, network consulting, service provider support, and certification have shown me that there is a common thread that frustrates people in all of these arenas. That common thread is documentation. There are many factors that cause documentation to be frustrating but the most common are amount, clarity, and completeness. The amount of documentation available, especially in regards to OSPF, can be overwhelming. For a person who is beginning to learn OSPF, the question is, "Where do I begin?" There are very good books, RFCs, white papers, and command references available, but it is difficult to know where to start. The clarity of documentation depends on your personal situation. For a seasoned OSPF designer, the documentation may be clear and concise. To an individual preparing for a professional certification such as the CCIE, the same documentation may be confusing. Even if the documentation is clear it is sometimes not complete. You may understand the words but be confused by the application. The purpose of this book is to provide an OSPF handbook that is clear, concise, and complete. This book is not meant to be read from cover to cover. The way you use this book will depend on your objectives. If you are preparing for the CCIE written and lab exams, this book can be used as a laboratory guide to learn the purpose and proper use of every OSPF command. If you are a network designer then this book can be used as a ready reference for any OSPF command. In order to satisfy these varying audiences the structure of this book is reasonably simple. Each OSPF command is illustrated using the following structure:

- Listing of the command structure and syntax
- Syntax description for the command with an explanation of all command parameters
- The purpose of the command and the situation where the command is used
- The first release of the IOS in which the command appeared
- One or more configuration examples to demonstrate the proper use of the command
- Procedures and examples to verify that the command is working properly
- How to troubleshoot the command when things are not working as intended

The example scenarios that demonstrate the proper use of the OSPF commands can be implemented on a minimum number of routers. This will allow you to learn each command without requiring an extensive and expensive lab configuration. The scenarios are presented so that the purpose and use of each command can be presented without clouding the issue. Some of the examples lead you into common non-working situations in order to reinforce the understanding of the operation of the particular OSPF command.

My hope is that this handbook will help you prepare for the CCIE exam, allow you to properly use OSPF in your network, or both.

Recommended Reading

This book assumes that you have a working knowledge of OSPF theory of operation and OSPF terminology. The following references can be used to supplement your knowledge of OSPF.

OSPF Network Design Solutions, Thomas M. Thomas II, Cisco Press (second edition will be released December 2002)

Routing TCP/IP Volume 1, Jeff Doyle, Cisco Press

Icons Used in This Book

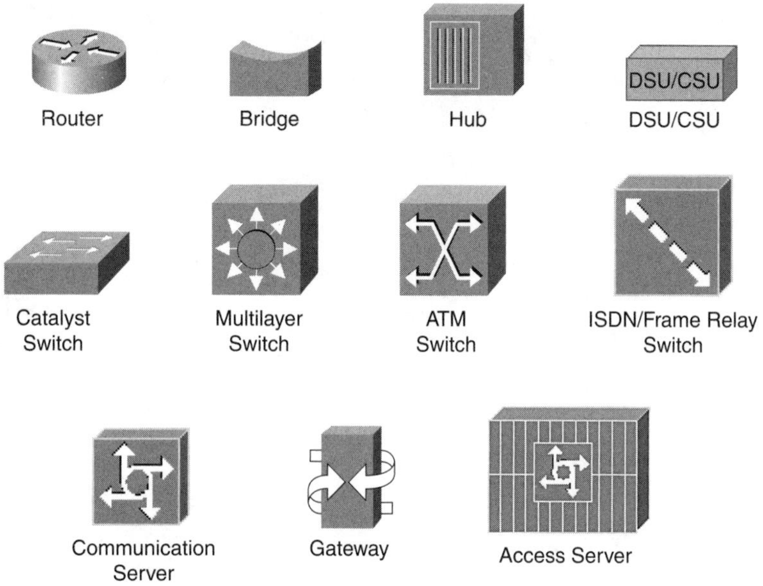

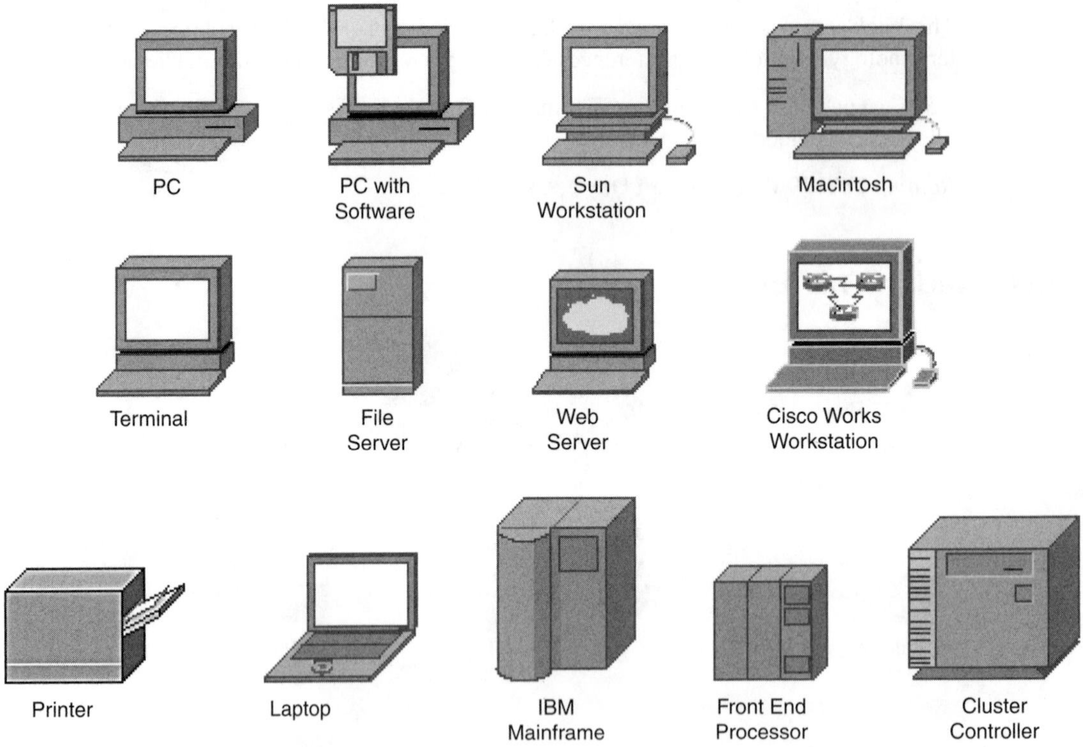
PC
PC with Software
Sun Workstation
Macintosh
Terminal
File Server
Web Server
Cisco Works Workstation
Printer
Laptop
IBM Mainframe
Front End Processor
Cluster Controller

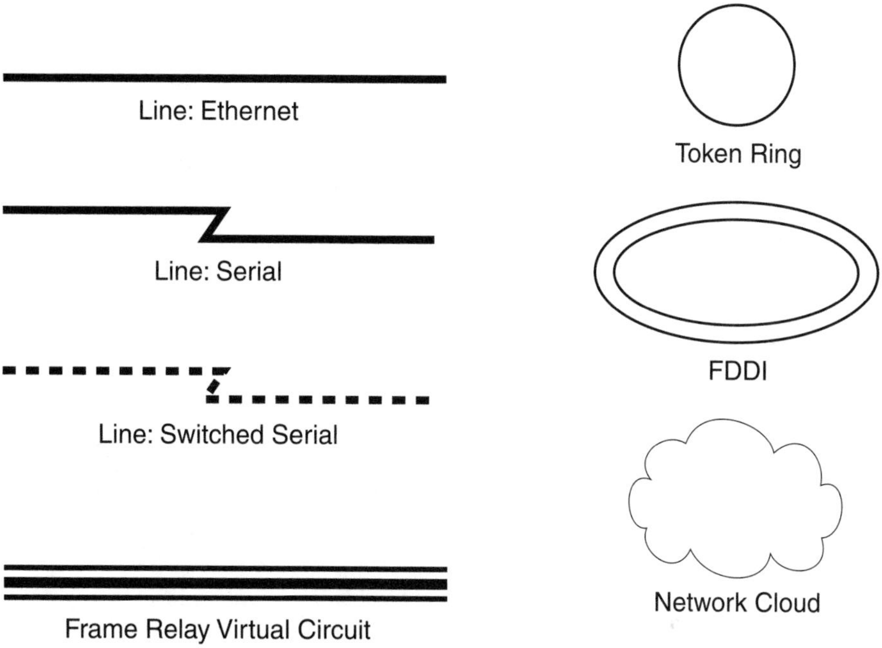

Command Syntax Conventions

The conventions used to present command syntax in this book are the same conventions used in the Cisco IOS Software Command Reference. The Command Reference describes these conventions as follows:

- Vertical bars (|) separate alternative, mutually exclusive elements.
- Square brackets [ ] indicate optional elements.
- Braces { } indicate a required choice.
- Braces within brackets [{ }] indicate a required choice within an optional element.
- **Boldface** indicates commands and keywords that are entered literally as shown. In actual configuration examples and output (not general command syntax), boldface indicates commands that are manually input by the user (such as a **show** command).
- *Italics* indicate arguments for which you supply actual values.

CHAPTER 1

OSPF Process Configuration Commands

1-1: router ospf *process-id*

Syntax Description:

- *process-id*—The OSPF process ID. The range of values is 1 to 65535.

Purpose: Used to enable one or more OSPF processes on a router. The process ID is only significant on the local router. Use the **no** form of the command to remove an OSPF process.

Initial IOS Software Release: 10.0

Configuration Example: Enabling an OSPF Process

Before you enable an OSPF process, there must be at least one active interface with an assigned IP address. OSPF uses the highest IP address assigned to an active interface as the OSPF Router ID. If loopback interfaces have been configured, then OSPF will use the highest loopback address as the Router ID even if the highest loopback IP address is smaller than the IP address of any active physical interface. Using a loopback interface on an OSPF router is recommended because a loopback interface is never down. A loopback interface will produce a stable OSPF router ID. The network in Figure 1-1 demonstrates that the OSPF Router ID (RID) is the highest IP address assigned to an active physical interface. If a loopback interface is used, then OSPF will use the loopback IP address as the OSPF RID.

Figure 1-1 *OSPF Router ID Selection*

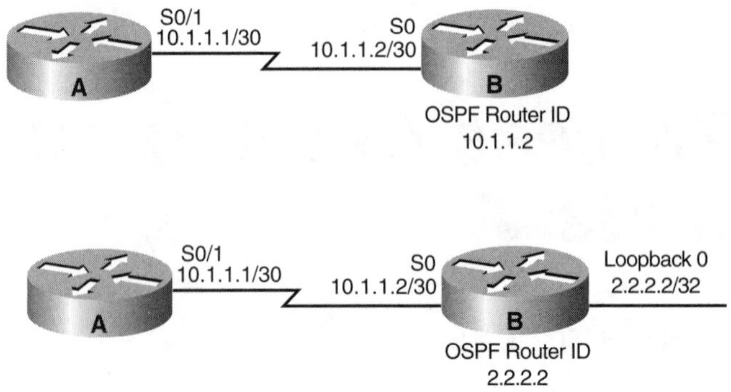

Start by removing all IP addresses and loopback interfaces from Router B. Now, attempt to configure an OSPF process on Router B.

```
rtrB#configure terminal
Enter configuration commands, one per line.  End with CNTL/Z.
rtrB(config)#router ospf 1
OSPF: Could not allocate router id
```

OSPF cannot be enabled on Router B because OSPF needs a RID and there are no IP addresses assigned on Router B. Configure the serial interfaces on Routers A and B and then configure an OSPF process on Router B.

```
Router A
interface Serial0/1
 bandwidth 64
 ip address 10.1.1.1 255.255.255.252
 clockrate 64000
```

```
Router B
interface Serial0
 ip address 10.1.1.2 255.255.255.252
 bandwidth 64

router ospf 1
```

The configuration of the OSPF process on Router B was successful. Examine the OSPF RID on Router B using the **show ip ospf** command.

```
rtrB#show ip ospf
 Routing Process "ospf 1" with ID 10.1.1.2
 Supports only single TOS(TOS0) routes
 SPF schedule delay 5 secs, Hold time between two SPFs 10 secs
```

```
 Number of DCbitless external LSA 0
 Number of DoNotAge external LSA 0
 Number of areas in this router is 0. 0 normal 0 stub 0 nssa
```

The only active interface on Router B is Serial0, so OSPF will use the IP address assigned to Serial0 for the router ID. Add a loopback interface to Router B and then re-examine the OSPF RID on Router B.

```
Router B
interface Loopback0
 ip address 2.2.2.2 255.255.255.255
rtrB#show ip ospf
 Routing Process "ospf 1" with ID 10.1.1.2
 Supports only single TOS(TOS0) routes
 SPF schedule delay 5 secs, Hold time between two SPFs 10 secs
 Number of DCbitless external LSA 0
 Number of DoNotAge external LSA 0
 Number of areas in this router is 0. 0 normal 0 stub 0 nssa
```

The OSPF RID has not changed. This is a stability feature of OSPF. The router ID will not change unless the OSPF process is restarted or if the interface used for the RID goes down. Shut down the serial interface on Router B, re-enable the serial interface on Router B, and examine the effect on the OSPF RID.

Verification

Verify that the OSPF RID on Router B is equal to the IP address assigned to the loopback interface.

```
rtrB#show ip ospf
 Routing Process "ospf 1" with ID 2.2.2.2
 Supports only single TOS(TOS0) routes
 SPF schedule delay 5 secs, Hold time between two SPFs 10 secs
 Number of DCbitless external LSA 0
 Number of DoNotAge external LSA 0
 Number of areas in this router is 0. 0 normal 0 stub 0 nssa
```

Troubleshooting

Verify that a loopback interface has been configured and an IP address assigned before configuring OSPF. A loopback interface is not mandatory, but it will add stability to your OSPF network.

1-2: router ospf *process-id* vrf *name*

Syntax Description:

- *process-id*—The OSPF process ID. The range of values is 1 to 65535.
- *name*—VPN Routing/Forwarding Instance (VRF) name. Routes learned by the OSPF process will be placed in the VRF instead of the global IP routing table.

Purpose: In a Multiprotocol Label Switching (MPLS) virtual private network (VPN) environment, this form of the OSPF router command is used to transfer VPN customer routes between the service provider and the VPN customer. In an MPLS/VPN environment, there are three types of routers, as shown in Figure 1-2.

- Provider (P) routers
- Customer edge (CE) routers
- Provider edge (PE) routers

Figure 1-2 *General MPLS/VPN Architecture*

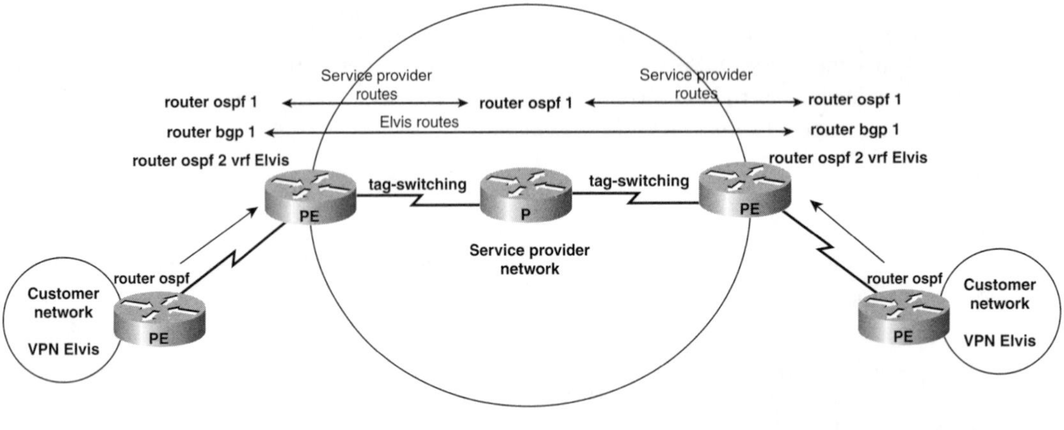

P routers are routers in the service provider network that have no connections to CE routers. PE routers are the interface routers between the customer and the service provider. Tag or label switching and an interior gateway protocol (IGP), such as OSPF, are run between P and PE routers to exchange internal service provider routes. These routes are installed in the global IP routing table on the P and PE routers. The PE routers have additional IP routing tables, one for each attached VPN customer. These routing tables are called *VRF*

instances. When OSPF is configured using the **vrf** option, routes learned from the CE will be placed into the appropriate VRF on the PE router. These VPN routes will be exchanged between PE routers via multiprotocol IBGP. For a detailed discussion of MPLS and MPLS VPNs, see the Cisco Press book *MPLS and VPN Architectures* by Ivan Pepelnjak and Jim Guichard.

Initial IOS Software Release: 12.0

CHAPTER 2

OSPF Area Commands

2-1: area *area-id* authentication

NOTE This command requires the following additional commands:

For a physical interface: **ip ospf authentication-key** *password* (see Section 19-2)

For a virtual link if authentication is used in area 0: **area** *transit-area* **virtual-link** *router-id* **authentication-key** *password* (see Section 2-17)

Syntax Description:

- *area-id*—OSPF area ID. This value can be entered as a decimal number in the range of 0 to 4,294,967,295 or in IP address format in the range 0.0.0.0 to 255.255.255.255. This command will enable simple password authentication in the indicated OSPF area. By default, authentication is not enabled.
- *transit-area*—The OSPF area across which the virtual link is configured.
- *password*—Clear-text password to be used for authentication in the selected area on the selected interface or virtual link. The password is an alphanumeric string from 1 to 8 characters.
- *router-id*—OSPF router ID of the router at the remote end of the virtual link.

Purpose: To enable simple clear-text password authentication in an OSPF area. OSPF simple authentication requires the use of the router configuration command to enable authentication in an area and the interface or virtual-link command for password configuration. Because this router configuration command enables authentication in an area, you must configure every interface in the area for authentication if using Cisco IOS Software Release 11.X or earlier. In Cisco IOS Software Release 12.X, the authentication used on an interface can be different than the authentication enabled for an area. When using Cisco IOS Software Release 12.X, the authentication method used on different interfaces in the same area does not need to be the same. You can remove authentication from selected interfaces using the interface command **ip ospf authentication null** (see Section 19-1). The password does not need to be the same on every interface in the area, but both ends of a common link must use the same password. Authentication is enabled by area (Cisco IOS Software Release 11.X and earlier), so it is possible to employ authentication in one area without using authentication in other areas. The clear-text password is not encrypted, so it will be possible for someone to intercept OSPF protocol packets and compromise the password.

Initial Cisco IOS Software Release: 10.0

Configuration Example: Simple Password Authentication

For the network in Figure 2-1, start by configuring OSPF without authentication in Area 0.

Figure 2-1 *Network Used to Demonstrate OSPF Authentication Configuration and Troubleshooting*

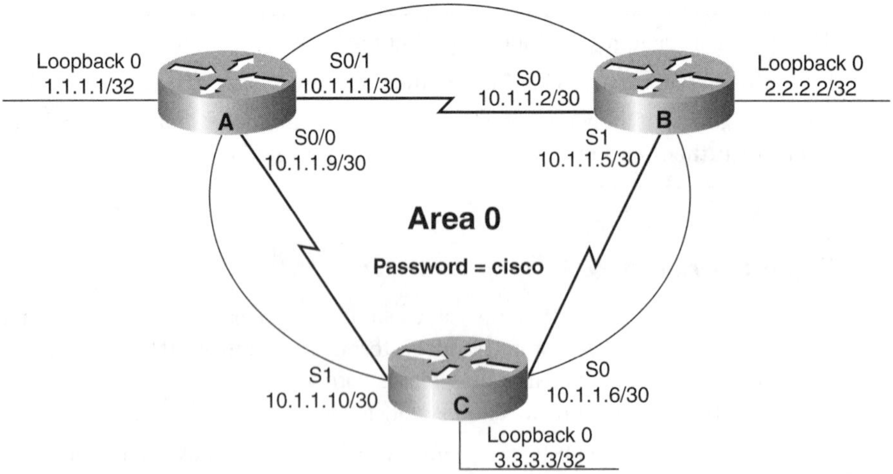


```
Router A
interface Loopback0
 ip address 1.1.1.1 255.255.255.255
!
interface Serial0/0
 ip address 10.1.1.9 255.255.255.252
!
interface Serial0/1
 ip address 10.1.1.1 255.255.255.252
 clock rate 64000
!
router ospf 1
 network 10.1.1.0 0.0.0.15 area 0
```

```
Router B
interface Loopback0
```

```
 ip address 2.2.2.2 255.255.255.255
!
interface Serial0
 ip address 10.1.1.2 255.255.255.252
!
interface Serial1
 ip address 10.1.1.5 255.255.255.252
 clock rate 64000
!
router ospf 1
 network 10.1.1.0 0.0.0.15 area 0
```

```
Router C
interface Loopback0
 ip address 3.3.3.3 255.255.255.255
!
interface Serial0
 ip address 10.1.1.6 255.255.255.252
!
interface Serial1
 ip address 10.1.1.10 255.255.255.252
 clock rate 64000
!
router ospf 1
 network 10.1.1.0 0.0.0.15 area 0
```

Verify the OSPF configuration on Routers A, B, and C by displaying the state of each router's OSPF neighbors.

```
rtrA#show ip ospf neighbor

Neighbor ID     Pri   State           Dead Time   Address         Interface
3.3.3.3           1   FULL/  -        00:00:38    10.1.1.10       Serial0/0
2.2.2.2           1   FULL/  -        00:00:37    10.1.1.2        Serial0/1
```

```
rtrB#show ip ospf neighbor

Neighbor ID     Pri   State           Dead Time   Address         Interface
1.1.1.1           1   FULL/  -        00:00:35    10.1.1.1        Serial0
3.3.3.3           1   FULL/  -        00:00:30    10.1.1.6        Serial1
```

```
rtrC#show ip ospf neighbor

Neighbor ID     Pri   State           Dead Time   Address         Interface
2.2.2.2           1   FULL/  -        00:00:30    10.1.1.5        Serial0
1.1.1.1           1   FULL/  -        00:00:37    10.1.1.9        Serial1
```

Verify that OSPF is not using authentication.

```
rtrA#show ip ospf
 Routing Process "ospf 1" with ID 1.1.1.1
 Supports only single TOS(TOS0) routes
 SPF schedule delay 5 secs, Hold time between two SPFs 10 secs
 Minimum LSA interval 5 secs. Minimum LSA arrival 1 secs
 Number of external LSA 0. Checksum Sum 0x0
 Number of DCbitless external LSA 0
 Number of DoNotAge external LSA 0
 Number of areas in this router is 1. 1 normal 0 stub 0 nssa
    Area BACKBONE(0)
        Number of interfaces in this area is 2
        Area has no authentication
        SPF algorithm executed 6 times
        Area ranges are
        Number of LSA 3. Checksum Sum 0x25F8D
        Number of DCbitless LSA 0
        Number of indication LSA 0
        Number of DoNotAge LSA 0
```

Modify the configurations on Routers A, B, and C by adding simple password authentication to Area 0. For this example, you will use the clear-text password "cisco".

```
Router A
interface Loopback0
 ip address 1.1.1.1 255.255.255.255
!
interface Serial0/0
 ip address 10.1.1.9 255.255.255.252
 ip ospf authentication-key cisco
!
interface Serial0/1
 ip address 10.1.1.1 255.255.255.252
 ip ospf authentication-key cisco
 clock rate 64000
!
router ospf 1
 area 0 authentication
 network 10.1.1.0 0.0.0.15 area 0
```

```
Router B
interface Loopback0
 ip address 2.2.2.2 255.255.255.255
!
interface Serial0
 ip address 10.1.1.2 255.255.255.252
 ip ospf authentication-key cisco
!
```

```
interface Serial1
 ip address 10.1.1.5 255.255.255.252
 ip ospf authentication-key cisco
 clock rate 64000
!
router ospf 1
 area 0 authentication
 network 10.1.1.0 0.0.0.15 area 0
```

```
Router C
interface Loopback0
 ip address 3.3.3.3 255.255.255.255
!
interface Serial0
 ip address 10.1.1.6 255.255.255.252
 ip ospf authentication-key cisco
!
interface Serial1
 ip address 10.1.1.10 255.255.255.252
 ip ospf authentication-key cisco
 clock rate 64000
!
router ospf 1
 area 0 authentication
 network 10.1.1.0 0.0.0.15 area 0
```

Verification

Verify that the OSPF neighbor relationships are still active.

```
rtrA#show ip ospf neighbor

Neighbor ID     Pri   State           Dead Time   Address         Interface
3.3.3.3           1   FULL/  -        00:00:31    10.1.1.10       Serial0/0
2.2.2.2           1   FULL/  -        00:00:30    10.1.1.2        Serial0/1
```

```
rtrB#show ip ospf neighbor

Neighbor ID     Pri   State           Dead Time   Address         Interface
1.1.1.1           1   FULL/  -        00:00:38    10.1.1.1        Serial0
3.3.3.3           1   FULL/  -        00:00:33    10.1.1.6        Serial1
```

```
rtrC#show ip ospf neighbor

Neighbor ID     Pri   State           Dead Time   Address         Interface
2.2.2.2           1   FULL/  -        00:00:33    10.1.1.5        Serial0
1.1.1.1           1   FULL/  -        00:00:30    10.1.1.9        Serial1
```

Verify that simple authentication is enabled for Area 0.

```
rtrA#show ip ospf
 Routing Process "ospf 1" with ID 1.1.1.1
 Supports only single TOS(TOS0) routes
 SPF schedule delay 5 secs, Hold time between two SPFs 10 secs
 Minimum LSA interval 5 secs. Minimum LSA arrival 1 secs
 Number of external LSA 0. Checksum Sum 0x0
 Number of DCbitless external LSA 0
 Number of DoNotAge external LSA 0
 Number of areas in this router is 1. 1 normal 0 stub 0 nssa
    Area BACKBONE(0)
        Number of interfaces in this area is 2
        Area has simple password authentication
        SPF algorithm executed 9 times
        Area ranges are
        Number of LSA 3. Checksum Sum 0x24F95
        Number of DCbitless LSA 0
        Number of indication LSA 0
        Number of DoNotAge LSA 0
```

The password used can be seen by anyone looking at your configuration. For added security, the password in the configuration can be encrypted using the global configuration command **service password-encryption**, as shown in the following configuration.

```
Router A
service password-encryption
```

Listing the configuration will show that the password has been encrypted. Although the password is encrypted in the configuration, it will still be sent in clear text by OSPF.

```
rtrA#show running-config
Building configuration...

Current configuration:
!
version 12.0
service timestamps debug uptime
service timestamps log uptime
service password-encryption
!
hostname rtrA
!
ip subnet-zero
!
interface Loopback0
 ip address 1.1.1.1 255.255.255.255
 no ip directed-broadcast
```

```
!
interface Serial0/0
 ip address 10.1.1.9 255.255.255.252
 no ip directed-broadcast
 ip ospf authentication-key 7 121A0C041104
 no ip mroute-cache
!
interface Serial0/1
 ip address 10.1.1.1 255.255.255.252
 no ip directed-broadcast
 ip ospf authentication-key 7 02050D480809
 clockrate 64000
```

Troubleshooting

Step 1 Before enabling authentication in an OSPF area, verify that there is a neighbor relationship among all OSPF routers by using the **show ip ospf neighbor** command.

Step 2 Verify that authentication has been enabled for every OSPF router with an interface in the area where authentication is being deployed.

Step 3 Verify that every interface in an OSPF area that is using authentication is configured with the proper password.

Step 4 If any OSPF neighbor relationships disappear after configuring authentication, then debugging can be used to determine the problem. For example, change the password on Router A, Interface Serial 0/0, to bosco, as shown here.

```
Router A
interface Serial0/0
 ip address 10.1.1.9 255.255.255.252
 ip ospf authentication-key bosco
```

List the OSPF neighbors for Router A.

```
rtrA#show ip ospf neighbor

Neighbor ID     Pri   State           Dead Time   Address         Interface
2.2.2.2           1   FULL/  -        00:00:36    10.1.1.2        Serial0/1
```

Router A has lost Router C as a neighbor. Enable debugging on Router A to see if the problem can be determined.

```
rtrA#debug ip ospf events
OSPF events debugging is on
rtrA#
03:41:09: OSPF: Rcv hello from 2.2.2.2 area 0 from Serial0/1 10.1.1.2
03:41:09: OSPF: End of hello processing
03:41:09: OSPF: Rcv pkt from 10.1.1.10, Serial0/0 : Mismatch Authentication Key
- Clear Text
```

Be careful when configuring passwords. A space is a valid character, so if you use the password **cisco<space>** then there will be a password mismatch, but you won't be able to tell by looking at the configuration.

Change the password on Router A, serial 0/0, back to cisco and remove the OSPF router configuration command **area 0 authentication**.

```
Router A
interface Serial0/0
 ip address 10.1.1.9 255.255.255.252
 ip ospf authentication-key cisco
!
router ospf 1
 no area 0 authentication
```

Router A should drop both OSPF neighbors.

```
rtrA#show ip ospf neighbor
Neighbor ID     Pri   State           Dead Time   Address         Interface
3.3.3.3           1   INIT/  -        00:00:38    10.1.1.10       Serial0/0
2.2.2.2           1   INIT/  -        00:00:39    10.1.1.2        Serial0/1
```

Now debug the OSPF traffic on Router B or C to determine the problem.

```
rtrB#debug ip ospf events
OSPF events debugging is on
rtrB#
03:55:35: OSPF: Rcv pkt from 10.1.1.1, Serial0 : Mismatch Authentication type. I
nput packet specified type 0, we use type 1
03:55:40: OSPF: Rcv hello from 3.3.3.3 area 0 from Serial1 10.1.1.6
03:55:40: OSPF: End of hello processing
```

Routers B and C are using type 1 authentication (simple password) and Router A is using type 0 authentication (none).

2-2: area *area-id* authentication message-digest

NOTE This command requires the following additional commands:

For a physical interface: **ip ospf message-digest-key** *key-id* **md5** *password* (see Section 19-9)

For a virtual link if authentication is used in Area 0: **area** *transit-area* **virtual-link** *router-id* **message-digest-key** *key-id* **md5** *password* (see Section 2-20)

Syntax Description:

- *area-id*—OSPF area ID. This value can be entered as a decimal number in the range of 0 to 4,294,967,295 or in IP address format in the range 0.0.0.0 to 255.255.255.255. This command will enable simple password authentication in the indicated OSPF area. By default, authentication is not enabled.
- *key-id*—Key used to encrypt a password. The range of values is 1 to 255. Both ends of a link must use the same key and password.
- *password*—Password to be used for authentication in the selected area on the selected interface or virtual link. The password is an alphanumeric string from 1 to 8 characters.
- *transit-area*—The OSPF area across which the virtual link is configured.
- *router-id*—OSPF router ID of the router at the remote end of the virtual link.

Purpose: To enable MD5 password authentication in an OSPF area. OSPF MD5 authentication requires the use of the router configuration command to enable authentication in an area and the interface or virtual link command for key and password configuration. Since this router configuration command enables authentication in an area, every interface in the area must be configured with an authentication key and password if using Cisco IOS Software Release 11.X or earlier. In Cisco IOS Software Release 12.X, the authentication used on an interface can be different from the authentication enabled for an area. When using Cisco IOS Software Release 12.X, the authentication method used on different interfaces in the same area does not need to be the same. Authentication can be turned off on selected interfaces using the command **ip ospf authentication null** (see Section 19-1). The key and password do not need to be the same on every interface, but both ends of a common link need to use the same key and password. Authentication is enabled by area (Cisco IOS Software Release 11.X and earlier) so it is possible to employ authentication in one area without using authentication in other areas. The password is encrypted, so it is extremely difficult for someone to intercept OSPF protocol packets and compromise the password.

Initial Cisco IOS Software Release: 11.0

Configuration Example 1: MD5 Password Authentication

For the network in Figure 2-2, initially configure OSPF without authentication in Area 0.

Figure 2-2 *Network Used to Demonstrate OSPF MD5 Authentication Configuration and Troubleshooting*

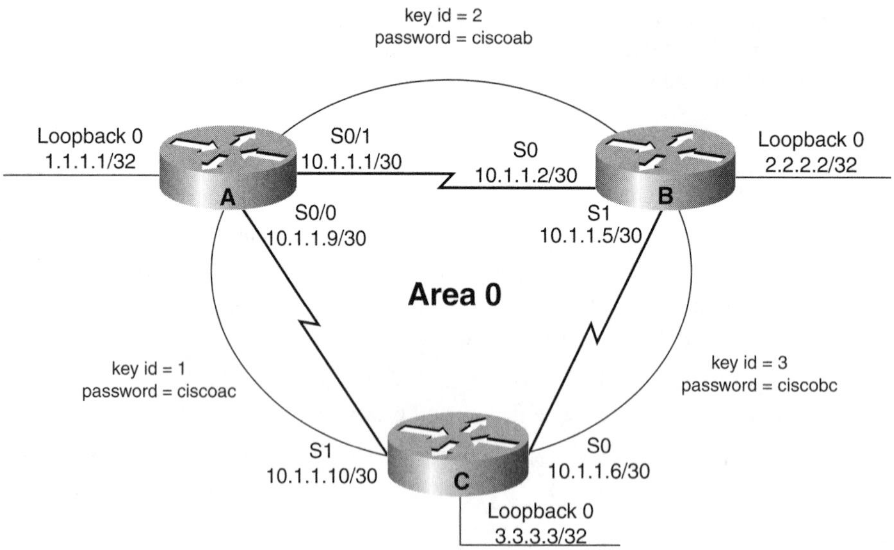


```
Router A
interface Loopback0
 ip address 1.1.1.1 255.255.255.255
!
interface Serial0/0
 ip address 10.1.1.9 255.255.255.252
!
interface Serial0/1
 ip address 10.1.1.1 255.255.255.252
 clock rate 64000
!
router ospf 1
 network 10.1.1.0 0.0.0.15 area 0
```

```
Router B
interface Loopback0
```

```
 ip address 2.2.2.2 255.255.255.255
!
interface Serial0
 ip address 10.1.1.2 255.255.255.252
!
interface Serial1
 ip address 10.1.1.5 255.255.255.252
 clock rate 64000
!
router ospf 1
 network 10.1.1.0 0.0.0.15 area 0
```

```
Router C
interface Loopback0
 ip address 3.3.3.3 255.255.255.255
!
interface Serial0
 ip address 10.1.1.6 255.255.255.252
!
interface Serial1
 ip address 10.1.1.10 255.255.255.252
 clock rate 64000
!
router ospf 1
 network 10.1.1.0 0.0.0.15 area 0
```

Verify the OSPF configuration on Routers A, B, and C by displaying the state of each router's OSPF neighbors.

```
rtrA#show ip ospf neighbor

Neighbor ID     Pri   State           Dead Time   Address         Interface
3.3.3.3           1   FULL/  -        00:00:38    10.1.1.10       Serial0/0
2.2.2.2           1   FULL/  -        00:00:37    10.1.1.2        Serial0/1
```

```
rtrB#show ip ospf neighbor

Neighbor ID     Pri   State           Dead Time   Address         Interface
1.1.1.1           1   FULL/  -        00:00:35    10.1.1.1        Serial0
3.3.3.3           1   FULL/  -        00:00:30    10.1.1.6        Serial1
```

```
rtrC#show ip ospf neighbor

Neighbor ID     Pri   State           Dead Time   Address         Interface
2.2.2.2           1   FULL/  -        00:00:30    10.1.1.5        Serial0
1.1.1.1           1   FULL/  -        00:00:37    10.1.1.9        Serial1
```

Verify that OSPF is not using authentication.

```
rtrA#show ip ospf
 Routing Process "ospf 1" with ID 1.1.1.1
 Supports only single TOS(TOS0) routes
 SPF schedule delay 5 secs, Hold time between two SPFs 10 secs
 Minimum LSA interval 5 secs. Minimum LSA arrival 1 secs
 Number of external LSA 0. Checksum Sum 0x0
 Number of DCbitless external LSA 0
 Number of DoNotAge external LSA 0
 Number of areas in this router is 1. 1 normal 0 stub 0 nssa
    Area BACKBONE(0)
        Number of interfaces in this area is 2
        Area has no authentication
        SPF algorithm executed 6 times
        Area ranges are
        Number of LSA 3. Checksum Sum 0x25F8D
        Number of DCbitless LSA 0
        Number of indication LSA 0
        Number of DoNotAge LSA 0
```

Modify the configurations on Routers A, B, and C by adding MD5 password authentication to area 0. For this example, use the passwords ciscoab, ciscobc, and ciscoac to demonstrate that multiple passwords can be used in an area.

```
Router A
interface Loopback0
 ip address 1.1.1.1 255.255.255.255
!
interface Serial0/0
 ip address 10.1.1.9 255.255.255.252
 ip ospf message-digest-key 1 md5 ciscoac
!
interface Serial0/1
 ip address 10.1.1.1 255.255.255.252
 ip ospf message-digest-key 2 ciscoab
 clock rate 64000
!
router ospf 1
 area 0 authentication message-digest
 network 10.1.1.0 0.0.0.15 area 0
```

```
Router B
interface Loopback0
 ip address 2.2.2.2 255.255.255.255
!
interface Serial0
 ip address 10.1.1.2 255.255.255.252
 ip ospf message-digest-key 2 md5 ciscoab
```

```
!
interface Serial1
 ip address 10.1.1.5 255.255.255.252
 ip ospf message-digest-key 3 md5 ciscobc
 clock rate 64000
!
router ospf 1
 area 0 authentication message-digest
 network 10.1.1.0 0.0.0.15 area 0
```

```
Router C
interface Loopback0
 ip address 3.3.3.3 255.255.255.255
!
interface Serial0
 ip address 10.1.1.6 255.255.255.252
 ip ospf message-digest-key 3 ciscobc
!
interface Serial1
 ip address 10.1.1.10 255.255.255.252
 ip ospf message-digest-key 1 md5 ciscoac
clock rate 64000
!
router ospf 1
 area 0 authentication message-digest
 network 10.1.1.0 0.0.0.15 area 0
```

Verification

Verify that the OSPF neighbor relationships are still active.

```
rtrA#show ip ospf neighbor

Neighbor ID     Pri   State          Dead Time   Address        Interface
3.3.3.3           1   FULL/  -       00:00:31    10.1.1.10      Serial0/0
2.2.2.2           1   FULL/  -       00:00:30    10.1.1.2       Serial0/1
```

```
rtrB#show ip ospf neighbor

Neighbor ID     Pri   State          Dead Time   Address        Interface
1.1.1.1           1   FULL/  -       00:00:38    10.1.1.1       Serial0
3.3.3.3           1   FULL/  -       00:00:33    10.1.1.6       Serial1
```

```
rtrC#show ip ospf neighbor

Neighbor ID     Pri   State          Dead Time   Address        Interface
2.2.2.2           1   FULL/  -       00:00:33    10.1.1.5       Serial0
1.1.1.1           1   FULL/  -       00:00:30    10.1.1.9       Serial1
```

Verify that MD5 authentication is enabled for Area 0.

```
rtrA#show ip ospf
Routing Process "ospf 1" with ID 1.1.1.1
 Supports only single TOS(TOS0) routes
 SPF schedule delay 5 secs, Hold time between two SPFs 10 secs
 Minimum LSA interval 5 secs. Minimum LSA arrival 1 secs
 Number of external LSA 0. Checksum Sum 0x0
 Number of DCbitless external LSA 0
 Number of DoNotAge external LSA 0
 Number of areas in this router is 1. 1 normal 0 stub 0 nssa
    Area BACKBONE(0)
        Number of interfaces in this area is 2
        Area has message digest authentication
        SPF algorithm executed 2 times
        Area ranges are
        Number of LSA 3. Checksum Sum 0x14A19
        Number of DCbitless LSA 0
        Number of indication LSA 0
        Number of DoNotAge LSA 0
```

The password used can be seen by anyone looking at your configuration. For added security, the password in the configuration can be encrypted using the global configuration command **service password-encryption**, as shown in the following configuration.

```
Router A
service password-encryption
```

Listing the configuration will show that the password has been encrypted.

```
rtrA#show running-config
Building configuration...

Current configuration:
!
version 12.0
service timestamps debug uptime
service timestamps log uptime
service password-encryption
!
hostname rtrA
!
ip subnet-zero
!
```

```
interface Loopback0
 ip address 1.1.1.1 255.255.255.255
 no ip directed-broadcast
!
interface Serial0/0
 ip address 10.1.1.9 255.255.255.252
 no ip directed-broadcast
 ip ospf message-digest-key 1 md5 7 02050D4808090E22
 no ip mroute-cache
!
interface Serial0/1
 ip address 10.1.1.1 255.255.255.252
 no ip directed-broadcast
 ip ospf message-digest-key 2 md5 7 045802150C2E4D4C
 clockrate 64000
```

Configuration Example 2: Changing Keys and Passwords

For additional security, you may choose to periodically change the key and password. With clear-text authentication, changing passwords will cause a loss of OSPF connectivity from the time you change the password on one interface until you change the password at the other end of the link. With MD5 authentication, you can configure a new key and password on a link while leaving the old key and password in place. The old key and password will continue to be used until the new key and password are configured on the other end of the link. Modify the key and password on the link between Routers A and B. Add a new key and password on Router A in order to observe the behavior when the new key and password have only been configured on one end of the link.

```
Router A
interface Serial0/1
 ip address 10.1.1.1 255.255.255.252
 no ip directed-broadcast
 ip ospf message-digest-key 2 md5 ciscoab
 ip ospf message-digest-key 4 md5 cisconew
 clockrate 64000
```

Verify that the OSPF neighbor relationship between Routers A and B is still active.

```
rtrA#show ip ospf neighbor

Neighbor ID     Pri   State           Dead Time   Address         Interface
3.3.3.3           1   FULL/  -        00:00:34    10.1.1.10       Serial0/0
2.2.2.2           1   FULL/  -        00:00:35    10.1.1.2        Serial0/1
```

You can determine if Router A is using both keys when communicating with Router B by viewing the interface properties or by enabling OSPF debugging.

```
rtrA#show ip ospf interface s0/1
Serial0/1 is up, line protocol is up
  Internet Address 10.1.1.1/30, Area 0
  Process ID 1, Router ID 1.1.1.1, Network Type POINT_TO_POINT, Cost: 64
  Transmit Delay is 1 sec, State POINT_TO_POINT,
  Timer intervals configured, Hello 10, Dead 40, Wait 40, Retransmit 5
    Hello due in 00:00:08
  Neighbor Count is 1, Adjacent neighbor count is 1
    Adjacent with neighbor 2.2.2.2
  Suppress hello for 0 neighbor(s)
  Message digest authentication enabled
    Youngest key id is 4
    Rollover in progress, 1 neighbor(s) using the old key(s):
      key id 2

rtrA#debug ip ospf events
OSPF events debugging is on
rtrA#
01:30:25: OSPF: Rcv hello from 3.3.3.3 area 0 from Serial0/0 10.1.1.10
01:30:25: OSPF: End of hello processing
01:30:26: OSPF: Rcv hello from 2.2.2.2 area 0 from Serial0/1 10.1.1.2
01:30:26: OSPF: End of hello processing
01:30:30: OSPF: Send with youngest Key 1
01:30:30: OSPF: Send with key 2
01:30:30: OSPF: Send with key 4
```

Notice that both keys are being used for authentication. Configure the new key and password on Router B while leaving the old key and password in place.

```
Router B
interface Serial0
 ip address 10.1.1.2 255.255.255.252
 no ip directed-broadcast
 ip ospf message-digest-key 2 md5 ciscoab
 ip ospf message-digest-key 4 md5 cisconew
```

Routers A and B will now use the youngest key (the last key configured).

```
rtrA#show ip ospf interface s0/1
Serial0/1 is up, line protocol is up
  Internet Address 10.1.1.1/30, Area 0
  Process ID 1, Router ID 1.1.1.1, Network Type POINT_TO_POINT, Cost: 64
  Transmit Delay is 1 sec, State POINT_TO_POINT,
```

```
  Timer intervals configured, Hello 10, Dead 40, Wait 40, Retransmit 5
    Hello due in 00:00:02
  Neighbor Count is 1, Adjacent neighbor count is 1
    Adjacent with neighbor 2.2.2.2
  Suppress hello for 0 neighbor(s)
  Message digest authentication enabled
    Youngest key id is 4
```

The old key and password can now be removed from routers A and B using the **no** form of the interface command.

Troubleshooting

Step 1 Before enabling authentication in an OSPF area, verify that there is a neighbor relationship among all OSPF routers by using the **show ip ospf neighbor** command.

Step 2 Verify that authentication has been enabled for every OSPF router with an interface in the area where authentication is being deployed.

Step 3 Verify that every interface using authentication in an OSPF area has been configured with the proper key and password.

Step 4 If any OSPF neighbor relationships disappear after configuring md5 authentication, debugging can be used to determine the problem. For example, change the key-id on router B, interface Serial 0, to 5. Use the **no** form of the command to remove the original key and password before applying the new key.

```
Router B
interface Serial0
 ip address 10.1.1.2 255.255.255.252
 no ip ospf message-digest-key 2 md5 ciscoab
 ip ospf message-digest-key 5 md5 ciscoab
```

List the OSPF neighbors for Router A.

```
rtrA#show ip ospf neighbor

Neighbor ID     Pri   State           Dead Time   Address         Interface
3.3.3.3           1   FULL/  -        00:00:31    10.1.1.10       Serial0/0
```

Router A has lost Router C as a neighbor. Enable debugging on Router A to see if you can determine the problem.

```
rtrA#debug ip ospf events
OSPF events debugging is on
rtrA#
00:09:34: OSPF: Rcv pkt from 10.1.1.2, Serial0/1 : Mismatch Authentication Key -
 No message digest key 5 on interface
```

Be careful when configuring passwords. A space is a valid character, so if you use the password **cisco<space>** then there will be a password mismatch, but you won't be able to tell by looking at the configuration, especially if the password is encrypted in the configuration.

On Router A, remove the OSPF router configuration command **area 0 authentication message-digest**. Restore the proper key on Serial0 on Router B.

```
Router A
interface Serial0/0
 ip address 10.1.1.9 255.255.255.252
 ip ospf authentication-key cisco
!
router ospf 1
 no area 0 authentication message-digest
```

```
Router B
interface Serial0
 ip address 10.1.1.2 255.255.255.252
 no ip ospf message-digest-key 5 md5 ciscoab
 ip ospf message-digest-key 2 md5 ciscoab
```

Router A should drop both OSPF neighbors.

```
rtrA#show ip ospf neighbor
Neighbor ID     Pri   State           Dead Time   Address         Interface
3.3.3.3           1   INIT/  -        00:00:38    10.1.1.10       Serial0/0
2.2.2.2           1   INIT/  -        00:00:39    10.1.1.2        Serial0/1
```

Now debug the OSPF traffic on Router B or C to determine the problem.

```
rtrB#debug ip ospf events
OSPF events debugging is on
rtrB#
21:43:04: OSPF: Rcv hello from 3.3.3.3 area 0 from Serial1 10.1.1.6
```

```
21:43:04: OSPF: End of hello processing
21:43:05: OSPF: Send with youngest Key 4
21:43:05: OSPF: Send with youngest Key 3
21:43:08: OSPF: Rcv pkt from 10.1.1.1, Serial0 : Mismatch Authentication type. I
nput packet specified type 0, we use type 2
```

Routers B and C are using type 2 authentication (MD5) and Router A is using type 0 authentication (none).

2-3: area *area-id* default-cost *cost*

NOTE This command requires the following additional commands:

area *area-id* **nssa** (see Section 2-4)

or

area *area-id* **stub** (see Section 2-11)

Syntax Description:

- *area-id*—OSPF area ID. This value can be entered as a decimal number in the range of 0 to 4,294,967,295 or in IP address form in the range 0.0.0.0 to 255.255.255.255.
- *cost*—The default cost of an OSPF stub area's advertised external default route metric. The range of values is 0 to 16,777,215. The default value is 1. The cost value will be added to the cost of reaching the Area Border Router (ABR) that is advertising the default route.

Purpose: External networks will not be advertised into a stub or totally stubby area. External networks are networks that have been redistributed into OSPF. External OSPF routes and inter-area OSPF routes are not advertised into a totally stubby area. When an OSPF area is configured as a stub area, a default route will be generated by the ABR into the stub area in place of the external routes. When an OSPF area is configured as a totally stubby area, the default route replaces the external and inter-area routes. The purpose of this command is to set the cost of the default route advertised into a stubby, totally stubby, or not-so-stubby area. If this command is not used, then the cost of the default route will be 1. When configuring stub areas, all routers with interfaces in the stub area must be configured with the same stub area type.

Initial Cisco IOS Software Release: 10.0

Configuration Example: Setting the Default Cost for a Stub Area

Initially, the network in Figure 2-3 is configured without a stubby area to compare the differences between the routes advertised into a normal area with those advertised into a stubby area. You will redistribute the loopback interface on Router C in order to generate an external route on Routers A and B.

Figure 2-3 *External OSPF Routes Are Not Advertised into an OSPF Stub Area. Inter-area and External Routes Are Not Advertised into a Totally Stubby Area*

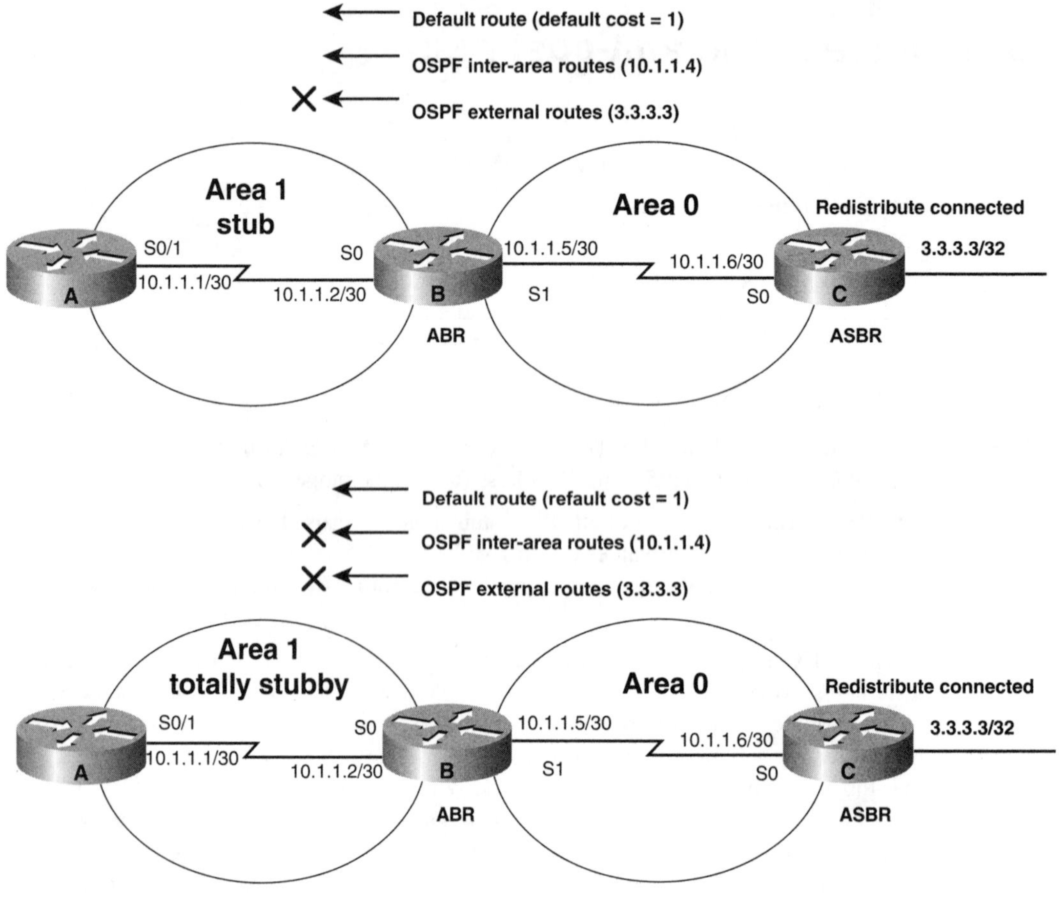


```
Router A
interface Loopback0
 ip address 1.1.1.1 255.255.255.255
!
interface Serial0/1
```

```
 ip address 10.1.1.1 255.255.255.252
 clock rate 64000
!
router ospf 1
 network 10.1.1.0 0.0.0.3 area 1
```

```
Router B
interface Loopback0
 ip address 2.2.2.2 255.255.255.255
!
interface Serial0
 ip address 10.1.1.2 255.255.255.252
!
interface Serial1
 ip address 10.1.1.5 255.255.255.252
 clock rate 64000
!
router ospf 1
 network 10.1.1.0 0.0.0.3 area 1
 network 10.1.1.4 0.0.0.3 area 0
```

```
Router C
interface Loopback0
 ip address 3.3.3.3 255.255.255.255
!
interface Serial0
 ip address 10.1.1.6 255.255.255.252
!
router ospf 1
 redistribute connected subnets
 network 10.1.1.4 0.0.0.3 area 0
```

If you examine the IP routing table on Router A, you can see that all OSPF routes are being advertised into Area 1.

```
rtrA#show ip route
Codes: C - connected, S - static, I - IGRP, R - RIP, M - mobile, B - BGP
       D - EIGRP, EX - EIGRP external, O - OSPF, IA - OSPF inter area
       N1 - OSPF NSSA external type 1, N2 - OSPF NSSA external type 2
       E1 - OSPF external type 1, E2 - OSPF external type 2, E - EGP
       i - IS-IS, L1 - IS-IS level-1, L2 - IS-IS level-2, * - candidate default
       U - per-user static route, o - ODR

Gateway of last resort is not set

     1.0.0.0/32 is subnetted, 1 subnets
C       1.1.1.1 is directly connected, Loopback0
     3.0.0.0/32 is subnetted, 1 subnets
O E2    3.3.3.3 [110/20] via 10.1.1.2, 00:00:04, Serial0/1
```

continues

```
     10.0.0.0/30 is subnetted, 3 subnets
C       10.1.1.0 is directly connected, Serial0/1
O IA    10.1.1.4 [110/128] via 10.1.1.2, 00:00:04, Serial0/1
```

Modify the configurations on Routers A and B so that Area 1 is a stub area.

```
Router A
router ospf 1
 area 1 stub
 network 10.1.1.0 0.0.0.3 area 1
```

```
Router B
router ospf 1
 area 1 stub
 network 10.1.1.0 0.0.0.3 area 1
 network 10.1.1.4 0.0.0.3 area 0
```

Re-examine the IP routing table on Router A.

```
rtrA#show ip route
Codes: C - connected, S - static, I - IGRP, R - RIP, M - mobile, B - BGP
       D - EIGRP, EX - EIGRP external, O - OSPF, IA - OSPF inter area
       N1 - OSPF NSSA external type 1, N2 - OSPF NSSA external type 2
       E1 - OSPF external type 1, E2 - OSPF external type 2, E - EGP
       i - IS-IS, L1 - IS-IS level-1, L2 - IS-IS level-2, * - candidate default
       U - per-user static route, o - ODR

Gateway of last resort is 10.1.1.2 to network 0.0.0.0

     1.0.0.0/32 is subnetted, 1 subnets
C       1.1.1.1 is directly connected, Loopback0
     10.0.0.0/30 is subnetted, 3 subnets
C       10.1.1.0 is directly connected, Serial0/1
O IA    10.1.1.4 [110/128] via 10.1.1.2, 00:00:06, Serial0/1
O*IA 0.0.0.0/0 [110/65] via 10.1.1.2, 00:00:06, Serial0/1
```

Notice that the cost of the default route is 65. This is the sum of the cost to the ABR of 64 and the cost of the default route, which has the default value of 1. You can verify the default cost by using the command **show ip ospf** on Router B.

```
rtrB#show ip ospf
 Routing Process "ospf 1" with ID 2.2.2.2
 Supports only single TOS(TOS0) routes
 It is an area border router
 SPF schedule delay 5 secs, Hold time between two SPFs 10 secs
 Minimum LSA interval 5 secs. Minimum LSA arrival 1 secs
```

```
Number of external LSA 3. Checksum Sum 0x14B45
Number of DCbitless external LSA 0
Number of DoNotAge external LSA 0
Number of areas in this router is 2. 1 normal 1 stub 0 nssa
   Area BACKBONE(0)
       Number of interfaces in this area is 1
       Area has no authentication
       SPF algorithm executed 21 times
       Area ranges are
       Number of LSA 3. Checksum Sum 0x14F55
       Number of DCbitless LSA 0
       Number of indication LSA 0
       Number of DoNotAge LSA 0
   Area 1
       Number of interfaces in this area is 1
       It is a stub area
         generates stub default route with cost 1
       Area has no authentication
       SPF algorithm executed 37 times
       Area ranges are
       Number of LSA 4. Checksum Sum 0x1E701
       Number of DCbitless LSA 0
       Number of indication LSA 0
       Number of DoNotAge LSA 0
```

Modify the cost of the default route being generated by Router B.

```
Router B
router ospf 1
 area 1 stub
 area 1 default-cost 15
 network 10.1.1.0 0.0.0.3 area 1
 network 10.1.1.4 0.0.0.3 area 0
```

Verification

Verify the new cost for the default route on Router A by using the **show ip route** command or the **show ip route 0.0.0.0** command. You can also verify the cost of the default route on Router B by using the **show ip ospf** command.

```
rtrA#show ip route
Codes: C - connected, S - static, I - IGRP, R - RIP, M - mobile, B - BGP
       D - EIGRP, EX - EIGRP external, O - OSPF, IA - OSPF inter area
       N1 - OSPF NSSA external type 1, N2 - OSPF NSSA external type 2
       E1 - OSPF external type 1, E2 - OSPF external type 2, E - EGP
       i - IS-IS, L1 - IS-IS level-1, L2 - IS-IS level-2, * - candidate default
       U - per-user static route, o - ODR

Gateway of last resort is 10.1.1.2 to network 0.0.0.0
```

continues

```
     1.0.0.0/32 is subnetted, 1 subnets
C       1.1.1.1 is directly connected, Loopback0
     10.0.0.0/30 is subnetted, 3 subnets
C       10.1.1.0 is directly connected, Serial0/1
O IA    10.1.1.4 [110/128] via 10.1.1.2, 00:03:39, Serial0/1
O*IA 0.0.0.0/0 [110/79] via 10.1.1.2, 00:00:09, Serial0/1

rtrA#show ip route 0.0.0.0
Routing entry for 0.0.0.0/0, supernet
  Known via "ospf 1", distance 110, metric 79, candidate default path, type inte
r area
  Redistributing via ospf 1
  Last update from 10.1.1.2 on Serial0/1, 00:01:05 ago
  Routing Descriptor Blocks:
  * 10.1.1.2, from 2.2.2.2, 00:01:05 ago, via Serial0/1
      Route metric is 79, traffic share count is 1
```

```
rtrB#show ip ospf
 Routing Process "ospf 1" with ID 2.2.2.2
 Supports only single TOS(TOS0) routes
 It is an area border router
 SPF schedule delay 5 secs, Hold time between two SPFs 10 secs
 Minimum LSA interval 5 secs. Minimum LSA arrival 1 secs
 Number of external LSA 3. Checksum Sum 0x14B45
 Number of DCbitless external LSA 0
 Number of DoNotAge external LSA 0
 Number of areas in this router is 2. 1 normal 1 stub 0 nssa
    Area BACKBONE(0)
        Number of interfaces in this area is 1
        Area has no authentication
        SPF algorithm executed 21 times
        Area ranges are
        Number of LSA 3. Checksum Sum 0x14F55
        Number of DCbitless LSA 0
        Number of indication LSA 0
        Number of DoNotAge LSA 0
    Area 1
        Number of interfaces in this area is 1
        It is a stub area
          generates stub default route with cost 15
        Area has no authentication
        SPF algorithm executed 37 times
        Area ranges are
        Number of LSA 4. Checksum Sum 0x27068
        Number of DCbitless LSA 0
        Number of indication LSA 0
        Number of DoNotAge LSA 0
```

The new cost is now 64 + 15 or 79.

Troubleshooting

Step 1 Verify that there is a neighbor relationship between the OSPF routers by using the **show ip ospf neighbor** command.

Step 2 Verify that the ABR to the stub area and all routers in the stub area have been configured as a stub using the router configuration command **area** *x* **stub**.

Step 3 Verify that the **default-cost** command has been configured on the ABR(s) for the stub area. The **default-cost** command will only work on the stub area ABR.

2-4: area *area-id* nssa

Syntax Description:

- *area-id*—OSPF area ID. This value can be entered as a decimal number in the range of 1 to 4,294,967,295 or in IP address form in the range 0.0.0.1 to 255.255.255.255. Area 0 can be entered but Area 0 cannot be configured as a not-so-stubby area (NSSA).

Purpose: In a stub or totally stubby area, the ABR to the stub area will prevent OSPF external routes (type 5) from being advertised into the stub area. This implies that an Autonomous System Boundary Router (ASBR) cannot be part of a stubby or totally stubby area because an ASBR generates OSPF external type 5 routes. There will be situations where you want to create a stubby or totally stubby area relative to OSPF and also want to advertise redistributed routes from an ASBR across the area. An OSPF area that has these properties is an NSSA. In Figure 2-4, you want Router B, the ABR to block OSPF external routes from Area 1. You also want the routes redistributed by Router C, the ASBR, to be allowed into the area. If you configure Area 1 as an NSSA, then the external OSPF routes that Router B receives from Area 0 will be blocked from Area 1. The redistributed routes from the ASBR will be sent as OSPF type 7 routes. Router B will convert these type 7 routes to OSPF type 5 routes and advertise them into Area 0. Routes are normally redistributed into OSPF as type 5 routes. An ASBR that has been configured as an NSSA will generate type 7 routes instead of type 5 routes.

Initial Cisco IOS Software Release: 11.2

Configuration Example: Configuring an OSPF NSSA

In Figure 2-4, Routers C and D are running RIP Version 2. Router D is advertising the networks 156.26.32.0/24 and 156.26.33.0/24 to Router C via RIP. Router C will redistribute the RIP routes, including the 10.1.1.8/30 network, into OSPF. Because Area 1 has been defined as an NSSA, the redistributed RIP routes will be advertised into Area 1 as OSPF type 7 routes. Initially you will configure Area 1 as a normal OSPF area in order to see the routes that are advertised.

Figure 2-4 *An OSPF NSSA*

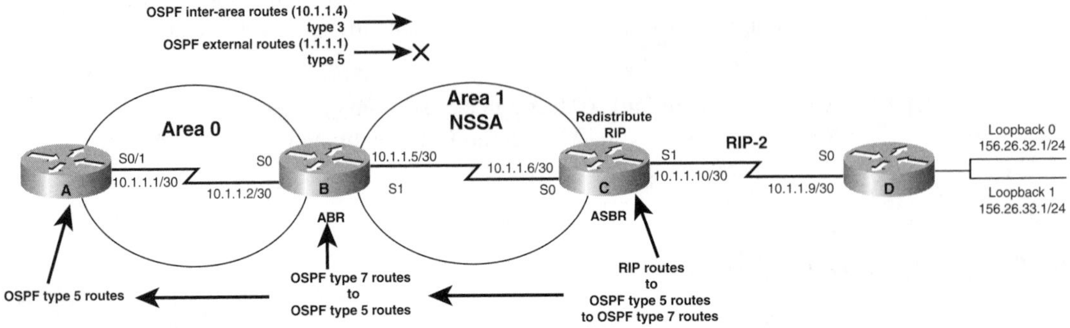


```
Router A
interface Loopback0
 ip address 1.1.1.1 255.255.255.255
!
interface Serial0/1
 ip address 10.1.1.1 255.255.255.252
 clockrate 64000
!
router ospf 1
 redistribute connected subnets
 network 10.1.1.0 0.0.0.3 area 0
```

```
Router B
interface Loopback0
 ip address 2.2.2.2 255.255.255.255
!
interface Serial0
 ip address 10.1.1.2 255.255.255.252
!
interface Serial1
 ip address 10.1.1.5 255.255.255.252
 lockrate 64000
!
router ospf 1
 network 10.1.1.0 0.0.0.3 area 0
 network 10.1.1.4 0.0.0.3 area 1
```

```
Router C
interface Loopback0
 ip address 3.3.3.3 255.255.255.255
!
```

```
interface Serial0
 ip address 10.1.1.6 255.255.255.252
!
interface Serial1
 ip address 10.1.1.10 255.255.255.252
 clockrate 64000
!
router ospf 1
 redistribute rip subnets
 network 10.1.1.4 0.0.0.3 area 1
!
router rip
 version 2
 passive-interface Serial0
 network 10.0.0.0
```

```
Router D
interface Loopback0
 ip address 156.26.32.1 255.255.255.0
!
interface Loopback1
 ip address 156.26.33.1 255.255.255.0
!
interface Serial0/0
 ip address 10.1.1.9 255.255.255.252
!
router rip
 version 2
 network 10.0.0.0
 network 156.26.0.0
 no auto-summary
```

Router A is advertising Loopback 0 as an OSPF type 5 external route because this route was injected into OSPF through redistribution. Routers A and B are also learning the redistributed RIP routes as external type 5 OSPF routes.

```
rtrA#show ip route
Codes: C - connected, S - static, I - IGRP, R - RIP, M - mobile, B - BGP
       D - EIGRP, EX - EIGRP external, O - OSPF, IA - OSPF inter area
       N1 - OSPF NSSA external type 1, N2 - OSPF NSSA external type 2
       E1 - OSPF external type 1, E2 - OSPF external type 2, E - EGP
       i - IS-IS, L1 - IS-IS level-1, L2 - IS-IS level-2, * - candidate default
       U - per-user static route, o - ODR

Gateway of last resort is not set

     1.0.0.0/32 is subnetted, 1 subnets
C       1.1.1.1 is directly connected, Loopback0
```

continues

```
     156.26.0.0/24 is subnetted, 2 subnets
O E2    156.26.32.0 [110/20] via 10.1.1.2, 00:02:25, Serial0/1
O E2    156.26.33.0 [110/20] via 10.1.1.2, 00:02:25, Serial0/1
     10.0.0.0/30 is subnetted, 3 subnets
O E2    10.1.1.8 [110/20] via 10.1.1.2, 00:02:25, Serial0/1
C       10.1.1.0 is directly connected, Serial0/1
O IA    10.1.1.4 [110/128] via 10.1.1.2, 00:02:25, Serial0/1
```

```
rtrB#show ip route
Codes: C - connected, S - static, I - IGRP, R - RIP, M - mobile, B - BGP
       D - EIGRP, EX - EIGRP external, O - OSPF, IA - OSPF inter area
       N1 - OSPF NSSA external type 1, N2 - OSPF NSSA external type 2
       E1 - OSPF external type 1, E2 - OSPF external type 2, E - EGP
       i - IS-IS, L1 - IS-IS level-1, L2 - IS-IS level-2, * - candidate default
       U - per-user static route, o - ODR

Gateway of last resort is not set

     1.0.0.0/32 is subnetted, 1 subnets
O E2    1.1.1.1 [110/20] via 10.1.1.1, 00:04:14, Serial0
     2.0.0.0/32 is subnetted, 1 subnets
C       2.2.2.2 is directly connected, Loopback0
     156.26.0.0/24 is subnetted, 2 subnets
O E2    156.26.32.0 [110/20] via 10.1.1.6, 00:04:14, Serial1
O E2    156.26.33.0 [110/20] via 10.1.1.6, 00:04:14, Serial1
     10.0.0.0/30 is subnetted, 3 subnets
O E2    10.1.1.8 [110/20] via 10.1.1.6, 00:04:14, Serial1
C       10.1.1.0 is directly connected, Serial0
C       10.1.1.4 is directly connected, Serial1
```

Router C is learning the network redistributed by Router A as an OSPF external type 5 route.

```
rtrC#show ip route
Codes: C - connected, S - static, I - IGRP, R - RIP, M - mobile, B - BGP
       D - EIGRP, EX - EIGRP external, O - OSPF, IA - OSPF inter area
       N1 - OSPF NSSA external type 1, N2 - OSPF NSSA external type 2
       E1 - OSPF external type 1, E2 - OSPF external type 2, E - EGP
       i - IS-IS, L1 - IS-IS level-1, L2 - IS-IS level-2, * - candidate default
       U - per-user static route, o - ODR

Gateway of last resort is not set

     1.0.0.0/32 is subnetted, 1 subnets
O E2    1.1.1.1 [110/20] via 10.1.1.5, 00:06:24, Serial0
     3.0.0.0/24 is subnetted, 1 subnets
C       3.3.3.0 is directly connected, Loopback0
     156.26.0.0/24 is subnetted, 2 subnets
R       156.26.32.0 [120/1] via 10.1.1.9, 00:00:18, Serial1
R       156.26.33.0 [120/1] via 10.1.1.9, 00:00:18, Serial1
     10.0.0.0/30 is subnetted, 3 subnets
```

```
C       10.1.1.8 is directly connected, Serial1
O IA    10.1.1.0 [110/128] via 10.1.1.5, 00:06:24, Serial0
C       10.1.1.4 is directly connected, Serial0
```

Now modify the OSPF configurations on Routers B and C in order to create the NSSA.

```
Router B
router ospf 1
 area 1 nssa
 network 10.1.1.0 0.0.0.3 area 0
 network 10.1.1.4 0.0.0.3 area 1
```

```
Router C
router ospf 1
 area 1 nssa
 redistribute rip subnets
 network 10.1.1.4 0.0.0.3 area 1
```

Verification

Verify that Area 1 has been configured as an NSSA.

```
rtrB#show ip ospf
 Routing Process "ospf 1" with ID 2.2.2.2
 Supports only single TOS(TOS0) routes
 It is an area border and autonomous system boundary router
 Redistributing External Routes from,
 SPF schedule delay 5 secs, Hold time between two SPFs 10 secs
 Minimum LSA interval 5 secs. Minimum LSA arrival 1 secs
 Number of external LSA 5. Checksum Sum 0x324D4
 Number of DCbitless external LSA 0
 Number of DoNotAge external LSA 0
 Number of areas in this router is 2. 1 normal 0 stub 1 nssa
    Area BACKBONE(0)
        Number of interfaces in this area is 1
        Area has no authentication
        SPF algorithm executed 11 times
        Area ranges are
        Number of LSA 3. Checksum Sum 0x20790
        Number of DCbitless LSA 0
        Number of indication LSA 0
        Number of DoNotAge LSA 0
    Area 1
        Number of interfaces in this area is 1
        It is a NSSA area
        Perform type-7/type-5 LSA translation
        Area has no authentication
        SPF algorithm executed 22 times
        Area ranges are
```

continues

```
        Number of LSA 7. Checksum Sum 0x26D1D
        Number of DCbitless LSA 0
        Number of indication LSA 0
        Number of DoNotAge LSA 0
```

Now inspect the routing tables on Routers A, B, and C to view the effect of configuring Area 1 as an NSSA.

```
rtrB#show ip route
Codes: C - connected, S - static, I - IGRP, R - RIP, M - mobile, B - BGP
       D - EIGRP, EX - EIGRP external, O - OSPF, IA - OSPF inter area
       N1 - OSPF NSSA external type 1, N2 - OSPF NSSA external type 2
       E1 - OSPF external type 1, E2 - OSPF external type 2, E - EGP
       i - IS-IS, L1 - IS-IS level-1, L2 - IS-IS level-2, * - candidate default
       U - per-user static route, o - ODR

Gateway of last resort is not set

     1.0.0.0/32 is subnetted, 1 subnets
O E2    1.1.1.1 [110/20] via 10.1.1.1, 00:03:55, Serial0
     2.0.0.0/32 is subnetted, 1 subnets
C       2.2.2.2 is directly connected, Loopback0
     156.26.0.0/24 is subnetted, 2 subnets
O N2    156.26.32.0 [110/20] via 10.1.1.6, 00:03:55, Serial1
O N2    156.26.33.0 [110/20] via 10.1.1.6, 00:03:55, Serial1
     10.0.0.0/30 is subnetted, 3 subnets
O N2    10.1.1.8 [110/20] via 10.1.1.6, 00:03:55, Serial1
C       10.1.1.0 is directly connected, Serial0
C       10.1.1.4 is directly connected, Serial1
```

The redistributed RIP routes have been converted from OSPF E2 routes to OSPF N2 routes. This means that the redistributed RIP routes are now being advertised as type 7 routes instead of type 5 routes. On Router A, these routes should still be OSPF type 5 routes because Router B is converting them from type 7 to type 5.

```
rtrA#show ip route
Codes: C - connected, S - static, I - IGRP, R - RIP, M - mobile, B - BGP
       D - EIGRP, EX - EIGRP external, O - OSPF, IA - OSPF inter area
       N1 - OSPF NSSA external type 1, N2 - OSPF NSSA external type 2
       E1 - OSPF external type 1, E2 - OSPF external type 2, E - EGP
       i - IS-IS, L1 - IS-IS level-1, L2 - IS-IS level-2, * - candidate default
       U - per-user static route, o - ODR

Gateway of last resort is not set

     1.0.0.0/32 is subnetted, 1 subnets
```

```
C       1.1.1.1 is directly connected, Loopback0
     156.26.0.0/24 is subnetted, 2 subnets
O E2    156.26.32.0 [110/20] via 10.1.1.2, 00:07:28, Serial0/1
O E2    156.26.33.0 [110/20] via 10.1.1.2, 00:07:28, Serial0/1
     10.0.0.0/30 is subnetted, 3 subnets
O E2    10.1.1.8 [110/20] via 10.1.1.2, 00:07:28, Serial0/1
C       10.1.1.0 is directly connected, Serial0/1
O IA    10.1.1.4 [110/128] via 10.1.1.2, 00:08:31, Serial0/1
```

Finally, inspect the IP routing table on Router C.

```
rtrC#show ip route
Codes: C - connected, S - static, I - IGRP, R - RIP, M - mobile, B - BGP
       D - EIGRP, EX - EIGRP external, O - OSPF, IA - OSPF inter area
       N1 - OSPF NSSA external type 1, N2 - OSPF NSSA external type 2
       E1 - OSPF external type 1, E2 - OSPF external type 2, E - EGP
       i - IS-IS, L1 - IS-IS level-1, L2 - IS-IS level-2, * - candidate default
       U - per-user static route, o - ODR

Gateway of last resort is not set

     3.0.0.0/24 is subnetted, 1 subnets
C       3.3.3.0 is directly connected, Loopback0
     156.26.0.0/24 is subnetted, 2 subnets
R       156.26.32.0 [120/1] via 10.1.1.9, 00:00:10, Serial1
R       156.26.33.0 [120/1] via 10.1.1.9, 00:00:10, Serial1
     10.0.0.0/30 is subnetted, 3 subnets
C       10.1.1.8 is directly connected, Serial1
O IA    10.1.1.0 [110/128] via 10.1.1.5, 00:08:58, Serial0
C       10.1.1.4 is directly connected, Serial0
```

The 1.1.1.1 route that Router A was advertising as an OSPF external type 5 route has been blocked from entering the NSSA area by Router B, but the inter-area routes have been permitted. Also notice that unlike a stub or totally stubby area, there is no default route advertised by the ABR or ASBR.

Troubleshooting

Step 1 Verify that there is a neighbor relationship between the OSPF routers by using the **show ip ospf neighbor** command.

Step 2 Verify that every router in the NSSA has been configured with the command **area** *x* **nssa**.

2-5: area *area-id* nssa default-information-originate

Syntax Description:

- *area-id*—OSPF area ID. This value can be entered as a decimal number in the range of 1 to 4,294,967,295 or in IP address form in the range 0.0.0.1 to 255.255.255.255. Area 0 can be entered, but Area 0 cannot be configured as an NSSA.

Purpose: This command is used on an OSPF ABR or an OSPF ASBR to generate an OSPF NSSA external type 2 default route into an NSSA. A default route does not need to be defined when using this command on an ABR. If this command is configured on an ASBR, then a default route needs to be configured. In a stub or totally stubby area, the ABR to the stub area will prevent OSPF external routes (type 5) from being advertised into the stub area. This implies that an ASBR cannot be part of a stubby or totally stubby area since an ASBR generates OSPF external type 5 routes. Situations arise where you want to create a stubby or totally stubby area relative to OSPF but also want to advertise redistributed routes from an ASBR across the area. An OSPF area that has these properties is an NSSA. In Figure 2-5, you want Router B, the ABR, to block OSPF external routes from Area 1 and advertise a default route into the NSSA. You also want the routes redistributed by Router C, the ASBR, to be allowed into the area. If you configure Area 1 as an NSSA, then the external OSPF routes that Router B receives from Area 0 will be blocked from Area 1. The redistributed routes from the ASBR will be sent as OSPF type 7 routes. Router B will convert these type 7 routes to OSPF type 5 routes and advertise them into Area 0. Normally, routes redistributed into OSPF are type 5 routes. An ASBR that has been configured as an NSSA will generate type 7 routes instead of type 5 routes. By default, an ABR does not generate a default route into an NSSA.

Initial Cisco IOS Software Release: 11.2

Configuration Example: Advertising an OSPF NSSA Default Route into an OSPF NSSA

In Figure 2-5, Routers C and D are running RIP Version 2. Router D is advertising the networks 156.26.32.0/24 and 156.26.33.0/24 to Router C via RIP. Router C will redistribute the RIP routes, including the 10.1.1.8/30 network, into OSPF. Because Area 1 has been defined as an NSSA, the redistributed RIP routes will be advertised into Area 1 as OSPF type 7 routes. Initially, you will configure Area 1 as a normal OSPF area in order to see the routes that are advertised.

Figure 2-5 *The* **default-information-originate** *Command Generates an OSPF NSSA Default Route into an OSPF NSSA*

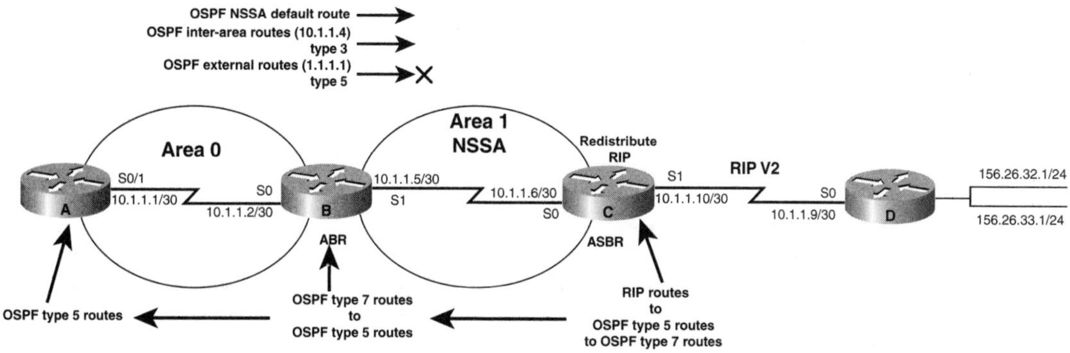


```
Router A
interface Loopback0
 ip address 1.1.1.1 255.255.255.255
!
interface Serial0/1
 ip address 10.1.1.1 255.255.255.252
 clockrate 64000
!
router ospf 1
 redistribute connected subnets
 network 10.1.1.0 0.0.0.3 area 0
```

```
Router B
interface Loopback0
 ip address 2.2.2.2 255.255.255.255
!
interface Serial0
 ip address 10.1.1.2 255.255.255.252
!
interface Serial1
 ip address 10.1.1.5 255.255.255.252
 lockrate 64000
!
router ospf 1
 network 10.1.1.0 0.0.0.3 area 0
 network 10.1.1.4 0.0.0.3 area 1
```

```
Router C
interface Loopback0
 ip address 3.3.3.3 255.255.255.255
!
interface Serial0
 ip address 10.1.1.6 255.255.255.252
```

continues

```
!
interface Serial1
 ip address 10.1.1.10 255.255.255.252
 clockrate 64000
!
router ospf 1
 redistribute rip subnets
 network 10.1.1.4 0.0.0.3 area 1
!
router rip
 version 2
 passive-interface Serial0
 network 10.0.0.0
```

```
Router D
interface Loopback0
 ip address 156.26.32.1 255.255.255.0
!
interface Loopback1
 ip address 156.26.33.1 255.255.255.0
!
interface Serial0/0
 ip address 10.1.1.9 255.255.255.252
!
router rip
 version 2
 network 10.0.0.0
 network 156.26.0.0
 no auto-summary
```

Router A is advertising Loopback 0 as an OSPF type 5 external route because this route was injected into OSPF through redistribution. Routers A and B are also learning the redistributed RIP routes as external type 5 OSPF routes.

```
rtrA#show ip route
Codes: C - connected, S - static, I - IGRP, R - RIP, M - mobile, B - BGP
       D - EIGRP, EX - EIGRP external, O - OSPF, IA - OSPF inter area
       N1 - OSPF NSSA external type 1, N2 - OSPF NSSA external type 2
       E1 - OSPF external type 1, E2 - OSPF external type 2, E - EGP
       i - IS-IS, L1 - IS-IS level-1, L2 - IS-IS level-2, * - candidate default
       U - per-user static route, o - ODR

Gateway of last resort is not set

     1.0.0.0/32 is subnetted, 1 subnets
C       1.1.1.1 is directly connected, Loopback0
     156.26.0.0/24 is subnetted, 2 subnets
O E2    156.26.32.0 [110/20] via 10.1.1.2, 00:02:25, Serial0/1
O E2    156.26.33.0 [110/20] via 10.1.1.2, 00:02:25, Serial0/1
     10.0.0.0/30 is subnetted, 3 subnets
```

```
O E2    10.1.1.8 [110/20] via 10.1.1.2, 00:02:25, Serial0/1
C       10.1.1.0 is directly connected, Serial0/1
O IA    10.1.1.4 [110/128] via 10.1.1.2, 00:02:25, Serial0/1
```

```
rtrB#show ip route
Codes: C - connected, S - static, I - IGRP, R - RIP, M - mobile, B - BGP
       D - EIGRP, EX - EIGRP external, O - OSPF, IA - OSPF inter area
       N1 - OSPF NSSA external type 1, N2 - OSPF NSSA external type 2
       E1 - OSPF external type 1, E2 - OSPF external type 2, E - EGP
       i - IS-IS, L1 - IS-IS level-1, L2 - IS-IS level-2, * - candidate default
       U - per-user static route, o - ODR

Gateway of last resort is not set

     1.0.0.0/32 is subnetted, 1 subnets
O E2    1.1.1.1 [110/20] via 10.1.1.1, 00:04:14, Serial0
     2.0.0.0/32 is subnetted, 1 subnets
C       2.2.2.2 is directly connected, Loopback0
     156.26.0.0/24 is subnetted, 2 subnets
O E2    156.26.32.0 [110/20] via 10.1.1.6, 00:04:14, Serial1
O E2    156.26.33.0 [110/20] via 10.1.1.6, 00:04:14, Serial1
     10.0.0.0/30 is subnetted, 3 subnets
O E2    10.1.1.8 [110/20] via 10.1.1.6, 00:04:14, Serial1
C       10.1.1.0 is directly connected, Serial0
C       10.1.1.4 is directly connected, Serial1
```

Router C is learning the network redistributed by Router A as an OSPF external type 5 route.

```
rtrC#show ip route
Codes: C - connected, S - static, I - IGRP, R - RIP, M - mobile, B - BGP
       D - EIGRP, EX - EIGRP external, O - OSPF, IA - OSPF inter area
       N1 - OSPF NSSA external type 1, N2 - OSPF NSSA external type 2
       E1 - OSPF external type 1, E2 - OSPF external type 2, E - EGP
       i - IS-IS, L1 - IS-IS level-1, L2 - IS-IS level-2, * - candidate default
       U - per-user static route, o - ODR

Gateway of last resort is not set

     1.0.0.0/32 is subnetted, 1 subnets
O E2    1.1.1.1 [110/20] via 10.1.1.5, 00:06:24, Serial0
     3.0.0.0/24 is subnetted, 1 subnets
C       3.3.3.0 is directly connected, Loopback0
     156.26.0.0/24 is subnetted, 2 subnets
R       156.26.32.0 [120/1] via 10.1.1.9, 00:00:18, Serial1
R       156.26.33.0 [120/1] via 10.1.1.9, 00:00:18, Serial1
     10.0.0.0/30 is subnetted, 3 subnets
C       10.1.1.8 is directly connected, Serial1
O IA    10.1.1.0 [110/128] via 10.1.1.5, 00:06:24, Serial0
C       10.1.1.4 is directly connected, Serial0
```

Now modify the OSPF configurations on Routers B and C in order to create the NSSA.

```
Router B
router ospf 1
 area 1 nssa
 network 10.1.1.0 0.0.0.3 area 0
 network 10.1.1.4 0.0.0.3 area 1
```

```
Router C
router ospf 1
 area 1 nssa
 redistribute rip subnets
 network 10.1.1.4 0.0.0.3 area 1
```

Verify that Area 1 has been configured as an NSSA.

```
rtrB#show ip ospf
 Routing Process "ospf 1" with ID 2.2.2.2
 Supports only single TOS(TOS0) routes
 It is an area border and autonomous system boundary router
 Redistributing External Routes from,
 SPF schedule delay 5 secs, Hold time between two SPFs 10 secs
 Minimum LSA interval 5 secs. Minimum LSA arrival 1 secs
 Number of external LSA 5. Checksum Sum 0x324D4
 Number of DCbitless external LSA 0
 Number of DoNotAge external LSA 0
 Number of areas in this router is 2. 1 normal 0 stub 1 nssa
    Area BACKBONE(0)
        Number of interfaces in this area is 1
        Area has no authentication
        SPF algorithm executed 11 times
        Area ranges are
        Number of LSA 3. Checksum Sum 0x20790
        Number of DCbitless LSA 0
        Number of indication LSA 0
        Number of DoNotAge LSA 0
    Area 1
        Number of interfaces in this area is 1
        It is a NSSA area
        Perform type-7/type-5 LSA translation
        Area has no authentication
        SPF algorithm executed 22 times
        Area ranges are
        Number of LSA 7. Checksum Sum 0x26D1D
        Number of DCbitless LSA 0
        Number of indication LSA 0
        Number of DoNotAge LSA 0
```

Now inspect the routing tables on Routers A, B, and C to view the effect of configuring Area 1 as an NSSA.

```
rtrB#show ip route
Codes: C - connected, S - static, I - IGRP, R - RIP, M - mobile, B - BGP
       D - EIGRP, EX - EIGRP external, O - OSPF, IA - OSPF inter area
       N1 - OSPF NSSA external type 1, N2 - OSPF NSSA external type 2
       E1 - OSPF external type 1, E2 - OSPF external type 2, E - EGP
       i - IS-IS, L1 - IS-IS level-1, L2 - IS-IS level-2, * - candidate default
       U - per-user static route, o - ODR

Gateway of last resort is not set

     1.0.0.0/32 is subnetted, 1 subnets
O E2    1.1.1.1 [110/20] via 10.1.1.1, 00:03:55, Serial0
     2.0.0.0/32 is subnetted, 1 subnets
C       2.2.2.2 is directly connected, Loopback0
     156.26.0.0/24 is subnetted, 2 subnets
O N2    156.26.32.0 [110/20] via 10.1.1.6, 00:03:55, Serial1
O N2    156.26.33.0 [110/20] via 10.1.1.6, 00:03:55, Serial1
     10.0.0.0/30 is subnetted, 3 subnets
O N2    10.1.1.8 [110/20] via 10.1.1.6, 00:03:55, Serial1
C       10.1.1.0 is directly connected, Serial0
C       10.1.1.4 is directly connected, Serial1
```

The redistributed RIP routes have been converted from OSPF E2 routes to OSPF N2 routes. This means that the redistributed RIP routes are now being advertised as type 7 routes instead of type 5 routes. On Router A, these routes should still be OSPF type 5 routes since Router B is converting them from type 7 to type 5.

```
rtrA#show ip route
Codes: C - connected, S - static, I - IGRP, R - RIP, M - mobile, B - BGP
       D - EIGRP, EX - EIGRP external, O - OSPF, IA - OSPF inter area
       N1 - OSPF NSSA external type 1, N2 - OSPF NSSA external type 2
       E1 - OSPF external type 1, E2 - OSPF external type 2, E - EGP
       i - IS-IS, L1 - IS-IS level-1, L2 - IS-IS level-2, * - candidate default
       U - per-user static route, o - ODR

Gateway of last resort is not set

     1.0.0.0/32 is subnetted, 1 subnets
C       1.1.1.1 is directly connected, Loopback0
     156.26.0.0/24 is subnetted, 2 subnets
O E2    156.26.32.0 [110/20] via 10.1.1.2, 00:07:28, Serial0/1
O E2    156.26.33.0 [110/20] via 10.1.1.2, 00:07:28, Serial0/1
     10.0.0.0/30 is subnetted, 3 subnets
O E2    10.1.1.8 [110/20] via 10.1.1.2, 00:07:28, Serial0/1
C       10.1.1.0 is directly connected, Serial0/1
O IA    10.1.1.4 [110/128] via 10.1.1.2, 00:08:31, Serial0/1
```

Finally, inspect the IP routing table on Router C.

```
rtrC#show ip route
Codes: C - connected, S - static, I - IGRP, R - RIP, M - mobile, B - BGP
       D - EIGRP, EX - EIGRP external, O - OSPF, IA - OSPF inter area
       N1 - OSPF NSSA external type 1, N2 - OSPF NSSA external type 2
       E1 - OSPF external type 1, E2 - OSPF external type 2, E - EGP
       i - IS-IS, L1 - IS-IS level-1, L2 - IS-IS level-2, * - candidate default
       U - per-user static route, o - ODR

Gateway of last resort is not set

     3.0.0.0/24 is subnetted, 1 subnets
C       3.3.3.0 is directly connected, Loopback0
     156.26.0.0/24 is subnetted, 2 subnets
R       156.26.32.0 [120/1] via 10.1.1.9, 00:00:10, Serial1
R       156.26.33.0 [120/1] via 10.1.1.9, 00:00:10, Serial1
     10.0.0.0/30 is subnetted, 3 subnets
C       10.1.1.8 is directly connected, Serial1
O IA    10.1.1.0 [110/128] via 10.1.1.5, 00:08:58, Serial0
C       10.1.1.4 is directly connected, Serial0
```

The 1.1.1.1 route that Router A was advertising as an OSPF external type 5 route has been blocked from entering the NSSA area by Router B but the inter-area routes have been permitted. Also notice that unlike a stub or totally stubby area, there is no default route advertised by the ABR or ASBR.

Modify the configuration on Router B in order to generate an OSPF NSSA default route into the NSSA.

```
Router B
router ospf 1
 area 1 nssa defalt-information-originate
 network 10.1.1.0 0.0.0.3 area 0
 network 10.1.1.4 0.0.0.3 area 1
```

Verification

Verify that a default route is being advertised into the NSSA by inspecting the routing table on Router C.

```
rtrC#show ip route
Codes: C - connected, S - static, I - IGRP, R - RIP, M - mobile, B - BGP
       D - EIGRP, EX - EIGRP external, O - OSPF, IA - OSPF inter area
       N1 - OSPF NSSA external type 1, N2 - OSPF NSSA external type 2
       E1 - OSPF external type 1, E2 - OSPF external type 2, E - EGP
       i - IS-IS, L1 - IS-IS level-1, L2 - IS-IS level-2, * - candidate default
       U - per-user static route, o - ODR
```

```
Gateway of last resort is 10.1.1.5 to network 0.0.0.0

     3.0.0.0/24 is subnetted, 1 subnets
C       3.3.3.0 is directly connected, Loopback0
     156.26.0.0/24 is subnetted, 2 subnets
R       156.26.32.0 [120/1] via 10.1.1.9, 00:00:23, Serial1
R       156.26.33.0 [120/1] via 10.1.1.9, 00:00:23, Serial1
     10.0.0.0/30 is subnetted, 3 subnets
C       10.1.1.8 is directly connected, Serial1
O IA    10.1.1.0 [110/128] via 10.1.1.5, 00:14:39, Serial0
C       10.1.1.4 is directly connected, Serial0
O*N2 0.0.0.0/0 [110/1] via 10.1.1.5, 00:14:39, Serial0
```

Troubleshooting

Step 1 Verify that there is a neighbor relationship between the OSPF routers by using the **show ip ospf neighbor** command.

Step 2 Verify that every router in the NSSA has been configured with the command **area** *x* **nssa**.

Step 3 The command option **default-information-originate** can only be used on the NSSA ABR or ASBR. Ensure that this command has been configured on either the ABR or ASBR.

2-6: area *area-id* nssa no-redistribution

Syntax Description:

- *area-id*—OSPF area ID. This value can be entered as a decimal number in the range of 1 to 4,294,967,295 or in IP address form in the range 0.0.0.1 to 255.255.255.255. Area 0 can be entered but Area 0 cannot be configured as an NSSA.

Purpose: In a stub or totally stubby area, the ABR to the stub area will prevent OSPF external routes (type 5) from being advertised into the stub area. This implies that an ASBR cannot be part of a stubby or totally stubby area because an ASBR generates OSPF external type 5 routes. Situations arise where you want to create a stubby or totally stubby area relative to OSPF but also want to advertise redistributed routes from an ASBR across the area. An OSPF area that has these properties is an NSSA. In Figure 2-6, you want Router B, the ABR, to block OSPF external routes from Area 1. You also want the routes redistributed by Router C, the ASBR, to be allowed into the area. Additionally, Router B is an ASBR for the EIGRP routes received from Router E. You want the EIGRP routes to be redistributed into Area 0 but you do not want them advertised into Area 1, the NSSA. If you configure Area 1 as an NSSA, then the external OSPF routes that Router B receives from Area 0 will be blocked from Area 1. The redistributed routes from the ASBR (Router C) will be sent as OSPF type 7 routes. Router B will convert these type 7 routes to OSPF type

5 routes and advertise them into Area 0. If you use the **no-redistribute** keyword on Router B, then the EIGRP routes will not be converted to OSPF type 7 routes. This will prevent them from entering Area 1 but will allow them to be advertised into Area 0. Normally, routes redistributed into OSPF are type 5 routes. An ASBR that has been configured as an NSSA will generate type 7 routes instead of type 5 routes.

Initial Cisco IOS Software Release: 11.2

Configuration Example: Preventing Redistributed Routes from Entering an OSPF NSSA

In Figure 2-6, Routers C and D are running RIP Version 2. Router D is advertising the networks 156.26.32.0/24 and 156.26.33.0/24 to Router C via RIP. Router C will redistribute the RIP routes, including the 10.1.1.8/30 network, into OSPF. Routers B and E are running EIGRP. Router B will redistribute the EIGRP routes into OSPF. Since Area 1 has been defined as an NSSA, the redistributed RIP and EIGRP routes will be advertised into Area 1 as OSPF type 7 routes. Initially, you will configure Area 1 as a normal OSPF area in order to see the routes that are advertised.

Figure 2-6 *An OSPF ABR/ASBR Can Control the Redistribution of Routes into an NSSA*

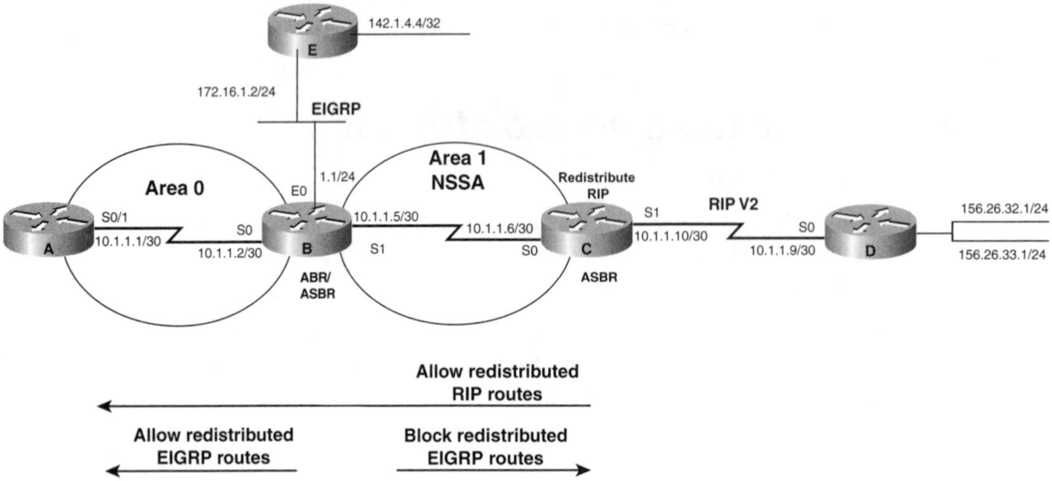

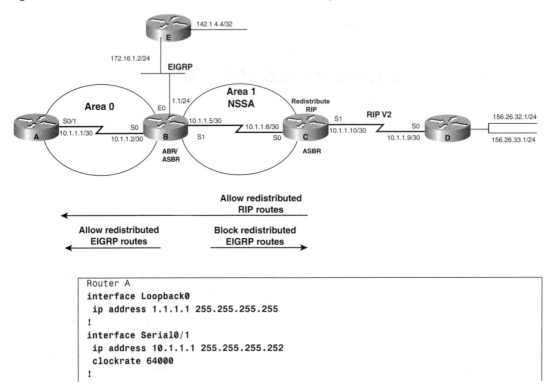

```
Router A
interface Loopback0
 ip address 1.1.1.1 255.255.255.255
!
interface Serial0/1
 ip address 10.1.1.1 255.255.255.252
 clockrate 64000
!
```

```
router ospf 1
 redistribute connected subnets
 network 10.1.1.0 0.0.0.3 area 0
```

```
Router B
interface Loopback0
 ip address 2.2.2.2 255.255.255.255
!
interface Ethernet0
 ip address 172.16.1.1 255.255.255.0
!
interface Serial0
 ip address 10.1.1.2 255.255.255.252
!
interface Serial1
 ip address 10.1.1.5 255.255.255.252
 lockrate 64000
!
router eigrp 1
 network 172.16.0.0
!
router ospf 1
 redistribute eigrp 1 subnets
 network 10.1.1.0 0.0.0.3 area 0
 network 10.1.1.4 0.0.0.3 area 1
```

```
Router C
interface Loopback0
 ip address 3.3.3.3 255.255.255.255
!
interface Serial0
 ip address 10.1.1.6 255.255.255.252
!
interface Serial1
 ip address 10.1.1.10 255.255.255.252
 clockrate 64000
!
router ospf 1
 redistribute rip subnets
 network 10.1.1.4 0.0.0.3 area 1
!
router rip
 version 2
 passive-interface Serial0
 network 10.0.0.0
```

```
Router D
interface Loopback0
 ip address 156.26.32.1 255.255.255.0
!
interface Loopback1
```

continues

```
 ip address 156.26.33.1 255.255.255.0
!
interface Serial0/0
 ip address 10.1.1.9 255.255.255.252
!
router rip
 version 2
 network 10.0.0.0
 network 156.26.0.0
 no auto-summary
```

```
Router E
interface Loopback0
 ip address 142.1.4.4 255.255.255.255
!
interface Ethernet0/0
 ip address 172.16.1.2 255.255.255.0
!
router eigrp 1
 network 142.1.0.0
 network 172.16.0.0
 no-auto-summary
```

Router A is advertising Loopback0 as an OSPF type 5 external route since this route was injected into OSPF through redistribution. Routers A and B are also learning the redistributed RIP routes as external type 5 OSPF routes. Routers A and C are learning the EIGRP routes that were redistributed by Router B.

```
rtrA#show ip route
Codes: C - connected, S - static, I - IGRP, R - RIP, M - mobile, B - BGP
       D - EIGRP, EX - EIGRP external, O - OSPF, IA - OSPF inter area
       N1 - OSPF NSSA external type 1, N2 - OSPF NSSA external type 2
       E1 - OSPF external type 1, E2 - OSPF external type 2, E - EGP
       i - IS-IS, L1 - IS-IS level-1, L2 - IS-IS level-2, * - candidate default
       U - per-user static route, o - ODR

Gateway of last resort is not set

     1.0.0.0/32 is subnetted, 1 subnets
C       1.1.1.1 is directly connected, Loopback0
     156.26.0.0/24 is subnetted, 2 subnets
O E2    156.26.32.0 [110/20] via 10.1.1.2, 00:02:29, Serial0/1
O E2    156.26.33.0 [110/20] via 10.1.1.2, 00:02:29, Serial0/1
     172.16.0.0/24 is subnetted, 1 subnets
O E2    172.16.1.0 [110/20] via 10.1.1.2, 00:01:28, Serial0/1
     142.1.0.0/32 is subnetted, 1 subnets
O E2    142.1.4.4 [110/20] via 10.1.1.2, 00:01:28, Serial0/1
     10.0.0.0/30 is subnetted, 3 subnets
O E2    10.1.1.8 [110/20] via 10.1.1.2, 00:02:29, Serial0/1
```

```
C        10.1.1.0 is directly connected, Serial0/1
O IA     10.1.1.4 [110/128] via 10.1.1.2, 00:02:30, Serial0/1
```

```
rtrB#show ip route
Codes: C - connected, S - static, I - IGRP, R - RIP, M - mobile, B - BGP
       D - EIGRP, EX - EIGRP external, O - OSPF, IA - OSPF inter area
       N1 - OSPF NSSA external type 1, N2 - OSPF NSSA external type 2
       E1 - OSPF external type 1, E2 - OSPF external type 2, E - EGP
       i - IS-IS, L1 - IS-IS level-1, L2 - IS-IS level-2, * - candidate default
       U - per-user static route, o - ODR

Gateway of last resort is not set

     1.0.0.0/32 is subnetted, 1 subnets
O E2    1.1.1.1 [110/20] via 10.1.1.1, 00:09:03, Serial0
     2.0.0.0/32 is subnetted, 1 subnets
C       2.2.2.2 is directly connected, Loopback0
     156.26.0.0/24 is subnetted, 2 subnets
O E2    156.26.32.0 [110/20] via 10.1.1.6, 00:09:03, Serial1
O E2    156.26.33.0 [110/20] via 10.1.1.6, 00:09:03, Serial1
     172.16.0.0/24 is subnetted, 1 subnets
C       172.16.1.0 is directly connected, Ethernet0
     142.1.0.0/32 is subnetted, 1 subnets
D       142.1.4.4 [90/409600] via 172.16.1.2, 00:09:41, Ethernet0
     10.0.0.0/30 is subnetted, 3 subnets
O E2    10.1.1.8 [110/20] via 10.1.1.6, 00:09:03, Serial1
C       10.1.1.0 is directly connected, Serial0
C       10.1.1.4 is directly connected, Serial1
```

Router C is learning the networks redistributed by Routers A and B as an OSPF external type 5 route.

```
rtrC#show ip route
Codes: C - connected, S - static, I - IGRP, R - RIP, M - mobile, B - BGP
       D - EIGRP, EX - EIGRP external, O - OSPF, IA - OSPF inter area
       N1 - OSPF NSSA external type 1, N2 - OSPF NSSA external type 2
       E1 - OSPF external type 1, E2 - OSPF external type 2, E - EGP
       i - IS-IS, L1 - IS-IS level-1, L2 - IS-IS level-2, * - candidate default
       U - per-user static route, o - ODR

Gateway of last resort is not set

     1.0.0.0/32 is subnetted, 1 subnets
O E2    1.1.1.1 [110/20] via 10.1.1.5, 00:12:02, Serial0
     3.0.0.0/24 is subnetted, 1 subnets
C       3.3.3.0 is directly connected, Loopback0
     156.26.0.0/24 is subnetted, 2 subnets
R       156.26.32.0 [120/1] via 10.1.1.9, 00:00:27, Serial1
R       156.26.33.0 [120/1] via 10.1.1.9, 00:00:27, Serial1
     172.16.0.0/24 is subnetted, 1 subnets
O E2    172.16.1.0 [110/20] via 10.1.1.5, 00:10:43, Serial0
     142.1.0.0/32 is subnetted, 1 subnets
```

continues

```
O E2    142.1.4.4 [110/20] via 10.1.1.5, 00:10:43, Serial0
     10.0.0.0/30 is subnetted, 3 subnets
C       10.1.1.8 is directly connected, Serial1
O IA    10.1.1.0 [110/128] via 10.1.1.5, 00:12:03, Serial0
C       10.1.1.4 is directly connected, Serial0
```

Now modify the OSPF configurations on Routers B and C in order to create the NSSA.

```
Router B
router ospf 1
 area 1 nssa
 redistribute eigrp 1 subnets
 network 10.1.1.0 0.0.0.3 area 0
 network 10.1.1.4 0.0.0.3 area 1
```

```
Router C
router ospf 1
 area 1 nssa
 redistribute rip subnets
 network 10.1.1.4 0.0.0.3 area 1
```

Verification

Verify that Area 1 has been configured as an NSSA.

```
rtrB#show ip ospf
 Routing Process "ospf 1" with ID 2.2.2.2
 Supports only single TOS(TOS0) routes
 It is an area border and autonomous system boundary router
 Redistributing External Routes from,
    eigrp 1, includes subnets in redistribution
 SPF schedule delay 5 secs, Hold time between two SPFs 10 secs
 Minimum LSA interval 5 secs. Minimum LSA arrival 1 secs
 Number of external LSA 7. Checksum Sum 0x3F1B4
 Number of DCbitless external LSA 0
 Number of DoNotAge external LSA 0
 Number of areas in this router is 2. 1 normal 0 stub 1 nssa
    Area BACKBONE(0)
        Number of interfaces in this area is 1
        Area has no authentication
        SPF algorithm executed 10 times
        Area ranges are
        Number of LSA 3. Checksum Sum 0x275D9
        Number of DCbitless LSA 0
        Number of indication LSA 0
        Number of DoNotAge LSA 0
    Area 1
        Number of interfaces in this area is 1
        It is a NSSA area
        Perform type-7/type-5 LSA translation
        Area has no authentication
        SPF algorithm executed 23 times
        Area ranges are
```

```
        Number of LSA 9. Checksum Sum 0x4AE6A
        Number of DCbitless LSA 0
        Number of indication LSA 0
        Number of DoNotAge LSA 0
```

Now inspect the routing tables on Routers A, B, and C to view the effect of configuring Area 1 as an NSSA.

```
rtrB#show ip route
Codes: C - connected, S - static, I - IGRP, R - RIP, M - mobile, B - BGP
       D - EIGRP, EX - EIGRP external, O - OSPF, IA - OSPF inter area
       N1 - OSPF NSSA external type 1, N2 - OSPF NSSA external type 2
       E1 - OSPF external type 1, E2 - OSPF external type 2, E - EGP
       i - IS-IS, L1 - IS-IS level-1, L2 - IS-IS level-2, * - candidate default
       U - per-user static route, o - ODR

Gateway of last resort is not set

     1.0.0.0/32 is subnetted, 1 subnets
O E2    1.1.1.1 [110/20] via 10.1.1.1, 00:02:19, Serial0
     2.0.0.0/32 is subnetted, 1 subnets
C       2.2.2.2 is directly connected, Loopback0
     156.26.0.0/24 is subnetted, 2 subnets
O N2    156.26.32.0 [110/20] via 10.1.1.6, 00:02:20, Serial1
O N2    156.26.33.0 [110/20] via 10.1.1.6, 00:02:20, Serial1
     172.16.0.0/24 is subnetted, 1 subnets
C       172.16.1.0 is directly connected, Ethernet0
     142.1.0.0/32 is subnetted, 1 subnets
D       142.1.4.4 [90/409600] via 172.16.1.2, 00:18:28, Ethernet0
     10.0.0.0/30 is subnetted, 3 subnets
O N2    10.1.1.8 [110/20] via 10.1.1.6, 00:02:20, Serial1
C       10.1.1.0 is directly connected, Serial0
C       10.1.1.4 is directly connected, Serial1
```

```
rtrC#show ip route
Codes: C - connected, S - static, I - IGRP, R - RIP, M - mobile, B - BGP
       D - EIGRP, EX - EIGRP external, O - OSPF, IA - OSPF inter area
       N1 - OSPF NSSA external type 1, N2 - OSPF NSSA external type 2
       E1 - OSPF external type 1, E2 - OSPF external type 2, E - EGP
       i - IS-IS, L1 - IS-IS level-1, L2 - IS-IS level-2, * - candidate default
       U - per-user static route, o - ODR

Gateway of last resort is not set

     3.0.0.0/24 is subnetted, 1 subnets
C       3.3.3.0 is directly connected, Loopback0
     156.26.0.0/24 is subnetted, 2 subnets
R       156.26.32.0 [120/1] via 10.1.1.9, 00:00:06, Serial1
R       156.26.33.0 [120/1] via 10.1.1.9, 00:00:06, Serial1
     172.16.0.0/24 is subnetted, 1 subnets
O N2    172.16.1.0 [110/20] via 10.1.1.5, 00:04:52, Serial0
```

continues

```
     142.1.0.0/32 is subnetted, 1 subnets
O N2     142.1.4.4 [110/20] via 10.1.1.5, 00:04:53, Serial0
     10.0.0.0/30 is subnetted, 3 subnets
C        10.1.1.8 is directly connected, Serial1
O IA     10.1.1.0 [110/128] via 10.1.1.5, 00:04:53, Serial0
C        10.1.1.4 is directly connected, Serial0
```

The redistributed RIP and EIGRP routes have been converted from OSPF E2 routes to OSPF N2 routes. This means that the redistributed RIP and EIGRP routes are now being advertised as type 7 routes instead of type 5 routes. On Router A, these routes should still be OSPF type 5 routes. Router B is converting the external routes learned via Router C from type 7 to type 5. Router B is also advertising the redistributed EIGRP routes as type 5 into Area 0 and type 7 into Area 1.

```
rtrA#show ip route
Codes: C - connected, S - static, I - IGRP, R - RIP, M - mobile, B - BGP
       D - EIGRP, EX - EIGRP external, O - OSPF, IA - OSPF inter area
       N1 - OSPF NSSA external type 1, N2 - OSPF NSSA external type 2
       E1 - OSPF external type 1, E2 - OSPF external type 2, E - EGP
       i - IS-IS, L1 - IS-IS level-1, L2 - IS-IS level-2, * - candidate default
       U - per-user static route, o - ODR

Gateway of last resort is not set

     1.0.0.0/32 is subnetted, 1 subnets
C       1.1.1.1 is directly connected, Loopback0
     156.26.0.0/24 is subnetted, 2 subnets
O E2    156.26.32.0 [110/20] via 10.1.1.2, 00:06:14, Serial0/1
O E2    156.26.33.0 [110/20] via 10.1.1.2, 00:06:14, Serial0/1
     172.16.0.0/24 is subnetted, 1 subnets
O E2    172.16.1.0 [110/20] via 10.1.1.2, 00:06:46, Serial0/1
     142.1.0.0/32 is subnetted, 1 subnets
O E2    142.1.4.4 [110/20] via 10.1.1.2, 00:06:46, Serial0/1
     10.0.0.0/30 is subnetted, 3 subnets
O E2    10.1.1.8 [110/20] via 10.1.1.2, 00:06:14, Serial0/1
C       10.1.1.0 is directly connected, Serial0/1
```

The 1.1.1.1 route that Router A was advertising as an OSPF external type 5 route has been blocked from entering the NSSA area by Router B, but the inter-area routes have been permitted. Also, notice that unlike a stub or totally stubby area there is no default route advertised by the ABR or ASBR.

Finally, modify the configuration on Router B to prevent the redistributed EIGRP routes from being advertised into Area 1, but still allow them to be advertised into Area 0.

```
Router B
router ospf 1
 area 1 nssa no-redistribution
 redistribute eigrp 1 subnets
```

```
network 10.1.1.0 0.0.0.3 area 0
network 10.1.1.4 0.0.0.3 area 1
```

Verify that Router B is no longer advertising the redistributed EIGRP routes into Area 1.

```
rtrB#show ip ospf
 Routing Process "ospf 1" with ID 2.2.2.2
 Supports only single TOS(TOS0) routes
 It is an area border and autonomous system boundary router
 Redistributing External Routes from,
    eigrp 1, includes subnets in redistribution
 SPF schedule delay 5 secs, Hold time between two SPFs 10 secs
 Minimum LSA interval 5 secs. Minimum LSA arrival 1 secs
 Number of external LSA 7. Checksum Sum 0x3EFB5
 Number of DCbitless external LSA 0
 Number of DoNotAge external LSA 0
 Number of areas in this router is 2. 1 normal 0 stub 1 nssa
    Area BACKBONE(0)
        Number of interfaces in this area is 1
        Area has no authentication
        SPF algorithm executed 11 times
        Area ranges are
        Number of LSA 3. Checksum Sum 0x26FDC
        Number of DCbitless LSA 0
        Number of indication LSA 0
        Number of DoNotAge LSA 0
    Area 1
        Number of interfaces in this area is 1
        It is a NSSA area, no redistribution into this area
        Perform type-7/type-5 LSA translation
        Area has no authentication
        SPF algorithm executed 26 times
        Area ranges are
        Number of LSA 7. Checksum Sum 0x31A46
        Number of DCbitless LSA 0
        Number of indication LSA 0
        Number of DoNotAge LSA 0
```

```
rtrC#show ip route
Codes: C - connected, S - static, I - IGRP, R - RIP, M - mobile, B - BGP
       D - EIGRP, EX - EIGRP external, O - OSPF, IA - OSPF inter area
       N1 - OSPF NSSA external type 1, N2 - OSPF NSSA external type 2
       E1 - OSPF external type 1, E2 - OSPF external type 2, E - EGP
       i - IS-IS, L1 - IS-IS level-1, L2 - IS-IS level-2, * - candidate default
       U - per-user static route, o - ODR

Gateway of last resort is not set

     3.0.0.0/24 is subnetted, 1 subnets
C       3.3.3.0 is directly connected, Loopback0
     156.26.0.0/24 is subnetted, 2 subnets
```

continues

```
R        156.26.32.0 [120/1] via 10.1.1.9, 00:00:02, Serial1
R        156.26.33.0 [120/1] via 10.1.1.9, 00:00:02, Serial1
     10.0.0.0/30 is subnetted, 3 subnets
C        10.1.1.8 is directly connected, Serial1
O IA     10.1.1.0 [110/128] via 10.1.1.5, 00:04:37, Serial0
C        10.1.1.4 is directly connected, Serial0
```

Verify that the redistributed EIGRP routes are being advertised into Area 0.

```
rtrA#show ip route
Codes: C - connected, S - static, I - IGRP, R - RIP, M - mobile, B - BGP
       D - EIGRP, EX - EIGRP external, O - OSPF, IA - OSPF inter area
       N1 - OSPF NSSA external type 1, N2 - OSPF NSSA external type 2
       E1 - OSPF external type 1, E2 - OSPF external type 2, E - EGP
       i - IS-IS, L1 - IS-IS level-1, L2 - IS-IS level-2, * - candidate default
       U - per-user static route, o - ODR

Gateway of last resort is not set

     1.0.0.0/32 is subnetted, 1 subnets
C       1.1.1.1 is directly connected, Loopback0
     156.26.0.0/24 is subnetted, 2 subnets
O E2    156.26.32.0 [110/20] via 10.1.1.2, 00:02:45, Serial0/1
O E2    156.26.33.0 [110/20] via 10.1.1.2, 00:02:45, Serial0/1
     172.16.0.0/24 is subnetted, 1 subnets
O E2    172.16.1.0 [110/20] via 10.1.1.2, 00:14:41, Serial0/1
     142.1.0.0/32 is subnetted, 1 subnets
O E2    142.1.4.4 [110/20] via 10.1.1.2, 00:14:41, Serial0/1
     10.0.0.0/30 is subnetted, 3 subnets
O E2    10.1.1.8 [110/20] via 10.1.1.2, 00:02:45, Serial0/1
C       10.1.1.0 is directly connected, Serial0/1
O IA    10.1.1.4 [110/128] via 10.1.1.2, 00:14:42, Serial0/1
```

Troubleshooting

Step 1 Verify that there is a neighbor relationship between the OSPF routers by using the **show ip ospf neighbor** command.

Step 2 Verify that every router in the NSSA has been configured with the command **area** *x* **nssa**.

Step 3 The **no-redistribute** keyword should only be used on the ASBR performing the route redistribution.

2-7: area *area-id* nssa no-summary

Syntax Description:

- *area-id*—OSPF area ID. This value can be entered as a decimal number in the range of 1 to 4,294,967,295 or in IP address form in the range 0.0.0.1 to 255.255.255.255. Area 0 can be entered, but Area 0 cannot be configured as an NSSA.

Purpose: This command is used on an OSPF ABR to block OSPF inter-area routes from entering an NSSA. This command will also generate an OSPF inter-area default route into the NSSA. This will make the NSSA a totally stubby area. In a stub or totally stubby area, the ABR to the stub area will prevent OSPF external routes (type 5) from being advertised into the stub area. This implies that an ASBR cannot be part of a stubby or totally stubby area because an ASBR generates OSPF external type 5 routes. Situations arise where you want to create a stubby or totally stubby area relative to OSPF but also want to advertise redistributed routes from an ASBR across the area. An OSPF area that has these properties is an NSSA. In Figure 2-7, you want Router B, the ABR, to block OSPF external routes and OSPF inter-area routes from Area 1 and advertise a default route into the NSSA. You also want the routes redistributed by Router C, the ASBR, to be allowed into the area. If you configure Area 1 as an NSSA, then the external OSPF routes that Router B receives from Area 0 will be blocked from Area 1. The redistributed routes from the ASBR will be sent as OSPF type 7 routes. Router B will convert these type 7 routes to OSPF type 5 routes and advertise them into Area 0. Normally, routes redistributed into OSPF are type 5 routes. An ASBR that has been configured as an NSSA will generate type 7 routes instead of type 5 routes. By default, an ABR does not generate a default route into an NSSA.

Initial Cisco IOS Software Release: 11.2

Configuration Example: Creating a Totally Stubby NSSA

In Figure 2-7, Routers C and D are running RIP version 2. Router D is advertising the networks 156.26.32.0/24 and 156.26.33.0/24 to Router C via RIP. Router C will redistribute the RIP routes, including the 10.1.1.8/30 network, into OSPF. Because Area 1 has been defined as an NSSA, the redistributed RIP routes will be advertised into Area 1 as OSPF type 7 routes. Initially we will configure Area 1 as a normal OSPF area in order to see the routes that are advertised.

Figure 2-7 *A Totally Stubby NSSA*

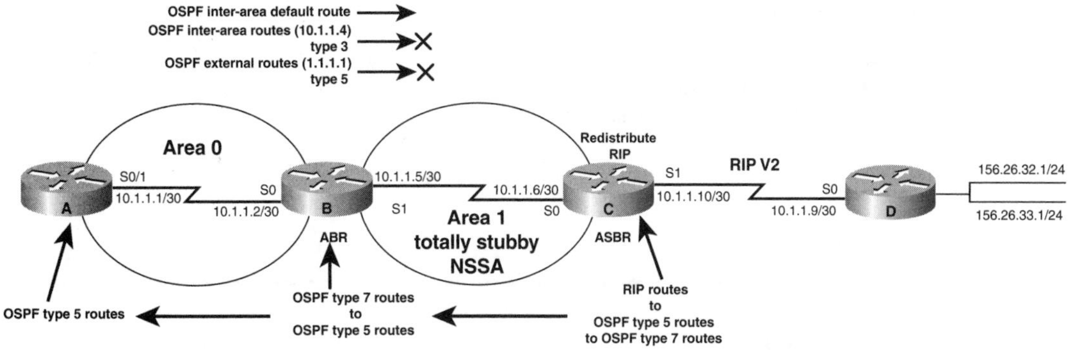

```
Router A
interface Loopback0
 ip address 1.1.1.1 255.255.255.255
!
interface Serial0/1
 ip address 10.1.1.1 255.255.255.252
 clockrate 64000
!
router ospf 1
 redistribute connected subnets
 network 10.1.1.0 0.0.0.3 area 0
```

```
Router B
interface Loopback0
 ip address 2.2.2.2 255.255.255.255
!
interface Serial0
 ip address 10.1.1.2 255.255.255.252
!
interface Serial1
 ip address 10.1.1.5 255.255.255.252
 lockrate 64000
!
router ospf 1
 network 10.1.1.0 0.0.0.3 area 0
 network 10.1.1.4 0.0.0.3 area 1
```

```
Router C
interface Loopback0
 ip address 3.3.3.3 255.255.255.255
!
interface Serial0
 ip address 10.1.1.6 255.255.255.252
!
interface Serial1
 ip address 10.1.1.10 255.255.255.252
 clockrate 64000
!
router ospf 1
 redistribute rip subnets
 network 10.1.1.4 0.0.0.3 area 1
!
router rip
 version 2
 passive-interface Serial0
 network 10.0.0.0
```

```
Router D
interface Loopback0
 ip address 156.26.32.1 255.255.255.0
!
```

```
interface Loopback1
 ip address 156.26.33.1 255.255.255.0
!
interface Serial0/0
 ip address 10.1.1.9 255.255.255.252
!
router rip
 version 2
 network 10.0.0.0
 network 156.26.0.0
 no auto-summary
```

Router A is advertising Loopback0 as an OSPF type 5 external route because this route was injected into OSPF through redistribution. Routers A and B are also learning the redistributed RIP routes as external type 5 OSPF routes.

```
rtrA#show ip route
Codes: C - connected, S - static, I - IGRP, R - RIP, M - mobile, B - BGP
       D - EIGRP, EX - EIGRP external, O - OSPF, IA - OSPF inter area
       N1 - OSPF NSSA external type 1, N2 - OSPF NSSA external type 2
       E1 - OSPF external type 1, E2 - OSPF external type 2, E - EGP
       i - IS-IS, L1 - IS-IS level-1, L2 - IS-IS level-2, * - candidate default
       U - per-user static route, o - ODR

Gateway of last resort is not set

     1.0.0.0/32 is subnetted, 1 subnets
C       1.1.1.1 is directly connected, Loopback0
     156.26.0.0/24 is subnetted, 2 subnets
O E2    156.26.32.0 [110/20] via 10.1.1.2, 00:02:25, Serial0/1
O E2    156.26.33.0 [110/20] via 10.1.1.2, 00:02:25, Serial0/1
     10.0.0.0/30 is subnetted, 3 subnets
O E2    10.1.1.8 [110/20] via 10.1.1.2, 00:02:25, Serial0/1
C       10.1.1.0 is directly connected, Serial0/1
O IA    10.1.1.4 [110/128] via 10.1.1.2, 00:02:25, Serial0/1
```

```
rtrB#show ip route
Codes: C - connected, S - static, I - IGRP, R - RIP, M - mobile, B - BGP
       D - EIGRP, EX - EIGRP external, O - OSPF, IA - OSPF inter area
       N1 - OSPF NSSA external type 1, N2 - OSPF NSSA external type 2
       E1 - OSPF external type 1, E2 - OSPF external type 2, E - EGP
       i - IS-IS, L1 - IS-IS level-1, L2 - IS-IS level-2, * - candidate default
       U - per-user static route, o - ODR

Gateway of last resort is not set

     1.0.0.0/32 is subnetted, 1 subnets
O E2    1.1.1.1 [110/20] via 10.1.1.1, 00:04:14, Serial0
     2.0.0.0/32 is subnetted, 1 subnets
C       2.2.2.2 is directly connected, Loopback0
```

continues

```
     156.26.0.0/24 is subnetted, 2 subnets
O E2    156.26.32.0 [110/20] via 10.1.1.6, 00:04:14, Serial1
O E2    156.26.33.0 [110/20] via 10.1.1.6, 00:04:14, Serial1
     10.0.0.0/30 is subnetted, 3 subnets
O E2    10.1.1.8 [110/20] via 10.1.1.6, 00:04:14, Serial1
C       10.1.1.0 is directly connected, Serial0
C       10.1.1.4 is directly connected, Serial1
```

Router C is learning the network redistributed by Router A as an OSPF external type 5 route.

```
rtrC#show ip route
Codes: C - connected, S - static, I - IGRP, R - RIP, M - mobile, B - BGP
       D - EIGRP, EX - EIGRP external, O - OSPF, IA - OSPF inter area
       N1 - OSPF NSSA external type 1, N2 - OSPF NSSA external type 2
       E1 - OSPF external type 1, E2 - OSPF external type 2, E - EGP
       i - IS-IS, L1 - IS-IS level-1, L2 - IS-IS level-2, * - candidate default
       U - per-user static route, o - ODR

Gateway of last resort is not set

     1.0.0.0/32 is subnetted, 1 subnets
O E2    1.1.1.1 [110/20] via 10.1.1.5, 00:06:24, Serial0
     3.0.0.0/24 is subnetted, 1 subnets
C       3.3.3.0 is directly connected, Loopback0
     156.26.0.0/24 is subnetted, 2 subnets
R       156.26.32.0 [120/1] via 10.1.1.9, 00:00:18, Serial1
R       156.26.33.0 [120/1] via 10.1.1.9, 00:00:18, Serial1
     10.0.0.0/30 is subnetted, 3 subnets
C       10.1.1.8 is directly connected, Serial1
O IA    10.1.1.0 [110/128] via 10.1.1.5, 00:06:24, Serial0
C       10.1.1.4 is directly connected, Serial0
```

Now modify the OSPF configurations on Routers B and C in order to create the NSSA.

```
Router B
router ospf 1
 area 1 nssa
 network 10.1.1.0 0.0.0.3 area 0
 network 10.1.1.4 0.0.0.3 area 1
```

```
Router C
router ospf 1
 area 1 nssa
 redistribute rip subnets
 network 10.1.1.4 0.0.0.3 area 1
```

Verify that Area 1 has been configured as an NSSA.

```
rtrB#show ip ospf
 Routing Process "ospf 1" with ID 2.2.2.2
 Supports only single TOS(TOS0) routes
 It is an area border and autonomous system boundary router
 Redistributing External Routes from,
 SPF schedule delay 5 secs, Hold time between two SPFs 10 secs
 Minimum LSA interval 5 secs. Minimum LSA arrival 1 secs
 Number of external LSA 5. Checksum Sum 0x324D4
 Number of DCbitless external LSA 0
 Number of DoNotAge external LSA 0
 Number of areas in this router is 2. 1 normal 0 stub 1 nssa
    Area BACKBONE(0)
        Number of interfaces in this area is 1
        Area has no authentication
        SPF algorithm executed 11 times
        Area ranges are
        Number of LSA 3. Checksum Sum 0x20790
        Number of DCbitless LSA 0
        Number of indication LSA 0
        Number of DoNotAge LSA 0
    Area 1
        Number of interfaces in this area is 1
        It is a NSSA area
        Perform type-7/type-5 LSA translation
        Area has no authentication
        SPF algorithm executed 22 times
        Area ranges are
        Number of LSA 7. Checksum Sum 0x26D1D
        Number of DCbitless LSA 0
        Number of indication LSA 0
        Number of DoNotAge LSA 0
```

Now inspect the routing tables on Routers A, B, and C to view the effect of configuring Area 1 as an NSSA.

```
rtrB#show ip route
Codes: C - connected, S - static, I - IGRP, R - RIP, M - mobile, B - BGP
       D - EIGRP, EX - EIGRP external, O - OSPF, IA - OSPF inter area
       N1 - OSPF NSSA external type 1, N2 - OSPF NSSA external type 2
       E1 - OSPF external type 1, E2 - OSPF external type 2, E - EGP
       i - IS-IS, L1 - IS-IS level-1, L2 - IS-IS level-2, * - candidate default
       U - per-user static route, o - ODR

Gateway of last resort is not set

     1.0.0.0/32 is subnetted, 1 subnets
O E2    1.1.1.1 [110/20] via 10.1.1.1, 00:03:55, Serial0
     2.0.0.0/32 is subnetted, 1 subnets
```

continues

```
C       2.2.2.2 is directly connected, Loopback0
     156.26.0.0/24 is subnetted, 2 subnets
O N2    156.26.32.0 [110/20] via 10.1.1.6, 00:03:55, Serial1
O N2    156.26.33.0 [110/20] via 10.1.1.6, 00:03:55, Serial1
     10.0.0.0/30 is subnetted, 3 subnets
O N2    10.1.1.8 [110/20] via 10.1.1.6, 00:03:55, Serial1
C       10.1.1.0 is directly connected, Serial0
C       10.1.1.4 is directly connected, Serial1
```

The redistributed RIP routes have been converted from OSPF E2 routes to OSPF N2 routes. This means that the redistributed RIP routes are now being advertised as type 7 routes instead of type 5 routes. On Router A, these routes should still be OSPF type 5 routes because Router B is converting them from type 7 to type 5.

```
rtrA#show ip route
Codes: C - connected, S - static, I - IGRP, R - RIP, M - mobile, B - BGP
       D - EIGRP, EX - EIGRP external, O - OSPF, IA - OSPF inter area
       N1 - OSPF NSSA external type 1, N2 - OSPF NSSA external type 2
       E1 - OSPF external type 1, E2 - OSPF external type 2, E - EGP
       i - IS-IS, L1 - IS-IS level-1, L2 - IS-IS level-2, * - candidate default
       U - per-user static route, o - ODR

Gateway of last resort is not set

     1.0.0.0/32 is subnetted, 1 subnets
C       1.1.1.1 is directly connected, Loopback0
     156.26.0.0/24 is subnetted, 2 subnets
O E2    156.26.32.0 [110/20] via 10.1.1.2, 00:07:28, Serial0/1
O E2    156.26.33.0 [110/20] via 10.1.1.2, 00:07:28, Serial0/1
     10.0.0.0/30 is subnetted, 3 subnets
O E2    10.1.1.8 [110/20] via 10.1.1.2, 00:07:28, Serial0/1
C       10.1.1.0 is directly connected, Serial0/1
O IA    10.1.1.4 [110/128] via 10.1.1.2, 00:08:31, Serial0/1
```

Finally, inspect the IP routing table on Router C.

```
rtrC#show ip route
Codes: C - connected, S - static, I - IGRP, R - RIP, M - mobile, B - BGP
       D - EIGRP, EX - EIGRP external, O - OSPF, IA - OSPF inter area
       N1 - OSPF NSSA external type 1, N2 - OSPF NSSA external type 2
       E1 - OSPF external type 1, E2 - OSPF external type 2, E - EGP
       i - IS-IS, L1 - IS-IS level-1, L2 - IS-IS level-2, * - candidate default
       U - per-user static route, o - ODR

Gateway of last resort is not set

     3.0.0.0/24 is subnetted, 1 subnets
C       3.3.3.0 is directly connected, Loopback0
     156.26.0.0/24 is subnetted, 2 subnets
```

```
R       156.26.32.0 [120/1] via 10.1.1.9, 00:00:10, Serial1
R       156.26.33.0 [120/1] via 10.1.1.9, 00:00:10, Serial1
     10.0.0.0/30 is subnetted, 3 subnets
C       10.1.1.8 is directly connected, Serial1
O IA    10.1.1.0 [110/128] via 10.1.1.5, 00:08:58, Serial0
C       10.1.1.4 is directly connected, Serial0
```

The 1.1.1.1 route that Router A was advertising as an OSPF external type 5 route has been blocked from entering the NSSA area by Router B, but the inter-area routes have been permitted. Also notice that unlike a stub or totally stubby area, there is no default route advertised by the ABR or ASBR.

Modify the configuration on Router B in order to generate a default route into the NSSA and to block OSPF inter-area routes.

```
Router B
router ospf 1
 area 1 nssa no-summary
 network 10.1.1.0 0.0.0.3 area 0
 network 10.1.1.4 0.0.0.3 area 1
```

Verification

Verify that a default route is being advertised into the NSSA and that OSPF inter-area routes are being blocked by the ABR by inspecting the routing table on Router C.

```
rtrC#show ip route
Codes: C - connected, S - static, I - IGRP, R - RIP, M - mobile, B - BGP
       D - EIGRP, EX - EIGRP external, O - OSPF, IA - OSPF inter area
       N1 - OSPF NSSA external type 1, N2 - OSPF NSSA external type 2
       E1 - OSPF external type 1, E2 - OSPF external type 2, E - EGP
       i - IS-IS, L1 - IS-IS level-1, L2 - IS-IS level-2, * - candidate default
       U - per-user static route, o - ODR

Gateway of last resort is 10.1.1.5 to network 0.0.0.0

     3.0.0.0/24 is subnetted, 1 subnets
C       3.3.3.0 is directly connected, Loopback0
     156.26.0.0/24 is subnetted, 2 subnets
R       156.26.32.0 [120/1] via 10.1.1.9, 00:00:25, Serial1
R       156.26.33.0 [120/1] via 10.1.1.9, 00:00:25, Serial1
     10.0.0.0/30 is subnetted, 2 subnets
C       10.1.1.8 is directly connected, Serial1
C       10.1.1.4 is directly connected, Serial0
O*IA 0.0.0.0/0 [110/65] via 10.1.1.5, 00:00:03, Serial0
```

Troubleshooting

Step 1 Verify that there is a neighbor relationship between the OSPF routers by using the **show ip ospf neighbor** command.

Step 2 Verify that every router in the NSSA has been configured with the command **area** *x* **nssa**.

Step 3 The command option **no-summary** can only be used on the NSSA ABR. Ensure that this command has been configured on the ABR.

2-8: area *area-id* range *ip-address mask*

2-9: area *area-id* range *ip-address mask* advertise

2-10: area *area-id* range *ip-address mask* not-advertise

Syntax Description:

- *area-id*—OSPF area ID. This value can be entered as a decimal number in the range of 0 to 4,294,967,295 or in IP address form in the range 0.0.0.0 to 255.255.255.255.
- *ip-address*—IP address of the summary route.
- *mask*—Subnet mask used to generate the summary.

Purpose: OSPF can summarize OSPF routes from the backbone or Area 0 into a non-zero OSPF area or from a non-zero area into the backbone. OSPF route summarization can only occur on an ABR. An ABR is a router than has at least one interface in Area 0 and at least one interface in a non-zero OSPF area. Commands 2-8 and 2-9 are equivalent. Using the keyword **not-advertise** will suppress the advertisement of the summary route by the ABR.

Initial Cisco IOS Software Release: 10.0

Configuration Example 1: Summarizing OSPF Routes from a Non-zero OSPF Area into the Backbone

In Figure 2-8, Router B will summarize the four Area 1 routes into Area 0. This example simulates four networks on Router B using loopback interfaces. These four networks will then be summarized into the backbone using the **area range** command.

Figure 2-8 *An ABR Can Summarize OSPF Routes from a Non-zero Area into the Backbone or Area 0*

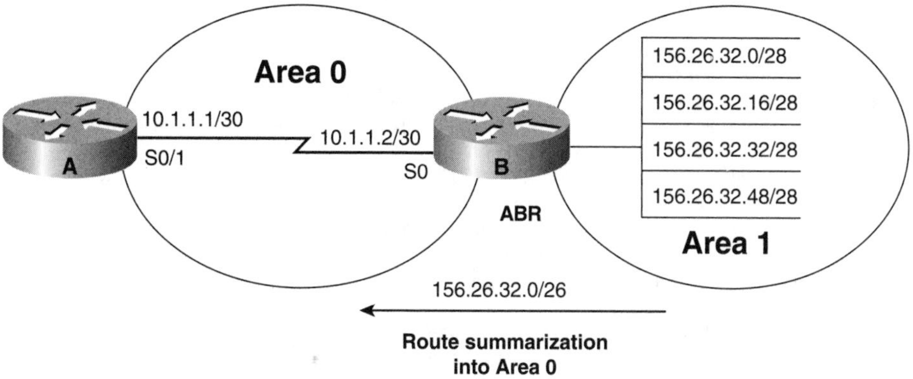


```
Router A
interface Loopback0
 ip address 1.1.1.1 255.255.255.255
!
interface Serial0/1
 ip address 10.1.1.1 255.255.255.252
 clockrate 64000
!
router ospf 1
 network 10.1.1.0 0.0.0.3 area 0
```

```
Router B
interface Loopback0
 ip address 2.2.2.2 255.255.255.255
!
interface Loopback1
 ip address 156.26.32.1 255.255.255.240
!
interface Loopback2
 ip address 156.26.32.17 255.255.255.240
!
interface Loopback3
 ip address 156.26.32.33 255.255.255.240
!
interface Loopback4
 ip address 156.26.32.49 255.255.255.240
!
interface Serial0
 ip address 10.1.1.2 255.255.255.252
!
router ospf 1
 network 10.1.1.0 0.0.0.3 area 0
 network 156.26.32.0 0.0.0.63 area 1
```

Before summarizing the routes, inspect the IP routing table on Router A to verify that the four networks are being advertised.

```
rtrA#show ip route
Codes: C - connected, S - static, I - IGRP, R - RIP, M - mobile, B - BGP
       D - EIGRP, EX - EIGRP external, O - OSPF, IA - OSPF inter area
       N1 - OSPF NSSA external type 1, N2 - OSPF NSSA external type 2
       E1 - OSPF external type 1, E2 - OSPF external type 2, E - EGP
       i - IS-IS, L1 - IS-IS level-1, L2 - IS-IS level-2, * - candidate default
       U - per-user static route, o - ODR

Gateway of last resort is not set

     1.0.0.0/32 is subnetted, 1 subnets
C       1.1.1.1 is directly connected, Loopback0
     156.26.0.0/32 is subnetted, 4 subnets
O IA    156.26.32.33 [110/65] via 10.1.1.2, 00:06:57, Serial0/1
O IA    156.26.32.49 [110/65] via 10.1.1.2, 00:06:57, Serial0/1
O IA    156.26.32.1 [110/65] via 10.1.1.2, 00:06:57, Serial0/1
O IA    156.26.32.17 [110/65] via 10.1.1.2, 00:06:57, Serial0/1
     10.0.0.0/30 is subnetted, 2 subnets
C       10.1.1.0 is directly connected, Serial0/1
```

A 26-bit subnet mask is required to summarize the four loopback addresses being advertised by Router B. Modify the configuration on Router B in order to summarize the four loopback addresses.

```
Router B
router ospf 1
 area 1 range 156.26.32.0 255.255.255.192
 network 10.1.1.0 0.0.0.3 area 0
 network 156.26.32.0 0.0.0.63 area 1
```

There are two important components to notice in the **area range** command. The first is the area ID. This is the area where the routes originated. In this example, the originating area is Area 1. The second component is the mask that is used with the **area range** command. The format of the mask is the opposite of the format used with the OSPF **network** command.

Verification

Verify that the four loopback networks have been summarized by Router B by inspecting the IP routing table on Router A.

```
rtrA#show ip route
Codes: C - connected, S - static, I - IGRP, R - RIP, M - mobile, B - BGP
       D - EIGRP, EX - EIGRP external, O - OSPF, IA - OSPF inter area
       N1 - OSPF NSSA external type 1, N2 - OSPF NSSA external type 2
       E1 - OSPF external type 1, E2 - OSPF external type 2, E - EGP
       i - IS-IS, L1 - IS-IS level-1, L2 - IS-IS level-2, * - candidate default
       U - per-user static route, o - ODR

Gateway of last resort is not set

     1.0.0.0/32 is subnetted, 1 subnets
C       1.1.1.1 is directly connected, Loopback0
     156.26.0.0/26 is subnetted, 1 subnets
O IA    156.26.32.0 [110/65] via 10.1.1.2, 00:04:57, Serial0/1
     10.0.0.0/30 is subnetted, 2 subnets
C       10.1.1.8 is directly connected, Serial0/0
C       10.1.1.0 is directly connected, Serial0/1
```

Configuration Example 2: Summarizing OSPF Routes from Area 0 into a Non-zero OSPF Area

In Figure 2-9, Router B will summarize the four Area 0 routes into Area 1. This example simulates four networks on Router B using loopback interfaces. These four networks will then be summarized into Area 1 from Area 0 using the **area range** command. The configuration changes from the previous example are highlighted in the following listing.

Figure 2-9 *An ABR Can Summarize OSPF Routes from the Backbone or Area 0 into a Non-Zero Area*

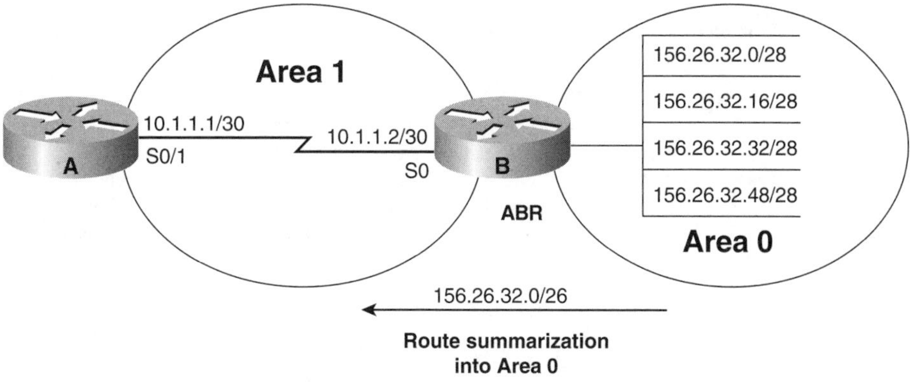

```
Router A
interface Loopback0
 ip address 1.1.1.1 255.255.255.255
!
interface Serial0/1
 ip address 10.1.1.1 255.255.255.252
 clockrate 64000
!
router ospf 1
 network 10.1.1.0 0.0.0.3 area 1
```

```
Router B
interface Loopback0
 ip address 2.2.2.2 255.255.255.255
!
interface Loopback1
 ip address 156.26.32.1 255.255.255.240
!
interface Loopback2
 ip address 156.26.32.17 255.255.255.240
!
interface Loopback3
 ip address 156.26.32.33 255.255.255.240
!
interface Loopback4
 ip address 156.26.32.49 255.255.255.240
!
interface Serial0
 ip address 10.1.1.2 255.255.255.252
!
router ospf 1
 network 10.1.1.0 0.0.0.3 area 1
 network 156.26.32.0 0.0.0.63 area 0
```

Before summarizing the routes, inspect the IP routing table on Router A to verify that the four networks are being advertised.

```
rtrA#show ip route
Codes: C - connected, S - static, I - IGRP, R - RIP, M - mobile, B - BGP
       D - EIGRP, EX - EIGRP external, O - OSPF, IA - OSPF inter area
       N1 - OSPF NSSA external type 1, N2 - OSPF NSSA external type 2
       E1 - OSPF external type 1, E2 - OSPF external type 2, E - EGP
       i - IS-IS, L1 - IS-IS level-1, L2 - IS-IS level-2, * - candidate default
       U - per-user static route, o - ODR

Gateway of last resort is not set

     1.0.0.0/32 is subnetted, 1 subnets
C       1.1.1.1 is directly connected, Loopback0
     156.26.0.0/32 is subnetted, 4 subnets
```

```
O IA     156.26.32.33 [110/65] via 10.1.1.2, 00:06:29, Serial0/1
O IA     156.26.32.49 [110/65] via 10.1.1.2, 00:06:29, Serial0/1
O IA     156.26.32.1 [110/65] via 10.1.1.2, 00:06:29, Serial0/1
O IA     156.26.32.17 [110/65] via 10.1.1.2, 00:06:29, Serial0/1
     10.0.0.0/30 is subnetted, 2 subnets
C       10.1.1.8 is directly connected, Serial0/0
C       10.1.1.0 is directly connected, Serial0/1
```

A 26-bit subnet mask is required to summarize the four loopback addresses being advertised by Router B. Modify the configuration on Router B in order to summarize the four loopback addresses.

```
Router B
router ospf 1
 area 0 range 156.26.32.0 255.255.255.192
 network 10.1.1.0 0.0.0.3 area 1
 network 156.26.32.0 0.0.0.63 area 0
```

Verification

Verify that the four loopback networks have been summarized by Router B by inspecting the IP routing table on Router A.

```
rtrA#show ip route
Codes: C - connected, S - static, I - IGRP, R - RIP, M - mobile, B - BGP
       D - EIGRP, EX - EIGRP external, O - OSPF, IA - OSPF inter area
       N1 - OSPF NSSA external type 1, N2 - OSPF NSSA external type 2
       E1 - OSPF external type 1, E2 - OSPF external type 2, E - EGP
       i - IS-IS, L1 - IS-IS level-1, L2 - IS-IS level-2, * - candidate default
       U - per-user static route, o - ODR

Gateway of last resort is not set

     1.0.0.0/32 is subnetted, 1 subnets
C       1.1.1.1 is directly connected, Loopback0
     156.26.0.0/26 is subnetted, 1 subnets
O IA     156.26.32.0 [110/65] via 10.1.1.2, 00:04:57, Serial0/1
     10.0.0.0/30 is subnetted, 2 subnets
C       10.1.1.8 is directly connected, Serial0/0
C       10.1.1.0 is directly connected, Serial0/1
```

Configuration Example 3: Using a Static Route to Null 0 for the Summary Address

If the ABR has a default static route pointing to the router that is receiving the summary for the four loopback addresses, then this could create a forwarding loop. In Figure 2-10, the network 156.26.32.0/28 is down. Also, Router B has a default static route pointing to Router A. Router A is receiving a summary from Router B that contains the network 156.26.32.0/28.

Figure 2-10 *A Forwarding Loop Can Be Created If the Router Advertising the Summary Has a Default Static Route*

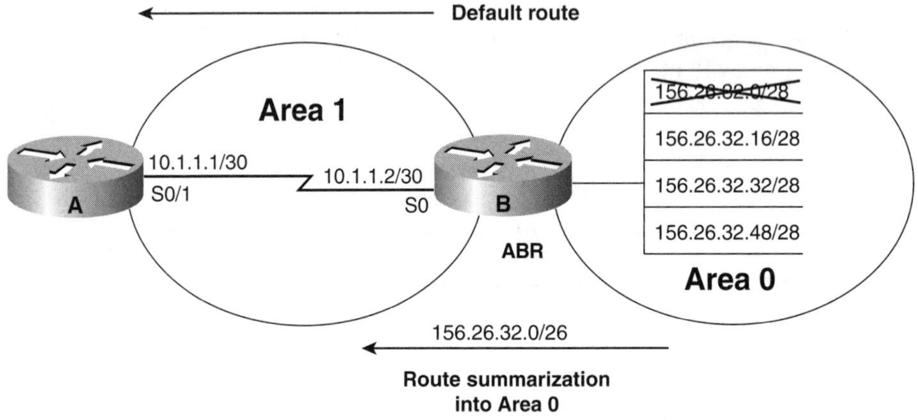


```
Router A
interface Loopback0
 ip address 1.1.1.1 255.255.255.255
!
interface Serial0/1
 ip address 10.1.1.1 255.255.255.252
 clockrate 64000
!
router ospf 1
 network 10.1.1.0 0.0.0.3 area 1
```

```
Router B
interface Loopback0
 ip address 2.2.2.2 255.255.255.255
!
interface Loopback1
 ip address 156.26.32.1 255.255.255.240
 shutdown
!
interface Loopback2
 ip address 156.26.32.17 255.255.255.240
!
interface Loopback3
 ip address 156.26.32.33 255.255.255.240
!
interface Loopback4
 ip address 156.26.32.49 255.255.255.240
```

```
!
interface Serial0
 ip address 10.1.1.2 255.255.255.252
 no ip directed-broadcast
!
router ospf 1
 network 10.1.1.0 0.0.0.3 area 1
 network 156.26.32.0 0.0.0.63 area 0
!
ip route 0.0.0.0 0.0.0.0 Serial0
```

When Router A sends traffic to Router B for host 156.26.32.1, Router B will not find this specific network in the IP routing table. Router B will then use the default route and send the traffic back to Router A as seen in the following ping trace.

```
rtrA#trace 156.26.32.1

Type escape sequence to abort.
Tracing the route to 156.26.32.1

  1 10.1.1.2 16 msec 16 msec 16 msec
  2 10.1.1.1 28 msec 28 msec 28 msec
```

To prevent this situation, create a static route to Null0 for every summary that the ABR is advertising. In IOS 12.X, OSPF will automatically create the route to Null0 for the summary.

```
Router B
ip route 0.0.0.0 0.0.0.0 Serial0
ip route 156.26.32.0 255.255.255.192 Null0
```

Even if the ABR does not have a default route, it is always a good idea to create a static route to Null0 for every summary that the ABR is advertising. If you now perform a ping trace from Router A you can see that Router B is discarding the traffic since the specific route for 156.26.32.1 is no longer in the IP routing table. Router B will look up the best match for the route, which is now Null0. The traffic will be discarded.

```
rtrA#trace 156.26.32.1

Type escape sequence to abort.
Tracing the route to 156.26.32.1

  1 10.1.1.2 16 msec 16 msec 16 msec
  2 10.1.1.2 !H  !H  *
```

Troubleshooting

Step 1 Verify that there is a neighbor relationship between the OSPF routers by using the **show ip ospf neighbor** command.

Step 2 The **area** *area-id* **range** command will only work on an OSPF ABR.

Step 3 Verify that you are using the proper area ID in the **area** *area-id* **range** command.

Step 4 Verify that you are using the correct IP address and mask with the **area range** command.

2-11: area *area-id* stub

Syntax Description:

- *area-id*—OSPF area ID. This value can be entered as a decimal number in the range of 0 to 4,294,967,295 or in IP address form in the range 0.0.0.0 to 255.255.255.255.

Purpose: In Figure 2-11, Area 1 has one exit point. Routers in Area 1 do not need to know the specific external routes that are being redistributed into OSPF by the ASBR. Therefore, Area 1 can be configured as a stub area and the ABR will advertise a default route into Area 1.

In Figure 2-12, Area 1 has two exit points. If routing to the external networks that have been redistributed into OSPF by the ASBR can be sub-optimal, then Area 1 can be configured as a stub area. The routers in Area 1 will be receiving a default route advertisement from both ABRs. All routers in a stub area, including the ABR, must be configured with the command **area** *area-id* **stub**. Inter-area OSPF routes will be advertised into a stub area but external OSPF routes will be blocked. The ABR for the stub area will inject a default route into the stub area. The backbone or Area 0 cannot be configured as a stub area. An ASBR cannot be part of a stub area since the purpose of an ASBR is to inject external routes into OSPF. A stub area cannot be used as the transit area for a virtual link.

Initial Cisco IOS Software Release: 10.0

Figure 2-11 *An OSPF Stub Area with One Exit*

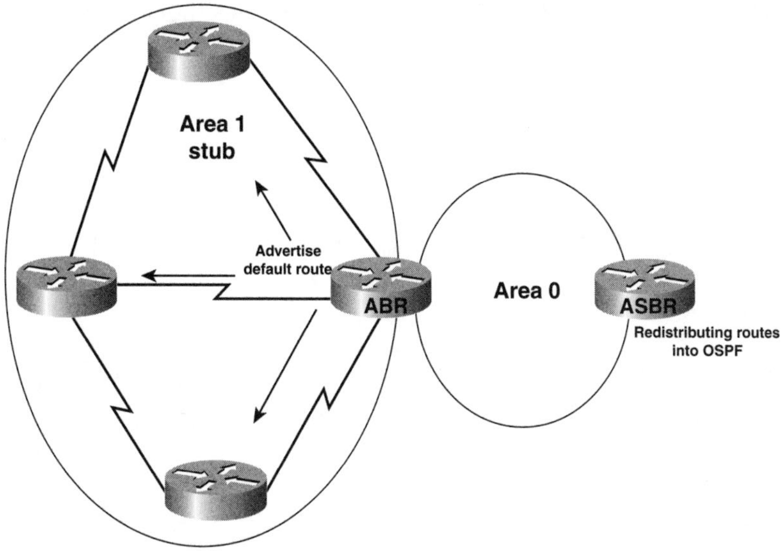

Figure 2-12 *An OSPF Stub Area with Multiple Exits*

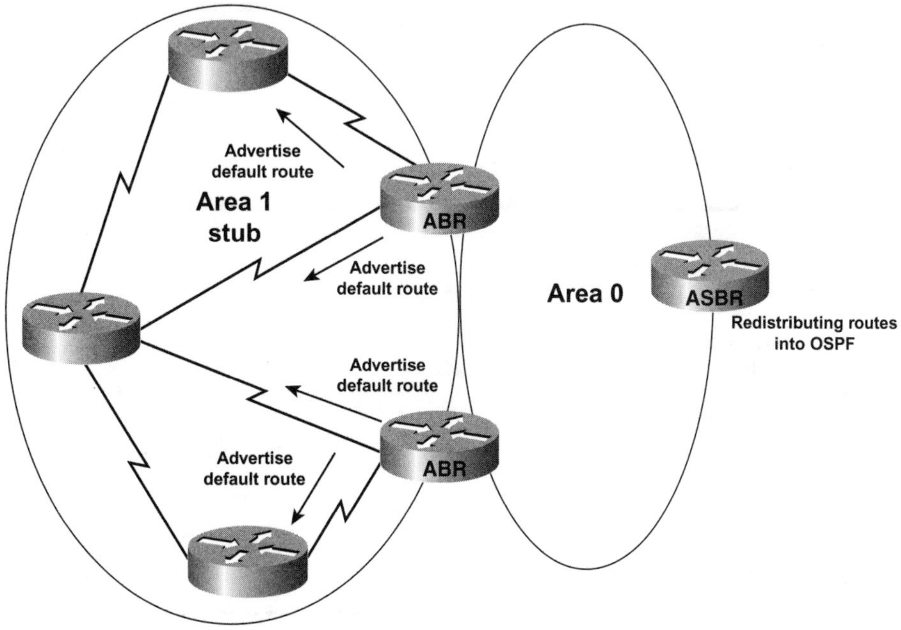

Configuration Example: Configuring an OSPF Stub Area

In Figure 2-13, Router C is redistributing connected interfaces into OSPF. These redistributed routes are OSPF external routes.

Figure 2-13 *An OSPF Stub Area*

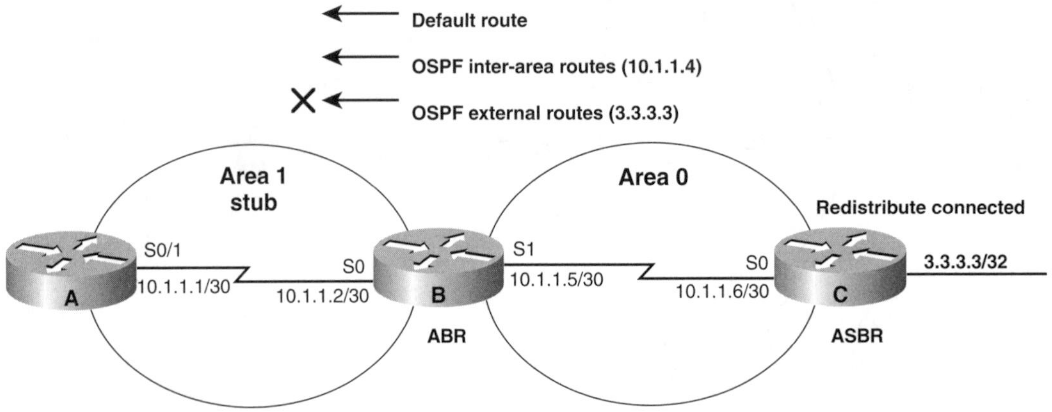


```
Router A
interface Loopback0
 ip address 1.1.1.1 255.255.255.255
!
interface Serial0/1
 ip address 10.1.1.1 255.255.255.252
 clockrate 64000
!
router ospf 1
 network 10.1.1.0 0.0.0.3 area 1
```

```
Router B
interface Loopback0
 ip address 2.2.2.2 255.255.255.255
!
interface Serial0
 ip address 10.1.1.2 255.255.255.252
!
interface Serial1
 ip address 10.1.1.5 255.255.255.252
 clock rate 64000
!
router ospf 1
 network 10.1.1.4 0.0.0.3 area 0
 network 10.1.1.0 0.0.0.3 area 1
```

```
Router C
interface Loopback0
 ip address 3.3.3.3 255.255.255.255
```

```
!
interface Serial0
 ip address 10.1.1.6 255.255.255.252
!
router ospf 1
 redistribute connected subnets
 network 10.1.1.4 0.0.0.15 area 0
```

Before configuring Area 1 as a stub area, verify that the redistributed routes are being advertised as OSPF external routes.

```
rtrA#show ip route
Codes: C - connected, S - static, I - IGRP, R - RIP, M - mobile, B - BGP
       D - EIGRP, EX - EIGRP external, O - OSPF, IA - OSPF inter area
       N1 - OSPF NSSA external type 1, N2 - OSPF NSSA external type 2
       E1 - OSPF external type 1, E2 - OSPF external type 2, E - EGP
       i - IS-IS, L1 - IS-IS level-1, L2 - IS-IS level-2, * - candidate default
       U - per-user static route, o - ODR

Gateway of last resort is not set

     1.0.0.0/32 is subnetted, 1 subnets
C       1.1.1.1 is directly connected, Loopback0
     3.0.0.0/32 is subnetted, 1 subnets
O E2    3.3.3.3 [110/20] via 10.1.1.2, 00:00:25, Serial0/1
     10.0.0.0/30 is subnetted, 3 subnets
C       10.1.1.8 is directly connected, Serial0/0
C       10.1.1.0 is directly connected, Serial0/1
O IA    10.1.1.4 [110/128] via 10.1.1.2, 00:00:25, Serial0/1
```

There is one OSPF external route and one OSPF inter-area route in the routing table on Router A. Configure Area 1 as a stub area by modifying the configurations on Routers A and B as shown in the following listing.

```
Router A
router ospf 1
 area 1 stub
 network 10.1.1.0 0.0.0.3 area 1
```

```
Router B
router ospf 1
 area 1 stub
 network 10.1.1.0 0.0.0.3 area 1
 network 10.1.1.4 0.0.0.3 area 0
```

Verification

Verify that OSPF inter-area routes are being advertised into the stub area. Also, verify that external OSPF routes have been blocked from being advertised into the stub area and that the ABR is injecting a default route into the stub area.

```
rtrA#show ip route
Codes: C - connected, S - static, I - IGRP, R - RIP, M - mobile, B - BGP
       D - EIGRP, EX - EIGRP external, O - OSPF, IA - OSPF inter area
       N1 - OSPF NSSA external type 1, N2 - OSPF NSSA external type 2
       E1 - OSPF external type 1, E2 - OSPF external type 2, E - EGP
       i - IS-IS, L1 - IS-IS level-1, L2 - IS-IS level-2, * - candidate default
       U - per-user static route, o - ODR

Gateway of last resort is 10.1.1.2 to network 0.0.0.0

     1.0.0.0/32 is subnetted, 1 subnets
C       1.1.1.1 is directly connected, Loopback0
     10.0.0.0/30 is subnetted, 3 subnets
C       10.1.1.8 is directly connected, Serial0/0
C       10.1.1.0 is directly connected, Serial0/1
O IA    10.1.1.4 [110/128] via 10.1.1.2, 00:00:04, Serial0/1
O*IA 0.0.0.0/0 [110/65] via 10.1.1.2, 00:00:04, Serial0/1
```

Verify that Area 1 is a stub area by using the command **show ip ospf** on Routers A and B.

```
rtrA#show ip ospf
 Routing Process "ospf 1" with ID 1.1.1.1
 Supports only single TOS(TOS0) routes
 SPF schedule delay 5 secs, Hold time between two SPFs 10 secs
 Minimum LSA interval 5 secs. Minimum LSA arrival 1 secs
 Number of external LSA 0. Checksum Sum 0x0
 Number of DCbitless external LSA 0
 Number of DoNotAge external LSA 0
 Number of areas in this router is 2. 1 normal 1 stub 0 nssa
    Area BACKBONE(0) (Inactive)
        Number of interfaces in this area is 0
        Area has no authentication
        SPF algorithm executed 2 times
        Area ranges are
        Number of LSA 1. Checksum Sum 0x51E9
        Number of DCbitless LSA 0
        Number of indication LSA 0
        Number of DoNotAge LSA 0
    Area 1
        Number of interfaces in this area is 1
        It is a stub area
        Area has no authentication
        SPF algorithm executed 6 times
        Area ranges are
```

```
        Number of LSA 9. Checksum Sum 0x38619
        Number of DCbitless LSA 0
        Number of indication LSA 0
        Number of DoNotAge LSA 0
```

```
rtrB#show ip ospf
 Routing Process "ospf 1" with ID 2.2.2.2
 Supports only single TOS(TOS0) routes
 It is an area border router
 SPF schedule delay 5 secs, Hold time between two SPFs 10 secs
 Minimum LSA interval 5 secs. Minimum LSA arrival 1 secs
 Number of external LSA 3. Checksum Sum 0x14F43
 Number of DCbitless external LSA 0
 Number of DoNotAge external LSA 3
 Number of areas in this router is 2. 1 normal 1 stub 0 nssa
    Area BACKBONE(0)
        Number of interfaces in this area is 1
        Area has no authentication
        SPF algorithm executed 15 times
        Area ranges are
        Number of LSA 4. Checksum Sum 0x20ABC
        Number of DCbitless LSA 0
        Number of indication LSA 0
        Number of DoNotAge LSA 0
    Area 1
        Number of interfaces in this area is 1
        It is a stub area
          generates stub default route with cost 1
        Area has no authentication
        SPF algorithm executed 18 times
        Area ranges are
        Number of LSA 8. Checksum Sum 0x34E69
        Number of DCbitless LSA 0
        Number of indication LSA 0
        Number of DoNotAge LSA 0
```

Troubleshooting

Step 1 Verify that there is a neighbor relationship between the OSPF routers by using the **show ip ospf neighbor** command.

Step 2 Ensure that every router in the stub area and the ABR to the stub area have the area configured as a stub using the router configuration command **area** *area-id* **stub**.

Step 3 An ASBR should not be part of a stub area.

Step 4 A stub area cannot be used as the transit area for a virtual link.

2-12: area *area-id* stub no-summary

Syntax Description:

- *area-id*—OSPF area ID. This value can be entered as a decimal number in the range of 0 to 4,294,967,295 or in IP address form in the range 0.0.0.0 to 255.255.255.255.

Purpose: Use of the **no-summary** keyword on the stub area's ABR creates a totally stubby area. In a totally stubby area, both external and inter-area OSPF routes are blocked from being advertised into the area. The backbone or Area 0 cannot be configured as a totally stubby area. An ASBR cannot be part of a totally stubby area, since the purpose of an ASBR is to inject external routes into OSPF. A totally stubby area cannot be used as the transit area for a virtual link.

Initial Cisco IOS Software Release: 10.0

Configuration Example: Configuring an OSPF Totally Stubby Area

In Figure 2-14, Router C is redistributing connected interfaces into OSPF. These redistributed routes are OSPF external routes.

Figure 2-14 *An OSPF Totally Stubby Area*

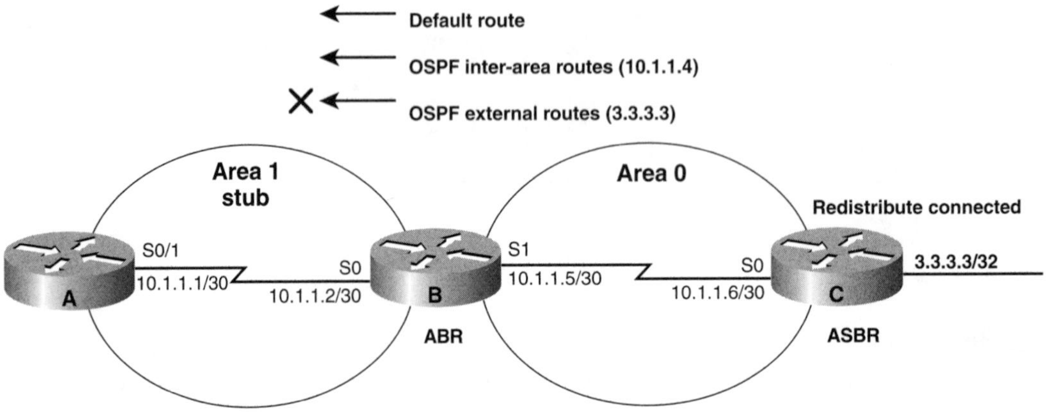


```
Router A
interface Loopback0
 ip address 1.1.1.1 255.255.255.255
!
interface Serial0/1
 ip address 10.1.1.1 255.255.255.252
 clockrate 64000
!
router ospf 1
 network 10.1.1.0 0.0.0.3 area 1
```

```
Router B
interface Loopback0
 ip address 2.2.2.2 255.255.255.255
!
interface Serial0
 ip address 10.1.1.2 255.255.255.252
!
interface Serial1
 ip address 10.1.1.5 255.255.255.252
 clock rate 64000
!
router ospf 1
network 10.1.1.4 0.0.0.3 area 0
network 10.1.1.0 0.0.0.3 area 1
```

```
Router C
interface Loopback0
 ip address 3.3.3.3 255.255.255.255
!
interface Serial0
 ip address 10.1.1.6 255.255.255.252
!
router ospf 1
 redistribute connected subnets
 network 10.1.1.4 0.0.0.15 area 0
```

Before configuring Area 1 as a totally stubby area, verify that the redistributed routes and OSPF inter-area routes are being advertised into Area 1.

```
rtrA#show ip route
Codes: C - connected, S - static, I - IGRP, R - RIP, M - mobile, B - BGP
       D - EIGRP, EX - EIGRP external, O - OSPF, IA - OSPF inter area
       N1 - OSPF NSSA external type 1, N2 - OSPF NSSA external type 2
       E1 - OSPF external type 1, E2 - OSPF external type 2, E - EGP
       i - IS-IS, L1 - IS-IS level-1, L2 - IS-IS level-2, * - candidate default
       U - per-user static route, o - ODR

Gateway of last resort is not set

     1.0.0.0/32 is subnetted, 1 subnets
C       1.1.1.1 is directly connected, Loopback0
     3.0.0.0/32 is subnetted, 1 subnets
O E2    3.3.3.3 [110/20] via 10.1.1.2, 00:00:02, Serial0/1
     10.0.0.0/30 is subnetted, 2 subnets
C       10.1.1.0 is directly connected, Serial0/1
O IA    10.1.1.4 [110/128] via 10.1.1.2, 00:00:02, Serial0/1
```

There is one OSPF external route and one OSPF inter-area route in the routing table on Router A. Configure Area 1 as a stub area by modifying the configurations on Routers A and B as shown in the following listing.

```
Router A
router ospf 1
 area 1 stub
 network 10.1.1.0 0.0.0.3 area 1
```

```
Router B
router ospf 1
 area 1 stub
 network 10.1.1.4 0.0.0.3 area 0
 network 10.1.1.0 0.0.0.3 area 1
```

Verification

Verify that the external OSPF routes have been blocked from being advertised into the stub area. Also verify that the ABR is injecting a default route into the stub area.

```
rtrA#show ip route
Codes: C - connected, S - static, I - IGRP, R - RIP, M - mobile, B - BGP
       D - EIGRP, EX - EIGRP external, O - OSPF, IA - OSPF inter area
       N1 - OSPF NSSA external type 1, N2 - OSPF NSSA external type 2
       E1 - OSPF external type 1, E2 - OSPF external type 2, E - EGP
       i - IS-IS, L1 - IS-IS level-1, L2 - IS-IS level-2, * - candidate default
       U - per-user static route, o - ODR

Gateway of last resort is 10.1.1.2 to network 0.0.0.0

     1.0.0.0/32 is subnetted, 1 subnets
C       1.1.1.1 is directly connected, Loopback0
     10.0.0.0/30 is subnetted, 2 subnets
C       10.1.1.0 is directly connected, Serial1
O IA    10.1.1.4 [110/128] via 10.1.1.2, 00:00:09, Serial0/1
O*IA 0.0.0.0/0 [110/65] via 10.1.1.2, 00:00:09, Serial0/1
```

Modify the configuration on Router B, the ABR, to create a totally stubby area.

```
Router B
router ospf 1
 area 1 stub no-summary
 network 10.1.1.4 0.0.0.3 area 0
 network 10.1.1.0 0.0.0.3 area 1
```

Verify that the OSPF inter-area routes are no longer being advertised by the ABR into the stub area.

```
rtrA#show ip route
Codes: C - connected, S - static, I - IGRP, R - RIP, M - mobile, B - BGP
       D - EIGRP, EX - EIGRP external, O - OSPF, IA - OSPF inter area
       N1 - OSPF NSSA external type 1, N2 - OSPF NSSA external type 2
       E1 - OSPF external type 1, E2 - OSPF external type 2, E - EGP
       i - IS-IS, L1 - IS-IS level-1, L2 - IS-IS level-2, * - candidate default
       U - per-user static route, o - ODR
Gateway of last resort is 10.1.1.2 to network 0.0.0.0

     1.0.0.0/32 is subnetted, 1 subnets
C       1.1.1.1 is directly connected, Loopback0
     10.0.0.0/30 is subnetted, 2 subnets
C       10.1.1.0 is directly connected, Serial0/1
O*IA 0.0.0.0/0 [110/65] via 10.1.1.2, 00:00:17, Serial0/1
```

You can also verify that Router B is blocking OSPF inter-area routes or summary LSAs by using the command **show ip ospf**.

```
rtrB#show ip ospf
 Routing Process "ospf 1" with ID 2.2.2.2
 Supports only single TOS(TOS0) routes
 It is an area border router
 SPF schedule delay 5 secs, Hold time between two SPFs 10 secs
 Minimum LSA interval 5 secs. Minimum LSA arrival 1 secs
 Number of external LSA 3. Checksum Sum 0x14946
 Number of DCbitless external LSA 0
 Number of DoNotAge external LSA 0
 Number of areas in this router is 2. 1 normal 1 stub 0 nssa
    Area BACKBONE(0)
        Number of interfaces in this area is 1
        Area has no authentication
        SPF algorithm executed 17 times
        Area ranges are
        Number of LSA 4. Checksum Sum 0x204BF
        Number of DCbitless LSA 0
        Number of indication LSA 0
        Number of DoNotAge LSA 0
    Area 1
        Number of interfaces in this area is 1
        It is a stub area, no summary LSA in this area
          generates stub default route with cost 1
        Area has no authentication
        SPF algorithm executed 25 times
        Area ranges are
        Number of LSA 7. Checksum Sum 0x424A1
        Number of DCbitless LSA 0
        Number of indication LSA 0
        Number of DoNotAge LSA 0
```

Troubleshooting

Step 1 Verify that there is a neighbor relationship between the OSPF routers by using the **show ip ospf neighbor** command.

Step 2 Ensure that every router in the stub area and the ABR to the stub area have the area configured as a stub by using the router configuration command **area** *area-id* **stub**.

Step 3 When creating a totally stubby area, verify that the keyword **no-summary** has been used on the ABR to the stub area.

Step 4 An ASBR should not be part of a totally stubby area.

Step 5 A totally stubby area cannot be used as the transit area for a virtual link.

2-13: area *transit-area-id* virtual-link *router-id*

Syntax Description:

- *transit-area-id*—The OSPF area ID of the area connecting the two ABRs that the virtual link will cross. This value can be entered as a decimal number in the range of 0 to 4,294,967,295 or in IP address form in the range 0.0.0.0 to 255.255.255.255.
- *router-id*—OSPF router ID of the router at the remote end of the virtual link.

Purpose: All non-zero OSPF areas must have a connection to the backbone or Area 0 and Area 0 must be contiguous. A virtual link is used to repair a segmented backbone or to connect a non-zero area that has been disconnected from Area 0. The transit area cannot be a stub area. Virtual links are used to repair a discontiguous backbone or to temporarily attach a disconnected non-zero area to the backbone. A virtual link should not be part of an initial OSPF design.

Initial Cisco IOS Software Release: 10.0

Configuration Example: Creating an OSPF Virtual Link

In Figure 2-15, Area 2 does not have a direct connection to Area 0. A virtual link is needed to repair this situation. Initially, you will configure the routers in Figure 2-15 without using a virtual link.

Figure 2-15 *OSPF Virtual Link*

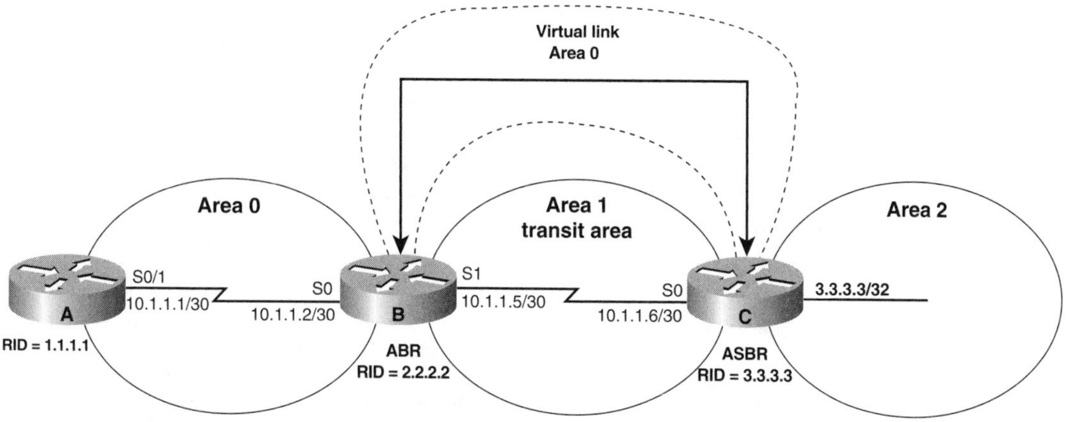


```
Router A
interface Loopback0
 ip address 1.1.1.1 255.255.255.255
!
interface Serial0/1
 ip address 10.1.1.1 255.255.255.252
 clockrate 64000
!
router ospf 1
 network 10.1.1.0 0.0.0.3 area 0
 network 1.1.1.1 0.0.0.0 area 0
```

```
Router B
interface Loopback0
 ip address 2.2.2.2 255.255.255.255
!
interface Serial0
 ip address 10.1.1.2 255.255.255.252
!
interface Serial1
 ip address 10.1.1.5 255.255.255.252
 clockrate 64000
!
router ospf 1
 network 10.1.1.0 0.0.0.3 area 0
 network 2.2.2.2 0.0.0.0 area 0
 network 10.1.1.4 0.0.0.3 area 1
```

```
Router C
interface Loopback0
 ip address 3.3.3.3 255.255.255.255
```

continues

```
!
interface Serial0
 ip address 10.1.1.6 255.255.255.252
!
router ospf 1
 network 3.3.3.3 0.0.0.0 area 2
 network 10.1.1.4 0.0.0.3 area 1
```

If you inspect the IP routing table on Router B, you will see that the 3.3.3.3 network from Router C is not present.

```
rtrB#show ip route
Codes: C - connected, S - static, I - IGRP, R - RIP, M - mobile, B - BGP
       D - EIGRP, EX - EIGRP external, O - OSPF, IA - OSPF inter area
       N1 - OSPF NSSA external type 1, N2 - OSPF NSSA external type 2
       E1 - OSPF external type 1, E2 - OSPF external type 2, E - EGP
       i - IS-IS, L1 - IS-IS level-1, L2 - IS-IS level-2, * - candidate default
       U - per-user static route, o - ODR

Gateway of last resort is not set

     1.0.0.0/32 is subnetted, 1 subnets
O IA    1.1.1.1 [110/65] via 10.1.1.1, 00:01:01, Serial0
     2.0.0.0/32 is subnetted, 1 subnets
C       2.2.2.2 is directly connected, Loopback0
     10.0.0.0/30 is subnetted, 2 subnets
C       10.1.1.0 is directly connected, Serial0
C       10.1.1.4 is directly connected, Serial1
```

Area 2 on Router C does not have a direct connection to Area 0. A virtual link needs to be configured to correct this situation. The transit area in this case is Area 1. You also need the router IDs of the two ABRs to be able to construct the virtual link. The first method to determine the router ID is to use the **show ip ospf neighbor** command. This will display the router ID of the remote end of the virtual link.

```
rtrB#show ip ospf neighbor

Neighbor ID     Pri   State           Dead Time   Address         Interface
1.1.1.1           1   FULL/  -        00:00:32    10.1.1.1        Serial0
3.3.3.3           1   FULL/  -        00:00:36    10.1.1.6        Serial1
```

```
rtrC#show ip ospf neighbor

Neighbor ID     Pri   State           Dead Time   Address         Interface
2.2.2.2           1   FULL/  -        00:00:35    10.1.1.5        Serial0
```

Router B has an ID of 2.2.2.2 and Router C has an ID of 3.3.3.3. The local router ID can be found by using the **show ip ospf** command.

```
rtrB#show ip ospf
 Routing Process "ospf 1" with ID 2.2.2.2
 Supports only single TOS(TOS0) routes
 It is an area border router
 SPF schedule delay 5 secs, Hold time between two SPFs 10 secs
 Minimum LSA interval 5 secs. Minimum LSA arrival 1 secs
 Number of external LSA 0. Checksum Sum 0x0
 Number of DCbitless external LSA 0
 Number of DoNotAge external LSA 0
 Number of areas in this router is 2. 2 normal 0 stub 0 nssa
    Area BACKBONE(0)
        Number of interfaces in this area is 2
        Area has no authentication
        SPF algorithm executed 3 times
        Area ranges are
        Number of LSA 3. Checksum Sum 0x1FD00
        Number of DCbitless LSA 0
        Number of indication LSA 0
        Number of DoNotAge LSA 0
    Area 1
        Number of interfaces in this area is 1
        Area has no authentication
        SPF algorithm executed 2 times
        Area ranges are
        Number of LSA 5. Checksum Sum 0x2B171
        Number of DCbitless LSA 0
        Number of indication LSA 0
        Number of DoNotAge LSA 0
```

```
rtrC#show ip ospf
 Routing Process "ospf 1" with ID 3.3.3.3
 Supports only single TOS(TOS0) routes
 SPF schedule delay 5 secs, Hold time between two SPFs 10 secs
 Minimum LSA interval 5 secs. Minimum LSA arrival 1 secs
 Number of external LSA 0. Checksum Sum 0x0
 Number of DCbitless external LSA 0
 Number of DoNotAge external LSA 0
 Number of areas in this router is 2. 2 normal 0 stub 0 nssa
    Area 1
        Number of interfaces in this area is 1
        Area has no authentication
        SPF algorithm executed 12 times
        Area ranges are
        Number of LSA 5. Checksum Sum 0x2B171
        Number of DCbitless LSA 0
        Number of indication LSA 0
        Number of DoNotAge LSA 0
    Area 2
```

continues

```
        Number of interfaces in this area is 1
        Area has no authentication
        SPF algorithm executed 1 times
        Area ranges are
        Number of LSA 1. Checksum Sum 0xDDE0
        Number of DCbitless LSA 0
        Number of indication LSA 0
        Number of DoNotAge LSA 0
```

We now have the information we need to configure the virtual link. On Router B, the form of the command is:

area *transit-area-id* **virtual-link** *router-C-ID*

And on Router C the command takes the form:

area *transit-area-id* **virtual-link** *router-B-ID*

Modify the configurations on Routers B and C to construct the virtual link.

```
Router B
router ospf 1
 area 1 virtual-link 3.3.3.3
 network 2.2.2.2 0.0.0.0 area 0
 network 10.1.1.0 0.0.0.3 area 0
 network 10.1.1.4 0.0.0.3 area 1
```

```
Router C
router ospf 1
 area 1 virtual-link 2.2.2.2
 network 3.3.3.3 0.0.0.0 area 2
 network 10.1.1.4 0.0.0.3 area 1
```

Verification

Verify that Router C has a connection to Area 0.

```
rtrC#show ip ospf
 Routing Process "ospf 1" with ID 3.3.3.3
 Supports only single TOS(TOS0) routes
 It is an area border router
 SPF schedule delay 5 secs, Hold time between two SPFs 10 secs
 Minimum LSA interval 5 secs. Minimum LSA arrival 1 secs
 Number of external LSA 0. Checksum Sum 0x0
 Number of DCbitless external LSA 0
 Number of DoNotAge external LSA 0
 Number of areas in this router is 3. 3 normal 0 stub 0 nssa
    Area BACKBONE(0)
        Number of interfaces in this area is 1
        Area has no authentication
```

```
        SPF algorithm executed 3 times
        Area ranges are
        Number of LSA 6. Checksum Sum 0x45CF4
        Number of DCbitless LSA 0
        Number of indication LSA 0
        Number of DoNotAge LSA 3
    Area 1
        Number of interfaces in this area is 1
        Area has no authentication
        SPF algorithm executed 14 times
        Area ranges are
        Number of LSA 10. Checksum Sum 0x4A8BD
        Number of DCbitless LSA 0
        Number of indication LSA 0
        Number of DoNotAge LSA 0
    Area 2
        Number of interfaces in this area is 1
        Area has no authentication
        SPF algorithm executed 3 times
        Area ranges are
        Number of LSA 5. Checksum Sum 0x2B425
        Number of DCbitless LSA 0
        Number of indication LSA 0
        Number of DoNotAge LSA 0
```

Router C now has an interface in Area 0 and this interface is the virtual link. Verify that the virtual link is active on Routers B and C.

```
rtrB#show ip ospf virtual-links
Virtual Link OSPF_VL0 to router 3.3.3.3 is up
  Run as demand circuit
  DoNotAge LSA allowed.
  Transit area 1, via interface Serial1, Cost of using 64
  Transmit Delay is 1 sec, State POINT_TO_POINT,
  Timer intervals configured, Hello 10, Dead 40, Wait 40, Retransmit 5
    Hello due in 00:00:09
    Adjacency State FULL (Hello suppressed)
```

```
rtrC#show ip ospf virtual-links
Virtual Link OSPF_VL0 to router 2.2.2.2 is up
  Run as demand circuit
  DoNotAge LSA allowed.
  Transit area 1, via interface Serial0, Cost of using 64
  Transmit Delay is 1 sec, State POINT_TO_POINT,
  Timer intervals configured, Hello 10, Dead 40, Wait 40, Retransmit 5
    Hello due in 00:00:00
    Adjacency State FULL (Hello suppressed)
```

Finally, verify that the loopback interfaces for Routers A, B, and C are being advertised to all OSPF neighbors.

```
rtrA#show ip route
Codes: C - connected, S - static, I - IGRP, R - RIP, M - mobile, B - BGP
       D - EIGRP, EX - EIGRP external, O - OSPF, IA - OSPF inter area
       N1 - OSPF NSSA external type 1, N2 - OSPF NSSA external type 2
       E1 - OSPF external type 1, E2 - OSPF external type 2, E - EGP
       i - IS-IS, L1 - IS-IS level-1, L2 - IS-IS level-2, * - candidate default
       U - per-user static route, o - ODR

Gateway of last resort is not set

     1.0.0.0/32 is subnetted, 1 subnets
C       1.1.1.1 is directly connected, Loopback0
     2.0.0.0/32 is subnetted, 1 subnets
O       2.2.2.2 [110/65] via 10.1.1.2, 00:09:04, Serial0/1
     3.0.0.0/32 is subnetted, 1 subnets
O IA    3.3.3.3 [110/129] via 10.1.1.2, 00:09:04, Serial0/1
     10.0.0.0/30 is subnetted, 2 subnets
C       10.1.1.0 is directly connected, Serial0/1
O IA    10.1.1.4 [110/128] via 10.1.1.2, 00:09:04, Serial0/1
```

```
rtrB#show ip route
Codes: C - connected, S - static, I - IGRP, R - RIP, M - mobile, B - BGP
       D - EIGRP, EX - EIGRP external, O - OSPF, IA - OSPF inter area
       N1 - OSPF NSSA external type 1, N2 - OSPF NSSA external type 2
       E1 - OSPF external type 1, E2 - OSPF external type 2, E - EGP
       i - IS-IS, L1 - IS-IS level-1, L2 - IS-IS level-2, * - candidate default
       U - per-user static route, o - ODR

Gateway of last resort is not set

     1.0.0.0/32 is subnetted, 1 subnets
O       1.1.1.1 [110/65] via 10.1.1.1, 00:10:19, Serial0
     2.0.0.0/32 is subnetted, 1 subnets
C       2.2.2.2 is directly connected, Loopback0
     3.0.0.0/32 is subnetted, 1 subnets
O IA    3.3.3.3 [110/65] via 10.1.1.6, 00:10:20, Serial1
     10.0.0.0/30 is subnetted, 2 subnets
C       10.1.1.0 is directly connected, Serial0
C       10.1.1.4 is directly connected, Serial1
```

```
rtrC#show ip route
Codes: C - connected, S - static, I - IGRP, R - RIP, M - mobile, B - BGP
       D - EIGRP, EX - EIGRP external, O - OSPF, IA - OSPF inter area
       N1 - OSPF NSSA external type 1, N2 - OSPF NSSA external type 2
       E1 - OSPF external type 1, E2 - OSPF external type 2, E - EGP
       i - IS-IS, L1 - IS-IS level-1, L2 - IS-IS level-2, * - candidate default
       U - per-user static route, o - ODR
```

```
Gateway of last resort is not set

     1.0.0.0/32 is subnetted, 1 subnets
O       1.1.1.1 [110/129] via 10.1.1.5, 00:11:10, Serial0
     2.0.0.0/32 is subnetted, 1 subnets
O       2.2.2.2 [110/65] via 10.1.1.5, 00:11:11, Serial0
     3.0.0.0/24 is subnetted, 1 subnets
C       3.3.3.0 is directly connected, Loopback0
     10.0.0.0/30 is subnetted, 2 subnets
O       10.1.1.0 [110/128] via 10.1.1.5, 00:11:11, Serial0
C       10.1.1.4 is directly connected, Serial0
```

Troubleshooting

Step 1 Verify that there is a neighbor relationship between the OSPF routers using the **show ip ospf neighbor** command.

Step 2 Verify that the transit area ID used in the **area virtual-link** command is the proper area.

Step 3 Verify that the router IDs used in the **area virtual-link** are correct.

2-14: area *transit-area-id* virtual-link *router-id* authentication authentication-key *password*

2-15: area *transit-area-id* virtual-link *router-id* authentication message-digest

2-16: area *transit-area-id* virtual-link *router-id* authentication null

NOTE Command 2-15 requires the use of the **area** *transit-area-id* **virtual-link** *router-id* **message-digest-key** *key-id* **md5** *password* command (see Section 2-20).

Syntax Description:

- *transit-area-id*—The OSPF area ID of the area connecting the two ABRs that the virtual link will cross. This value can be entered as a decimal number in the range of 0 to 4,294,967,295 or in IP address form in the range 0.0.0.0 to 255.255.255.255. The transit area cannot be a stub area.
- *router-id*—OSPF router ID of the router at the remote end of the virtual link.
- *key-id*—Key to use to encrypt a password. The range of values is 1 to 255. Both ends of a virtual link must use the same key and password.
- *password*—Password to be used for authentication in the selected area on the selected interface or virtual link. The password is an alphanumeric string from 1 to 8 characters.

Purpose: In Cisco IOS Software Releases prior to 12.0, if authentication was enabled in Area 0, then all virtual links had to be configured with the same authentication type. This command allows the configuration of authentication over a virtual link that is different from the authentication type being used in Area 0. If authentication is used, then both ends of the virtual link must be configured with the same authentication method. Also, the same password or key and password must be configured on both ends of the virtual link.

Initial Cisco IOS Software Release: 12.0

Configuration Example 1: Simple Password Authentication Over a Virtual Link

In Figure 2-16, Area 2 does not have a direct connection to Area 0. A virtual link is needed to repair this situation. Start by configuring the routers in Figure 2-16 without using authentication over the virtual link.

Figure 2-16 *The Authentication Type Used on an OSPF Virtual Link Can Be Different from the Type Used in Area 0*

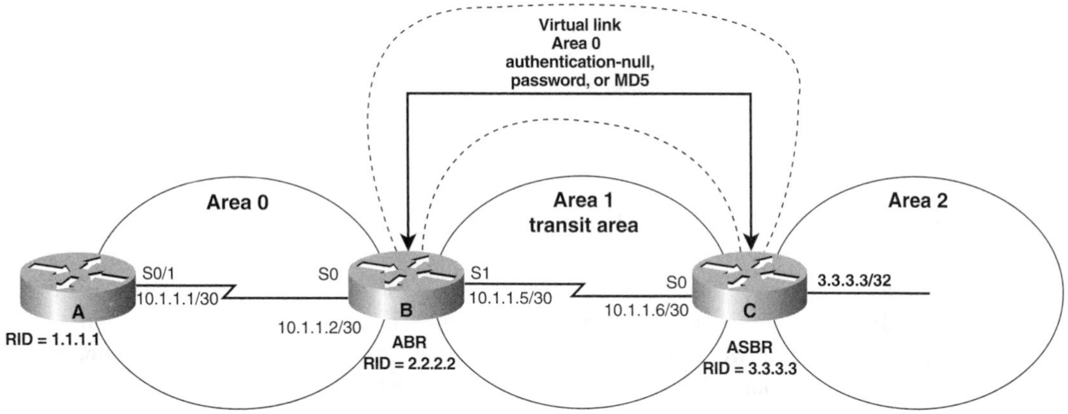


```
Router A
interface Loopback0
 ip address 1.1.1.1 255.255.255.255
!
interface Serial0/1
 ip address 10.1.1.1 255.255.255.252
 clockrate 64000
!
router ospf 1
 network 10.1.1.0 0.0.0.3 area 0
 network 1.1.1.1 0.0.0.0 area 0
```

```
Router B
interface Loopback0
 ip address 2.2.2.2 255.255.255.255
!
interface Serial0
 ip address 10.1.1.2 255.255.255.252
!
interface Serial1
 ip address 10.1.1.5 255.255.255.252
 clockrate 64000
!
router ospf 1
 area 1 virtual-link 3.3.3.3
 network 10.1.1.0 0.0.0.3 area 0
 network 2.2.2.2 0.0.0.0 area 0
 network 10.1.1.4 0.0.0.3 area 1
```

continues

```
Router C
interface Loopback0
 ip address 3.3.3.3 255.255.255.255
!
interface Serial0
 ip address 10.1.1.6 255.255.255.252
!
router ospf 1
 area 1 virtual-link 2.2.2.2
 network 3.3.3.3 0.0.0.0 area 2
 network 10.1.1.4 0.0.0.3 area 1
```

Area 2 on Router C does not have a direct connection to Area 0. A virtual link needs to be configured to correct this situation. The transit area in this case is Area 1. You also need the router IDs of the two ABRs to be able to construct the virtual link. The first method to determine the router ID is to use the **show ip ospf neighbor** command. This will display the router ID of the remote end of the virtual link.

```
rtrB#show ip ospf neighbor

Neighbor ID     Pri   State           Dead Time   Address         Interface
1.1.1.1           1   FULL/  -        00:00:32    10.1.1.1        Serial0
3.3.3.3           1   FULL/  -        00:00:36    10.1.1.6        Serial1
```

```
rtrC#show ip ospf neighbor

Neighbor ID     Pri   State           Dead Time   Address         Interface
2.2.2.2           1   FULL/  -        00:00:35    10.1.1.5        Serial0
```

Router B has an ID of 2.2.2.2 and Router C has an ID of 3.3.3.3. The local router ID can be found by using the **show ip ospf** command.

```
rtrB#show ip ospf
 Routing Process "ospf 1" with ID 2.2.2.2
 Supports only single TOS(TOS0) routes
 It is an area border router
 SPF schedule delay 5 secs, Hold time between two SPFs 10 secs
 Minimum LSA interval 5 secs. Minimum LSA arrival 1 secs
 Number of external LSA 0. Checksum Sum 0x0
 Number of DCbitless external LSA 0
 Number of DoNotAge external LSA 0
 Number of areas in this router is 2. 2 normal 0 stub 0 nssa
    Area BACKBONE(0)
        Number of interfaces in this area is 2
        Area has no authentication
        SPF algorithm executed 3 times
        Area ranges are
```

```
        Number of LSA 3. Checksum Sum 0x1FD00
        Number of DCbitless LSA 0
        Number of indication LSA 0
        Number of DoNotAge LSA 0
    Area 1
        Number of interfaces in this area is 1
        Area has no authentication
        SPF algorithm executed 2 times
        Area ranges are
        Number of LSA 5. Checksum Sum 0x2B171
        Number of DCbitless LSA 0
        Number of indication LSA 0
        Number of DoNotAge LSA 0
```

```
rtrC#show ip ospf
 Routing Process "ospf 1" with ID 3.3.3.3
 Supports only single TOS(TOS0) routes
 SPF schedule delay 5 secs, Hold time between two SPFs 10 secs
 Minimum LSA interval 5 secs. Minimum LSA arrival 1 secs
 Number of external LSA 0. Checksum Sum 0x0
 Number of DCbitless external LSA 0
 Number of DoNotAge external LSA 0
 Number of areas in this router is 2. 2 normal 0 stub 0 nssa
    Area 1
        Number of interfaces in this area is 1
        Area has no authentication
        SPF algorithm executed 12 times
        Area ranges are
        Number of LSA 5. Checksum Sum 0x2B171
        Number of DCbitless LSA 0
        Number of indication LSA 0
        Number of DoNotAge LSA 0
    Area 2
        Number of interfaces in this area is 1
        Area has no authentication
        SPF algorithm executed 1 times
        Area ranges are
        Number of LSA 1. Checksum Sum 0xDDE0
        Number of DCbitless LSA 0
        Number of indication LSA 0
        Number of DoNotAge LSA 0
```

You want to add simple password authentication to the virtual link but you do not want to configure authentication over any other link in Area 0. Modify the configurations on

Routers B and C to enable simple password authentication over the virtual link using the password cisco.

```
Router B
router ospf 1
 area 1 virtual-link 3.3.3.3 authentication authentication-key cisco
 network 2.2.2.2 0.0.0.0 area 0
 network 10.1.1.0 0.0.0.3 area 0
 network 10.1.1.4 0.0.0.3 area 1
```

```
Router C
router ospf 1
 area 1 virtual-link 2.2.2.2 authentication authentication-key cisco
 network 3.3.3.3 0.0.0.0 area 2
 network 10.1.1.4 0.0.0.3 area 1
```

Verification

Router C now has an interface in Area 0 and this interface is the virtual link. Verify that the virtual link is active on Routers B and C.

```
rtrB#show ip ospf virtual-links
Virtual Link OSPF_VL0 to router 3.3.3.3 is up
  Run as demand circuit
  DoNotAge LSA allowed.
  Transit area 1, via interface Serial1, Cost of using 64
  Transmit Delay is 1 sec, State POINT_TO_POINT,
  Timer intervals configured, Hello 10, Dead 40, Wait 40, Retransmit 5
    Hello due in 00:00:09
    Adjacency State FULL (Hello suppressed)
```

```
rtrC#show ip ospf virtual-links
Virtual Link OSPF_VL1 to router 2.2.2.2 is up
  Run as demand circuit
  DoNotAge LSA allowed.
  Transit area 1, via interface Serial0, Cost of using 64
  Transmit Delay is 1 sec, State POINT_TO_POINT,
  Timer intervals configured, Hello 10, Dead 40, Wait 40, Retransmit 5
    Hello due in 00:00:06
    Adjacency State FULL (Hello suppressed)
```

Also, verify that the loopback interfaces for Routers A, B, and C are being advertised to all OSPF neighbors.

```
rtrA#show ip route
Codes: C - connected, S - static, I - IGRP, R - RIP, M - mobile, B - BGP
       D - EIGRP, EX - EIGRP external, O - OSPF, IA - OSPF inter area
       N1 - OSPF NSSA external type 1, N2 - OSPF NSSA external type 2
       E1 - OSPF external type 1, E2 - OSPF external type 2, E - EGP
       i - IS-IS, L1 - IS-IS level-1, L2 - IS-IS level-2, * - candidate default
       U - per-user static route, o - ODR

Gateway of last resort is not set

     1.0.0.0/32 is subnetted, 1 subnets
C       1.1.1.1 is directly connected, Loopback0
     2.0.0.0/32 is subnetted, 1 subnets
O       2.2.2.2 [110/65] via 10.1.1.2, 00:09:04, Serial0/1
     3.0.0.0/32 is subnetted, 1 subnets
O IA    3.3.3.3 [110/129] via 10.1.1.2, 00:09:04, Serial0/1
     10.0.0.0/30 is subnetted, 2 subnets
C       10.1.1.0 is directly connected, Serial0/1
O IA    10.1.1.4 [110/128] via 10.1.1.2, 00:09:04, Serial0/1
```

```
rtrB#show ip route
Codes: C - connected, S - static, I - IGRP, R - RIP, M - mobile, B - BGP
       D - EIGRP, EX - EIGRP external, O - OSPF, IA - OSPF inter area
       N1 - OSPF NSSA external type 1, N2 - OSPF NSSA external type 2
       E1 - OSPF external type 1, E2 - OSPF external type 2, E - EGP
       i - IS-IS, L1 - IS-IS level-1, L2 - IS-IS level-2, * - candidate default
       U - per-user static route, o - ODR

Gateway of last resort is not set

     1.0.0.0/32 is subnetted, 1 subnets
O       1.1.1.1 [110/65] via 10.1.1.1, 00:10:19, Serial0
     2.0.0.0/32 is subnetted, 1 subnets
C       2.2.2.2 is directly connected, Loopback0
     3.0.0.0/32 is subnetted, 1 subnets
O IA    3.3.3.3 [110/65] via 10.1.1.6, 00:10:20, Serial1
     10.0.0.0/30 is subnetted, 2 subnets
C       10.1.1.0 is directly connected, Serial0
C       10.1.1.4 is directly connected, Serial1
```

```
rtrC#show ip route
Codes: C - connected, S - static, I - IGRP, R - RIP, M - mobile, B - BGP
       D - EIGRP, EX - EIGRP external, O - OSPF, IA - OSPF inter area
       N1 - OSPF NSSA external type 1, N2 - OSPF NSSA external type 2
       E1 - OSPF external type 1, E2 - OSPF external type 2, E - EGP
       i - IS-IS, L1 - IS-IS level-1, L2 - IS-IS level-2, * - candidate default
       U - per-user static route, o - ODR
```

continues

```
Gateway of last resort is not set

     1.0.0.0/32 is subnetted, 1 subnets
O       1.1.1.1 [110/129] via 10.1.1.5, 00:11:10, Serial0
     2.0.0.0/32 is subnetted, 1 subnets
O       2.2.2.2 [110/65] via 10.1.1.5, 00:11:11, Serial0
     3.0.0.0/24 is subnetted, 1 subnets
C       3.3.3.0 is directly connected, Loopback0
     10.0.0.0/30 is subnetted, 2 subnets
O       10.1.1.0 [110/128] via 10.1.1.5, 00:11:11, Serial0
C       10.1.1.4 is directly connected, Serial0
```

Configuration Example 2: MD5 Authentication Over a Virtual Link

Modify the configurations on Routers B and C by adding MD5 password authentication to the virtual link. For this example, use the password cisco.

```
Router B
router ospf 1
 area 1 virtual-link 3.3.3.3 authentication message-digest
 area 1 virtual-link 3.3.3.3 message-digest-key 1 md5 cisco
 network 2.2.2.2 0.0.0.0 area 0
 network 10.1.1.0 0.0.0.3 area 0
 network 10.1.1.4 0.0.0.3 area 1
```

```
Router C
router ospf 1
 area 1 virtual-link 2.2.2.2 authentication message-digest
 area 1 virtual-link 2.2.2.2 message-digest-key 1 md5 cisco
 network 3.3.3.3 0.0.0.0 area 2
 network 10.1.1.4 0.0.0.3 area 1
```

Verification

Verify that the virtual link is still active and that MD5 authentication is enabled.

```
rtrB#show ip ospf virtual-links
Virtual Link OSPF_VL3 to router 3.3.3.3 is up
  Run as demand circuit
  DoNotAge LSA allowed.
  Transit area 1, via interface Serial1, Cost of using 64
  Transmit Delay is 1 sec, State POINT_TO_POINT,
  Timer intervals configured, Hello 10, Dead 40, Wait 40, Retransmit 5
    Hello due in 00:00:01
    Adjacency State FULL (Hello suppressed)
  Message digest authentication enabled
    Youngest key id is 1
```

```
rtrC#show ip ospf virtual-links
Virtual Link OSPF_VL4 to router 2.2.2.2 is up
  Run as demand circuit
  DoNotAge LSA allowed.
  Transit area 1, via interface Serial0, Cost of using 64
  Transmit Delay is 1 sec, State POINT_TO_POINT,
  Timer intervals configured, Hello 10, Dead 40, Wait 40, Retransmit 5
    Hello due in 00:00:02
    Adjacency State FULL (Hello suppressed)
  Message digest authentication enabled
    Youngest key id is 1
```

Also, verify that the loopback interfaces for Routers A, B, and C are being advertised to all OSPF neighbors.

```
rtrA#show ip route
Codes: C - connected, S - static, I - IGRP, R - RIP, M - mobile, B - BGP
       D - EIGRP, EX - EIGRP external, O - OSPF, IA - OSPF inter area
       N1 - OSPF NSSA external type 1, N2 - OSPF NSSA external type 2
       E1 - OSPF external type 1, E2 - OSPF external type 2, E - EGP
       i - IS-IS, L1 - IS-IS level-1, L2 - IS-IS level-2, * - candidate default
       U - per-user static route, o - ODR

Gateway of last resort is not set

     1.0.0.0/32 is subnetted, 1 subnets
C       1.1.1.1 is directly connected, Loopback0
     2.0.0.0/32 is subnetted, 1 subnets
O       2.2.2.2 [110/65] via 10.1.1.2, 00:09:04, Serial0/1
     3.0.0.0/32 is subnetted, 1 subnets
O IA    3.3.3.3 [110/129] via 10.1.1.2, 00:09:04, Serial0/1
     10.0.0.0/30 is subnetted, 2 subnets
C       10.1.1.0 is directly connected, Serial0/1
O IA    10.1.1.4 [110/128] via 10.1.1.2, 00:09:04, Serial0/1
```

```
rtrB#show ip route
Codes: C - connected, S - static, I - IGRP, R - RIP, M - mobile, B - BGP
       D - EIGRP, EX - EIGRP external, O - OSPF, IA - OSPF inter area
       N1 - OSPF NSSA external type 1, N2 - OSPF NSSA external type 2
       E1 - OSPF external type 1, E2 - OSPF external type 2, E - EGP
       i - IS-IS, L1 - IS-IS level-1, L2 - IS-IS level-2, * - candidate default
       U - per-user static route, o - ODR

Gateway of last resort is not set

     1.0.0.0/32 is subnetted, 1 subnets
O       1.1.1.1 [110/65] via 10.1.1.1, 00:10:19, Serial0
     2.0.0.0/32 is subnetted, 1 subnets
C       2.2.2.2 is directly connected, Loopback0
     3.0.0.0/32 is subnetted, 1 subnets
```

continues

```
O IA    3.3.3.3 [110/65] via 10.1.1.6, 00:10:20, Serial1
     10.0.0.0/30 is subnetted, 2 subnets
C       10.1.1.0 is directly connected, Serial0
C       10.1.1.4 is directly connected, Serial1
```

```
rtrC#show ip route
Codes: C - connected, S - static, I - IGRP, R - RIP, M - mobile, B - BGP
       D - EIGRP, EX - EIGRP external, O - OSPF, IA - OSPF inter area
       N1 - OSPF NSSA external type 1, N2 - OSPF NSSA external type 2
       E1 - OSPF external type 1, E2 - OSPF external type 2, E - EGP
       i - IS-IS, L1 - IS-IS level-1, L2 - IS-IS level-2, * - candidate default
       U - per-user static route, o - ODR

Gateway of last resort is not set

     1.0.0.0/32 is subnetted, 1 subnets
O       1.1.1.1 [110/129] via 10.1.1.5, 00:11:10, Serial0
     2.0.0.0/32 is subnetted, 1 subnets
O       2.2.2.2 [110/65] via 10.1.1.5, 00:11:11, Serial0
     3.0.0.0/24 is subnetted, 1 subnets
C       3.3.3.0 is directly connected, Loopback0
     10.0.0.0/30 is subnetted, 2 subnets
O       10.1.1.0 [110/128] via 10.1.1.5, 00:11:11, Serial0
C       10.1.1.4 is directly connected, Serial0
```

Configuration Example 3: Changing Keys and Passwords

For additional security you may choose to periodically change the key and password. With clear-text authentication, when you change passwords there will be a loss of OSPF connectivity from the time you change the password on one end of the virtual link until you change the password at the other end of the virtual link. With MD5 authentication, you can configure a new key and password on a virtual link while leaving the old key and password in place. The old key and password will continue to be used until the new key and password are configured on the other end of the virtual link. Modify the key and password on the virtual link between Routers B and C. First add a new key and password to Router B in order to observe the behavior when the new key and password have been configured on only one end of the virtual link.

```
Router B
router ospf 1
 area 1 virtual-link 3.3.3.3 authentication message-digest
 area 1 virtual-link 3.3.3.3 message-digest-key 1 md5 cisco
 area 1 virtual-link 3.3.3.3 message-digest-key 2 md5 bosco
 network 2.2.2.2 0.0.0.0 area 0
 network 10.1.1.0 0.0.0.3 area 0
 network 10.1.1.4 0.0.0.3 area 1
```

Examine the effect of adding a new key and password on only one end of the virtual link.

```
rtrB#show ip ospf virtual-links
Virtual Link OSPF_VL3 to router 3.3.3.3 is up
  Run as demand circuit
  DoNotAge LSA allowed.
  Transit area 1, via interface Serial1, Cost of using 64
  Transmit Delay is 1 sec, State POINT_TO_POINT,
  Timer intervals configured, Hello 10, Dead 40, Wait 40, Retransmit 5
    Hello due in 00:00:08
    Adjacency State FULL (Hello suppressed)
  Message digest authentication enabled
    Youngest key id is 2
    Rollover in progress, 1 neighbor(s) using the old key(s):
      key id 1
```

Notice that both keys are being used for authentication. Configure the new key and password on Router C while leaving the old key and password in place.

```
Router C
router ospf 1
 area 1 virtual-link 2.2.2.2 authentication message-digest
 area 1 virtual-link 2.2.2.2 message-digest-key 1 md5 cisco
 area 1 virtual-link 2.2.2.2 message-digest-key 2 md5 bosco
 network 3.3.3.3 0.0.0.0 area 2
 network 10.1.1.4 0.0.0.3 area 1
```

Verify that Router C is now using the new key and password.

```
rtrC#show ip ospf virtual-links
Virtual Link OSPF_VL4 to router 2.2.2.2 is up
  Run as demand circuit
  DoNotAge LSA allowed.
  Transit area 1, via interface Serial0, Cost of using 64
  Transmit Delay is 1 sec, State POINT_TO_POINT,
  Timer intervals configured, Hello 10, Dead 40, Wait 40, Retransmit 5
    Hello due in 00:00:09
    Adjacency State FULL (Hello suppressed)
  Message digest authentication enabled
    Youngest key id is 2
    Rollover in progress, 1 neighbor(s) using the old key(s):
      key id 1
```

You can now remove the old key and password from Routers B and C.

```
Router B
router ospf 1
 no area 1 virtual-link 3.3.3.3 message-digest-key 1
```

```
Router C
router ospf 1
 no area 1 virtual-link 2.2.2.2 message-digest-key 1
```

Verification

Verify that Routers B and C are using the new key and password.

```
rtrB#show ip ospf virtual-links
Virtual Link OSPF_VL3 to router 3.3.3.3 is up
  Run as demand circuit
  DoNotAge LSA allowed.
  Transit area 1, via interface Serial1, Cost of using 64
  Transmit Delay is 1 sec, State POINT_TO_POINT,
  Timer intervals configured, Hello 10, Dead 40, Wait 40, Retransmit 5
    Hello due in 00:00:04
    Adjacency State INIT (Hello suppressed)
  Message digest authentication enabled
    Youngest key id is 2
```

```
rtrC#show ip ospf virtual-links
Virtual Link OSPF_VL4 to router 2.2.2.2 is up
  Run as demand circuit
  DoNotAge LSA allowed.
  Transit area 1, via interface Serial0, Cost of using 64
  Transmit Delay is 1 sec, State POINT_TO_POINT,
  Timer intervals configured, Hello 10, Dead 40, Wait 40, Retransmit 5
    Hello due in 00:00:08
    Adjacency State FULL (Hello suppressed)
  Message digest authentication enabled
    Youngest key id is 2
```

Configuration Example 4: Null Authentication

If authentication, either clear text or md5, is configured for Area 0, then authentication must be enabled on all virtual links. If authentication is not required on a virtual link, then NULL authentication can be employed to override the authentication that has been configured for

Area 0. Configure the routers in Figure 2-16 with simple password authentication on Area 0.

```
Router A
interface Loopback0
 ip address 1.1.1.1 255.255.255.255
!
interface Serial0/1
 ip address 10.1.1.1 255.255.255.252
 ip ospf authentication-key cisco
 clockrate 64000
!
router ospf 1
 area 0 authentication
 network 1.1.1.1 0.0.0.0 area 0
 network 10.1.1.0 0.0.0.3 area 0
```

```
Router B
interface Loopback0
 ip address 2.2.2.2 255.255.255.255
!
interface Serial0
 ip address 10.1.1.2 255.255.255.252
 ip ospf authentication-key cisco
!
interface Serial1
 ip address 10.1.1.5 255.255.255.252
 clockrate 64000
!
router ospf 1
 area 0 authentication
 area 1 virtual-link 3.3.3.3
 network 2.2.2.2 0.0.0.0 area 0
 network 10.1.1.0 0.0.0.3 area 0
 network 10.1.1.4 0.0.0.3 area 1
```

```
Router C
interface Loopback0
 ip address 3.3.3.3 255.255.255.255
!
interface Serial0
 ip address 10.1.1.6 255.255.255.252
!
router ospf 1
 area 1 virtual-link 2.2.2.2
 network 3.3.3.3 0.0.0.0 area 2
 network 10.1.1.4 0.0.0.3 area 1
```

When authentication is enabled for Area 0, then the same authentication type is automatically enabled for the virtual link. Because the virtual link is not using authentication, routing updates will not be accepted over the virtual link. This can be seen by enabling OSPF debugging on either Router B or C.

```
rtrB#debug ip ospf adj
OSPF adjacency events debugging is on
rtrB#
23:13:13: OSPF: Rcv pkt from 10.1.1.6, Serial1 : Mismatch Authentication type. I
nput packet specified type 0, we use type 1
```

This situation can be fixed by either configuring the same authentication type on the virtual link (see Sections 2-17 and 2-20) or by explicitly configuring the virtual link to use NULL authentication. Modify the configurations on routers B and C to use NULL authentication on the virtual link.

```
Router B
router ospf 1
 area 0 authentication
 area 1 virtual-link 3.3.3.3 authentication null
 network 2.2.2.2 0.0.0.0 area 0
 network 10.1.1.0 0.0.0.3 area 0
 network 10.1.1.4 0.0.0.3 area 1
```

```
Router C
router ospf 1
 area 1 virtual-link 2.2.2.2 authentication null
 network 3.3.3.3 0.0.0.0 area 2
 network 10.1.1.4 0.0.0.3 area 1
```

Verification

Verify that all OSPF routes are being advertised.

```
rtrA#show ip route
Codes: C - connected, S - static, I - IGRP, R - RIP, M - mobile, B - BGP
       D - EIGRP, EX - EIGRP external, O - OSPF, IA - OSPF inter area
       N1 - OSPF NSSA external type 1, N2 - OSPF NSSA external type 2
       E1 - OSPF external type 1, E2 - OSPF external type 2, E - EGP
       i - IS-IS, L1 - IS-IS level-1, L2 - IS-IS level-2, * - candidate default
       U - per-user static route, o - ODR

Gateway of last resort is not set

     1.0.0.0/32 is subnetted, 1 subnets
C       1.1.1.1 is directly connected, Loopback0
```

```
     2.0.0.0/32 is subnetted, 1 subnets
O       2.2.2.2 [110/65] via 10.1.1.2, 00:03:46, Serial0/1
     3.0.0.0/32 is subnetted, 1 subnets
O IA    3.3.3.3 [110/129] via 10.1.1.2, 00:03:46, Serial0/1
     10.0.0.0/30 is subnetted, 2 subnets
C       10.1.1.0 is directly connected, Serial0/1
O IA    10.1.1.4 [110/128] via 10.1.1.2, 00:03:46, Serial0/1
```

```
rtrB#show ip route
Codes: C - connected, S - static, I - IGRP, R - RIP, M - mobile, B - BGP
       D - EIGRP, EX - EIGRP external, O - OSPF, IA - OSPF inter area
       N1 - OSPF NSSA external type 1, N2 - OSPF NSSA external type 2
       E1 - OSPF external type 1, E2 - OSPF external type 2, E - EGP
       i - IS-IS, L1 - IS-IS level-1, L2 - IS-IS level-2, * - candidate default
       U - per-user static route, o - ODR

Gateway of last resort is not set

     1.0.0.0/32 is subnetted, 1 subnets
O       1.1.1.1 [110/65] via 10.1.1.1, 00:04:48, Serial0
     2.0.0.0/32 is subnetted, 1 subnets
C       2.2.2.2 is directly connected, Loopback0
     3.0.0.0/32 is subnetted, 1 subnets
O IA    3.3.3.3 [110/65] via 10.1.1.6, 00:04:49, Serial1
     10.0.0.0/30 is subnetted, 2 subnets
C       10.1.1.0 is directly connected, Serial0
C       10.1.1.4 is directly connected, Serial1
```

```
rtrC#show ip route
Codes: C - connected, S - static, I - IGRP, R - RIP, M - mobile, B - BGP
       D - EIGRP, EX - EIGRP external, O - OSPF, IA - OSPF inter area
       N1 - OSPF NSSA external type 1, N2 - OSPF NSSA external type 2
       E1 - OSPF external type 1, E2 - OSPF external type 2, E - EGP
       i - IS-IS, L1 - IS-IS level-1, L2 - IS-IS level-2, * - candidate default
       U - per-user static route, o - ODR

Gateway of last resort is not set

     1.0.0.0/32 is subnetted, 1 subnets
O       1.1.1.1 [110/129] via 10.1.1.5, 00:05:33, Serial0
     2.0.0.0/32 is subnetted, 1 subnets
O       2.2.2.2 [110/65] via 10.1.1.5, 00:05:33, Serial0
     3.0.0.0/24 is subnetted, 1 subnets
C       3.3.3.0 is directly connected, Loopback0
     10.0.0.0/30 is subnetted, 2 subnets
O       10.1.1.0 [110/128] via 10.1.1.5, 00:05:34, Serial0
C       10.1.1.4 is directly connected, Serial0
```

Troubleshooting

Step 1 Verify that there is a neighbor relationship between the OSPF routers by using the **show ip ospf neighbor** command.

Step 2 Verify that the transit area ID used in the **area virtual-link** command is proper.

Step 3 Verify that the router IDs used in the **area virtual-link** are correct.

Step 4 If using simple password authentication, verify that the same password is being used on each side of the virtual link.

Step 5 If using MD5 authentication, verify that the same key and password are being used on each side of the virtual link.

2-17: area *transit-area-id* virtual-link *router-id* authentication-key *password*

Syntax Description:

- *transit-area-id*—The OSPF area ID of the area connecting the two ABRs that the virtual link will cross. This value can be entered as a decimal number in the range of 0 to 4,294,967,295 or in IP address form in the range 0.0.0.0 to 255.255.255.255. The transit area cannot be a stub area.
- *router-id*—OSPF router ID of the router at the remote end of the virtual link.
- *password*—Password to be used for authentication in the selected area on the selected interface or virtual link. The password is an alphanumeric string from 1 to 8 characters.

Purpose: If simple password authentication is enabled in Area 0, then all virtual links need to be configured with the same authentication type. This command is used to configure simple password authentication over a virtual link. In Cisco IOS Software Release 12.0 and later, virtual link authentication can be configured independently of Area 0 (see Section 2-14).

Initial Cisco IOS Software Release: 10.0

Configuration Example 1: Simple Password Authentication Over a Virtual Link

In Figure 2-17, simple password authentication has been enabled for Area 0. Initially, authentication is not enabled over the virtual link so you can see the effect of enabling authentication in Area 0 but not over the virtual link.

Figure 2-17 *Prior to Cisco IOS Software Release 12.0, if Authentication Is Enabled in Area 0 Then the Same Authentication Must Be Enabled Over the Virtual Link*

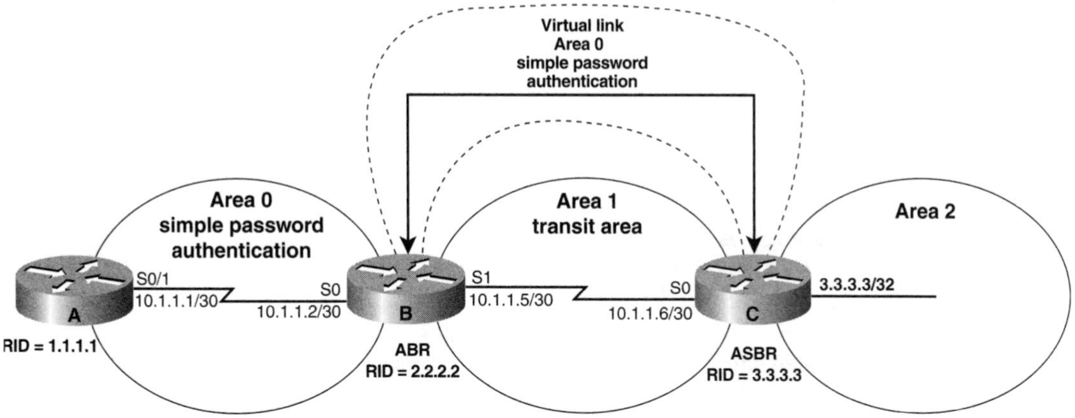


```
Router A
interface Loopback0
 ip address 1.1.1.1 255.255.255.255
!
interface Serial0/1
 ip address 10.1.1.1 255.255.255.252
 ip ospf authentication-key cisco
 clockrate 64000
!
router ospf 1
 area 0 authentication
 network 10.1.1.0 0.0.0.3 area 0
 network 1.1.1.1 0.0.0.0 area 0
```

```
Router B
interface Loopback0
 ip address 2.2.2.2 255.255.255.255
!
interface Serial0
 ip address 10.1.1.2 255.255.255.252
 ip ospf authentication-key cisco
!
interface Serial1
 ip address 10.1.1.5 255.255.255.252
 clockrate 64000
!
router ospf 1
 area 0 authentication
 area 1 virtual-link 3.3.3.3
 network 10.1.1.0 0.0.0.3 area 0
```

continues

```
 network 2.2.2.2 0.0.0.0 area 0
 network 10.1.1.4 0.0.0.3 area 1
```

```
Router C
interface Loopback0
 ip address 3.3.3.3 255.255.255.255
!
interface Serial0
 ip address 10.1.1.6 255.255.255.252
!
router ospf 1
 area 1 virtual-link 2.2.2.2
 network 3.3.3.3 0.0.0.0 area 2
 network 10.1.1.4 0.0.0.3 area 1
```

Verify that authentication has been enabled for Area 0.

```
rtrA#show ip ospf
 Routing Process "ospf 1" with ID 1.1.1.1
 Supports only single TOS(TOS0) routes
 SPF schedule delay 5 secs, Hold time between two SPFs 10 secs
 Minimum LSA interval 5 secs. Minimum LSA arrival 1 secs
 Number of external LSA 0. Checksum Sum 0x0
 Number of DCbitless external LSA 0
 Number of DoNotAge external LSA 0
 Number of areas in this router is 1. 1 normal 0 stub 0 nssa
    Area BACKBONE(0)
        Number of interfaces in this area is 2
        Area has simple password authentication
        SPF algorithm executed 2 times
        Area ranges are
        Number of LSA 6. Checksum Sum 0x3B837
        Number of DCbitless LSA 0
        Number of indication LSA 0
        Number of DoNotAge LSA 3
```

```
rtrB#show ip ospf
 Routing Process "ospf 1" with ID 2.2.2.2
 Supports only single TOS(TOS0) routes
 It is an area border router
 SPF schedule delay 5 secs, Hold time between two SPFs 10 secs
 Minimum LSA interval 5 secs. Minimum LSA arrival 1 secs
 Number of external LSA 0. Checksum Sum 0x0
 Number of DCbitless external LSA 0
 Number of DoNotAge external LSA 0
 Number of areas in this router is 2. 2 normal 0 stub 0 nssa
    Area BACKBONE(0)
        Number of interfaces in this area is 3
        Area has simple password authentication
        SPF algorithm executed 8 times
```

```
        Area ranges are
        Number of LSA 6. Checksum Sum 0x3B837
        Number of DCbitless LSA 0
        Number of indication LSA 0
        Number of DoNotAge LSA 3
    Area 1
        Number of interfaces in this area is 1
        Area has no authentication
        SPF algorithm executed 4 times
        Area ranges are
        Number of LSA 6. Checksum Sum 0x364E1
        Number of DCbitless LSA 0
        Number of indication LSA 0
        Number of DoNotAge LSA 0
```

When authentication is enabled in Area 0, then this authentication type will be applied to all interfaces in Area 0, including virtual links. Any routing updates from neighbors in Area 0 will be rejected if the authentication type and password do not match. Because a virtual link is considered to be in Area 0, routing updates passing over the virtual link will be rejected. This can be verified by examining the IP routing table on Router B.

```
rtrB#show ip route
Codes: C - connected, S - static, I - IGRP, R - RIP, M - mobile, B - BGP
       D - EIGRP, EX - EIGRP external, O - OSPF, IA - OSPF inter area
       N1 - OSPF NSSA external type 1, N2 - OSPF NSSA external type 2
       E1 - OSPF external type 1, E2 - OSPF external type 2, E - EGP
       i - IS-IS, L1 - IS-IS level-1, L2 - IS-IS level-2, * - candidate default
       U - per-user static route, o - ODR

Gateway of last resort is not set

     1.0.0.0/32 is subnetted, 1 subnets
O       1.1.1.1 [110/65] via 10.1.1.1, 00:06:34, Serial0
     2.0.0.0/32 is subnetted, 1 subnets
C       2.2.2.2 is directly connected, Loopback0
     10.0.0.0/30 is subnetted, 2 subnets
C       10.1.1.0 is directly connected, Serial0
C       10.1.1.4 is directly connected, Serial1
```

Router B has learned the routes being advertised by Router A but not the routes advertised by Router C. Simple password authentication needs to be enabled on the virtual link so that routing updates can be exchanged between routers B and C. You can also use a different authentication type on the virtual link using command 2-14, 2-15, or 2-16. In this case, configure the same authentication type that is being used in Area 0. Change the password over the virtual link to demonstrate that the passwords for different interfaces do not need to be the same. Remember that the password for a common link must be the same at both ends of the link. Modify the configurations on Routers B and C to enable simple password authentication over the virtual link using the password bosco.

```
Router B
router ospf 1
 area 0 authentication
 area 1 virtual-link 3.3.3.3 authentication-key bosco
 network 2.2.2.2 0.0.0.0 area 0
 network 10.1.1.0 0.0.0.3 area 0
 network 10.1.1.4 0.0.0.3 area 1
```

```
Router C
router ospf 1
 area 0 authentication
 area 1 virtual-link 2.2.2.2 authentication-key bosco
 network 3.3.3.3 0.0.0.0 area 2
 network 10.1.1.4 0.0.0.3 area 1
```

Notice that the command **area 0 authentication** was used on Router C because the virtual link is in Area 0.

Verification

Verify that authentication has been enabled over the virtual link.

```
rtrC#show ip ospf
 Routing Process "ospf 1" with ID 3.3.3.3
 Supports only single TOS(TOS0) routes
 It is an area border router
 SPF schedule delay 5 secs, Hold time between two SPFs 10 secs
 Minimum LSA interval 5 secs. Minimum LSA arrival 1 secs
 Number of external LSA 0. Checksum Sum 0x0
 Number of DCbitless external LSA 0
 Number of DoNotAge external LSA 0
 Number of areas in this router is 3. 3 normal 0 stub 0 nssa
    Area BACKBONE(0)
        Number of interfaces in this area is 1
        Area has simple password authentication
        SPF algorithm executed 4 times
        Area ranges are
        Number of LSA 6. Checksum Sum 0x3CFAD
        Number of DCbitless LSA 0
        Number of indication LSA 0
        Number of DoNotAge LSA 3
    Area 1
        Number of interfaces in this area is 1
        Area has no authentication
        SPF algorithm executed 22 times
```

```
        Area ranges are
        Number of LSA 10. Checksum Sum 0x4ACBB
        Number of DCbitless LSA 0
        Number of indication LSA 0
        Number of DoNotAge LSA 0
    Area 2
        Number of interfaces in this area is 1
        Area has no authentication
        SPF algorithm executed 18 times
        Area ranges are
        Number of LSA 5. Checksum Sum 0x238E3
        Number of DCbitless LSA 0
        Number of indication LSA 0
        Number of DoNotAge LSA 0
```

Verify that all OSPF routes are now being exchanged.

```
rtrA#show ip route
Codes: C - connected, S - static, I - IGRP, R - RIP, M - mobile, B - BGP
       D - EIGRP, EX - EIGRP external, O - OSPF, IA - OSPF inter area
       N1 - OSPF NSSA external type 1, N2 - OSPF NSSA external type 2
       E1 - OSPF external type 1, E2 - OSPF external type 2, E - EGP
       i - IS-IS, L1 - IS-IS level-1, L2 - IS-IS level-2, * - candidate default
       U - per-user static route, o - ODR

Gateway of last resort is not set

     1.0.0.0/32 is subnetted, 1 subnets
C       1.1.1.1 is directly connected, Loopback0
     2.0.0.0/32 is subnetted, 1 subnets
O       2.2.2.2 [110/65] via 10.1.1.2, 00:09:04, Serial0/1
     3.0.0.0/32 is subnetted, 1 subnets
O IA    3.3.3.3 [110/129] via 10.1.1.2, 00:09:04, Serial0/1
     10.0.0.0/30 is subnetted, 2 subnets
C       10.1.1.0 is directly connected, Serial0/1
O IA    10.1.1.4 [110/128] via 10.1.1.2, 00:09:04, Serial0/1
```

```
rtrB#show ip route
Codes: C - connected, S - static, I - IGRP, R - RIP, M - mobile, B - BGP
       D - EIGRP, EX - EIGRP external, O - OSPF, IA - OSPF inter area
       N1 - OSPF NSSA external type 1, N2 - OSPF NSSA external type 2
       E1 - OSPF external type 1, E2 - OSPF external type 2, E - EGP
       i - IS-IS, L1 - IS-IS level-1, L2 - IS-IS level-2, * - candidate default
       U - per-user static route, o - ODR

Gateway of last resort is not set

     1.0.0.0/32 is subnetted, 1 subnets
O       1.1.1.1 [110/65] via 10.1.1.1, 00:10:19, Serial0
     2.0.0.0/32 is subnetted, 1 subnets
C       2.2.2.2 is directly connected, Loopback0
```

continues

```
     3.0.0.0/32 is subnetted, 1 subnets
O IA    3.3.3.3 [110/65] via 10.1.1.6, 00:10:20, Serial1
     10.0.0.0/30 is subnetted, 2 subnets
C       10.1.1.0 is directly connected, Serial0
C       10.1.1.4 is directly connected, Serial1
```

```
rtrC#show ip route
Codes: C - connected, S - static, I - IGRP, R - RIP, M - mobile, B - BGP
       D - EIGRP, EX - EIGRP external, O - OSPF, IA - OSPF inter area
       N1 - OSPF NSSA external type 1, N2 - OSPF NSSA external type 2
       E1 - OSPF external type 1, E2 - OSPF external type 2, E - EGP
       i - IS-IS, L1 - IS-IS level-1, L2 - IS-IS level-2, * - candidate default
       U - per-user static route, o - ODR

Gateway of last resort is not set

     1.0.0.0/32 is subnetted, 1 subnets
O       1.1.1.1 [110/129] via 10.1.1.5, 00:11:10, Serial0
     2.0.0.0/32 is subnetted, 1 subnets
O       2.2.2.2 [110/65] via 10.1.1.5, 00:11:11, Serial0
     3.0.0.0/24 is subnetted, 1 subnets
C       3.3.3.0 is directly connected, Loopback0
     10.0.0.0/30 is subnetted, 2 subnets
O       10.1.1.0 [110/128] via 10.1.1.5, 00:11:11, Serial0
C       10.1.1.4 is directly connected, Serial0
```

Troubleshooting

Step 1 Verify that there is a neighbor relationship between the OSPF routers using the **show ip ospf neighbor** command.

Step 2 Verify that the transit area ID used in the **area virtual-link** command is proper.

Step 3 Verify that the router IDs used in the **area virtual-link** are correct.

Step 4 Verify that the same password is being used on each side of the virtual link.

2-18: area *transit-area-id* virtual-link *router-id* dead-interval *seconds*

Syntax Description:

- *transit-area-id*—The OSPF area ID of the area connecting the two ABRs that the virtual link will cross. This value can be entered as a decimal number in the range of 0 to 4,294,967,295 or in IP address form in the range 0.0.0.0 to 255.255.255.255. The transit area cannot be a stub area.

- *router-id*—OSPF router ID of the router at the remote end of the virtual link.
- *seconds*—If Hello packets from a neighbor are not received during a period of time equal to the dead interval, then the neighbor will be declared down. The range of values is 1–8192 seconds. The default value is 40 seconds.

Purpose: When an OSPF router receives a Hello packet from an OSPF neighbor, the receiving router assumes that the neighbor is active. The dead interval is used to determine when an OSPF neighbor has become inactive. If a Hello packet has not been received during the time set for the dead interval, then the neighbor will be declared down. By default, the dead interval is four times the Hello interval. The dead interval should always be greater than the Hello interval.

Initial Cisco IOS Software Release: 10.0

Configuration Example: Modifying the Dead Interval Over a Virtual Link

Configure the network in Figure 2-18 to observe the default timer values over the virtual link. You will then experiment with adjusting the values of the dead interval.

Figure 2-18 *The Dead Interval Must Be Configured with the Same Value at Both Ends of an OSPF Virtual Link*

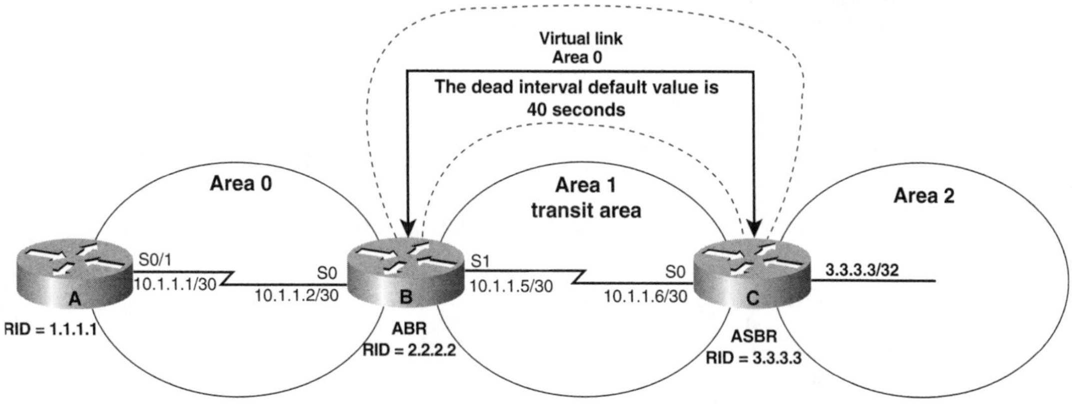


```
Router A
interface Loopback0
 ip address 1.1.1.1 255.255.255.255
!
interface Serial0/1
 ip address 10.1.1.1 255.255.255.252
 clockrate 64000
!
router ospf 1
```

continues

```
 network 10.1.1.0 0.0.0.3 area 0
 network 1.1.1.1 0.0.0.0 area 0
```

```
Router B
interface Loopback0
 ip address 2.2.2.2 255.255.255.255
!
interface Serial0
 ip address 10.1.1.2 255.255.255.252
!
interface Serial1
 ip address 10.1.1.5 255.255.255.252
 clockrate 64000
!
router ospf 1
 area 1 virtual-link 3.3.3.3
 network 10.1.1.0 0.0.0.3 area 0
 network 2.2.2.2 0.0.0.0 area 0
 network 10.1.1.4 0.0.0.3 area 1
```

```
Router C
interface Loopback0
 ip address 3.3.3.3 255.255.255.255
!
interface Serial0
 ip address 10.1.1.6 255.255.255.252
!
router ospf 1
 area 1 virtual-link 2.2.2.2
 network 3.3.3.3 0.0.0.0 area 2
 network 10.1.1.4 0.0.0.3 area 1
```

Verify that the virtual link is active and that all OSPF routes are being exchanged.

```
rtrB#show ip ospf virtual-links
Virtual Link OSPF_VL0 to router 3.3.3.3 is up
  Run as demand circuit
  DoNotAge LSA allowed.
  Transit area 1, via interface Serial1, Cost of using 64
  Transmit Delay is 1 sec, State POINT_TO_POINT,
  Timer intervals configured, Hello 10, Dead 40, Wait 40, Retransmit 5
    Hello due in 00:00:03
    Adjacency State FULL (Hello suppressed)
```

```
rtrC#show ip ospf virtual-links
Virtual Link OSPF_VL7 to router 2.2.2.2 is up
  Run as demand circuit
  DoNotAge LSA allowed.
  Transit area 1, via interface Serial0, Cost of using 64
```

```
  Transmit Delay is 1 sec, State POINT_TO_POINT,
  Timer intervals configured, Hello 10, Dead 40, Wait 40, Retransmit 5
    Hello due in 00:00:06
    Adjacency State FULL (Hello suppressed)

rtrC#show ip route
Codes: C - connected, S - static, I - IGRP, R - RIP, M - mobile, B - BGP
       D - EIGRP, EX - EIGRP external, O - OSPF, IA - OSPF inter area
       N1 - OSPF NSSA external type 1, N2 - OSPF NSSA external type 2
       E1 - OSPF external type 1, E2 - OSPF external type 2, E - EGP
       i - IS-IS, L1 - IS-IS level-1, L2 - IS-IS level-2, * - candidate default
       U - per-user static route, o - ODR

Gateway of last resort is not set

     1.0.0.0/32 is subnetted, 1 subnets
O       1.1.1.1 [110/129] via 10.1.1.5, 00:02:25, Serial0
     2.0.0.0/32 is subnetted, 1 subnets
O       2.2.2.2 [110/65] via 10.1.1.5, 00:02:26, Serial0
     3.0.0.0/24 is subnetted, 1 subnets
C       3.3.3.0 is directly connected, Loopback0
     10.0.0.0/30 is subnetted, 2 subnets
O       10.1.1.0 [110/128] via 10.1.1.5, 00:02:26, Serial0
C       10.1.1.4 is directly connected, Serial0
```

Notice that the default Hello interval is 10 seconds and the default dead interval is 40 seconds. Modify the configuration on Router B to change the dead interval to 41 seconds while leaving the value for the dead interval on Router C set to the default of 40 seconds.

```
Router B
router ospf 1
 area 1 virtual-link 3.3.3.3 dead-interval 41
 network 2.2.2.2 0.0.0.0 area 0
 network 10.1.1.0 0.0.0.3 area 0
 network 10.1.1.4 0.0.0.3 area 1
```

Is the virtual link still active?

```
rtrB#show ip ospf virtual-links
Virtual Link OSPF_VL0 to router 3.3.3.3 is up
  Run as demand circuit
  DoNotAge LSA allowed.
  Transit area 1, via interface Serial1, Cost of using 64
  Transmit Delay is 1 sec, State POINT_TO_POINT,
  Timer intervals configured, Hello 10, Dead 41, Wait 40, Retransmit 5
    Hello due in 00:00:07
```

The virtual link is up. Now check to see if the OSPF routes are being exchanged.

```
rtrB#show ip route
Codes: C - connected, S - static, I - IGRP, R - RIP, M - mobile, B - BGP
       D - EIGRP, EX - EIGRP external, O - OSPF, IA - OSPF inter area
       N1 - OSPF NSSA external type 1, N2 - OSPF NSSA external type 2
       E1 - OSPF external type 1, E2 - OSPF external type 2, E - EGP
       i - IS-IS, L1 - IS-IS level-1, L2 - IS-IS level-2, * - candidate default
       U - per-user static route, o - ODR

Gateway of last resort is not set

     1.0.0.0/32 is subnetted, 1 subnets
O       1.1.1.1 [110/65] via 10.1.1.1, 00:07:49, Serial0
     2.0.0.0/32 is subnetted, 1 subnets
C       2.2.2.2 is directly connected, Loopback0
     10.0.0.0/30 is subnetted, 2 subnets
C       10.1.1.0 is directly connected, Serial0
C       10.1.1.4 is directly connected, Serial1
```

Router B has learned the routes being advertised by Router A but not the routes advertised by Router C. Because the dead interval time on Router B does not match the dead interval on Router C, routes will not be exchanged over the virtual link. Modify the dead interval time on Router C to match the dead interval time on Router B.

```
Router C
router ospf 1
router ospf 1
 area 1 virtual-link 2.2.2.2 dead-interval 41
 network 3.3.3.3 0.0.0.0 area 2
 network 10.1.1.4 0.0.0.3 area 1
```

Verification

Verify that the dead interval on Router C matches the dead interval on Router B.

```
rtrC#show ip ospf virtual-links
Virtual Link OSPF_VL7 to router 2.2.2.2 is up
  Run as demand circuit
  DoNotAge LSA allowed.
  Transit area 1, via interface Serial0, Cost of using 64
  Transmit Delay is 1 sec, State POINT_TO_POINT,
  Timer intervals configured, Hello 10, Dead 41, Wait 40, Retransmit 5
    Hello due in 00:00:00
    Adjacency State FULL (Hello suppressed)
```

Verify that all OSPF routes are now being exchanged.

```
rtrA#show ip route
Codes: C - connected, S - static, I - IGRP, R - RIP, M - mobile, B - BGP
       D - EIGRP, EX - EIGRP external, O - OSPF, IA - OSPF inter area
       N1 - OSPF NSSA external type 1, N2 - OSPF NSSA external type 2
       E1 - OSPF external type 1, E2 - OSPF external type 2, E - EGP
       i - IS-IS, L1 - IS-IS level-1, L2 - IS-IS level-2, * - candidate default
       U - per-user static route, o - ODR

Gateway of last resort is not set

     1.0.0.0/32 is subnetted, 1 subnets
C       1.1.1.1 is directly connected, Loopback0
     2.0.0.0/32 is subnetted, 1 subnets
O       2.2.2.2 [110/65] via 10.1.1.2, 00:09:04, Serial0/1
     3.0.0.0/32 is subnetted, 1 subnets
O IA    3.3.3.3 [110/129] via 10.1.1.2, 00:09:04, Serial0/1
     10.0.0.0/30 is subnetted, 2 subnets
C       10.1.1.0 is directly connected, Serial0/1
O IA    10.1.1.4 [110/128] via 10.1.1.2, 00:09:04, Serial0/1
```

```
rtrB#show ip route
Codes: C - connected, S - static, I - IGRP, R - RIP, M - mobile, B - BGP
       D - EIGRP, EX - EIGRP external, O - OSPF, IA - OSPF inter area
       N1 - OSPF NSSA external type 1, N2 - OSPF NSSA external type 2
       E1 - OSPF external type 1, E2 - OSPF external type 2, E - EGP
       i - IS-IS, L1 - IS-IS level-1, L2 - IS-IS level-2, * - candidate default
       U - per-user static route, o - ODR

Gateway of last resort is not set

     1.0.0.0/32 is subnetted, 1 subnets
O       1.1.1.1 [110/65] via 10.1.1.1, 00:10:19, Serial0
     2.0.0.0/32 is subnetted, 1 subnets
C       2.2.2.2 is directly connected, Loopback0
     3.0.0.0/32 is subnetted, 1 subnets
O IA    3.3.3.3 [110/65] via 10.1.1.6, 00:10:20, Serial1
     10.0.0.0/30 is subnetted, 2 subnets
C       10.1.1.0 is directly connected, Serial0
C       10.1.1.4 is directly connected, Serial1
```

```
rtrC#show ip route
Codes: C - connected, S - static, I - IGRP, R - RIP, M - mobile, B - BGP
       D - EIGRP, EX - EIGRP external, O - OSPF, IA - OSPF inter area
       N1 - OSPF NSSA external type 1, N2 - OSPF NSSA external type 2
       E1 - OSPF external type 1, E2 - OSPF external type 2, E - EGP
       i - IS-IS, L1 - IS-IS level-1, L2 - IS-IS level-2, * - candidate default
       U - per-user static route, o - ODR

Gateway of last resort is not set
```

continues

```
     1.0.0.0/32 is subnetted, 1 subnets
O       1.1.1.1 [110/129] via 10.1.1.5, 00:11:10, Serial0
     2.0.0.0/32 is subnetted, 1 subnets
O       2.2.2.2 [110/65] via 10.1.1.5, 00:11:11, Serial0
     3.0.0.0/24 is subnetted, 1 subnets
C       3.3.3.0 is directly connected, Loopback0
     10.0.0.0/30 is subnetted, 2 subnets
O       10.1.1.0 [110/128] via 10.1.1.5, 00:11:11, Serial0
C       10.1.1.4 is directly connected, Serial0
```

Troubleshooting

Step 1 Verify that there is a neighbor relationship between the OSPF routers using the **show ip ospf neighbor** command.

Step 2 Verify that the transit area ID used in the **area virtual-link** command is the proper area.

Step 3 Verify that the router IDs used in the **area virtual-link** are correct.

Step 4 Verify that the dead interval is being used on both ends of the virtual link.

2-19: area *transit-area-id* virtual-link *router-id* hello-interval *seconds*

Syntax Description:

- *transit-area-id*—The OSPF area ID of the area connecting the two ABRs that the virtual link will cross. This value can be entered as a decimal number in the range of 0 to 4,294,967,295 or in IP address form in the range 0.0.0.0 to 255.255.255.255. The transit area cannot be a stub area.
- *router-id*—OSPF router ID of the router at the remote end of the virtual link.
- *seconds*—The time in seconds between sending Hello packets over the virtual link. The range of values is 1–8192 seconds. The default value is 10 seconds (30 seconds on a nonbroadcast multiaccess [NBMA] network).

Purpose: OSPF Hello packets are used to initially establish the neighbor relationship. Once the neighbor relationship is established, the packets are used as a keepalive mechanism to determine if the neighbor at the other end of the virtual link is still active. The Hello interval should be less than the dead interval (see Command 2-18).

Initial Cisco IOS Software Release: 10.0

Configuration Example: Modifying the Hello Interval Over a Virtual Link

Configure the network in Figure 2-19 to observe the default timer values over the virtual link. You will then experiment with adjusting the values of the Hello interval.

Figure 2-19 *The Hello Interval Must Be Configured with the Same Value at Both Ends of an OSPF Virtual Link*

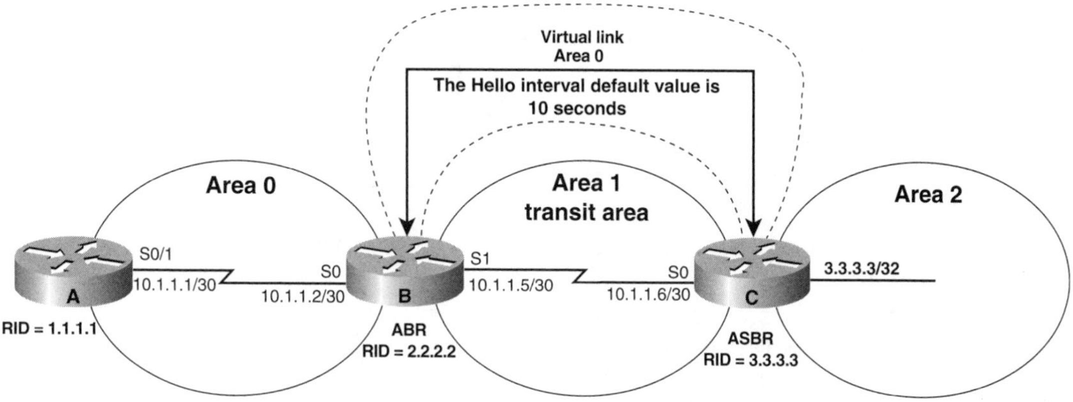


```
Router A
interface Loopback0
 ip address 1.1.1.1 255.255.255.255
!
interface Serial0/1
 ip address 10.1.1.1 255.255.255.252
 clockrate 64000
!
router ospf 1
 network 10.1.1.0 0.0.0.3 area 0
 network 1.1.1.1 0.0.0.0 area 0
```

```
Router B
interface Loopback0
 ip address 2.2.2.2 255.255.255.255
!
interface Serial0
 ip address 10.1.1.2 255.255.255.252
!
interface Serial1
 ip address 10.1.1.5 255.255.255.252
 clockrate 64000
!
router ospf 1
 area 1 virtual-link 3.3.3.3
```

continues

```
 network 10.1.1.0 0.0.0.3 area 0
 network 2.2.2.2 0.0.0.0 area 0
 network 10.1.1.4 0.0.0.3 area 1
```

```
Router C
interface Loopback0
 ip address 3.3.3.3 255.255.255.255
!
interface Serial0
 ip address 10.1.1.6 255.255.255.252
!
router ospf 1
 area 1 virtual-link 2.2.2.2
 network 3.3.3.3 0.0.0.0 area 2
 network 10.1.1.4 0.0.0.3 area 1
```

Verify that the virtual link is active and that all OSPF routes are being exchanged.

```
rtrB#show ip ospf virtual-links
Virtual Link OSPF_VL0 to router 3.3.3.3 is up
  Run as demand circuit
  DoNotAge LSA allowed.
  Transit area 1, via interface Serial1, Cost of using 64
  Transmit Delay is 1 sec, State POINT_TO_POINT,
  Timer intervals configured, Hello 10, Dead 40, Wait 40, Retransmit 5
    Hello due in 00:00:03
    Adjacency State FULL (Hello suppressed)
```

```
rtrC#show ip ospf virtual-links
Virtual Link OSPF_VL7 to router 2.2.2.2 is up
  Run as demand circuit
  DoNotAge LSA allowed.
  Transit area 1, via interface Serial0, Cost of using 64
  Transmit Delay is 1 sec, State POINT_TO_POINT,
  Timer intervals configured, Hello 10, Dead 40, Wait 40, Retransmit 5
    Hello due in 00:00:06
    Adjacency State FULL (Hello suppressed)

rtrC#show ip route
Codes: C - connected, S - static, I - IGRP, R - RIP, M - mobile, B - BGP
       D - EIGRP, EX - EIGRP external, O - OSPF, IA - OSPF inter area
       N1 - OSPF NSSA external type 1, N2 - OSPF NSSA external type 2
       E1 - OSPF external type 1, E2 - OSPF external type 2, E - EGP
       i - IS-IS, L1 - IS-IS level-1, L2 - IS-IS level-2, * - candidate default
       U - per-user static route, o - ODR

Gateway of last resort is not set

     1.0.0.0/32 is subnetted, 1 subnets
O       1.1.1.1 [110/129] via 10.1.1.5, 00:02:25, Serial0
     2.0.0.0/32 is subnetted, 1 subnets
```

```
O       2.2.2.2 [110/65] via 10.1.1.5, 00:02:26, Serial0
     3.0.0.0/24 is subnetted, 1 subnets
C       3.3.3.0 is directly connected, Loopback0
     10.0.0.0/30 is subnetted, 2 subnets
O       10.1.1.0 [110/128] via 10.1.1.5, 00:02:26, Serial0
C       10.1.1.4 is directly connected, Serial0
```

Notice that the default Hello interval is 10 seconds and the default dead interval is 40 seconds. Modify the configuration on Router B to change the Hello interval to 11 seconds while leaving the value for the Hello interval on Router C set to the default of 10 seconds.

```
Router B
router ospf 1
 area 1 virtual-link 3.3.3.3 hello-interval 11
 network 2.2.2.2 0.0.0.0 area 0
 network 10.1.1.0 0.0.0.3 area 0
 network 10.1.1.4 0.0.0.3 area 1
```

Is the virtual link still active?

```
rtrB#show ip ospf virtual-links
Virtual Link OSPF_VL0 to router 3.3.3.3 is up
  Run as demand circuit
  DoNotAge LSA allowed.
  Transit area 1, via interface Serial1, Cost of using 64
  Transmit Delay is 1 sec, State POINT_TO_POINT,
  Timer intervals configured, Hello 11, Dead 40, Wait 40, Retransmit 5
    Hello due in 00:00:07
```

The virtual link is up. Now check to see if the OSPF routes are being exchanged.

```
rtrB#show ip route
Codes: C - connected, S - static, I - IGRP, R - RIP, M - mobile, B - BGP
       D - EIGRP, EX - EIGRP external, O - OSPF, IA - OSPF inter area
       N1 - OSPF NSSA external type 1, N2 - OSPF NSSA external type 2
       E1 - OSPF external type 1, E2 - OSPF external type 2, E - EGP
       i - IS-IS, L1 - IS-IS level-1, L2 - IS-IS level-2, * - candidate default
       U - per-user static route, o - ODR

Gateway of last resort is not set

     1.0.0.0/32 is subnetted, 1 subnets
O       1.1.1.1 [110/65] via 10.1.1.1, 00:07:49, Serial0
     2.0.0.0/32 is subnetted, 1 subnets
C       2.2.2.2 is directly connected, Loopback0
     10.0.0.0/30 is subnetted, 2 subnets
C       10.1.1.0 is directly connected, Serial0
C       10.1.1.4 is directly connected, Serial1
```

Router B has learned the routes being advertised by Router A but not the routes advertised by Router C. Because the Hello interval time on Router B does not match the Hello interval on Router C, routes will not be exchanged over the virtual link. Modify the Hello interval time on Router C to match the Hello interval time on Router B.

```
Router C
router ospf 1
router ospf 1
 area 1 virtual-link 2.2.2.2 hello-interval 11
 network 3.3.3.3 0.0.0.0 area 2
 network 10.1.1.4 0.0.0.3 area 1
```

Verification

Verify that the Hello interval on Router C matches the dead interval on Router B.

```
rtrC#show ip ospf virtual-links
Virtual Link OSPF_VL7 to router 2.2.2.2 is up
  Run as demand circuit
  DoNotAge LSA allowed.
  Transit area 1, via interface Serial0, Cost of using 64
  Transmit Delay is 1 sec, State POINT_TO_POINT,
  Timer intervals configured, Hello 11, Dead 41, Wait 40, Retransmit 5
    Hello due in 00:00:00
    Adjacency State FULL (Hello suppressed)
```

Verify that all OSPF routes are now being exchanged.

```
rtrA#show ip route
Codes: C - connected, S - static, I - IGRP, R - RIP, M - mobile, B - BGP
       D - EIGRP, EX - EIGRP external, O - OSPF, IA - OSPF inter area
       N1 - OSPF NSSA external type 1, N2 - OSPF NSSA external type 2
       E1 - OSPF external type 1, E2 - OSPF external type 2, E - EGP
       i - IS-IS, L1 - IS-IS level-1, L2 - IS-IS level-2, * - candidate default
       U - per-user static route, o - ODR

Gateway of last resort is not set

     1.0.0.0/32 is subnetted, 1 subnets
C       1.1.1.1 is directly connected, Loopback0
     2.0.0.0/32 is subnetted, 1 subnets
O       2.2.2.2 [110/65] via 10.1.1.2, 00:09:04, Serial0/1
     3.0.0.0/32 is subnetted, 1 subnets
O IA    3.3.3.3 [110/129] via 10.1.1.2, 00:09:04, Serial0/1
     10.0.0.0/30 is subnetted, 2 subnets
C       10.1.1.0 is directly connected, Serial0/1
O IA    10.1.1.4 [110/128] via 10.1.1.2, 00:09:04, Serial0/1
```

```
rtrB#show ip route
Codes: C - connected, S - static, I - IGRP, R - RIP, M - mobile, B - BGP
       D - EIGRP, EX - EIGRP external, O - OSPF, IA - OSPF inter area
       N1 - OSPF NSSA external type 1, N2 - OSPF NSSA external type 2
       E1 - OSPF external type 1, E2 - OSPF external type 2, E - EGP
       i - IS-IS, L1 - IS-IS level-1, L2 - IS-IS level-2, * - candidate default
       U - per-user static route, o - ODR

Gateway of last resort is not set

     1.0.0.0/32 is subnetted, 1 subnets
O       1.1.1.1 [110/65] via 10.1.1.1, 00:10:19, Serial0
     2.0.0.0/32 is subnetted, 1 subnets
C       2.2.2.2 is directly connected, Loopback0
     3.0.0.0/32 is subnetted, 1 subnets
O IA    3.3.3.3 [110/65] via 10.1.1.6, 00:10:20, Serial1
     10.0.0.0/30 is subnetted, 2 subnets
C       10.1.1.0 is directly connected, Serial0
C       10.1.1.4 is directly connected, Serial1
```

```
rtrC#show ip route
Codes: C - connected, S - static, I - IGRP, R - RIP, M - mobile, B - BGP
       D - EIGRP, EX - EIGRP external, O - OSPF, IA - OSPF inter area
       N1 - OSPF NSSA external type 1, N2 - OSPF NSSA external type 2
       E1 - OSPF external type 1, E2 - OSPF external type 2, E - EGP
       i - IS-IS, L1 - IS-IS level-1, L2 - IS-IS level-2, * - candidate default
       U - per-user static route, o - ODR

Gateway of last resort is not set

     1.0.0.0/32 is subnetted, 1 subnets
O       1.1.1.1 [110/129] via 10.1.1.5, 00:11:10, Serial0
     2.0.0.0/32 is subnetted, 1 subnets
O       2.2.2.2 [110/65] via 10.1.1.5, 00:11:11, Serial0
     3.0.0.0/24 is subnetted, 1 subnets
C       3.3.3.0 is directly connected, Loopback0
     10.0.0.0/30 is subnetted, 2 subnets
O       10.1.1.0 [110/128] via 10.1.1.5, 00:11:11, Serial0
C       10.1.1.4 is directly connected, Serial0
```

Troubleshooting

Step 1 Verify that there is a neighbor relationship between the OSPF routers by using the **show ip ospf neighbor** command.

Step 2 Verify that the transit area ID used in the **area virtual-link** command is the proper area.

Step 3 Verify that the router IDs used in the **area virtual-link** are correct.

Step 4 Verify that the Hello interval is being used on both ends of the virtual link.

2-20: area *transit-area-id* virtual-link *router-id* message-digest-key *key-id* md5 *password*

Syntax Description:

- *transit-area-id*—The OSPF area ID of the area connecting the two ABRs that the virtual link will cross. This value can be entered as a decimal number in the range of 0 to 4,294,967,295 or in IP address form in the range 0.0.0.0 to 255.255.255.255. The transit area cannot be a stub area.
- *router-id*—OSPF router ID of the router at the remote end of the virtual link.
- *key-id*—Key to use to encrypt a password. The range of values is 1 to 255. Both ends of a virtual link must use the same key and password.
- *password*—Password to be used for authentication in the selected area on the selected interface or virtual link. The password is an alphanumeric string from 1 to 8 characters.

Purpose: If message digest authentication is enabled in Area 0, then all virtual links need to be configured with the same authentication type. This command is used to configure message digest authentication over a virtual link. In Cisco IOS Software Release 12.0 and later, virtual link authentication can be configured independent of Area 0 (see Section 2-15).

Initial Cisco IOS Software Release: 11.0

Configuration Example 1: Message Digest Authentication Over a Virtual Link

In Figure 2-20, message authentication has been enabled for Area 0. Initially, authentication is not enabled over the virtual link so you can see the effect of enabling authentication in Area 0 but not over the virtual link.

Figure 2-20 *Prior to Cisco IOS Software Release 12.0, if Message Digest Authentication Is Enabled in Area 0 Then Message Digest Authentication Must Be Enabled Over the Virtual Link*

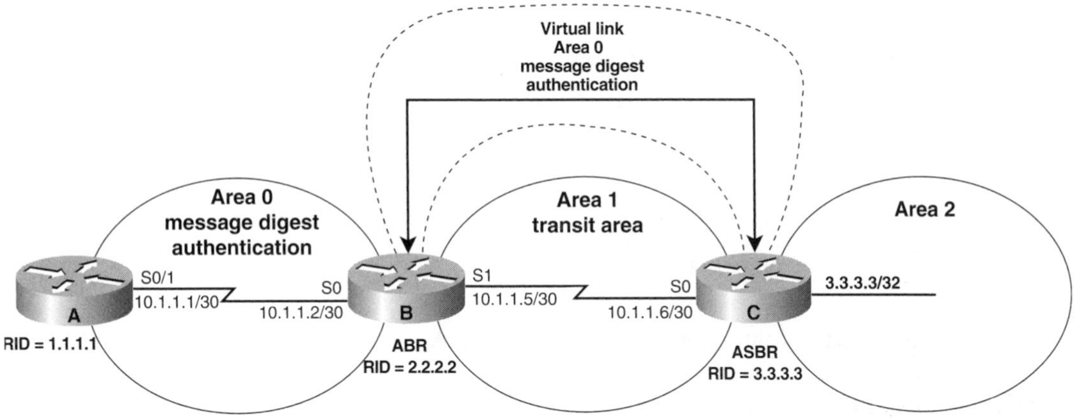


```
Router A
interface Loopback0
 ip address 1.1.1.1 255.255.255.255
!
interface Serial0/1
 ip address 10.1.1.1 255.255.255.252
ip ospf message-digest-key 1 md5 cisco
 clockrate 64000
!
router ospf 1
 area 0 authentication-message digest
 network 10.1.1.0 0.0.0.3 area 0
 network 1.1.1.1 0.0.0.0 area 0
```

```
Router B
interface Loopback0
 ip address 2.2.2.2 255.255.255.255
!
interface Serial0
 ip address 10.1.1.2 255.255.255.252
ip ospf message-digest-key 1 md5 cisco
!
interface Serial1
 ip address 10.1.1.5 255.255.255.252
 clockrate 64000
!
router ospf 1
 area 0 authentication message-digest
 area 1 virtual-link 3.3.3.3
 network 10.1.1.0 0.0.0.3 area 0
 network 2.2.2.2 0.0.0.0 area 0
```

continues

```
 network 10.1.1.4 0.0.0.3 area 1
```

```
Router C
interface Loopback0
 ip address 3.3.3.3 255.255.255.255
!
interface Serial0
 ip address 10.1.1.6 255.255.255.252
!
router ospf 1
 area 1 virtual-link 2.2.2.2
 network 3.3.3.3 0.0.0.0 area 2
 network 10.1.1.4 0.0.0.3 area 1
```

Verify that authentication has been enabled for Area 0.

```
rtrA#show ip ospf
Routing Process "ospf 1" with ID 1.1.1.1
 Supports only single TOS(TOS0) routes
 SPF schedule delay 5 secs, Hold time between two SPFs 10 secs
 Minimum LSA interval 5 secs. Minimum LSA arrival 1 secs
 Number of external LSA 0. Checksum Sum 0x0
 Number of DCbitless external LSA 0
 Number of DoNotAge external LSA 0
 Number of areas in this router is 1. 1 normal 0 stub 0 nssa
    Area BACKBONE(0)
        Number of interfaces in this area is 2
        Area has message digest authentication
        SPF algorithm executed 8 times
        Area ranges are
        Number of LSA 6. Checksum Sum 0x4AC3C
        Number of DCbitless LSA 0
        Number of indication LSA 0
        Number of DoNotAge LSA 3
```

```
rtrB#show ip ospf
 Routing Process "ospf 1" with ID 2.2.2.2
 Supports only single TOS(TOS0) routes
 It is an area border router
 SPF schedule delay 5 secs, Hold time between two SPFs 10 secs
 Minimum LSA interval 5 secs. Minimum LSA arrival 1 secs
 Number of external LSA 0. Checksum Sum 0x0
 Number of DCbitless external LSA 0
 Number of DoNotAge external LSA 0
 Number of areas in this router is 2. 2 normal 0 stub 0 nssa
    Area BACKBONE(0)
        Number of interfaces in this area is 3
        Area has message digest authentication
        SPF algorithm executed 14 times
        Area ranges are
```

```
        Number of LSA 6. Checksum Sum 0x4AC3C
        Number of DCbitless LSA 0
        Number of indication LSA 0
        Number of DoNotAge LSA 3
    Area 1
        Number of interfaces in this area is 1
        Area has no authentication
        SPF algorithm executed 4 times
        Area ranges are
        Number of LSA 8. Checksum Sum 0x4AED7
        Number of DCbitless LSA 0
        Number of indication LSA 0
        Number of DoNotAge LSA 0
```

When authentication is enabled in Area 0, then this authentication type will be applied to all interfaces in Area 0, including virtual links. Any routing updates from neighbors in Area 0 will be rejected if the authentication type and password do not match. Because a virtual link is considered to be in Area 0, routing updates passing over the virtual link will be rejected. This can be verified by examining the IP routing table on Router B.

```
rtrB#show ip route
Codes: C - connected, S - static, I - IGRP, R - RIP, M - mobile, B - BGP
       D - EIGRP, EX - EIGRP external, O - OSPF, IA - OSPF inter area
       N1 - OSPF NSSA external type 1, N2 - OSPF NSSA external type 2
       E1 - OSPF external type 1, E2 - OSPF external type 2, E - EGP
       i - IS-IS, L1 - IS-IS level-1, L2 - IS-IS level-2, * - candidate default
       U - per-user static route, o - ODR

Gateway of last resort is not set

     1.0.0.0/32 is subnetted, 1 subnets
O       1.1.1.1 [110/65] via 10.1.1.1, 00:06:34, Serial0
     2.0.0.0/32 is subnetted, 1 subnets
C       2.2.2.2 is directly connected, Loopback0
     10.0.0.0/30 is subnetted, 2 subnets
C       10.1.1.0 is directly connected, Serial0
C       10.1.1.4 is directly connected, Serial1
```

Router B has learned the routes being advertised by Router A, but not the routes advertised by Router C. You must enable message digest authentication on the virtual link so that routing updates can be exchanged between Routers B and C. You can also use a different authentication type on the virtual link using command 2-14, 2-15, or 2-16. In this case, you will configure the same authentication type that is being used in Area 0. Change the key and password used over the virtual link to demonstrate that the keys and passwords for different interfaces do not need to be the same. Remember that the key and password for a common link must be the same at both ends of the link. Modify the configurations on Routers B and

C to enable message digest authentication over the virtual link using a key of 2 and the password bosco.

```
Router B
router ospf 1
 area 0 authentication
 area 1 virtual-link 3.3.3.3 message-digest-key 2 md5 bosco
 network 2.2.2.2 0.0.0.0 area 0
 network 10.1.1.0 0.0.0.3 area 0
 network 10.1.1.4 0.0.0.3 area 1
```

```
Router C
router ospf 1
 area 0 authentication
 area 1 virtual-link 2.2.2.2 message-digest-key 2 md5 bosco
 network 3.3.3.3 0.0.0.0 area 2
 network 10.1.1.4 0.0.0.3 area 1
```

Notice that the command **area 0 authentication message-digest** was used on Router C because the virtual link is in Area 0.

Verification

Verify that message digest authentication has been enabled over the virtual link.

```
rtrC#show ip ospf virtual-links
Virtual Link OSPF_VL7 to router 2.2.2.2 is up
  Run as demand circuit
  DoNotAge LSA allowed.
  Transit area 1, via interface Serial0, Cost of using 64
  Transmit Delay is 1 sec, State POINT_TO_POINT,
  Timer intervals configured, Hello 10, Dead 40, Wait 40, Retransmit 5
    Hello due in 00:00:06
    Adjacency State FULL (Hello suppressed)
  Message digest authentication enabled
    Youngest key id is 2
```

Verify that all OSPF routes are now being exchanged.

```
rtrA#show ip route
Codes: C - connected, S - static, I - IGRP, R - RIP, M - mobile, B - BGP
       D - EIGRP, EX - EIGRP external, O - OSPF, IA - OSPF inter area
       N1 - OSPF NSSA external type 1, N2 - OSPF NSSA external type 2
       E1 - OSPF external type 1, E2 - OSPF external type 2, E - EGP
       i - IS-IS, L1 - IS-IS level-1, L2 - IS-IS level-2, * - candidate default
       U - per-user static route, o - ODR
```

```
Gateway of last resort is not set

     1.0.0.0/32 is subnetted, 1 subnets
C       1.1.1.1 is directly connected, Loopback0
     2.0.0.0/32 is subnetted, 1 subnets
O       2.2.2.2 [110/65] via 10.1.1.2, 00:09:04, Serial0/1
     3.0.0.0/32 is subnetted, 1 subnets
O IA    3.3.3.3 [110/129] via 10.1.1.2, 00:09:04, Serial0/1
     10.0.0.0/30 is subnetted, 2 subnets
C       10.1.1.0 is directly connected, Serial0/1
O IA    10.1.1.4 [110/128] via 10.1.1.2, 00:09:04, Serial0/1
```

```
rtrB#show ip route
Codes: C - connected, S - static, I - IGRP, R - RIP, M - mobile, B - BGP
       D - EIGRP, EX - EIGRP external, O - OSPF, IA - OSPF inter area
       N1 - OSPF NSSA external type 1, N2 - OSPF NSSA external type 2
       E1 - OSPF external type 1, E2 - OSPF external type 2, E - EGP
       i - IS-IS, L1 - IS-IS level-1, L2 - IS-IS level-2, * - candidate default
       U - per-user static route, o - ODR

Gateway of last resort is not set

     1.0.0.0/32 is subnetted, 1 subnets
O       1.1.1.1 [110/65] via 10.1.1.1, 00:10:19, Serial0
     2.0.0.0/32 is subnetted, 1 subnets
C       2.2.2.2 is directly connected, Loopback0
     3.0.0.0/32 is subnetted, 1 subnets
O IA    3.3.3.3 [110/65] via 10.1.1.6, 00:10:20, Serial1
     10.0.0.0/30 is subnetted, 2 subnets
C       10.1.1.0 is directly connected, Serial0
C       10.1.1.4 is directly connected, Serial1
```

```
rtrC#show ip route
Codes: C - connected, S - static, I - IGRP, R - RIP, M - mobile, B - BGP
       D - EIGRP, EX - EIGRP external, O - OSPF, IA - OSPF inter area
       N1 - OSPF NSSA external type 1, N2 - OSPF NSSA external type 2
       E1 - OSPF external type 1, E2 - OSPF external type 2, E - EGP
       i - IS-IS, L1 - IS-IS level-1, L2 - IS-IS level-2, * - candidate default
       U - per-user static route, o - ODR

Gateway of last resort is not set

     1.0.0.0/32 is subnetted, 1 subnets
O       1.1.1.1 [110/129] via 10.1.1.5, 00:11:10, Serial0
     2.0.0.0/32 is subnetted, 1 subnets
O       2.2.2.2 [110/65] via 10.1.1.5, 00:11:11, Serial0
     3.0.0.0/24 is subnetted, 1 subnets
C       3.3.3.0 is directly connected, Loopback0
     10.0.0.0/30 is subnetted, 2 subnets
O       10.1.1.0 [110/128] via 10.1.1.5, 00:11:11, Serial0
C       10.1.1.4 is directly connected, Serial0
```

Configuration Example 2: Changing Keys and Passwords

For additional security you may choose to periodically change the key and password. With clear-text authentication, when you change passwords there will be a loss of OSPF connectivity from the time you change the password on one end of the virtual link until you change the password at the other end of the virtual link. With MD5 authentication you can configure a new key and password on a virtual link while leaving the old key and password in place. The old key and password will continue to be used until the new key and password are configured on the other end of the virtual link. Modify the key and password on the virtual link between Routers B and C. First, add a new key and password to Router B in order to observe the behavior when the new key and password have only been configured on one end of the virtual link.

```
Router B
router ospf 1
area 0 authentication message-digest
 area 1 virtual-link 3.3.3.3 message-digest-key 2 md5 bosco
 area 1 virtual-link 3.3.3.3 message-digest-key 3 md5 newton
 network 2.2.2.2 0.0.0.0 area 0
 network 10.1.1.0 0.0.0.3 area 0
 network 10.1.1.4 0.0.0.3 area 1
```

Examine the effect of adding a new key and password on only one end of the virtual link.

```
rtrB#show ip ospf virtual-links
Virtual Link OSPF_VL1 to router 3.3.3.3 is up
  Run as demand circuit
  DoNotAge LSA allowed.
  Transit area 1, via interface Serial1, Cost of using 64
  Transmit Delay is 1 sec, State POINT_TO_POINT,
  Timer intervals configured, Hello 10, Dead 40, Wait 40, Retransmit 5
    Hello due in 00:00:03
    Adjacency State FULL (Hello suppressed)
  Message digest authentication enabled
    Youngest key id is 3
    Rollover in progress, 1 neighbor(s) using the old key(s):
      key id 2
```

Notice that both keys are being used for authentication. Configure the new key and password on Router C while leaving the old key and password in place.

```
Router C
router ospf 1
 area 0 authentication message-digest
 area 1 virtual-link 2.2.2.2 message-digest-key 2 md5 bosco
```

```
 area 1 virtual-link 2.2.2.2 message-digest-key 3 md5 newton
 network 3.3.3.3 0.0.0.0 area 2
 network 10.1.1.4 0.0.0.3 area 1
```

Verify that Router C is now using the new key and password.

```
rtrC#show ip ospf virtual-links
Virtual Link OSPF_VL7 to router 2.2.2.2 is up
  Run as demand circuit
  DoNotAge LSA allowed.
  Transit area 1, via interface Serial0, Cost of using 64
  Transmit Delay is 1 sec, State POINT_TO_POINT,
  Timer intervals configured, Hello 10, Dead 40, Wait 40, Retransmit 5
    Hello due in 00:00:04
    Adjacency State FULL (Hello suppressed)
  Message digest authentication enabled
    Youngest key id is 3
    Rollover in progress, 1 neighbor(s) using the old key(s):
      key id 2
```

You can now remove the old key and password from Routers B and C.

```
Router B
router ospf 1
 no area 1 virtual-link 3.3.3.3 message-digest-key 2
```

```
Router C
router ospf 1
 no area 1 virtual-link 2.2.2.2 message-digest-key 2
```

Verification

Verify that only the new key and password are being used over the virtual link.

```
rtrB#show ip ospf virtual-links
Virtual Link OSPF_VL0 to router 3.3.3.3 is up
  Run as demand circuit
  DoNotAge LSA allowed.
  Transit area 1, via interface Serial1, Cost of using 64
  Transmit Delay is 1 sec, State POINT_TO_POINT,
  Timer intervals configured, Hello 10, Dead 40, Wait 40, Retransmit 5
    Hello due in 00:00:01
    Adjacency State INIT (Hello suppressed)
  Message digest authentication enabled
    Youngest key id is 3
```

Troubleshooting

Step 1 Verify that there is a neighbor relationship between the OSPF routers using the **show ip ospf neighbor** command.

Step 2 Verify that the transit area ID used in the **area virtual-link** command is the proper area.

Step 3 Verify that the router IDs used in the **area virtual-link** are correct.

Step 4 Verify that the same key and password are being used on each side of the virtual link.

2-21: area *transit-area-id* virtual-link *router-id* retransmit-interval *seconds*

Syntax Description:

- *transit-area-id*—The OSPF area ID of the area connecting the two ABRs that the virtual link will cross. This value can be entered as a decimal number in the range of 0 to 4,294,967,295 or in IP address form in the range 0.0.0.0 to 255.255.255.255. The transit area cannot be a stub area.
- *router-id*—OSPF router ID of the router at the remote end of the virtual link.
- *seconds*—The range of values is 1–8192 seconds. The default value is 5 seconds.

Purpose: When a router advertises a link-state advertisement (LSA) over a virtual link, the LSA is added to a retransmission list for the virtual link. The LSA will be retransmitted until the LSA is acknowledged. The number of seconds between the advertisements is called the retransmit interval.

Initial Cisco IOS Software Release: 10.0

Configuration Example: Modifying the Retransmit Interval Over a Virtual Link

Configure the network in Figure 2-21 to observe the default timer values over the virtual link. You will then experiment with adjusting the values of the retransmit interval.

Figure 2-21 *The Retransmit Interval Is the Time Between Resending Unacknowledged LSAs*

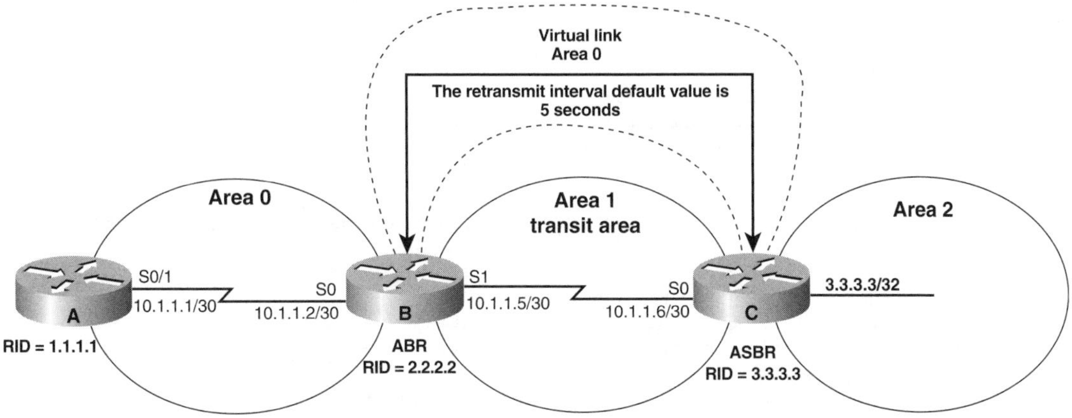


```
Router A
interface Loopback0
 ip address 1.1.1.1 255.255.255.255
!
interface Serial0/1
 ip address 10.1.1.1 255.255.255.252
 clockrate 64000
!
router ospf 1
 network 10.1.1.0 0.0.0.3 area 0
 network 1.1.1.1 0.0.0.0 area 0
```

```
Router B
interface Loopback0
 ip address 2.2.2.2 255.255.255.255
!
interface Serial0
 ip address 10.1.1.2 255.255.255.252
!
interface Serial1
 ip address 10.1.1.5 255.255.255.252
 clockrate 64000
!
router ospf 1
 area 1 virtual-link 3.3.3.3
 network 10.1.1.0 0.0.0.3 area 0
 network 2.2.2.2 0.0.0.0 area 0
 network 10.1.1.4 0.0.0.3 area 1
```

```
Router C
interface Loopback0
 ip address 3.3.3.3 255.255.255.255
```

continues

```
!
interface Serial0
 ip address 10.1.1.6 255.255.255.252
!
router ospf 1
 area 1 virtual-link 2.2.2.2
 network 3.3.3.3 0.0.0.0 area 2
 network 10.1.1.4 0.0.0.3 area 1
```

Verify that the virtual link is active and that all OSPF routes are being exchanged.

```
rtrB#show ip ospf virtual-links
Virtual Link OSPF_VL0 to router 3.3.3.3 is up
  Run as demand circuit
  DoNotAge LSA allowed.
  Transit area 1, via interface Serial1, Cost of using 64
  Transmit Delay is 1 sec, State POINT_TO_POINT,
  Timer intervals configured, Hello 10, Dead 40, Wait 40, Retransmit 5
    Hello due in 00:00:03
    Adjacency State FULL (Hello suppressed)
```

```
rtrC#show ip ospf virtual-links
Virtual Link OSPF_VL7 to router 2.2.2.2 is up
  Run as demand circuit
  DoNotAge LSA allowed.
  Transit area 1, via interface Serial0, Cost of using 64
  Transmit Delay is 1 sec, State POINT_TO_POINT,
  Timer intervals configured, Hello 10, Dead 40, Wait 40, Retransmit 5
    Hello due in 00:00:06
    Adjacency State FULL (Hello suppressed)

rtrC#show ip route
Codes: C - connected, S - static, I - IGRP, R - RIP, M - mobile, B - BGP
       D - EIGRP, EX - EIGRP external, O - OSPF, IA - OSPF inter area
       N1 - OSPF NSSA external type 1, N2 - OSPF NSSA external type 2
       E1 - OSPF external type 1, E2 - OSPF external type 2, E - EGP
       i - IS-IS, L1 - IS-IS level-1, L2 - IS-IS level-2, * - candidate default
       U - per-user static route, o - ODR

Gateway of last resort is not set

     1.0.0.0/32 is subnetted, 1 subnets
O       1.1.1.1 [110/129] via 10.1.1.5, 00:02:25, Serial0
     2.0.0.0/32 is subnetted, 1 subnets
O       2.2.2.2 [110/65] via 10.1.1.5, 00:02:26, Serial0
     3.0.0.0/24 is subnetted, 1 subnets
C       3.3.3.0 is directly connected, Loopback0
     10.0.0.0/30 is subnetted, 2 subnets
O       10.1.1.0 [110/128] via 10.1.1.5, 00:02:26, Serial0
C       10.1.1.4 is directly connected, Serial0
```

Notice that the default retransmit interval is 5 seconds. Modify the configuration on Router B to change the retransmit interval to 6 seconds while leaving the value for the retransmit interval on Router C set to the default of 5 seconds.

```
Router B
router ospf 1
 area 1 virtual-link 3.3.3.3 retransmit-interval 6
 network 2.2.2.2 0.0.0.0 area 0
 network 10.1.1.0 0.0.0.3 area 0
 network 10.1.1.4 0.0.0.3 area 1
```

Is the virtual link still active?

```
rtrB#show ip ospf virtual-links
Virtual Link OSPF_VL0 to router 3.3.3.3 is up
  Run as demand circuit
  DoNotAge LSA allowed.
  Transit area 1, via interface Serial1, Cost of using 64
  Transmit Delay is 1 sec, State POINT_TO_POINT,
  Timer intervals configured, Hello 10, Dead 40, Wait 40, Retransmit 6
    Hello due in 00:00:07
```

The virtual link is up. Now check to see if the OSPF routes are being exchanged.

```
rtrB#show ip route
Codes: C - connected, S - static, I - IGRP, R - RIP, M - mobile, B - BGP
       D - EIGRP, EX - EIGRP external, O - OSPF, IA - OSPF inter area
       N1 - OSPF NSSA external type 1, N2 - OSPF NSSA external type 2
       E1 - OSPF external type 1, E2 - OSPF external type 2, E - EGP
       i - IS-IS, L1 - IS-IS level-1, L2 - IS-IS level-2, * - candidate default
       U - per-user static route, o - ODR

Gateway of last resort is not set

     1.0.0.0/32 is subnetted, 1 subnets
O       1.1.1.1 [110/65] via 10.1.1.1, 00:03:53, Serial0
     2.0.0.0/32 is subnetted, 1 subnets
C       2.2.2.2 is directly connected, Loopback0
     3.0.0.0/32 is subnetted, 1 subnets
O IA    3.3.3.3 [110/65] via 10.1.1.6, 00:03:54, Serial1
     10.0.0.0/30 is subnetted, 2 subnets
C       10.1.1.0 is directly connected, Serial0
C       10.1.1.4 is directly connected, Serial1
```

Router B has learned the routes being advertised by Router A and the routes advertised by Router C. Unlike the Hello interval (see Section 2-19) and the dead interval (see Section

2-18), the virtual link does not need to have the same retransmit interval configured on both ends of the link.

Verification

Verify that the new retransmit interval has been configured on Router C.

```
rtrC#show ip ospf virtual-links
Virtual Link OSPF_VL7 to router 2.2.2.2 is up
  Run as demand circuit
  DoNotAge LSA allowed.
  Transit area 1, via interface Serial0, Cost of using 64
  Transmit Delay is 1 sec, State POINT_TO_POINT,
  Timer intervals configured, Hello 10, Dead 40, Wait 40, Retransmit 6
    Hello due in 00:00:00
    Adjacency State FULL (Hello suppressed)
```

Verify that all OSPF routes are now being exchanged.

```
rtrA#show ip route
Codes: C - connected, S - static, I - IGRP, R - RIP, M - mobile, B - BGP
       D - EIGRP, EX - EIGRP external, O - OSPF, IA - OSPF inter area
       N1 - OSPF NSSA external type 1, N2 - OSPF NSSA external type 2
       E1 - OSPF external type 1, E2 - OSPF external type 2, E - EGP
       i - IS-IS, L1 - IS-IS level-1, L2 - IS-IS level-2, * - candidate default
       U - per-user static route, o - ODR

Gateway of last resort is not set

     1.0.0.0/32 is subnetted, 1 subnets
C       1.1.1.1 is directly connected, Loopback0
     2.0.0.0/32 is subnetted, 1 subnets
O       2.2.2.2 [110/65] via 10.1.1.2, 00:09:04, Serial0/1
     3.0.0.0/32 is subnetted, 1 subnets
O IA    3.3.3.3 [110/129] via 10.1.1.2, 00:09:04, Serial0/1
     10.0.0.0/30 is subnetted, 2 subnets
C       10.1.1.0 is directly connected, Serial0/1
O IA    10.1.1.4 [110/128] via 10.1.1.2, 00:09:04, Serial0/1
```

```
rtrB#show ip route
Codes: C - connected, S - static, I - IGRP, R - RIP, M - mobile, B - BGP
       D - EIGRP, EX - EIGRP external, O - OSPF, IA - OSPF inter area
       N1 - OSPF NSSA external type 1, N2 - OSPF NSSA external type 2
       E1 - OSPF external type 1, E2 - OSPF external type 2, E - EGP
       i - IS-IS, L1 - IS-IS level-1, L2 - IS-IS level-2, * - candidate default
       U - per-user static route, o - ODR
```

```
Gateway of last resort is not set

     1.0.0.0/32 is subnetted, 1 subnets
O       1.1.1.1 [110/65] via 10.1.1.1, 00:10:19, Serial0
     2.0.0.0/32 is subnetted, 1 subnets
C       2.2.2.2 is directly connected, Loopback0
     3.0.0.0/32 is subnetted, 1 subnets
O IA    3.3.3.3 [110/65] via 10.1.1.6, 00:10:20, Serial1
     10.0.0.0/30 is subnetted, 2 subnets
C       10.1.1.0 is directly connected, Serial0
C       10.1.1.4 is directly connected, Serial1
```

```
rtrC#show ip route
Codes: C - connected, S - static, I - IGRP, R - RIP, M - mobile, B - BGP
       D - EIGRP, EX - EIGRP external, O - OSPF, IA - OSPF inter area
       N1 - OSPF NSSA external type 1, N2 - OSPF NSSA external type 2
       E1 - OSPF external type 1, E2 - OSPF external type 2, E - EGP
       i - IS-IS, L1 - IS-IS level-1, L2 - IS-IS level-2, * - candidate default
       U - per-user static route, o - ODR

Gateway of last resort is not set

     1.0.0.0/32 is subnetted, 1 subnets
O       1.1.1.1 [110/129] via 10.1.1.5, 00:11:10, Serial0
     2.0.0.0/32 is subnetted, 1 subnets
O       2.2.2.2 [110/65] via 10.1.1.5, 00:11:11, Serial0
     3.0.0.0/24 is subnetted, 1 subnets
C       3.3.3.0 is directly connected, Loopback0
     10.0.0.0/30 is subnetted, 2 subnets
O       10.1.1.0 [110/128] via 10.1.1.5, 00:11:11, Serial0
C       10.1.1.4 is directly connected, Serial0
```

Verification

The retransmit interval can be verified by using the **show ip ospf virtual-links** command.

```
rtrC#show ip ospf virtual-links
Virtual Link OSPF_VL7 to router 2.2.2.2 is up
  Run as demand circuit
  DoNotAge LSA allowed.
  Transit area 1, via interface Serial0, Cost of using 64
  Transmit Delay is 1 sec, State POINT_TO_POINT,
  Timer intervals configured, Hello 10, Dead 40, Wait 40, Retransmit 5
    Hello due in 00:00:04
    Adjacency State FULL (Hello suppressed)
```

Troubleshooting

Step 1 Verify that there is a neighbor relationship between the OSPF routers using the **show ip ospf** neighbors command.

Step 2 Verify that the transit area ID used in the **area virtual-link** command is the proper area.

Step 3 Verify that the router IDs used in the **area virtual-link** are correct.

Step 4 Verify that the desired retransmit interval has been configured by using the command **show ip ospf virtual-links**.

2-22: area *transit-area-id* virtual-link *router-id* transmit-delay *seconds*

Syntax Description:

- *transit-area-id*—The OSPF area ID of the area connecting the two ABRs that the virtual link will cross. This value can be entered as a decimal number in the range of 0 to 4,294,967,295 or in IP address form in the range 0.0.0.0 to 255.255.255.255. The transit area cannot be a stub area.
- *router-id*—OSPF router ID of the router at the remote end of the virtual link.
- *seconds*—The range of values is 1–8192 seconds. The default value is 1 second.

Purpose: When an LSA is created, the router will set the LS age field to 0. The transmit delay value is added to the age field of the LSA. This initial value represents the time delay of propagating the LSA over the virtual link.

Initial Cisco IOS Software Release: 10.0

Configuration Example: Modifying the Transmit Delay Value for a Virtual Link

Configure the network in Figure 2-22 and set the transmit delay value to 2 seconds.

Figure 2-22 *Transmit Delay Represents the LSA Propagation Delay Over a Virtual Link*

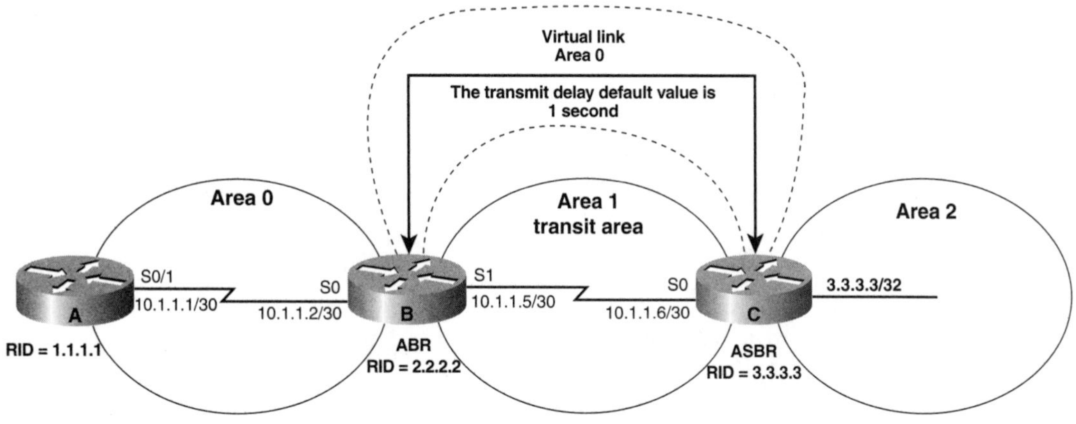


```
Router A
interface Loopback0
 ip address 1.1.1.1 255.255.255.255
!
interface Serial0/1
 ip address 10.1.1.1 255.255.255.252
 clockrate 64000
!
router ospf 1
 network 10.1.0.0 0.0.0.3 area 0
 network 1.1.1.1 0.0.0.0 area 0
```

```
Router B
interface Loopback0
 ip address 2.2.2.2 255.255.255.255
!
interface Serial0
 ip address 10.1.1.2 255.255.255.252
!
interface Serial1
 ip address 10.1.1.5 255.255.255.252
 clockrate 64000
!
router ospf 1
 area 1 virtual-link 3.3.3.3 transmit-delay 2
 network 10.1.1.0 0.0.0.3 area 0
 network 2.2.2.2 0.0.0.0 area 0
 network 10.1.1.4 0.0.0.3 area 1
```

```
Router C
interface Loopback0
```

continues

```
 ip address 3.3.3.3 255.255.255.255
!
interface Serial0
 ip address 10.1.1.6 255.255.255.252
!
router ospf 1
 area 1 virtual-link 2.2.2.2 transmit-delay 2
 network 3.3.3.3 0.0.0.0 area 2
 network 10.1.1.4 0.0.0.3 area 1
```

Verification

Verify that the transmit delay value has been modified, that the virtual link is active, and that all OSPF routes are being exchanged.

```
rtrB#show ip ospf virtual-links
Virtual Link OSPF_VL0 to router 3.3.3.3 is up
  Run as demand circuit
  DoNotAge LSA allowed.
  Transit area 1, via interface Serial1, Cost of using 64
  Transmit Delay is 2 sec, State POINT_TO_POINT,
  Timer intervals configured, Hello 10, Dead 40, Wait 40, Retransmit 6
    Hello due in 00:00:01
    Adjacency State FULL (Hello suppressed)
```

```
rtrC#show ip ospf virtual-links
Virtual Link OSPF_VL7 to router 2.2.2.2 is up
  Run as demand circuit
  DoNotAge LSA allowed.
  Transit area 1, via interface Serial0, Cost of using 64
  Transmit Delay is 2 sec, State POINT_TO_POINT,
  Timer intervals configured, Hello 10, Dead 40, Wait 40, Retransmit 5
    Hello due in 00:00:03
    Adjacency State FULL (Hello suppressed)

rtrC#show ip route
Codes: C - connected, S - static, I - IGRP, R - RIP, M - mobile, B - BGP
       D - EIGRP, EX - EIGRP external, O - OSPF, IA - OSPF inter area
       N1 - OSPF NSSA external type 1, N2 - OSPF NSSA external type 2
       E1 - OSPF external type 1, E2 - OSPF external type 2, E - EGP
       i - IS-IS, L1 - IS-IS level-1, L2 - IS-IS level-2, * - candidate default
       U - per-user static route, o - ODR

Gateway of last resort is not set

     1.0.0.0/32 is subnetted, 1 subnets
O       1.1.1.1 [110/129] via 10.1.1.5, 00:02:25, Serial0
     2.0.0.0/32 is subnetted, 1 subnets
O       2.2.2.2 [110/65] via 10.1.1.5, 00:02:26, Serial0
     3.0.0.0/24 is subnetted, 1 subnets
```

```
C        3.3.3.0 is directly connected, Loopback0
     10.0.0.0/30 is subnetted, 2 subnets
O        10.1.1.0 [110/128] via 10.1.1.5, 00:02:26, Serial0
C        10.1.1.4 is directly connected, Serial0
```

Troubleshooting

Step 1 Verify that there is a neighbor relationship between the OSPF routers by using the **show ip ospf neighbor** command.

Step 2 Verify that the transit area ID used in the **area virtual-link** command is the proper area.

Step 3 Verify that the router IDs used in the **area virtual-link** are correct.

Step 4 Verify that the desired transmit delay value has been configured by using the command **show ip ospf virtual-links**.

CHAPTER 3

Auto Cost

3-1: auto-cost reference-bandwidth *bandwidth*

Syntax Description:

- *bandwidth*—Value to use as the reference bandwidth when calculating the cost of an OSPF route. Range of values is 1 to 4,294,967 Mbps. The default value is 100 Mbps.

Purpose: By default, OSPF calculates the cost of an interface by dividing the bandwidth of the interface into 100,000,000. Table 3-1 lists the costs for various interface types. Using the default value when your network has interfaces with a bandwidth greater than 100,000,000 is not recommended. OSPF will not be able to differentiate between a 100-Mbps interface and any interface with a bandwidth greater than 100 Mbps. This command allows you to change the OSPF reference value globally so the calculated cost for every interface is updated. The cost for individual interfaces can be adjusted using the interface command **ip ospf cost** (see Section 19-5). The use of the **ip ospf cost** interface command is not recommended.

Table 3-1 *Default OSPF Cost for Selected Interfaces*

Interface Type	Interface Bandwidth	OSPF Cost
Loopback	8,000,000,000	1
Serial	56,000	1785
T1	1,544,000	64
Ethernet	10,000,000	10
Fast Ethernet	100,000,000	1
Gigabit Ethernet	1,000,000,000	1
OC48	2,500,000,000	1

Initial Cisco IOS Software Release: 11.2

Configuration Example: Globally Modifying OSPF Interface Costs

Configure the routers in Figure 3-1 using the default reference value of 100,000,000 to investigate the costs of the various interfaces.

Figure 3-1 *OSPF Cost Is Based on the Interface Bandwidth*

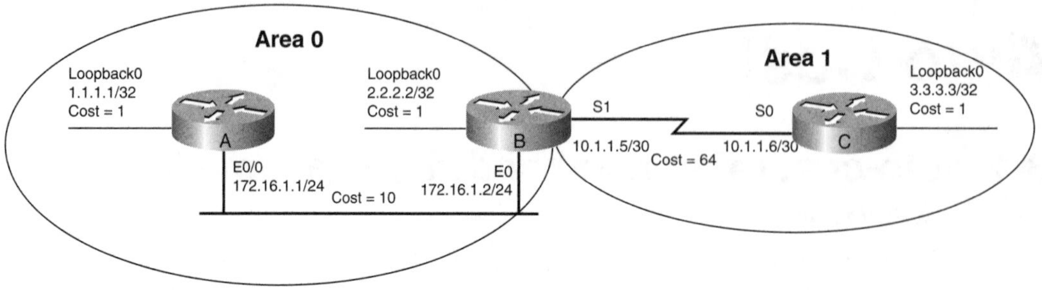


```
Router A
interface Loopback0
 ip address 1.1.1.1 255.255.255.255
!
interface Ethernet0/0
 ip address 172.16.1.1 255.255.255.0
!
router ospf 1
 network 1.1.1.1 0.0.0.0 area 0
 network 172.16.1.0 0.0.0.255 area 0
```

```
Router B
interface Loopback0
 ip address 2.2.2.2 255.255.255.255
!
interface Ethernet0
 ip address 172.16.1.2 255.255.255.0
!
interface Serial1
 ip address 10.1.1.5 255.255.255.252
 clockrate 64000
!
router ospf 1
 network 2.2.2.2 0.0.0.0 area 0
 network 10.1.1.4 0.0.0.3 area 1
 network 172.16.1.0 0.0.0.255 area 0
```

```
Router C
interface Loopback0
 ip address 3.3.3.3 255.255.255.255
!
interface Serial0
```

```
 ip address 10.1.1.6 255.255.255.252
!
router ospf 1
 network 3.3.3.3 0.0.0.0 area 1
 network 10.1.1.4 0.0.0.3 area 1
```

Verify that Routers A, B, and C have established OSPF neighbor relationships.

```
rtrA#show ip ospf neighbor

Neighbor ID     Pri   State           Dead Time   Address         Interface
2.2.2.2           1   FULL/BDR        00:00:30    172.16.1.2      Ethernet0/0
```

```
rtrB#show ip ospf neighbor

Neighbor ID     Pri   State           Dead Time   Address         Interface
1.1.1.1           1   FULL/DR         00:00:38    172.16.1.1      Ethernet0
3.3.3.3           1   FULL/  -        00:00:38    10.1.1.6        Serial1
```

```
rtrC#show ip ospf neighbor

Neighbor ID     Pri   State           Dead Time   Address         Interface
2.2.2.2           1   FULL/  -        00:00:34    10.1.1.5        Serial0
```

Now inspect the routing tables on Routers A, B, and C to determine the OSPF cost of the routes.

```
rtrA#show ip route
Codes: C - connected, S - static, I - IGRP, R - RIP, M - mobile, B - BGP
       D - EIGRP, EX - EIGRP external, O - OSPF, IA - OSPF inter area
       N1 - OSPF NSSA external type 1, N2 - OSPF NSSA external type 2
       E1 - OSPF external type 1, E2 - OSPF external type 2, E - EGP
       i - IS-IS, L1 - IS-IS level-1, L2 - IS-IS level-2, * - candidate default
       U - per-user static route, o - ODR

Gateway of last resort is not set

     1.0.0.0/32 is subnetted, 1 subnets
C       1.1.1.1 is directly connected, Loopback0
     2.0.0.0/32 is subnetted, 1 subnets
O       2.2.2.2 [110/11] via 172.16.1.2, 00:49:20, Ethernet0/0
     3.0.0.0/32 is subnetted, 1 subnets
O IA    3.3.3.3 [110/75] via 172.16.1.2, 00:49:20, Ethernet0/0
     172.16.0.0/24 is subnetted, 1 subnets
C       172.16.1.0 is directly connected, Ethernet0/0
     10.0.0.0/30 is subnetted, 1 subnets
O IA    10.1.1.4 [110/74] via 172.16.1.2, 00:49:20, Ethernet0/0
```

continues

```
rtrB#show ip route
Codes: C - connected, S - static, I - IGRP, R - RIP, M - mobile, B - BGP
       D - EIGRP, EX - EIGRP external, O - OSPF, IA - OSPF inter area
       N1 - OSPF NSSA external type 1, N2 - OSPF NSSA external type 2
       E1 - OSPF external type 1, E2 - OSPF external type 2, E - EGP
       i - IS-IS, L1 - IS-IS level-1, L2 - IS-IS level-2, * - candidate default
       U - per-user static route, o - ODR

Gateway of last resort is not set

     1.0.0.0/32 is subnetted, 1 subnets
O       1.1.1.1 [110/11] via 172.16.1.1, 01:06:18, Ethernet0
     2.0.0.0/32 is subnetted, 1 subnets
C       2.2.2.2 is directly connected, Loopback0
     3.0.0.0/32 is subnetted, 1 subnets
O       3.3.3.3 [110/65] via 10.1.1.6, 01:06:48, Serial1
     172.16.0.0/24 is subnetted, 1 subnets
C       172.16.1.0 is directly connected, Ethernet0
     10.0.0.0/30 is subnetted, 1 subnets
C       10.1.1.4 is directly connected, Serial1
```

```
rtrC#show ip route
Codes: C - connected, S - static, I - IGRP, R - RIP, M - mobile, B - BGP
       D - EIGRP, EX - EIGRP external, O - OSPF, IA - OSPF inter area
       N1 - OSPF NSSA external type 1, N2 - OSPF NSSA external type 2
       E1 - OSPF external type 1, E2 - OSPF external type 2, E - EGP
       i - IS-IS, L1 - IS-IS level-1, L2 - IS-IS level-2, * - candidate default
       U - per-user static route, o - ODR

Gateway of last resort is not set

     1.0.0.0/32 is subnetted, 1 subnets
O IA    1.1.1.1 [110/75] via 10.1.1.5, 01:07:11, Serial0
     2.0.0.0/32 is subnetted, 1 subnets
O IA    2.2.2.2 [110/65] via 10.1.1.5, 01:07:22, Serial0
     3.0.0.0/24 is subnetted, 1 subnets
C       3.3.3.0 is directly connected, Loopback0
     172.16.0.0/24 is subnetted, 1 subnets
O IA    172.16.1.0 [110/74] via 10.1.1.5, 01:07:41, Serial0
     10.0.0.0/30 is subnetted, 1 subnets
C       10.1.1.4 is directly connected, Serial0
```

For each OSPF route in the IP routing tables, there are two numbers that represent the cost of the route. For example, in the IP routing table on Router C the entry for network 1.1.1.1 is:

```
O IA    1.1.1.1 [110/75] via 10.1.1.5, 01:07:11, Serial0.
```

The first number, 110, represents the administrative distance for an OSPF route. The administrative distance is used if the router is learning about the same route from more than one IP routing protocol. The route with the lowest administrative distance will be considered the best route. The second number, 75, is the cost for Router C to reach network 1.1.1.1 on Router A. This figure consists of the cost to traverse the serial link between Routers B and C plus the cost to traverse the Ethernet link between Routers A and B plus the cost of the loopback interface on Router A. You can determine these individual costs by examining the interfaces on each router. First, view the cost associated with the serial interface between Routers B and C, as shown here:

```
rtrC#show ip ospf interface serial 0
Serial0 is up, line protocol is up
  Internet Address 10.1.1.6/30, Area 1
  Process ID 1, Router ID 3.3.3.3, Network Type POINT_TO_POINT, Cost: 64
  Transmit Delay is 1 sec, State POINT_TO_POINT,
  Timer intervals configured, Hello 10, Dead 40, Wait 40, Retransmit 5
    Hello due in 00:00:00
  Neighbor Count is 1, Adjacent neighbor count is 1
    Adjacent with neighbor 2.2.2.2
  Suppress hello for 0 neighbor(s)
```

The cost of the first link is 64. Now view the cost associated with the Ethernet network between Routers A and B.

```
rtrB#show ip ospf interface e0
Ethernet0 is up, line protocol is up
  Internet Address 172.16.1.2/24, Area 0
  Process ID 1, Router ID 2.2.2.2, Network Type BROADCAST, Cost: 10
  Transmit Delay is 1 sec, State BDR, Priority 1
  Designated Router (ID) 1.1.1.1, Interface address 172.16.1.1
  Backup Designated router (ID) 2.2.2.2, Interface address 172.16.1.2
  Timer intervals configured, Hello 10, Dead 40, Wait 40, Retransmit 5
    Hello due in 00:00:07
  Neighbor Count is 1, Adjacent neighbor count is 1
    Adjacent with neighbor 1.1.1.1  (Designated Router)
  Suppress hello for 0 neighbor(s)
```

Finally, view the cost of the loopback interface on Router A.

```
rtrA#show ip ospf interface loopback0
Loopback0 is up, line protocol is up
  Internet Address 1.1.1.1/32, Area 0
  Process ID 1, Router ID 1.1.1.1, Network Type LOOPBACK, Cost: 1
  Loopback interface is treated as a stub Host
```

The three costs are 64, 10, and 1, for a total cost of 75.

Because the default reference is 100,000,000, the cost of the Ethernet link is 100,000,000/10,000,000 = 10. By definition, the cost of a loopback interface is 1. The question is, why is the cost of the Serial interface 64? The clock rate on the Serial link is 64,000, so shouldn't the cost be 100,000,000/64,000 = 1562? Even though we have set a clock rate on the interface, the bandwidth is not 64,000, as can be seen by inspecting the interface properties.

```
rtrB#show interfaces serial 1
Serial1 is up, line protocol is up
  Hardware is HD64570
  Internet address is 10.1.1.5/30
  MTU 1500 bytes, BW 1544 Kbit, DLY 20000 usec, rely 255/255, load 1/255
  Encapsulation HDLC, loopback not set, keepalive set (10 sec)
  Last input 00:00:07, output 00:00:08, output hang never
  Last clearing of "show interface" counters never
  Input queue: 0/75/0 (size/max/drops); Total output drops: 0
  Queueing strategy: weighted fair
  Output queue: 0/1000/64/0 (size/max total/threshold/drops)
     Conversations  0/1/256 (active/max active/max total)
     Reserved Conversations 0/0 (allocated/max allocated)
  5 minute input rate 0 bits/sec, 0 packets/sec
  5 minute output rate 0 bits/sec, 0 packets/sec
     2559 packets input, 168890 bytes, 0 no buffer
     Received 1338 broadcasts, 0 runts, 0 giants, 0 throttles
     0 input errors, 0 CRC, 0 frame, 0 overrun, 0 ignored, 0 abort
     2589 packets output, 173462 bytes, 0 underruns
     0 output errors, 0 collisions, 1 interface resets
     0 output buffer failures, 0 output buffers swapped out
     2 carrier transitions
     DCD=up  DSR=up  DTR=up  RTS=up  CTS=up
```

The bandwidth is T1 or 1,544,000 bps. Therefore, the OSPF cost is 100,000,000/1,544,000 = 64. We can modify the cost of the serial interface by using the **bandwidth** command on Routers B and C.

```
Router B
interface Serial1
 bandwidth 64
 ip address 10.1.1.5 255.255.255.252
 clockrate 64000
```

```
Router C
interface Serial0
 bandwidth 64
 ip address 10.1.1.6 255.255.255.252
 no ip directed-broadcast
```

Re-examine the bandwidth of the serial link on Router B.

```
rtrB#show interfaces serial 1
Serial1 is up, line protocol is up
  Hardware is HD64570
  Internet address is 10.1.1.5/30
  MTU 1500 bytes, BW 64 Kbit, DLY 20000 usec, rely 255/255, load 1/255
  Encapsulation HDLC, loopback not set, keepalive set (10 sec)
  Last input 00:00:08, output 00:00:09, output hang never
  Last clearing of "show interface" counters never
  Input queue: 0/75/0 (size/max/drops); Total output drops: 0
  Queueing strategy: weighted fair
  Output queue: 0/1000/64/0 (size/max total/threshold/drops)
     Conversations  0/1/256 (active/max active/max total)
     Reserved Conversations 0/0 (allocated/max allocated)
  5 minute input rate 0 bits/sec, 0 packets/sec
  5 minute output rate 0 bits/sec, 0 packets/sec
     2599 packets input, 171490 bytes, 0 no buffer
     Received 1359 broadcasts, 0 runts, 0 giants, 0 throttles
     0 input errors, 0 CRC, 0 frame, 0 overrun, 0 ignored, 0 abort
     2630 packets output, 176116 bytes, 0 underruns
     0 output errors, 0 collisions, 1 interface resets
     0 output buffer failures, 0 output buffers swapped out
     2 carrier transitions
     DCD=up  DSR=up  DTR=up  RTS=up  CTS=up
```

Inspect the routing table on Router C to see if the OSPF costs have been updated.

```
rtrC#show ip route
Codes: C - connected, S - static, I - IGRP, R - RIP, M - mobile, B - BGP
       D - EIGRP, EX - EIGRP external, O - OSPF, IA - OSPF inter area
       N1 - OSPF NSSA external type 1, N2 - OSPF NSSA external type 2
       E1 - OSPF external type 1, E2 - OSPF external type 2, E - EGP
       i - IS-IS, L1 - IS-IS level-1, L2 - IS-IS level-2, * - candidate default
       U - per-user static route, o - ODR

Gateway of last resort is not set

     1.0.0.0/32 is subnetted, 1 subnets
O IA    1.1.1.1 [110/1573] via 10.1.1.5, 00:02:04, Serial0
     2.0.0.0/32 is subnetted, 1 subnets
O IA    2.2.2.2 [110/1563] via 10.1.1.5, 00:02:05, Serial0
     3.0.0.0/24 is subnetted, 1 subnets
C       3.3.3.0 is directly connected, Loopback0
     172.16.0.0/24 is subnetted, 1 subnets
O IA    172.16.1.0 [110/1572] via 10.1.1.5, 00:02:05, Serial0
     10.0.0.0/30 is subnetted, 1 subnets
C       10.1.1.4 is directly connected, Serial0
```

Now change the default OSPF cost reference so that an Ethernet network has a cost of 50. The cost equation is:

$$\text{Reference/Bandwidth} = \text{Cost}$$

Rearranging, we get this equation:

$$\text{Reference} = \text{Cost} \times \text{Bandwidth} = 50 \times 10{,}000{,}000 = 500{,}000{,}000$$

So we want to change the OSPF cost reference to 500 Mbps.

```
Router A
router ospf 1
 auto-cost reference-bandwidth 500
 network 1.1.1.1 0.0.0.0 area 0
 network 172.16.1.0 0.0.0.255 area 0
```

```
Router B
router ospf 1
 auto-cost reference-bandwidth 500
 network 2.2.2.2 0.0.0.0 area 0
 network 10.1.1.4 0.0.0.3 area 1
 network 172.16.1.0 0.0.0.255 area 0
```

```
Router C
router ospf 1
 auto-cost reference-bandwidth 500
 network 3.3.3.3 0.0.0.0 area 1
 network 10.1.1.4 0.0.0.3 area 1
```

When you configure the new cost reference, the router will give you a friendly reminder, as shown here:

```
rtrC(config-router)#auto-cost reference-bandwidth 500
% OSPF: Reference bandwidth is changed.
        Please ensure reference bandwidth is consistent across all routers.
```

Verification

Verify that the new cost reference is being used to calculate OSPF costs.

```
rtrA#show ip ospf interface ethernet 0/0
Ethernet0/0 is up, line protocol is up
  Internet Address 172.16.1.1/24, Area 0
  Process ID 1, Router ID 1.1.1.1, Network Type BROADCAST, Cost: 50
  Transmit Delay is 1 sec, State DR, Priority 1
  Designated Router (ID) 1.1.1.1, Interface address 172.16.1.1
```

```
  Backup Designated router (ID) 2.2.2.2, Interface address 172.16.1.2
  Timer intervals configured, Hello 10, Dead 40, Wait 40, Retransmit 5
    Hello due in 00:00:03
  Neighbor Count is 1, Adjacent neighbor count is 1
    Adjacent with neighbor 2.2.2.2  (Backup Designated Router)
  Suppress hello for 0 neighbor(s)

rtrA#show ip ospf interface loopback 0
Loopback0 is up, line protocol is up
  Internet Address 1.1.1.1/32, Area 0
  Process ID 1, Router ID 1.1.1.1, Network Type LOOPBACK, Cost: 1
  Loopback interface is treated as a stub Host
```

```
rtrC#show ip ospf interface serial 0
Serial0 is up, line protocol is up
  Internet Address 10.1.1.6/30, Area 1
  Process ID 1, Router ID 3.3.3.3, Network Type POINT_TO_POINT, Cost: 7812
  Transmit Delay is 1 sec, State POINT_TO_POINT,
  Timer intervals configured, Hello 10, Dead 40, Wait 40, Retransmit 5
    Hello due in 00:00:01
  Neighbor Count is 1, Adjacent neighbor count is 1
    Adjacent with neighbor 2.2.2.2
  Suppress hello for 0 neighbor(s)
```

Notice that the cost of the loopback interfaces remains 1.

Troubleshooting

Step 1 Verify that there is a neighbor relationship between the OSPF routers using the **show ip ospf neighbors** command.

Step 2 Verify that the same reference bandwidth has been configured on all OSPF routers in the same domain. Two different OSPF domains can use a different reference bandwidth.

CHAPTER 4

Default Route Generation

4-1: default-information originate

Syntax Description:

This form of the command has no arguments.

Purpose: To enable OSPF to advertise the default route 0.0.0.0 into the OSPF domain. This form of the command will only advertise the default route if the route exists in the local IP routing table.

Initial Cisco IOS Software Release: 10.0

Configuration Example: Advertising a Default Route into the OSPF Domain

Configure the routers in Figure 4-1 as shown in the following code.

Figure 4-1 *When OSPF Advertises a Default Route the Advertising Router Becomes an Autonomous System Border Router (ASBR)*

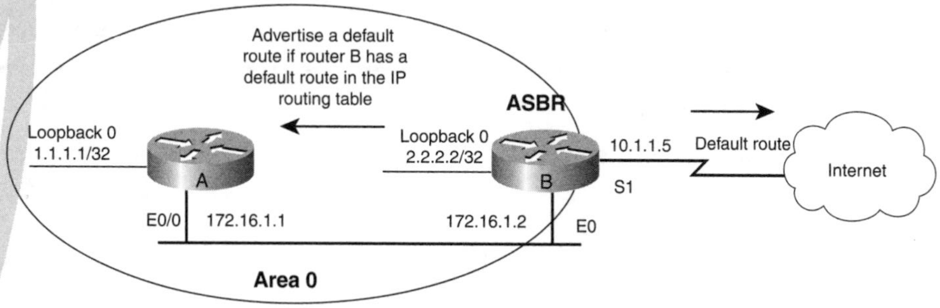

```
Router A
interface Loopback0
 ip address 1.1.1.1 255.255.255.255
!
interface Ethernet0/0
 ip address 172.16.1.1 255.255.255.0
!
router ospf 1
 network 1.1.1.1 0.0.0.0 area 0
 network 172.16.1.0 0.0.0.255 area 0
```

```
Router B
interface Loopback0
 ip address 2.2.2.2 255.255.255.255
!
interface Ethernet0
 ip address 172.16.1.2 255.255.255.0
!
interface Serial1
 bandwidth 64
 ip address 10.1.1.5 255.255.255.252
 clockrate 64000
!
router ospf 1
 network 2.2.2.2 0.0.0.0 area 0
 network 172.16.1.0 0.0.0.255 area 0
```

Verify that Routers A and B have established an OSPF neighbor relationship, as shown here:

```
rtrA#show ip ospf neighbor

Neighbor ID     Pri   State           Dead Time   Address         Interface
2.2.2.2           1   FULL/BDR        00:00:30    172.16.1.2      Ethernet0/0
```

```
rtrB#show ip ospf neighbor

Neighbor ID     Pri   State           Dead Time   Address         Interface
1.1.1.1           1   FULL/DR         00:00:38    172.16.1.1      Ethernet0
```

Modify the configuration on Router B so that OSPF will advertise a default route into the OSPF domain.

```
Router B
router ospf 1
 network 2.2.2.2 0.0.0.0 area 0
 network 172.16.1.0 0.0.0.255 area 0
 default-information originate
```

Inspect the routing table on Router A to see if the default route is being advertised.

```
rtrA#show ip route
Codes: C - connected, S - static, I - IGRP, R - RIP, M - mobile, B - BGP
       D - EIGRP, EX - EIGRP external, O - OSPF, IA - OSPF inter area
       N1 - OSPF NSSA external type 1, N2 - OSPF NSSA external type 2
       E1 - OSPF external type 1, E2 - OSPF external type 2, E - EGP
       i - IS-IS, L1 - IS-IS level-1, L2 - IS-IS level-2, * - candidate default
       U - per-user static route, o - ODR

Gateway of last resort is not set

     1.0.0.0/32 is subnetted, 1 subnets
C       1.1.1.1 is directly connected, Loopback0
     2.0.0.0/32 is subnetted, 1 subnets
O       2.2.2.2 [110/11] via 172.16.1.2, 00:05:30, Ethernet0/0
     172.16.0.0/24 is subnetted, 1 subnets
C       172.16.1.0 is directly connected, Ethernet0/0
```

Router B is not advertising the default route because there is not a default route in the routing table on Router B. Configure a static default route on Router B. Once the static route is configured, then Router B should advertise the default route to Router A.

```
Router B
ip route 0.0.0.0 0.0.0.0 Serial1
```

Verification

Verify that the default route is in the IP routing table on Router B.

```
rtrB#show ip route
Codes: C - connected, S - static, I - IGRP, R - RIP, M - mobile, B - BGP
       D - EIGRP, EX - EIGRP external, O - OSPF, IA - OSPF inter area
       N1 - OSPF NSSA external type 1, N2 - OSPF NSSA external type 2
       E1 - OSPF external type 1, E2 - OSPF external type 2, E - EGP
       i - IS-IS, L1 - IS-IS level-1, L2 - IS-IS level-2, * - candidate default
       U - per-user static route, o - ODR

Gateway of last resort is 0.0.0.0 to network 0.0.0.0

     1.0.0.0/32 is subnetted, 1 subnets
O       1.1.1.1 [110/11] via 172.16.1.1, 00:09:15, Ethernet0
     2.0.0.0/32 is subnetted, 1 subnets
C       2.2.2.2 is directly connected, Loopback0
     172.16.0.0/24 is subnetted, 1 subnets
C       172.16.1.0 is directly connected, Ethernet0
     10.0.0.0/30 is subnetted, 1 subnets
C       10.1.1.4 is directly connected, Serial1
S*   0.0.0.0/0 is directly connected, Serial1
```

Verify that the default route is being advertised to Router A.

```
rtrA#show ip route
Codes: C - connected, S - static, I - IGRP, R - RIP, M - mobile, B - BGP
       D - EIGRP, EX - EIGRP external, O - OSPF, IA - OSPF inter area
       N1 - OSPF NSSA external type 1, N2 - OSPF NSSA external type 2
       E1 - OSPF external type 1, E2 - OSPF external type 2, E - EGP
       i - IS-IS, L1 - IS-IS level-1, L2 - IS-IS level-2, * - candidate default
       U - per-user static route, o - ODR

Gateway of last resort is 172.16.1.2 to network 0.0.0.0

     1.0.0.0/32 is subnetted, 1 subnets
C       1.1.1.1 is directly connected, Loopback0
     2.0.0.0/32 is subnetted, 1 subnets
O       2.2.2.2 [110/11] via 172.16.1.2, 00:10:27, Ethernet0/0
     172.16.0.0/24 is subnetted, 1 subnets
C       172.16.1.0 is directly connected, Ethernet0/0
O*E2 0.0.0.0/0 [110/1] via 172.16.1.2, 00:01:17, Ethernet0/0
```

Troubleshooting:

Step 1 Verify that there is a neighbor relationship between the OSPF routers using the **show ip ospf** neighbors command.

Step 2 Verify that the router that is to advertise the default route has a default route in the IP routing table.

4-2: default-information originate always

Syntax Description:

This form of the command has no arguments.

Purpose: To enable OSPF to advertise the default route 0.0.0.0 into the OSPF domain. This form of the command will advertise the default route even if the route does not exist in the local IP routing table. If the **always** keyword is not used and the default route is flapping, then OSPF needs to send an update into the OSPF domain every time the route flaps. Using the **always** keyword will minimize OSPF database activity if the default route is flapping.

Initial Cisco IOS Software Release: 10.0

Configuration Example: Unconditionally Advertising a Default Route into the OSPF Domain

Configure the routers in Figure 4-2 as shown in the following code.

Figure 4-2 *When OSPF Advertises a Default Route, the Advertising Router Becomes an ASBR. The* **default-information-originate always** *Command Will Unconditionally Advertise a Default Route*

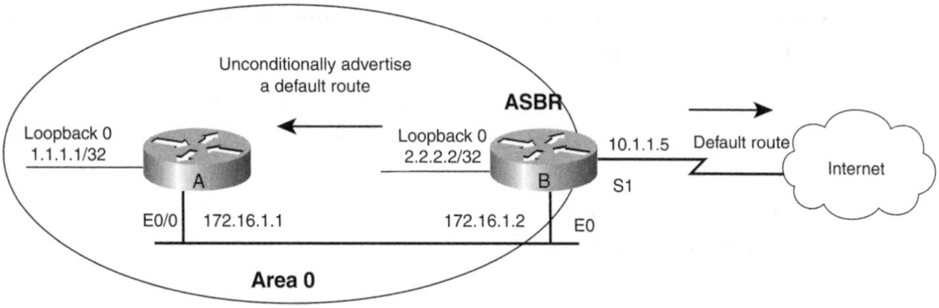


```
Router A
interface Loopback0
 ip address 1.1.1.1 255.255.255.255
!
interface Ethernet0/0
 ip address 172.16.1.1 255.255.255.0
!
router ospf 1
 network 1.1.1.1 0.0.0.0 area 0
 network 172.16.1.0 0.0.0.255 area 0
```

```
Router B
interface Loopback0
 ip address 2.2.2.2 255.255.255.255
!
interface Ethernet0
 ip address 172.16.1.2 255.255.255.0
!
interface Serial1
 bandwidth 64
 ip address 10.1.1.5 255.255.255.252
 clockrate 64000
!
router ospf 1
 network 2.2.2.2 0.0.0.0 area 0
 network 172.16.1.0 0.0.0.255 area 0
```

Verify that Routers A and B have established an OSPF neighbor relationship, as shown here.

```
rtrA#show ip ospf neighbor

Neighbor ID     Pri   State           Dead Time   Address         Interface
2.2.2.2           1   FULL/BDR        00:00:30    172.16.1.2      Ethernet0/0
```

```
rtrB#show ip ospf neighbor

Neighbor ID     Pri   State           Dead Time   Address         Interface
1.1.1.1           1   FULL/DR         00:00:38    172.16.1.1      Ethernet0
```

Modify the configuration on Router B so that OSPF will unconditionally advertise a default route into the OSPF domain.

```
Router B
router ospf 1
 network 2.2.2.2 0.0.0.0 area 0
 network 172.16.1.0 0.0.0.255 area 0
 default-information originate always
```

Verification

Verify that the default route is in the IP routing table on Router B.

```
rtrB#show ip route
Codes: C - connected, S - static, I - IGRP, R - RIP, M - mobile, B - BGP
       D - EIGRP, EX - EIGRP external, O - OSPF, IA - OSPF inter area
       N1 - OSPF NSSA external type 1, N2 - OSPF NSSA external type 2
       E1 - OSPF external type 1, E2 - OSPF external type 2, E - EGP
       i - IS-IS, L1 - IS-IS level-1, L2 - IS-IS level-2, * - candidate default
       U - per-user static route, o - ODR

Gateway of last resort is not set

     1.0.0.0/32 is subnetted, 1 subnets
O       1.1.1.1 [110/11] via 172.16.1.1, 16:23:59, Ethernet0
     2.0.0.0/32 is subnetted, 1 subnets
C       2.2.2.2 is directly connected, Loopback0
     172.16.0.0/24 is subnetted, 1 subnets
C       172.16.1.0 is directly connected, Ethernet0
     10.0.0.0/30 is subnetted, 1 subnets
C       10.1.1.4 is directly connected, Serial1
```

Router B does not have a default route in the IP routing table. Verify that a default route is being advertised to Router A.

```
rtrA#show ip route
Codes: C - connected, S - static, I - IGRP, R - RIP, M - mobile, B - BGP
       D - EIGRP, EX - EIGRP external, O - OSPF, IA - OSPF inter area
       N1 - OSPF NSSA external type 1, N2 - OSPF NSSA external type 2
       E1 - OSPF external type 1, E2 - OSPF external type 2, E - EGP
       i - IS-IS, L1 - IS-IS level-1, L2 - IS-IS level-2, * - candidate default
       U - per-user static route, o - ODR

Gateway of last resort is 172.16.1.2 to network 0.0.0.0

     1.0.0.0/32 is subnetted, 1 subnets
C       1.1.1.1 is directly connected, Loopback0
     2.0.0.0/32 is subnetted, 1 subnets
O       2.2.2.2 [110/11] via 172.16.1.2, 00:10:27, Ethernet0/0
     172.16.0.0/24 is subnetted, 1 subnets
C       172.16.1.0 is directly connected, Ethernet0/0
O*E2 0.0.0.0/0 [110/1] via 172.16.1.2, 00:01:17, Ethernet0/0
```

Troubleshooting

If there is an OSPF relationship between the OSPF routers, then this command should work as expected.

4-3: default-information originate metric *cost*

4-4: default-information originate always metric *cost*

Syntax Description:

- *cost*—The cost of the advertised external default route metric. The range of values is 0 to 16,777,214. The default value is 1.

Purpose: To set the external cost of the default route advertised into the OSPF domain. The first form of the command will advertise the default route only if the route exists in the local IP routing table. The second form will unconditionally advertise the default route. If more than one OSPF router is advertising a default route, the metric can be used to select the preferred default route. The default route with the lowest metric is considered the best route.

Initial Cisco IOS Software Release: 10.0

Configuration Example: Unconditionally Advertising a Default Route into the OSPF Domain

Configure the routers in Figure 4-3 as shown in the following listing.

Figure 4-3 *When OSPF Advertises a Default Route, the Advertising Router Becomes an ASBR. The Default Cost of the Default Route is 1*

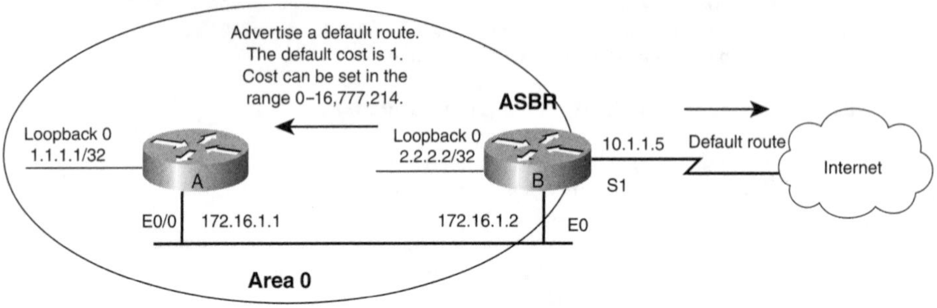


```
Router A
interface Loopback0
 ip address 1.1.1.1 255.255.255.255
!
interface Ethernet0/0
 ip address 172.16.1.1 255.255.255.0
!
router ospf 1
 network 1.1.1.1 0.0.0.0 area 0
 network 172.16.1.0 0.0.0.255 area 0
```

```
Router B
interface Loopback0
 ip address 2.2.2.2 255.255.255.255
!
interface Ethernet0
 ip address 172.16.1.2 255.255.255.0
!
interface Serial1
 bandwidth 64
 ip address 10.1.1.5 255.255.255.252
 clockrate 64000
!
router ospf 1
 network 2.2.2.2 0.0.0.0 area 0
 network 172.16.1.0 0.0.0.255 area 0
```

Verify that Routers A and B have established an OSPF neighbor relationship.

```
rtrA#show ip ospf neighbor

Neighbor ID     Pri   State           Dead Time   Address         Interface
2.2.2.2           1   FULL/BDR        00:00:30    172.16.1.2      Ethernet0/0
```

```
rtrB#show ip ospf neighbor

Neighbor ID     Pri   State           Dead Time   Address         Interface
1.1.1.1           1   FULL/DR         00:00:38    172.16.1.1      Ethernet0
```

Modify the configuration on Router B so that OSPF will unconditionally advertise a default route into the OSPF domain.

```
Router B
router ospf 1
 network 2.2.2.2 0.0.0.0 area 0
 network 172.16.1.0 0.0.0.255 area 0
 default-information originate always
```

Verify that the default route is in the IP routing table on Router B.

```
rtrB#show ip route
Codes: C - connected, S - static, I - IGRP, R - RIP, M - mobile, B - BGP
       D - EIGRP, EX - EIGRP external, O - OSPF, IA - OSPF inter area
       N1 - OSPF NSSA external type 1, N2 - OSPF NSSA external type 2
       E1 - OSPF external type 1, E2 - OSPF external type 2, E - EGP
       i - IS-IS, L1 - IS-IS level-1, L2 - IS-IS level-2, * - candidate default
       U - per-user static route, o - ODR

Gateway of last resort is not set

     1.0.0.0/32 is subnetted, 1 subnets
O       1.1.1.1 [110/11] via 172.16.1.1, 16:23:59, Ethernet0
     2.0.0.0/32 is subnetted, 1 subnets
C       2.2.2.2 is directly connected, Loopback0
     172.16.0.0/24 is subnetted, 1 subnets
C       172.16.1.0 is directly connected, Ethernet0
     10.0.0.0/30 is subnetted, 1 subnets
C       10.1.1.4 is directly connected, Serial1
```

Router B does not have a default route in the IP routing table. Verify that a default route is being advertised to Router A.

```
rtrA#show ip route
Codes: C - connected, S - static, I - IGRP, R - RIP, M - mobile, B - BGP
       D - EIGRP, EX - EIGRP external, O - OSPF, IA - OSPF inter area
       N1 - OSPF NSSA external type 1, N2 - OSPF NSSA external type 2
       E1 - OSPF external type 1, E2 - OSPF external type 2, E - EGP
       i - IS-IS, L1 - IS-IS level-1, L2 - IS-IS level-2, * - candidate default
       U - per-user static route, o - ODR

Gateway of last resort is 172.16.1.2 to network 0.0.0.0

     1.0.0.0/32 is subnetted, 1 subnets
C       1.1.1.1 is directly connected, Loopback0
     2.0.0.0/32 is subnetted, 1 subnets
O       2.2.2.2 [110/11] via 172.16.1.2, 00:10:27, Ethernet0/0
     172.16.0.0/24 is subnetted, 1 subnets
C       172.16.1.0 is directly connected, Ethernet0/0
O*E2 0.0.0.0/0 [110/1] via 172.16.1.2, 00:01:17, Ethernet0/0
```

Notice that the default cost of the default route is 1. Modify the configuration on Router B to give the default route a cost of 15.

```
Router B
router ospf 1
 network 2.2.2.2 0.0.0.0 area 0
 network 172.16.1.0 0.0.0.255 area 0
 default-information originate always metric 15
```

Verification

Verify that the cost of the default route has been modified.

```
rtrA#show ip route
Codes: C - connected, S - static, I - IGRP, R - RIP, M - mobile, B - BGP
       D - EIGRP, EX - EIGRP external, O - OSPF, IA - OSPF inter area
       N1 - OSPF NSSA external type 1, N2 - OSPF NSSA external type 2
       E1 - OSPF external type 1, E2 - OSPF external type 2, E - EGP
       i - IS-IS, L1 - IS-IS level-1, L2 - IS-IS level-2, * - candidate default
       U - per-user static route, o - ODR

Gateway of last resort is 172.16.1.2 to network 0.0.0.0

     1.0.0.0/32 is subnetted, 1 subnets
C       1.1.1.1 is directly connected, Loopback0
     2.0.0.0/32 is subnetted, 1 subnets
O       2.2.2.2 [110/11] via 172.16.1.2, 00:15:49, Ethernet0/0
```

```
     172.16.0.0/24 is subnetted, 1 subnets
C       172.16.1.0 is directly connected, Ethernet0/0
O*E2 0.0.0.0/0 [110/15] via 172.16.1.2, 00:01:56, Ethernet0/0

rtrA#show ip route 0.0.0.0
Routing entry for 0.0.0.0/0, supernet
  Known via "ospf 1", distance 110, metric 15, candidate default path
  Tag 1, type extern 2, forward metric 10
  Redistributing via ospf 1
  Last update from 172.16.1.2 on Ethernet0/0, 00:02:33 ago
  Routing Descriptor Blocks:
  * 172.16.1.2, from 2.2.2.2, 00:02:33 ago, via Ethernet0/0
      Route metric is 15, traffic share count is 1
```

Troubleshooting

Step 1 Verify that there is a neighbor relationship between the OSPF routers using the **show ip ospf neighbors** command.

Step 2 If using the **always** form of the command, then this command should work as expected.

Step 3 If you are not using the **always** form of the command, then verify that the advertising router has a default route in the IP routing table.

4-5: default-information originate metric-type *type*

4-6: default-information originate always metric-type *type*

Syntax Description:

- *type*—The type can be set to 1 or 2. The cost of a type 1 route includes both the external cost of the redistributed route and the OSPF cost. The cost of a type 2 route only includes the external cost. The default is type 2.

Purpose: When a route is redistributed into OSPF, the route is assigned a metric that represents the cost of reaching that route from the ASBR. In Figure 4-4, the external cost of the default route is 1. This is the value the ASBR would assign to the default route (see Sections 4-3 and 4-4). If the default route is advertised as a type 2 route (the default case), then the cost of the default route should be 1 on every router in the OSPF domain. If the default route is advertised as a type 1 route, then the cost of the default route would include the internal cost of reaching the ASBR and the external cost of the route that was set by the ASBR. If multiple paths exist to reach the ASBR across the OSPF domain, all routes would have an equal cost if advertised as type 2 routes. If the default route is advertised as a type 1 route, then OSPF can determine the best path to the ASBR.

Initial Cisco IOS Software Release: 10.0

Configuration Example: Setting the OSPF Metric Type for a Default Route

Configure the routers in Figure 4-4 as shown in the following listing.

Figure 4-4 *When OSPF Advertises a Default Route the Advertising Router Becomes an ASBR. A Type 1 Route Includes Both the Internal and External Cost of Reaching the Route. A Type 2 Route Only Includes the External Cost*

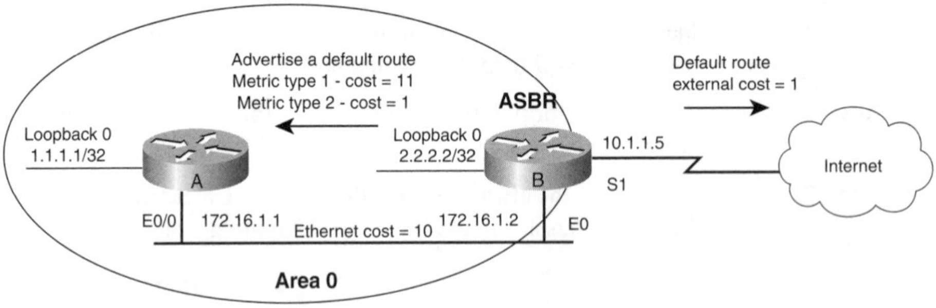


```
Router A
interface Loopback0
 ip address 1.1.1.1 255.255.255.255
!
interface Ethernet0/0
 ip address 172.16.1.1 255.255.255.0
!
router ospf 1
 network 1.1.1.1 0.0.0.0 area 0
 network 172.16.1.0 0.0.0.255 area 0
```

```
Router B
interface Loopback0
 ip address 2.2.2.2 255.255.255.255
!
interface Ethernet0
 ip address 172.16.1.2 255.255.255.0
!
interface Serial1
 bandwidth 64
 ip address 10.1.1.5 255.255.255.252
 clockrate 64000
```

```
!
router ospf 1
 network 2.2.2.2 0.0.0.0 area 0
 network 172.16.1.0 0.0.0.255 area 0
```

Verify that Routers A and B have established an OSPF neighbor relationship, as shown here.

```
rtrA#show ip ospf neighbor

Neighbor ID     Pri   State           Dead Time   Address         Interface
2.2.2.2           1   FULL/BDR        00:00:30    172.16.1.2      Ethernet0/0

rtrB#show ip ospf neighbor

Neighbor ID     Pri   State           Dead Time   Address         Interface
1.1.1.1           1   FULL/DR         00:00:38    172.16.1.1      Ethernet0
```

Modify the configuration on Router B so that OSPF will unconditionally advertise a default route into the OSPF domain.

```
Router B
router ospf 1
 network 2.2.2.2 0.0.0.0 area 0
 network 172.16.1.0 0.0.0.255 area 0
 default-information originate always
```

Verify that the default route is in the IP routing table on Router B.

```
rtrB#show ip route
Codes: C - connected, S - static, I - IGRP, R - RIP, M - mobile, B - BGP
       D - EIGRP, EX - EIGRP external, O - OSPF, IA - OSPF inter area
       N1 - OSPF NSSA external type 1, N2 - OSPF NSSA external type 2
       E1 - OSPF external type 1, E2 - OSPF external type 2, E - EGP
       i - IS-IS, L1 - IS-IS level-1, L2 - IS-IS level-2, * - candidate default
       U - per-user static route, o - ODR

Gateway of last resort is not set

     1.0.0.0/32 is subnetted, 1 subnets
O       1.1.1.1 [110/11] via 172.16.1.1, 16:23:59, Ethernet0
     2.0.0.0/32 is subnetted, 1 subnets
C       2.2.2.2 is directly connected, Loopback0
     172.16.0.0/24 is subnetted, 1 subnets
C       172.16.1.0 is directly connected, Ethernet0
     10.0.0.0/30 is subnetted, 1 subnets
C       10.1.1.4 is directly connected, Serial1
```

Router B does not have a default route in the IP routing table. Verify that a default route is being advertised to Router A.

```
rtrA#show ip route
Codes: C - connected, S - static, I - IGRP, R - RIP, M - mobile, B - BGP
       D - EIGRP, EX - EIGRP external, O - OSPF, IA - OSPF inter area
       N1 - OSPF NSSA external type 1, N2 - OSPF NSSA external type 2
       E1 - OSPF external type 1, E2 - OSPF external type 2, E - EGP
       i - IS-IS, L1 - IS-IS level-1, L2 - IS-IS level-2, * - candidate default
       U - per-user static route, o - ODR

Gateway of last resort is 172.16.1.2 to network 0.0.0.0

     1.0.0.0/32 is subnetted, 1 subnets
C       1.1.1.1 is directly connected, Loopback0
     2.0.0.0/32 is subnetted, 1 subnets
O       2.2.2.2 [110/11] via 172.16.1.2, 00:10:27, Ethernet0/0
     172.16.0.0/24 is subnetted, 1 subnets
C       172.16.1.0 is directly connected, Ethernet0/0
O*E2 0.0.0.0/0 [110/1] via 172.16.1.2, 00:01:17, Ethernet0/0

rtrA#show ip route 0.0.0.0
Routing entry for 0.0.0.0/0, supernet
  Known via "ospf 1", distance 110, metric 1, candidate default path
  Tag 1, type extern 2, forward metric 10
  Redistributing via ospf 1
  Last update from 172.16.1.2 on Ethernet0/0, 00:00:09 ago
  Routing Descriptor Blocks:
  * 172.16.1.2, from 2.2.2.2, 00:00:09 ago, via Ethernet0/0
      Route metric is 1, traffic share count is 1
```

Notice that the default cost of the default route is 1 and the route type is type 2 (the default). The type 2 route does not include the cost of reaching the ASBR over the Ethernet link. Modify the configuration on Router B to advertise the default route as a type 1 route.

```
Router B
router ospf 1
 network 2.2.2.2 0.0.0.0 area 0
 network 172.16.1.0 0.0.0.255 area 0
 default-information originate always metric-type 1
```

Verification

Verify that the metric type of the default route has been modified.

```
rtrA#show ip route
Codes: C - connected, S - static, I - IGRP, R - RIP, M - mobile, B - BGP
       D - EIGRP, EX - EIGRP external, O - OSPF, IA - OSPF inter area
       N1 - OSPF NSSA external type 1, N2 - OSPF NSSA external type 2
       E1 - OSPF external type 1, E2 - OSPF external type 2, E - EGP
       i - IS-IS, L1 - IS-IS level-1, L2 - IS-IS level-2, * - candidate default
       U - per-user static route, o - ODR

Gateway of last resort is 172.16.1.2 to network 0.0.0.0

     1.0.0.0/32 is subnetted, 1 subnets
C       1.1.1.1 is directly connected, Loopback0
     2.0.0.0/32 is subnetted, 1 subnets
O       2.2.2.2 [110/11] via 172.16.1.2, 00:02:09, Ethernet0/0
     172.16.0.0/24 is subnetted, 1 subnets
C       172.16.1.0 is directly connected, Ethernet0/0
O*E1 0.0.0.0/0 [110/11] via 172.16.1.2, 00:00:22, Ethernet0/0

rtrA#show ip route 0.0.0.0
Routing entry for 0.0.0.0/0, supernet
  Known via "ospf 1", distance 110, metric 11, candidate default path
  Tag 1, type extern 1
  Redistributing via ospf 1
  Last update from 172.16.1.2 on Ethernet0/0, 00:00:57 ago
  Routing Descriptor Blocks:
  * 172.16.1.2, from 2.2.2.2, 00:00:57 ago, via Ethernet0/0
      Route metric is 11, traffic share count is 1
```

The cost of the default route now includes the external cost (1) and the internal OSPF cost (10) for a total of 11.

Troubleshooting

Step 1 Verify that there is a neighbor relationship between the OSPF routers using the **show ip ospf neighbors** command.

Step 2 If using the **always** form of the command, then this command should work as expected.

Step 3 If you are not using the **always** form of the command, then verify that the advertising router has a default route in the IP routing table.

4-7: default-information originate route-map *route-map-name*

Syntax Description:

- *route-map-name*—OSPF will generate a default route only if the conditions of the route map are satisfied. If the keyword **always** is used, the default route will be advertised regardless of the conditions in the route map.

Purpose: The advertisement of a default route can be made conditional using a route map. If the conditions of the route map are satisfied, then the default route will be advertised into the OSPF domain.

Initial Cisco IOS Software Release: 10.0

Configuration Example: Using a Route Map for Conditional Default Route Advertisement

In Figure 4-5, Router B is receiving the route 3.3.3.0/30 from Router C via EIGRP. This network will carry all default traffic from the OPSF domain. If this network is down then you don't want the traffic from the OSPF domain to be sent to Router C. A route map can be used on Router B to make a conditional advertisement of a default route. For this example, the condition will be the existence of the 3.3.3.0/30 in the IP routing table on Router B.

Figure 4-5 *When OSPF Advertises a Default Route, the Advertising Router Becomes an ASBR. The Advertisement of a Default Route Can Be Made Conditional Using a Route Map*

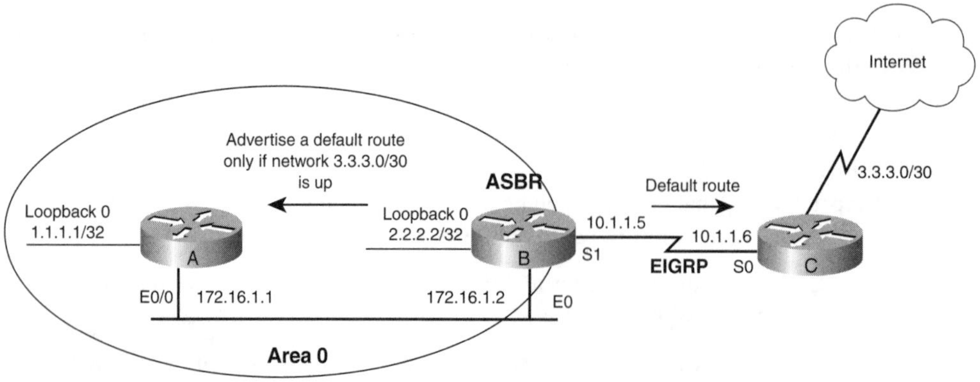

```
Router A
interface Loopback0
 ip address 1.1.1.1 255.255.255.255
!
interface Ethernet0/0
 ip address 172.16.1.1 255.255.255.0
!
router ospf 1
 network 1.1.1.1 0.0.0.0 area 0
 network 172.16.1.0 0.0.0.255 area 0
```

```
Router B
interface Loopback0
 ip address 2.2.2.2 255.255.255.255
!
interface Ethernet0
 ip address 172.16.1.2 255.255.255.0
!
interface Serial1
 bandwidth 64
 ip address 10.1.1.5 255.255.255.252
 clockrate 64000
!
router  eigrp 1
 network 10.0.0.0

router ospf 1
 network 2.2.2.2 0.0.0.0 area 0
 network 172.16.1.0 0.0.0.255 area 0
```

```
Router C
interface Loopback0
 description Simulate the network 3.3.3.0/30
 ip address 3.3.3.1 255.255.255.252
!
interface Serial0
 bandwidth 64
 ip address 10.1.1.6 255.255.255.252
!
router eigrp 1
 network 3.0.0.0
 network 10.0.0.0
 no auto-summary
```

Verify that Routers A and B have established an OSPF neighbor relationship.

```
rtrA#show ip ospf neighbor

Neighbor ID     Pri   State           Dead Time   Address         Interface
2.2.2.2           1   FULL/BDR        00:00:30    172.16.1.2      Ethernet0/0
```

```
rtrB#show ip ospf neighbor

Neighbor ID     Pri   State           Dead Time   Address         Interface
1.1.1.1           1   FULL/DR         00:00:38    172.16.1.1      Ethernet0
```

Verify that Routers B and C have formed an EIGRP relationship.

```
rtrB#show ip eigrp neighbors
IP-EIGRP neighbors for process 1
H   Address                 Interface   Hold Uptime   SRTT   RTO  Q  Seq
                                        (sec)         (ms)       Cnt Num
0   10.1.1.6                Se1           10 00:13:27  399  2394  0  4
```

```
rtrC#show ip eigrp neighbors
IP-EIGRP neighbors for process 1
H   Address                 Interface   Hold Uptime   SRTT   RTO  Q  Seq
                                        (sec)         (ms)       Cnt Num
0   10.1.1.5                Se0           11 00:13:53   28  2280  0  6
```

Verify that Router B is receiving the 3.3.3.0/30 network from Router C.

```
rtrB#show ip route
Codes: C - connected, S - static, I - IGRP, R - RIP, M - mobile, B - BGP
       D - EIGRP, EX - EIGRP external, O - OSPF, IA - OSPF inter area
       N1 - OSPF NSSA external type 1, N2 - OSPF NSSA external type 2
       E1 - OSPF external type 1, E2 - OSPF external type 2, E - EGP
       i - IS-IS, L1 - IS-IS level-1, L2 - IS-IS level-2, * - candidate default
       U - per-user static route, o - ODR

Gateway of last resort is not set

     1.0.0.0/32 is subnetted, 1 subnets
O       1.1.1.1 [110/11] via 172.16.1.1, 00:13:37, Ethernet0
     2.0.0.0/32 is subnetted, 1 subnets
C       2.2.2.2 is directly connected, Loopback0
     3.0.0.0/30 is subnetted, 1 subnets
D       3.3.3.0 [90/40640000] via 10.1.1.6, 00:13:38, Serial1
     172.16.0.0/24 is subnetted, 1 subnets
C       172.16.1.0 is directly connected, Ethernet0
     10.0.0.0/30 is subnetted, 1 subnets
C       10.1.1.4 is directly connected, Serial1
```

Modify the configuration on router B so that OSPF will conditionally advertise a default route into the OSPF domain based on the existence of the 3.3.3.0/30 network.

```
Router B
router ospf 1
 network 2.2.2.2 0.0.0.0 area 0
 network 172.16.1.0 0.0.0.255 area 0
 default-information originate route-map exist
!
access-list 1 permit 3.3.3.0 0.0.0.3
!
route-map exist permit 10
 match ip address 1
```

Verification

Verify that the default route is in the IP routing table on Router A.

```
rtrA#show ip route
Codes: C - connected, S - static, I - IGRP, R - RIP, M - mobile, B - BGP
       D - EIGRP, EX - EIGRP external, O - OSPF, IA - OSPF inter area
       N1 - OSPF NSSA external type 1, N2 - OSPF NSSA external type 2
       E1 - OSPF external type 1, E2 - OSPF external type 2, E - EGP
       i - IS-IS, L1 - IS-IS level-1, L2 - IS-IS level-2, * - candidate default
       U - per-user static route, o - ODR

Gateway of last resort is 172.16.1.2 to network 0.0.0.0

     1.0.0.0/32 is subnetted, 1 subnets
C       1.1.1.1 is directly connected, Loopback0
     2.0.0.0/32 is subnetted, 1 subnets
O       2.2.2.2 [110/11] via 172.16.1.2, 00:15:57, Ethernet0/0
     172.16.0.0/24 is subnetted, 1 subnets
C       172.16.1.0 is directly connected, Ethernet0/0
O*E2 0.0.0.0/0 [110/1] via 172.16.1.2, 00:15:57, Ethernet0/0
```

Test the route map by shutting down the loopback0 interface on Router C so the 3.3.3.0/30 will no longer be advertised by EIGRP. This should prevent Router B from advertising the default route.

```
Router C
interface Loopback0
 shutdown
```

Verify that the 3.3.3.0/30 network is not in the IP routing table on Router B.

```
rtrB#show ip route
Codes: C - connected, S - static, I - IGRP, R - RIP, M - mobile, B - BGP
       D - EIGRP, EX - EIGRP external, O - OSPF, IA - OSPF inter area
       N1 - OSPF NSSA external type 1, N2 - OSPF NSSA external type 2
       E1 - OSPF external type 1, E2 - OSPF external type 2, E - EGP
       i - IS-IS, L1 - IS-IS level-1, L2 - IS-IS level-2, * - candidate default
       U - per-user static route, o - ODR

Gateway of last resort is not set

     1.0.0.0/32 is subnetted, 1 subnets
O       1.1.1.1 [110/11] via 172.16.1.1, 00:19:58, Ethernet0
     2.0.0.0/32 is subnetted, 1 subnets
C       2.2.2.2 is directly connected, Loopback0
     172.16.0.0/24 is subnetted, 1 subnets
C       172.16.1.0 is directly connected, Ethernet0
     10.0.0.0/30 is subnetted, 1 subnets
C       10.1.1.4 is directly connected, Serial1
```

Verify that the default route is not being advertised to Router A.

```
rtrA#show ip route
Codes: C - connected, S - static, I - IGRP, R - RIP, M - mobile, B - BGP
       D - EIGRP, EX - EIGRP external, O - OSPF, IA - OSPF inter area
       N1 - OSPF NSSA external type 1, N2 - OSPF NSSA external type 2
       E1 - OSPF external type 1, E2 - OSPF external type 2, E - EGP
       i - IS-IS, L1 - IS-IS level-1, L2 - IS-IS level-2, * - candidate default
       U - per-user static route, o - ODR

Gateway of last resort is not set

     1.0.0.0/32 is subnetted, 1 subnets
C       1.1.1.1 is directly connected, Loopback0
     2.0.0.0/32 is subnetted, 1 subnets
O       2.2.2.2 [110/11] via 172.16.1.2, 00:20:13, Ethernet0/0
     172.16.0.0/24 is subnetted, 1 subnets
C       172.16.1.0 is directly connected, Ethernet0/0
```

Reenable the loopback interface on Router C and verify that the default route is being advertised.

```
Router C
interface Loopback0
 no shutdown
```

```
rtrB#show ip route
Codes: C - connected, S - static, I - IGRP, R - RIP, M - mobile, B - BGP
       D - EIGRP, EX - EIGRP external, O - OSPF, IA - OSPF inter area
       N1 - OSPF NSSA external type 1, N2 - OSPF NSSA external type 2
       E1 - OSPF external type 1, E2 - OSPF external type 2, E - EGP
       i - IS-IS, L1 - IS-IS level-1, L2 - IS-IS level-2, * - candidate default
       U - per-user static route, o - ODR

Gateway of last resort is not set

     1.0.0.0/32 is subnetted, 1 subnets
O       1.1.1.1 [110/11] via 172.16.1.1, 00:22:27, Ethernet0
     2.0.0.0/32 is subnetted, 1 subnets
C       2.2.2.2 is directly connected, Loopback0
     3.0.0.0/30 is subnetted, 1 subnets
D       3.3.3.0 [90/40640000] via 10.1.1.6, 00:00:05, Serial1
     172.16.0.0/24 is subnetted, 1 subnets
C       172.16.1.0 is directly connected, Ethernet0
     10.0.0.0/30 is subnetted, 1 subnets
C       10.1.1.4 is directly connected, Serial1
```

```
rtrA#show ip route
Codes: C - connected, S - static, I - IGRP, R - RIP, M - mobile, B - BGP
       D - EIGRP, EX - EIGRP external, O - OSPF, IA - OSPF inter area
       N1 - OSPF NSSA external type 1, N2 - OSPF NSSA external type 2
       E1 - OSPF external type 1, E2 - OSPF external type 2, E - EGP
       i - IS-IS, L1 - IS-IS level-1, L2 - IS-IS level-2, * - candidate default
       U - per-user static route, o - ODR

Gateway of last resort is 172.16.1.2 to network 0.0.0.0

     1.0.0.0/32 is subnetted, 1 subnets
C       1.1.1.1 is directly connected, Loopback0
     2.0.0.0/32 is subnetted, 1 subnets
O       2.2.2.2 [110/11] via 172.16.1.2, 00:22:44, Ethernet0/0
     172.16.0.0/24 is subnetted, 1 subnets
C       172.16.1.0 is directly connected, Ethernet0/0
O*E2 0.0.0.0/0 [110/1] via 172.16.1.2, 00:01:00, Ethernet0/0
```

Troubleshooting

Step 1 Verify that there is a neighbor relationship between the OSPF routers using the **show ip ospf neighbors** command.

Step 2 Verify the syntax and conditions of the route map.

Step 3 If you are using the **always** form of the command, then the default route will be advertised regardless of the conditions in the route map.

CHAPTER 5

Setting the Default Metric for Redistributed Protocols

5-1: default-metric *cost*

Syntax Description:

- *cost*—External cost assigned to routes redistributed into OSPF. The range of values is 1 to 4,294,967,295. The default metric for redistributed BGP routes is 1. The default metric for all other redistributed protocols is 20.

Purpose: Used to assign a cost to routes redistributed into OSPF that have not been assigned a metric by the **redistribute** command. Using the **default-metric** command will not affect routes that have been assigned a metric by the **redistribute** command.

Initial Cisco IOS Software Release: 10.0

Configuration Example: Setting the Default Cost for Redistributed Routes

In Figure 5-1, Router B is receiving the routes 3.3.3.0/24 and 10.1.1.4/30 from Router C via EIGRP. These EIGRP routes will be initially redistributed into OSPF using the default metric of 20. See Chapter 14, "Route Redistribution," for the use of the **redistribute** command.

Figure 5-1 *The Default Metric for* **redistributed** *BGP Routes Is 1 and the Default Metric for Other* **redistributed** *Routes Is 20*

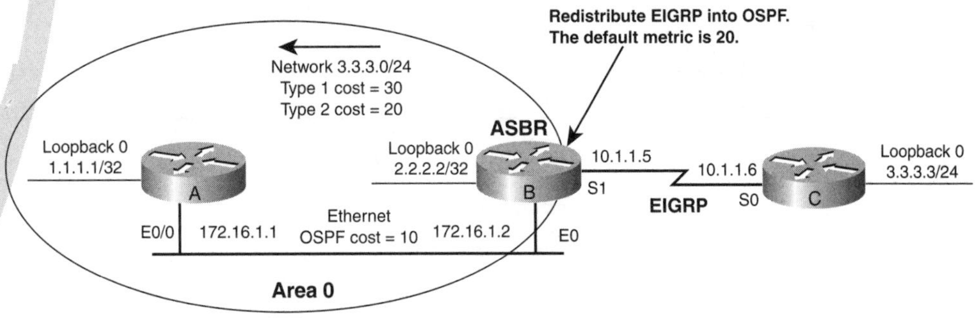

```
Router A
interface Loopback0
 ip address 1.1.1.1 255.255.255.255
!
interface Ethernet0/0
 ip address 172.16.1.1 255.255.255.0
!
router ospf 1
 network 1.1.1.1 0.0.0.0 area 0
 network 172.16.1.0 0.0.0.255 area 0
```

```
Router B
interface Loopback0
 ip address 2.2.2.2 255.255.255.255
!
interface Ethernet0
 ip address 172.16.1.2 255.255.255.0
!
interface Serial1
 bandwidth 64
 ip address 10.1.1.5 255.255.255.252
 clockrate 64000
!
router  eigrp 1
 network 10.0.0.0

router ospf 1
 redistribute eigrp 1 subnets
 network 2.2.2.2 0.0.0.0 area 0
 network 172.16.1.0 0.0.0.255 area 0
```

```
Router C
interface Loopback0
 description Simulate the network 3.3.3.0/24
 ip address 3.3.3.3 255.255.255.0
!
interface Serial0
 bandwidth 64
 ip address 10.1.1.6 255.255.255.252
!
router eigrp 1
 network 3.0.0.0
 network 10.0.0.0
 no auto-summary
```

Verify that Routers A and B have established an OSPF neighbor relationship, as shown here:

```
rtrA#show ip ospf neighbor

Neighbor ID     Pri   State           Dead Time   Address         Interface
2.2.2.2           1   FULL/BDR        00:00:30    172.16.1.2      Ethernet0/0
```

```
rtrB#show ip ospf neighbor

Neighbor ID     Pri   State           Dead Time   Address         Interface
1.1.1.1           1   FULL/DR         00:00:38    172.16.1.1      Ethernet0
```

Verify that Routers B and C have formed an EIGRP relationship.

```
rtrB#show ip eigrp neighbors
IP-EIGRP neighbors for process 1
H   Address                 Interface   Hold Uptime   SRTT   RTO  Q  Seq
                                        (sec)         (ms)       Cnt Num
0   10.1.1.6                Se1           10 00:13:27  399  2394  0  4
```

```
rtrC#show ip eigrp neighbors
IP-EIGRP neighbors for process 1
H   Address                 Interface   Hold Uptime   SRTT   RTO  Q  Seq
                                        (sec)         (ms)       Cnt Num
0   10.1.1.5                Se0           11 00:13:53   28  2280  0  6
```

Verify that Router B is receiving the 3.3.3.0/24 network from Router C.

```
rtrB#show ip route
Codes: C - connected, S - static, I - IGRP, R - RIP, M - mobile, B - BGP
       D - EIGRP, EX - EIGRP external, O - OSPF, IA - OSPF inter area
       N1 - OSPF NSSA external type 1, N2 - OSPF NSSA external type 2
       E1 - OSPF external type 1, E2 - OSPF external type 2, E - EGP
       i - IS-IS, L1 - IS-IS level-1, L2 - IS-IS level-2, * - candidate default
       U - per-user static route, o - ODR

Gateway of last resort is not set

     1.0.0.0/32 is subnetted, 1 subnets
O       1.1.1.1 [110/11] via 172.16.1.1, 00:13:37, Ethernet0
     2.0.0.0/32 is subnetted, 1 subnets
C       2.2.2.2 is directly connected, Loopback0
     3.0.0.0/24 is subnetted, 1 subnets
D       3.3.3.0 [90/40640000] via 10.1.1.6, 00:13:38, Serial1
     172.16.0.0/24 is subnetted, 1 subnets
C       172.16.1.0 is directly connected, Ethernet0
     10.0.0.0/30 is subnetted, 1 subnets
C       10.1.1.4 is directly connected, Serial1
```

Inspect the routing table on Router A to verify the default cost of the redistributed route.

```
rtrA#show ip route
Codes: C - connected, S - static, I - IGRP, R - RIP, M - mobile, B - BGP
       D - EIGRP, EX - EIGRP external, O - OSPF, IA - OSPF inter area
       N1 - OSPF NSSA external type 1, N2 - OSPF NSSA external type 2
       E1 - OSPF external type 1, E2 - OSPF external type 2, E - EGP
       i - IS-IS, L1 - IS-IS level-1, L2 - IS-IS level-2, * - candidate default
       U - per-user static route, o - ODR

Gateway of last resort is not set

     1.0.0.0/32 is subnetted, 1 subnets
C       1.1.1.1 is directly connected, Loopback0
     2.0.0.0/32 is subnetted, 1 subnets
O       2.2.2.2 [110/11] via 172.16.1.2, 00:27:10, Ethernet0/0
     3.0.0.0/24 is subnetted, 1 subnets
O E2    3.3.3.0 [110/20] via 172.16.1.2, 00:01:58, Ethernet0/0
     172.16.0.0/24 is subnetted, 1 subnets
C       172.16.1.0 is directly connected, Ethernet0/0
     10.0.0.0/30 is subnetted, 1 subnets
O E2    10.1.1.4 [110/20] via 172.16.1.2, 00:01:58, Ethernet0/0
```

The redistributed EIGRP routes have a cost or metric of 20. These routes were redistributed as type 2 routes (the default) so the cost of crossing the Ethernet network is not included. Modify the configuration on Router B so the redistributed EIGRP routes are assigned a cost of 55.

```
Router B
router ospf 1
 redistribute eigrp 1 subnets
 network 2.2.2.2 0.0.0.0 area 0
 network 172.16.1.0 0.0.0.255 area 0
 default-metric 55
```

Verification

Verify that the redistributed EIGRP routes have been assigned a cost of 55.

```
rtrA#show ip route
Codes: C - connected, S - static, I - IGRP, R - RIP, M - mobile, B - BGP
       D - EIGRP, EX - EIGRP external, O - OSPF, IA - OSPF inter area
       N1 - OSPF NSSA external type 1, N2 - OSPF NSSA external type 2
       E1 - OSPF external type 1, E2 - OSPF external type 2, E - EGP
       i - IS-IS, L1 - IS-IS level-1, L2 - IS-IS level-2, * - candidate default
       U - per-user static route, o - ODR


Gateway of last resort is not set

     1.0.0.0/32 is subnetted, 1 subnets
C       1.1.1.1 is directly connected, Loopback0
     2.0.0.0/32 is subnetted, 1 subnets
O       2.2.2.2 [110/11] via 172.16.1.2, 00:00:06, Ethernet0/0
     3.0.0.0/24 is subnetted, 1 subnets
O E2    3.3.3.0 [110/55] via 172.16.1.2, 00:00:06, Ethernet0/0
     172.16.0.0/24 is subnetted, 1 subnets
C       172.16.1.0 is directly connected, Ethernet0/0
     10.0.0.0/30 is subnetted, 1 subnets
O E2    10.1.1.4 [110/55] via 172.16.1.2, 00:00:06, Ethernet0/0
```

Troubleshooting

Step 1 Verify that there is a neighbor relationship between the OSPF routers using the **show ip ospf neighbors** command.

Step 2 Verify that the routes to be redistributed are in the IP routing table.

Step 3 Verify that you have used the desired metric with the **default-metric** command.

CHAPTER 6

Administrative Distance

6-1: distance *administrative-distance*

Syntax Description:

- *administrative-distance*—The supplied value will be applied to the administrative distance of all OSPF routes in the local routing table. The default administrative distance for OSPF routes is 110.

Purpose: If a router has learned about a network from more than one routing protocol, then the administrative distance is used to select the best route. The best route is the route that will be installed in the IP routing table. It is the route with the lowest administrative distance. The default administrative distances for the IP routing protocols are as follows:

- **connected**—0
- **static**—1
- **EBGP**—20
- **EIGRP**—90
- **IGRP**—100
- **OSPF**—110
- **IS-IS**—115
- **RIP**—120
- **IBGP**—200

Initial Cisco IOS Software Release: 10.0

Configuration Example: Adjusting the Administrative Distance to Influence Route Selection

In Figure 6-1, Router B is receiving the route 3.3.3.0/24 from Router A via OSPF and Router C via EIGRP. Because EIGRP has a lower administrative distance than OSPF, the EIGRP route will be installed in the routing table on Router B. A loopback address on Routers A and C is used to simulate the network that is being propagated by OSPF and

EIGRP. The **ip ospf network point-to-point** interface command (see Section 19-17) on Router A is used so the loopback is advertised as a /24 network and not a /32 network.

Figure 6-1 *When a Router Learns the Same Route via Two Different Routing Protocols, the Administrative Distance Is Used to Select the Best Route*

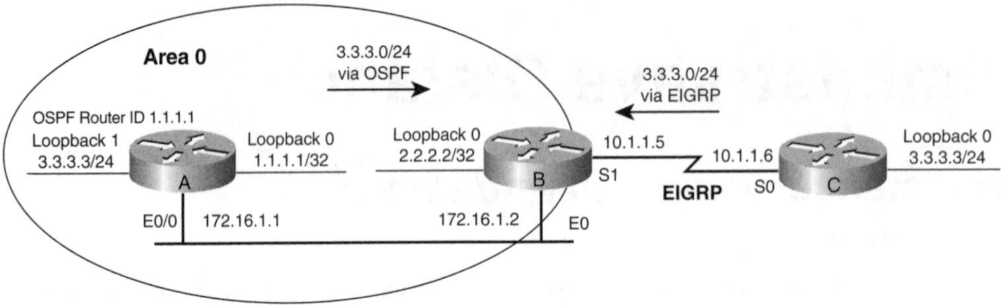


```
Router A
interface Loopback0
 ip address 1.1.1.1 255.255.255.255
!
interface Loopback1 description Simulate the network 3.3.3.0/24
 ip address 3.3.3.3 255.255.255.0
 ip ospf network point-to-point
!
interface Ethernet0/0
 ip address 172.16.1.1 255.255.255.0
!
router ospf 1
 router-id 1.1.1.1
 network 1.1.1.1 0.0.0.0 area 0
 network 3.3.3.0 0.0.0.255 area 0
 network 172.16.1.0 0.0.0.255 area 0
```

```
Router B
interface Loopback0
 ip address 2.2.2.2 255.255.255.255
!
interface Ethernet0
 ip address 172.16.1.2 255.255.255.0
!
interface Serial1
 bandwidth 64
 ip address 10.1.1.5 255.255.255.252
 clockrate 64000
!
router  eigrp 1
 network 10.0.0.0
```

```
router ospf 1
 network 2.2.2.2 0.0.0.0 area 0
 network 172.16.1.0 0.0.0.255 area 0
```

```
Router C
interface Loopback0
 description Simulate the network 3.3.3.0/24
 ip address 3.3.3.3 255.255.255.0
!
interface Serial0
 bandwidth 64
 ip address 10.1.1.6 255.255.255.252
!
router eigrp 1
 network 3.0.0.0
 network 10.0.0.0
 no auto-summary
```

Verify that Routers A and B have established an OSPF neighbor relationship.

```
rtrA#show ip ospf neighbor

Neighbor ID     Pri   State          Dead Time   Address        Interface
2.2.2.2           1   FULL/BDR       00:00:30    172.16.1.2     Ethernet0/0
```

```
rtrB#show ip ospf neighbor

Neighbor ID     Pri   State          Dead Time   Address        Interface
1.1.1.1           1   FULL/DR        00:00:38    172.16.1.1     Ethernet0
```

Verify that Routers B and C have formed an EIGRP relationship.

```
rtrB#show ip eigrp neighbors
IP-EIGRP neighbors for process 1
H   Address                 Interface   Hold Uptime   SRTT   RTO  Q  Seq
                                        (sec)         (ms)       Cnt Num
0   10.1.1.6                Se1           10 00:13:27  399  2394  0  4
```

```
rtrC#show ip eigrp neighbors
IP-EIGRP neighbors for process 1
H   Address                 Interface   Hold Uptime   SRTT   RTO  Q  Seq
                                        (sec)         (ms)       Cnt Num
0   10.1.1.5                Se0           11 00:13:53   28  2280  0  6
```

Verify that Router B is installing the 3.3.3.0/24 network learned via EIGRP from Router C.

```
rtrB#show ip route
Codes: C - connected, S - static, I - IGRP, R - RIP, M - mobile, B - BGP
       D - EIGRP, EX - EIGRP external, O - OSPF, IA - OSPF inter area
       N1 - OSPF NSSA external type 1, N2 - OSPF NSSA external type 2
       E1 - OSPF external type 1, E2 - OSPF external type 2, E - EGP
       i - IS-IS, L1 - IS-IS level-1, L2 - IS-IS level-2, * - candidate default
       U - per-user static route, o - ODR

Gateway of last resort is not set

     1.0.0.0/32 is subnetted, 1 subnets
O       1.1.1.1 [110/11] via 172.16.1.1, 00:13:37, Ethernet0
     2.0.0.0/32 is subnetted, 1 subnets
C       2.2.2.2 is directly connected, Loopback0
     3.0.0.0/24 is subnetted, 1 subnets
D       3.3.3.0 [90/40640000] via 10.1.1.6, 00:13:38, Serial1
     172.16.0.0/24 is subnetted, 1 subnets
C       172.16.1.0 is directly connected, Ethernet0
     10.0.0.0/30 is subnetted, 1 subnets
C       10.1.1.4 is directly connected, Serial1
```

Modify the configuration on Router B to set the administrative distance of all OSPF routes to 80. Because this value is less than the administrative distance for EIGRP (90), the OSPF route for 3.3.3.0/24 should be installed in the IP routing table on Router B.

```
Router B
router ospf 1
 network 2.2.2.2 0.0.0.0 area 0
 network 172.16.1.0 0.0.0.255 area 0
 distance 80
```

Verification

Verify that the OSPF route for 3.3.3.0/24 has been installed in the routing table on Router B.

```
rtrB#show ip route
Codes: C - connected, S - static, I - IGRP, R - RIP, M - mobile, B - BGP
       D - EIGRP, EX - EIGRP external, O - OSPF, IA - OSPF inter area
       N1 - OSPF NSSA external type 1, N2 - OSPF NSSA external type 2
       E1 - OSPF external type 1, E2 - OSPF external type 2, E - EGP
       i - IS-IS, L1 - IS-IS level-1, L2 - IS-IS level-2, * - candidate default
       U - per-user static route, o - ODR

Gateway of last resort is not set
```

```
        1.0.0.0/32 is subnetted, 1 subnets
O          1.1.1.1 [80/11] via 172.16.1.1, 00:01:22, Ethernet0
        2.0.0.0/32 is subnetted, 1 subnets
C          2.2.2.2 is directly connected, Loopback0
        3.0.0.0/24 is subnetted, 1 subnets
O          3.3.3.0 [80/11] via 172.16.1.1, 00:01:23, Ethernet0
        172.16.0.0/24 is subnetted, 1 subnets
C          172.16.1.0 is directly connected, Ethernet0
        10.0.0.0/30 is subnetted, 1 subnets
C          10.1.1.4 is directly connected, Serial1
```

Troubleshooting

Step 1 Verify that there is a neighbor relationship between the OSPF routers using the **show ip ospf neighbors** command.

Step 2 Verify that the correct administrative distance is being used with the **distance** command.

Step 3 Verify the administrative distance of the OSPF routes using the **show ip route** command.

6-2: distance *administrative-distance source-ip-address source-ip-mask*

6-3: distance *administrative-distance source-ip-address source-ip-mask access-list-number*

Syntax Description:

- *administrative-distance*—The supplied value will be applied to the administrative distance of selected OSPF routes in the local routing table. The default administrative distance for OSPF routes is 110.
- *source-ip-address*—IP address of the source of the OSPF routes. For OSPF, the source address is the OSPF router ID.
- *source-ip-mask*—IP mask for the source of the OSPF routes.
- *access-list-number*—Standard IP access number used to determine which routes learned from the source will have their administrative distance modified. The range of access list numbers is 1–99 and 1300–1999.

Purpose: If a router has learned about a network from more than one routing protocol, then the administrative distance is used to select the best route. The best route is the route that will be installed in the IP routing table, the route with the lowest administrative distance. The default administrative distances for the IP routing protocols are as follows:

- **connected**—0
- **static**—1
- **EBGP**—20
- **EIGRP**—90
- **IGRP**—100
- **OSPF**—110
- **IS-IS**—115
- **RIP**—120
- **IBGP**—200

Command 6-2 is used to modify the administrative distance of all routes learned from sources that match the source IP address/mask pair. Command 6-3 is used to modify the administrative distance of selected routes learned from sources that match the IP address/mask pair by using an IP access list.

Initial Cisco IOS Software Release: 10.0

Configuration Example 1: Adjusting the Administrative Distance of All Routes Learned from a Particular OSPF Neighbor

In Figure 6-2, Router B is receiving the route 3.3.3.0/24 from Router A via OSPF and Router C via EIGRP. Because EIGRP has a lower administrative distance than OSPF, the EIGRP route will be installed in the routing table on Router B. A loopback address on Routers A and C is used to simulate the network that is being propagated by OSPF and EIGRP. The **ip ospf network point-to-point interface** command (see Section 19-7) on Router A is used so the loopback is advertised as a /24 network and not a /32 network.

Figure 6-2 *The Administrative Distance of OSPF Routes Can Be Modified Based on the Neighbor Router's OSPF ID*

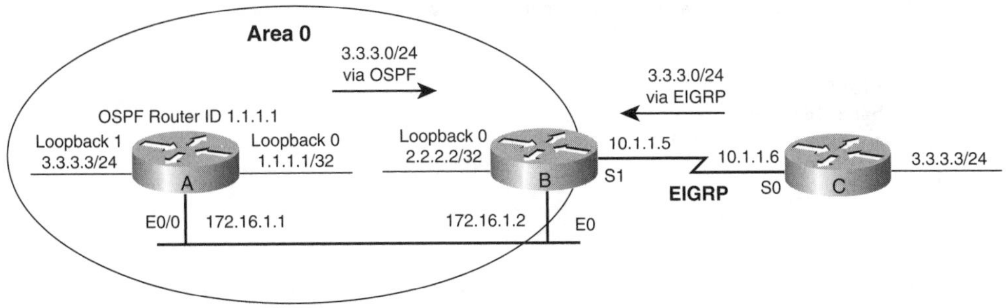


```
Router A
interface Loopback0
 ip address 1.1.1.1 255.255.255.255
!
interface Loopback1
 description Simulate the network 3.3.3.0/24
 ip address 3.3.3.3 255.255.255.0
 ip ospf network point-to-point
!
interface Ethernet0/0
 ip address 172.16.1.1 255.255.255.0
!
router ospf 1
 router-id 1.1.1.1
 network 1.1.1.1 0.0.0.0 area 0
 network 3.3.3.0 0.0.0.255 area 0
 network 172.16.1.0 0.0.0.255 area 0
```

```
Router B
interface Loopback0
 ip address 2.2.2.2 255.255.255.255
!
interface Ethernet0
 ip address 172.16.1.2 255.255.255.0
!
interface Serial1
 bandwidth 64
 ip address 10.1.1.5 255.255.255.252
 clockrate 64000
!
router  eigrp 1
 network 10.0.0.0

router ospf 1
 network 2.2.2.2 0.0.0.0 area 0
 network 172.16.1.0 0.0.0.255 area 0
```

continues

```
Router C
interface Loopback0
 description Simulate the network 3.3.3.0/24
 ip address 3.3.3.3 255.255.255.0
!
interface Serial0
 bandwidth 64
 ip address 10.1.1.6 255.255.255.252
!
router eigrp 1
 network 3.0.0.0
 network 10.0.0.0
 no auto-summary
```

Verify that Routers A and B have established an OSPF neighbor relationship.

```
rtrA#show ip ospf neighbor

Neighbor ID     Pri   State           Dead Time   Address         Interface
2.2.2.2           1   FULL/BDR        00:00:30    172.16.1.2      Ethernet0/0
```

```
rtrB#show ip ospf neighbor

Neighbor ID     Pri   State           Dead Time   Address         Interface
1.1.1.1           1   FULL/DR         00:00:38    172.16.1.1      Ethernet0
```

Verify that Routers B and C have formed an EIGRP relationship.

```
rtrB#show ip eigrp neighbors
IP-EIGRP neighbors for process 1
H   Address                 Interface   Hold Uptime   SRTT   RTO  Q  Seq
                                        (sec)         (ms)       Cnt Num
0   10.1.1.6                Se1           10 00:13:27  399  2394  0  4
```

```
rtrC#show ip eigrp neighbors
IP-EIGRP neighbors for process 1
H   Address                 Interface   Hold Uptime   SRTT   RTO  Q  Seq
                                        (sec)         (ms)       Cnt Num
0   10.1.1.5                Se0           11 00:13:53   28  2280  0  6
```

Verify that Router B is installing the 3.3.3.0/24 network learned via EIGRP from Router C.

```
rtrB#show ip route
Codes: C - connected, S - static, I - IGRP, R - RIP, M - mobile, B - BGP
       D - EIGRP, EX - EIGRP external, O - OSPF, IA - OSPF inter area
       N1 - OSPF NSSA external type 1, N2 - OSPF NSSA external type 2
       E1 - OSPF external type 1, E2 - OSPF external type 2, E - EGP
       i - IS-IS, L1 - IS-IS level-1, L2 - IS-IS level-2, * - candidate default
       U - per-user static route, o - ODR

Gateway of last resort is not set

     1.0.0.0/32 is subnetted, 1 subnets
O       1.1.1.1 [110/11] via 172.16.1.1, 00:13:37, Ethernet0
     2.0.0.0/32 is subnetted, 1 subnets
C       2.2.2.2 is directly connected, Loopback0
     3.0.0.0/24 is subnetted, 1 subnets
D       3.3.3.0 [90/40640000] via 10.1.1.6, 00:13:38, Serial1
     172.16.0.0/24 is subnetted, 1 subnets
C       172.16.1.0 is directly connected, Ethernet0
     10.0.0.0/30 is subnetted, 1 subnets
C       10.1.1.4 is directly connected, Serial1
```

Modify the configuration on Router B to set the administrative distance of all OSPF routes learned from neighbor 172.16.1.1 to 80. Because this value is less than the administrative distance for EIGRP (90), the OSPF route for 3.3.3.0/24 should be installed in the IP routing table on Router B. When using the distance command with OSPF, the source address is the OSPF router ID. The source mask is an inverse mask. Therefore, to set the administrative distance of OSPF routes learned from Router A, use the source address/mask pair 1.1.1.1/0.0.0.0.

```
Router B
router ospf 1
 network 2.2.2.2 0.0.0.0 area 0
 network 172.16.1.0 0.0.0.255 area 0
 distance 80 1.1.1.1 0.0.0.0
```

Verification

Verify that the OSPF route for 3.3.3.0/24 has been installed in the routing table on Router B.

```
rtrB#show ip route
Codes: C - connected, S - static, I - IGRP, R - RIP, M - mobile, B - BGP
       D - EIGRP, EX - EIGRP external, O - OSPF, IA - OSPF inter area
       N1 - OSPF NSSA external type 1, N2 - OSPF NSSA external type 2
       E1 - OSPF external type 1, E2 - OSPF external type 2, E - EGP
       i - IS-IS, L1 - IS-IS level-1, L2 - IS-IS level-2, * - candidate default
       U - per-user static route, o - ODR

Gateway of last resort is not set

     1.0.0.0/32 is subnetted, 1 subnets
O       1.1.1.1 [80/11] via 172.16.1.1, 00:01:22, Ethernet0
     2.0.0.0/32 is subnetted, 1 subnets
C       2.2.2.2 is directly connected, Loopback0
     3.0.0.0/24 is subnetted, 1 subnets
O       3.3.3.0 [80/11] via 172.16.1.1, 00:01:23, Ethernet0
     172.16.0.0/24 is subnetted, 1 subnets
C       172.16.1.0 is directly connected, Ethernet0
     10.0.0.0/30 is subnetted, 1 subnets
C       10.1.1.4 is directly connected, Serial1
```

Configuration Example 2: Adjusting the Administrative Distance of Selected Routes Learned from a Particular OSPF Neighbor

Modify the configuration on Router B to modify only the administrative distance of the network 3.3.3.0/24. The network 1.1.1.1/32 should maintain the default OSPF administrative distance of 110. The OSPF router ID of Router A can be found by using the **show ip ospf** command.

```
rtrA#show ip ospf
 Routing Process "ospf 1" with ID 1.1.1.1
Supports only single TOS(TOS0) routes
 SPF schedule delay 5 secs, Hold time between two SPFs 10 secs
 Minimum LSA interval 5 secs. Minimum LSA arrival 1 secs
 Number of external LSA 0. Checksum Sum 0x0
 Number of DCbitless external LSA 0
 Number of DoNotAge external LSA 0
 Number of areas in this router is 1. 1 normal 0 stub 0 nssa
    Area BACKBONE(0)
        Number of interfaces in this area is 3
        Area has no authentication
        SPF algorithm executed 32 times
        Area ranges are
        Number of LSA 3. Checksum Sum 0x15E77
        Number of DCbitless LSA 0
```

```
        Number of indication LSA 0
        Number of DoNotAge LSA 0
```

```
Router B
router ospf 1
 network 2.2.2.2 0.0.0.0 area 0
 network 172.16.1.0 0.0.0.255 area 0
 distance 80 1.1.1.1 0.0.0.0 1
!
access-list 1 permit 3.3.3.0 0.0.0.255
```

Verification

Verify that the administrative distance for the 3.3.3.0/24 network has been modified while the 1.1.1.1 network remains unchanged.

```
rtrB#show ip route
Codes: C - connected, S - static, I - IGRP, R - RIP, M - mobile, B - BGP
       D - EIGRP, EX - EIGRP external, O - OSPF, IA - OSPF inter area
       N1 - OSPF NSSA external type 1, N2 - OSPF NSSA external type 2
       E1 - OSPF external type 1, E2 - OSPF external type 2, E - EGP
       i - IS-IS, L1 - IS-IS level-1, L2 - IS-IS level-2, * - candidate default
       U - per-user static route, o - ODR

Gateway of last resort is not set

     1.0.0.0/32 is subnetted, 1 subnets
O       1.1.1.1 [110/11] via 172.16.1.1, 00:03:51, Ethernet0
     2.0.0.0/32 is subnetted, 1 subnets
C       2.2.2.2 is directly connected, Loopback0
     3.0.0.0/24 is subnetted, 1 subnets
O       3.3.3.0 [80/11] via 172.16.1.1, 00:03:52, Ethernet0
     172.16.0.0/24 is subnetted, 1 subnets
C       172.16.1.0 is directly connected, Ethernet0
     10.0.0.0/30 is subnetted, 1 subnets
C       10.1.1.4 is directly connected, Serial1
```

Troubleshooting

Step 1 Verify that there is a neighbor relationship between the OSPF routers using the **show ip ospf neighbors** command.

Step 2 Verify that the correct administrative distance is being used with the **distance** command.

Step 3 The source address for OSPF is the OSPF router ID. Ensure that the proper OSPF router ID is being used.

Step 4 Ensure that the source mask is an inverse mask.

Step 5 Verify the syntax of the access-list and make sure the distance command is referencing the correct access list.

6-4: distance ospf external *administrative-distance*

6-5: distance ospf inter-area *administrative-distance*

6-6: distance ospf intra-area *administrative-distance*

Syntax Description:

- *administrative-distance*—The supplied value will be applied to the administrative distance of either the external, inter-area, or intra-area OSPF routes in the local routing table. The default administrative distance for these OSPF routes is 110.

Purpose: If a router has learned about a network from more than one routing protocol, then the administrative distance is used to select the best route. The best route is the route that will be installed in the IP routing table, the route with the lowest administrative distance. The default administrative distances for the IP routing protocols are:

- **connected**—0
- **static**—1
- **EBGP**—20
- **EIGRP**—90
- **IGRP**—100
- **OSPF**—110
- **IS-IS**—115
- **RIP**—120
- **IBGP**—200

There are three types of OSPF routes. These types are external (either type 1 or 2), inter-area, and intra-area. External routes are those that have been redistributed into OSPF. A route to an area directly connected to the router is an intra-area route and a route to an area that is not directly connected to the router is an inter-area route. These commands are used to modify the administrative distance of all routes belonging to one of the three types of OSPF routes.

Initial Cisco IOS Software Release: 11.1

Configuration Example: Adjusting the Administrative Distance Based on the Type of OSPF Route

In Figure 6-3, Router A is receiving two OSPF external routes from the redistribution of EIGRP on Router B. Router A is also receiving an OSPF inter-area route and an OSPF intra-area route from Router B.

Figure 6-3 *The Three Types of OSPF Routes Are Inter-area, Intra-area, and External*

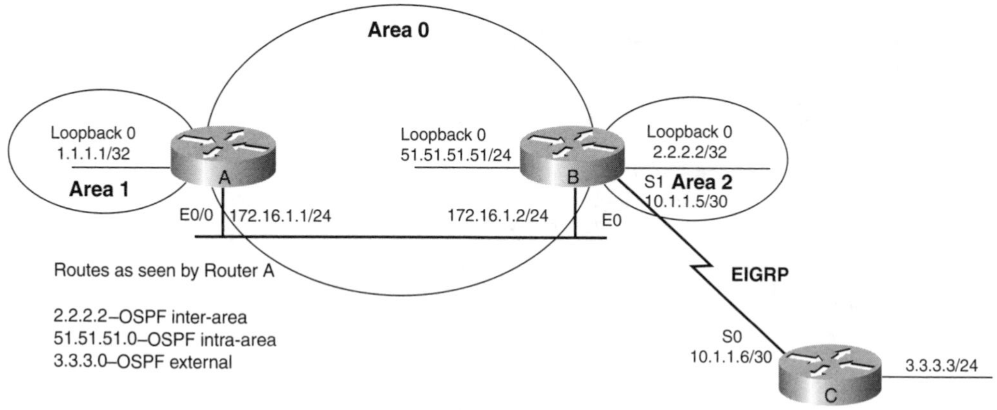


```
Router A
interface Loopback0
 ip address 1.1.1.1 255.255.255.255
!
interface Ethernet0/0
 ip address 172.16.1.1 255.255.255.0
!
router ospf 1
 network 1.1.1.1 0.0.0.0 area 1
 network 172.16.1.0 0.0.0.255 area 0
```

```
Router B
interface Loopback0
 ip address 2.2.2.2 255.255.255.255
!
interface Loopback1
 ip address 51.51.51.51 255.255.255.0
!
```

continues

```
interface Ethernet0
 ip address 172.16.1.2 255.255.255.0
!
interface Serial1
 bandwidth 64
 ip address 10.1.1.5 255.255.255.252
 clockrate 64000
!
router  eigrp 1
 network 10.0.0.0
!
router ospf 1
 router-id 2.2.2.2
 redistribute eigrp 1 subnets
 network 2.2.2.2 0.0.0.0 area 2
 network 51.51.51.51 0.0.0.0 area 0
 network 172.16.1.0 0.0.0.255 area 0
```

```
Router C
interface Loopback0
 ip address 3.3.3.3 255.255.255.0
!
interface Serial0
 bandwidth 64
 ip address 10.1.1.6 255.255.255.252
!
router eigrp 1
 network 3.0.0.0
 network 10.0.0.0
 no auto-summary
```

Verify that Routers A and B have established an OSPF neighbor relationship.

```
rtrA#show ip ospf neighbor

Neighbor ID     Pri   State           Dead Time   Address         Interface
2.2.2.2           1   FULL/BDR        00:00:30    172.16.1.2      Ethernet0/0
```

```
rtrB#show ip ospf neighbor

Neighbor ID     Pri   State           Dead Time   Address         Interface
1.1.1.1           1   FULL/DR         00:00:38    172.16.1.1      Ethernet0
```

Verify that Routers B and C have formed an EIGRP relationship.

```
rtrB#show ip eigrp neighbors
IP-EIGRP neighbors for process 1
H   Address                 Interface    Hold Uptime   SRTT   RTO  Q  Seq
                                         (sec)         (ms)       Cnt Num
0   10.1.1.6                Se1            10 00:13:27  399  2394  0  4
```

```
rtrC#show ip eigrp neighbors
IP-EIGRP neighbors for process 1
H   Address                 Interface    Hold Uptime   SRTT   RTO  Q  Seq
                                         (sec)         (ms)       Cnt Num
0   10.1.1.5                Se0            11 00:13:53   28  2280  0  6
```

Verify that Router A is learning each type of OSPF route.

```
rtrA#show ip route
Codes: C - connected, S - static, I - IGRP, R - RIP, M - mobile, B - BGP
       D - EIGRP, EX - EIGRP external, O - OSPF, IA - OSPF inter area
       N1 - OSPF NSSA external type 1, N2 - OSPF NSSA external type 2
       E1 - OSPF external type 1, E2 - OSPF external type 2, E - EGP
       i - IS-IS, L1 - IS-IS level-1, L2 - IS-IS level-2, * - candidate default
       U - per-user static route, o - ODR

Gateway of last resort is not set

     51.0.0.0/32 is subnetted, 1 subnets
O       51.51.51.51 [110/11] via 172.16.1.2, 00:21:44, Ethernet0/0
     1.0.0.0/32 is subnetted, 1 subnets
C       1.1.1.1 is directly connected, Loopback0
     2.0.0.0/32 is subnetted, 1 subnets
O IA    2.2.2.2 [110/11] via 172.16.1.2, 00:21:44, Ethernet0/0
     3.0.0.0/24 is subnetted, 1 subnets
O E2    3.3.3.0 [110/20] via 172.16.1.2, 00:21:44, Ethernet0/0
     172.16.0.0/24 is subnetted, 1 subnets
C       172.16.1.0 is directly connected, Ethernet0/0
     10.0.0.0/30 is subnetted, 1 subnets
O E2    10.1.1.4 [110/20] via 172.16.1.2, 00:21:44, Ethernet0/0
```

Modify the configuration on Router A to set the administrative distance of OSPF inter-area routes to 60, intra-area routes to 70, and external routes to 50.

```
Router A
router ospf 1
 network 1.1.1.1 0.0.0.0 area 1
 network 3.3.3.0 0.0.0.255 area 0
 network 172.16.1.0 0.0.0.255 area 0
 distance ospf intra-area 70 inter-area 60 external 50
```

Verification

Verify that the different OSPF route types have been configured with the proper administrative distance.

```
rtrA#show ip route
Codes: C - connected, S - static, I - IGRP, R - RIP, M - mobile, B - BGP
       D - EIGRP, EX - EIGRP external, O - OSPF, IA - OSPF inter area
       N1 - OSPF NSSA external type 1, N2 - OSPF NSSA external type 2
       E1 - OSPF external type 1, E2 - OSPF external type 2, E - EGP
       i - IS-IS, L1 - IS-IS level-1, L2 - IS-IS level-2, * - candidate default
       U - per-user static route, o - ODR

Gateway of last resort is not set

     51.0.0.0/32 is subnetted, 1 subnets
O       51.51.51.51 [70/11] via 172.16.1.2, 00:02:04, Ethernet0/0
     1.0.0.0/32 is subnetted, 1 subnets
C       1.1.1.1 is directly connected, Loopback0
     2.0.0.0/32 is subnetted, 1 subnets
O IA    2.2.2.2 [60/11] via 172.16.1.2, 00:02:04, Ethernet0/0
     3.0.0.0/24 is subnetted, 1 subnets
O E2    3.3.3.0 [50/20] via 172.16.1.2, 00:02:04, Ethernet0/0
     172.16.0.0/24 is subnetted, 1 subnets
C       172.16.1.0 is directly connected, Ethernet0/0
     10.0.0.0/30 is subnetted, 1 subnets
O E2    10.1.1.4 [50/20] via 172.16.1.2, 00:02:04, Ethernet0/0
```

Troubleshooting

Step 1 Verify that there is a neighbor relationship between the OSPF routers using the **show ip ospf neighbors** command.

Step 2 Verify that the correct administrative distance is being used with the **distance ospf** command and that the distance is being applied to the correct OSPF route type.

CHAPTER 7

Filtering Routes with Distribute Lists

7-1: distribute-list *access-list-number* in

Syntax Description:

- *access-list-number*—Standard IP access number used to determine which routes learned via OSPF will be prevented from being installed in the IP routing table. The range of access list numbers is 1–99 and 1300–2699.

Purpose: To prevent OSPF learned routes from being installed in the IP routing table. Even though an OSPF route may be prevented from being installed in the IP routing table, the route will still be in the OSPF database and advertised to OSPF neighbors. If you want to block a particular route or group of routes from entering the IP routing table, use a distribute list on all OSPF routers.

Initial Cisco IOS Software Release: 10.0

Configuration Example: Preventing OSPF Learned Routes from Being Installed in the IP Routing Table

In Figure 7-1, Router A is receiving the OSPF routes 2.2.2.2, 3.3.3.3, and 4.4.4.4 from Router B. Start by configuring Routers A and B as shown in the listing that follows.

Figure 7-1 *A Distribute List/Access List Controls Which OSPF Routes Are Transferred from the OSPF Database into the IP Routing Table*

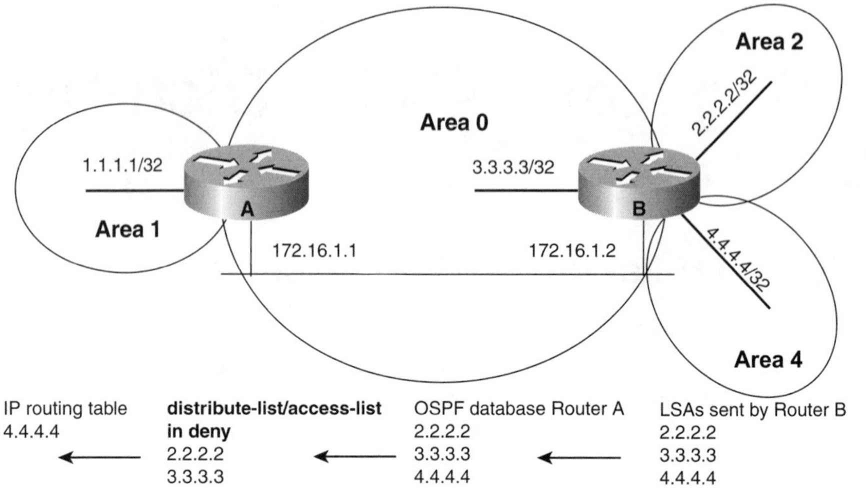


```
Router A
interface Loopback0
 ip address 1.1.1.1 255.255.255.255
!
interface Ethernet0/0
 ip address 172.16.1.1 255.255.255.0
!
router ospf 1
 network 1.1.1.1 0.0.0.0 area 1
 network 172.16.1.0 0.0.0.255 area 0
```

```
Router B

interface Loopback0
 ip address 2.2.2.2 255.255.255.255
!
interface Loopback1
 ip address 3.3.3.3 255.255.255.255
!
interface Loopback2
 ip address 4.4.4.4 255.255.255.255
!
interface Ethernet0
 ip address 172.16.1.2 255.255.255.0
!
router ospf 1
 router-id 2.2.2.2
 network 2.2.2.2 0.0.0.0 area 2
 network 3.3.3.3 0.0.0.0 area 0
 network 4.4.4.4 0.0.0.0 area 4
 network 172.16.1.2 0.0.0.0 area 0
```

Verify that Routers A and B have established a FULL OSPF neighbor relationship.

```
rtrA#show ip ospf neighbor

Neighbor ID     Pri   State           Dead Time   Address         Interface
2.2.2.2           1   FULL/BDR        00:00:30    172.16.1.2      Ethernet0/0
```

```
rtrB#show ip ospf neighbor

Neighbor ID     Pri   State           Dead Time   Address         Interface
1.1.1.1           1   FULL/DR         00:00:38    172.16.1.1      Ethernet0
```

Verify that Router A is receiving the routes 2.2.2.2, 3.3.3.3, and 4.4.4.4 from Router B.

```
rtrA#show ip route
Codes: C - connected, S - static, I - IGRP, R - RIP, M - mobile, B - BGP
       D - EIGRP, EX - EIGRP external, O - OSPF, IA - OSPF inter area
       N1 - OSPF NSSA external type 1, N2 - OSPF NSSA external type 2
       E1 - OSPF external type 1, E2 - OSPF external type 2, E - EGP
       i - IS-IS, L1 - IS-IS level-1, L2 - IS-IS level-2, ia - IS-IS inter area
       * - candidate default, U - per-user static route, o - ODR
       P - periodic downloaded static route

Gateway of last resort is not set

     1.0.0.0/32 is subnetted, 1 subnets
C       1.1.1.1 is directly connected, Loopback0
     2.0.0.0/32 is subnetted, 1 subnets
O IA    2.2.2.2 [110/11] via 172.16.1.2, 00:04:28, Ethernet0/0
     3.0.0.0/32 is subnetted, 1 subnets
O       3.3.3.3 [110/11] via 172.16.1.2, 00:04:28, Ethernet0/0
     4.0.0.0/32 is subnetted, 1 subnets
O IA    4.4.4.4 [110/11] via 172.16.1.2, 00:04:28, Ethernet0/0
     172.16.0.0/24 is subnetted, 1 subnets
C       172.16.1.0 is directly connected, Ethernet0/0
```

For illustrative purposes, verify that these three routes are in the OSPF database on Router A.

```
rtrA#show ip ospf database

            OSPF Router with ID (1.1.1.1) (Process ID 1)

                Router Link States (Area 0)

Link ID         ADV Router      Age         Seq#       Checksum Link count
1.1.1.1         1.1.1.1         493         0x800000A5 0x8F6F   1
```

continues

```
2.2.2.2         2.2.2.2         489         0x80000030 0x7ECF    2

                Net Link States (Area 0)

Link ID         ADV Router      Age         Seq#       Checksum
172.16.1.1      1.1.1.1         496         0x80000001 0x6DFD

                Summary Net Link States (Area 0)

Link ID         ADV Router      Age         Seq#       Checksum
1.1.1.1         1.1.1.1         714         0x80000033 0xE21F
2.2.2.2         2.2.2.2         487         0x80000049 0x6A79
4.4.4.4         2.2.2.2         490         0x80000001 0x9E85

                Router Link States (Area 1)

Link ID         ADV Router      Age         Seq#       Checksum Link count
1.1.1.1         1.1.1.1         726         0x80000001 0xD351    1

                Summary Net Link States (Area 1)

Link ID         ADV Router      Age         Seq#       Checksum
2.2.2.2         1.1.1.1         492         0x80000001 0x7DA8
3.3.3.3         1.1.1.1         492         0x80000001 0x4FD2
4.4.4.4         1.1.1.1         492         0x80000001 0x21FC
172.16.1.0      1.1.1.1         496         0x80000003 0x3B34
```

Modify the configuration on Router A to prevent the OSPF routes 2.2.2.2 and 3.3.3.3 from being installed in the IP routing table.

```
Router A

router ospf 1
 network 1.1.1.1 0.0.0.0 area 1
 network 172.16.1.0 0.0.0.255 area 0
 distribute-list 1 in
!
access-list 1 deny   2.2.2.0 0.0.0.255
access-list 1 deny   3.3.3.0 0.0.0.255
access-list 1 permit any
```

Verification

Verify that the OSPF routes 2.2.2.2 and 3.3.3.3 have been blocked from entering the IP routing table on Router A. They should be absent from the IP routing table.

```
rtrA#show ip route
Codes: C - connected, S - static, I - IGRP, R - RIP, M - mobile, B - BGP
       D - EIGRP, EX - EIGRP external, O - OSPF, IA - OSPF inter area
```

```
       N1 - OSPF NSSA external type 1, N2 - OSPF NSSA external type 2
       E1 - OSPF external type 1, E2 - OSPF external type 2, E - EGP
       i - IS-IS, L1 - IS-IS level-1, L2 - IS-IS level-2, ia - IS-IS inter area
       * - candidate default, U - per-user static route, o - ODR
       P - periodic downloaded static route

Gateway of last resort is not set

     1.0.0.0/32 is subnetted, 1 subnets
C       1.1.1.1 is directly connected, Loopback0
     4.0.0.0/32 is subnetted, 1 subnets
O IA    4.4.4.4 [110/11] via 172.16.1.2, 00:03:39, Ethernet0/0
     172.16.0.0/24 is subnetted, 1 subnets
C       172.16.1.0 is directly connected, Ethernet0/0
```

Verify that the routes 2.2.2.2 and 3.3.3.3 are still in the OSPF database on Router A.

```
rtrA#show ip ospf database

            OSPF Router with ID (1.1.1.1) (Process ID 1)

                Router Link States (Area 0)

Link ID         ADV Router      Age         Seq#       Checksum Link count
1.1.1.1         1.1.1.1         951         0x800000A5 0x8F6F   1
2.2.2.2         2.2.2.2         947         0x80000030 0x7ECF   2

                Net Link States (Area 0)

Link ID         ADV Router      Age         Seq#       Checksum
172.16.1.1      1.1.1.1         954         0x80000001 0x6DFD

                Summary Net Link States (Area 0)

Link ID         ADV Router      Age         Seq#       Checksum
1.1.1.1         1.1.1.1         1172        0x80000033 0xE21F
2.2.2.2         2.2.2.2         945         0x80000049 0x6A79
4.4.4.4         2.2.2.2         948         0x80000001 0x9E85

                Router Link States (Area 1)

Link ID         ADV Router      Age         Seq#       Checksum Link count
1.1.1.1         1.1.1.1         1184        0x80000001 0xD351   1

                Summary Net Link States (Area 1)

Link ID         ADV Router      Age         Seq#       Checksum
3.3.3.3         1.1.1.1         946         0x80000001 0x4FD2
4.4.4.4         1.1.1.1         946         0x80000001 0x21FC
172.16.1.0      1.1.1.1         950         0x80000003 0x3B34
```

Troubleshooting

Step 1 Verify that there is a neighbor relationship between the OSPF routers by using the **show ip ospf neighbor** command.

Step 2 Verify that the **distribute-list** command is referencing the correct access list number.

Step 3 Verify the syntax of the access list.

Step 4 Verify that the access list has been referenced by using the command **show ip access-lists** *access-list-number*. For example, for the preceding configuration, the output should be:

```
rtrA#show ip access-lists 1
Standard IP access list 1
    deny   2.2.2.0, wildcard bits 0.0.0.255 (1 match) check=4
    deny   3.3.3.0, wildcard bits 0.0.0.255 (1 match) check=3
    permit any (3 matches)
```

7-2: distribute-list *access-list-number* in *interface-type interface-number*

Syntax Description:

- *access-list-number*—Standard IP access number used to determine which routes learned via OSPF will be prevented from being installed in the IP routing table. The range of access list numbers is 1–99 and 1300–2699.
- *interface-type*—Optional parameter, along with the *interface-number*, used to apply the distribute list to OSPF routes learned through a particular interface.
- *interface-number*—Number of the interface type.

Purpose: To prevent OSPF routes learned over a specific interface from being installed in the IP routing table. Even though an OSPF route may be prevented from being installed in the IP routing table, the route will still be in the OSPF database. Because the filtered route will still be in the OSPF database, it is possible for the route to be received from another OSPF interface.

Initial Cisco IOS Software Release: 10.0. The *interface-type* and *interface-number* parameters were added in 11.2.

Configuration Example: Preventing Routes Learned via OSPF Over a Specific Interface from Being Installed in the IP Routing Table

In Figure 7-2, Router A is receiving the OSPF routes 2.2.2.2, 3.3.3.3, and 4.4.4.4 from Router B over two serial interfaces. Start by configuring Routers A and B as shown in the listing below the figure.

Figure 7-2 *A Distribute List/Access List Controls Which OSPF Routes, Learned Over a Specific Interface, Are Transferred from the OSPF Database into the IP Routing Table*

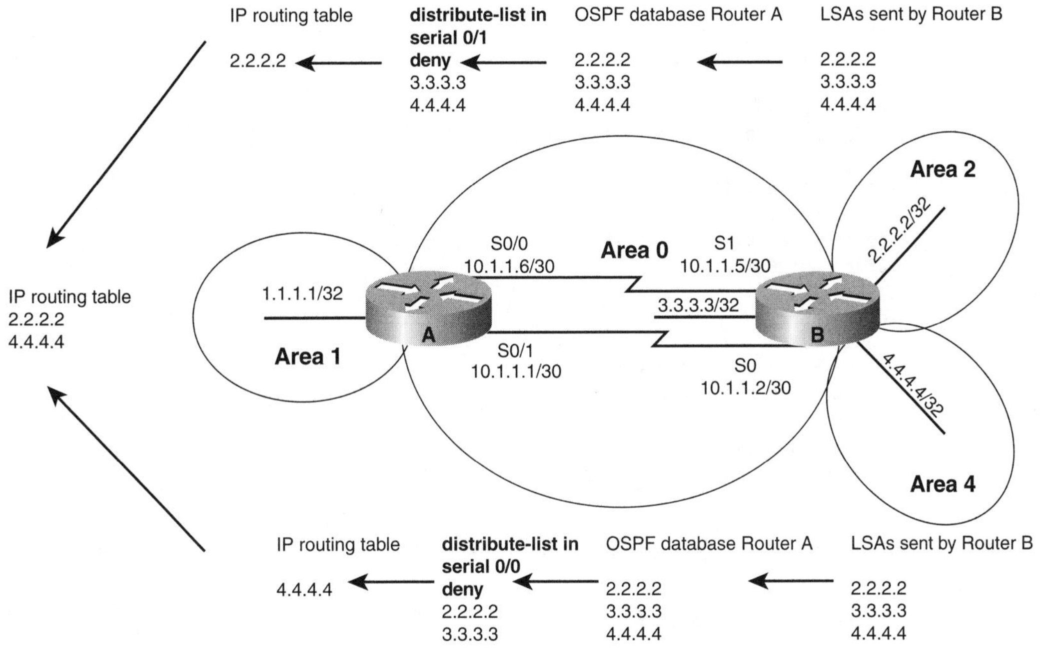


```
Router A

interface Loopback0
 ip address 1.1.1.1 255.255.255.255
!
interface Serial0/0
 ip address 10.1.1.6 255.255.255.252
!
interface Serial0/1
 ip address 10.1.1.1 255.255.255.252
 clockrate 64000
!
router ospf 1
 network 1.1.1.1 0.0.0.0 area 1
```

continues

```
 network 10.1.1.0 0.0.0.3 area 0
 network 10.1.1.4 0.0.0.3 area 0
```

```
Router B

interface Loopback0
 ip address 2.2.2.2 255.255.255.255
!
interface Loopback1
 ip address 3.3.3.3 255.255.255.255
!
interface Loopback2
 ip address 4.4.4.4 255.255.255.255
!
interface Serial0
 ip address 10.1.1.2 255.255.255.252
!
interface Serial1
 bandwidth 64
 ip address 10.1.1.5 255.255.255.252
 clockrate 64000
!
router ospf 1
 router-id 2.2.2.2
 network 2.2.2.2 0.0.0.0 area 2
 network 3.3.3.3 0.0.0.0 area 0
 network 4.4.4.4 0.0.0.0 area 4
 network 10.1.1.0 0.0.0.3 area 0
 network 10.1.1.4 0.0.0.3 area 0
```

Verify that Routers A and B have established a FULL OSPF neighbor relationship.

```
rtrA#show ip ospf neighbor

Neighbor ID     Pri   State           Dead Time   Address         Interface
2.2.2.2           1   FULL/  -        00:00:33    10.1.1.5        Serial0/0
2.2.2.2           1   FULL/  -        00:00:37    10.1.1.2        Serial0/1
```

```
rtrB#show ip ospf neighbor

Neighbor ID     Pri   State           Dead Time   Address         Interface
1.1.1.1           1   FULL/  -        00:00:38    10.1.1.1        Serial0
1.1.1.1           1   FULL/  -        00:00:36    10.1.1.6        Serial1
```

Verify that Router A is receiving the routes 2.2.2.2, 3.3.3.3, and 4.4.4.4 from Router B.

```
rtrA#show ip route
Codes: C - connected, S - static, I - IGRP, R - RIP, M - mobile, B - BGP
       D - EIGRP, EX - EIGRP external, O - OSPF, IA - OSPF inter area
       N1 - OSPF NSSA external type 1, N2 - OSPF NSSA external type 2
       E1 - OSPF external type 1, E2 - OSPF external type 2, E - EGP
       i - IS-IS, L1 - IS-IS level-1, L2 - IS-IS level-2, ia - IS-IS inter area
       * - candidate default, U - per-user static route, o - ODR
       P - periodic downloaded static route

Gateway of last resort is not set

     1.0.0.0/32 is subnetted, 1 subnets
C       1.1.1.1 is directly connected, Loopback0
     2.0.0.0/32 is subnetted, 1 subnets
O IA    2.2.2.2 [110/65] via 10.1.1.5, 00:00:10, Serial0/0
                [110/65] via 10.1.1.2, 00:00:10, Serial0/1
     3.0.0.0/32 is subnetted, 1 subnets
O       3.3.3.3 [110/65] via 10.1.1.5, 00:00:10, Serial0/0
                [110/65] via 10.1.1.2, 00:00:10, Serial0/1
     4.0.0.0/32 is subnetted, 1 subnets
O IA    4.4.4.4 [110/65] via 10.1.1.5, 00:00:10, Serial0/0
                [110/65] via 10.1.1.2, 00:00:11, Serial0/1
     10.0.0.0/30 is subnetted, 2 subnets
C       10.1.1.0 is directly connected, Serial0/1
C       10.1.1.4 is directly connected, Serial0/0
```

For illustrative purposes, verify that these three routes are in the OSPF database on Router A.

```
rtrA#show ip ospf database

            OSPF Router with ID (1.1.1.1) (Process ID 1)

                Router Link States (Area 0)


1.1.1.1         1.1.1.1         1423        0x800000C1 0xE80E   4
2.2.2.2         2.2.2.2         1451        0x80000050 0xA7E3   5

                Summary Net Link States (Area 0)

Link ID         ADV Router      Age         Seq#       Checksum
1.1.1.1         1.1.1.1         165         0x80000044 0xC030
2.2.2.2         2.2.2.2         707         0x80000057 0x4E87
4.4.4.4         2.2.2.2         707         0x8000000F 0x8293

                Router Link States (Area 1)
```

continues

```
Link ID         ADV Router      Age         Seq#       Checksum Link count
1.1.1.1         1.1.1.1         1666        0x80000008 0xC558   1

                Summary Net Link States (Area 1)

Link ID         ADV Router      Age         Seq#       Checksum
2.2.2.2         1.1.1.1         1423        0x80000006 0x9159
3.3.3.3         1.1.1.1         1669        0x80000009 0x5D86
4.4.4.4         1.1.1.1         1669        0x80000009 0x2FB0
10.1.1.0        1.1.1.1         168         0x80000007 0x36B3
10.1.1.4        1.1.1.1         1425        0x80000008 0xCD8
```

Modify the configuration on Router A to prevent the OSPF routes 2.2.2.2 and 3.3.3.3 received over interface Serial 0/0 and the routes 3.3.3.3 and 4.4.4.4 received over Serial 0/1 from being installed in the IP routing table.

```
Router A

router ospf 1
 network 1.1.1.1 0.0.0.0 area 1
 network 172.16.1.0 0.0.0.255 area 0
 distribute-list 1 in Serial0/0
 distribute-list 2 in Serial0/1
!
access-list 1 deny   2.2.2.0 0.0.0.255
access-list 1 deny   3.3.3.0 0.0.0.255
access-list 1 permit any
access-list 2 deny   3.3.3.0 0.0.0.255
access-list 2 deny   4.4.4.0 0.0.0.255
access-list 2 permit any
```

Verification

Determine the routes that have been filtered from reaching the IP routing table on Router A.

```
rtrA#show ip route
Codes: C - connected, S - static, I - IGRP, R - RIP, M - mobile, B - BGP
       D - EIGRP, EX - EIGRP external, O - OSPF, IA - OSPF inter area
       N1 - OSPF NSSA external type 1, N2 - OSPF NSSA external type 2
       E1 - OSPF external type 1, E2 - OSPF external type 2, E - EGP
       i - IS-IS, L1 - IS-IS level-1, L2 - IS-IS level-2, ia - IS-IS inter area
       * - candidate default, U - per-user static route, o - ODR
       P - periodic downloaded static route

Gateway of last resort is not set

     1.0.0.0/32 is subnetted, 1 subnets
C       1.1.1.1 is directly connected, Loopback0
     2.0.0.0/32 is subnetted, 1 subnets
```

```
O IA     2.2.2.2 [110/65] via 10.1.1.2, 00:01:15, Serial0/1
     4.0.0.0/32 is subnetted, 1 subnets
O IA     4.4.4.4 [110/65] via 10.1.1.5, 00:01:15, Serial0/0
     172.16.0.0/24 is subnetted, 1 subnets
C        172.16.1.0 is directly connected, Ethernet0/0
     10.0.0.0/30 is subnetted, 2 subnets
C        10.1.1.0 is directly connected, Serial0/1
C        10.1.1.4 is directly connected, Serial0/0
```

Access list 1 on Router A allows network 4.4.4.0. Access list 2 on Router A allows network 2.2.2.0. The only network that is filtered by both access lists is 3.3.3.0. Verify that routes 2.2.2.2, 3.3.3.3, and 4.4.4.4 are still in the OSPF database on Router A.

```
rtrA#show ip ospf database

              OSPF Router with ID (1.1.1.1) (Process ID 1)

                  Router Link States (Area 0)

Link ID         ADV Router      Age         Seq#       Checksum Link count
1.1.1.1         1.1.1.1         1815        0x800000C1 0xE80E   4
2.2.2.2         2.2.2.2         1843        0x80000050 0xA7E3   5

                  Summary Net Link States (Area 0)

Link ID         ADV Router      Age         Seq#       Checksum
1.1.1.1         1.1.1.1         557         0x80000044 0xC030
2.2.2.2         2.2.2.2         1099        0x80000057 0x4E87
4.4.4.4         2.2.2.2         1099        0x8000000F 0x8293

                  Router Link States (Area 1)

Link ID         ADV Router      Age         Seq#       Checksum Link count
1.1.1.1         1.1.1.1         43          0x80000009 0xC359   1

                  Summary Net Link States (Area 1)

Link ID         ADV Router      Age         Seq#       Checksum
2.2.2.2         1.1.1.1         1815        0x80000006 0x9159
3.3.3.3         1.1.1.1         45          0x8000000A 0x5B87
4.4.4.4         1.1.1.1         45          0x8000000A 0x2DB1
10.1.1.0        1.1.1.1         559         0x80000007 0x36B3
10.1.1.4        1.1.1.1         1816        0x80000008 0xCD8
```

Troubleshooting

Step 1 Verify that there is a neighbor relationship between the OSPF routers by using the **show ip ospf neighbor** command.

Step 2 Verify that the **distribute-list** command is referencing the correct access list number and interface.

Step 3 Verify the syntax of the access list.

Step 4 Verify that the access list has been referenced by using the command **show ip access-lists** *access-list-number*. For example, for the preceding configuration, the output would be the following:

```
rtrA#show ip access-lists 1
Standard IP access list 1
    deny   2.2.2.0, wildcard bits 0.0.0.255 (5 matches) check=15
    deny   3.3.3.0, wildcard bits 0.0.0.255 (5 matches) check=10
    permit any (10 matches)
Standard IP access list 2
    deny   3.3.3.0, wildcard bits 0.0.0.255 (4 matches) check=12
    deny   4.4.4.0, wildcard bits 0.0.0.255 (4 matches) check=8
    permit any (8 matches)
```

7-3: distribute-list *access-list-number* out

Syntax Description:

- *access-list-number*—Standard IP access number used to determine which routes learned via OSPF will be prevented from being installed in the IP routing table. The range of access list numbers is 1–99 and 1300–2699.

Purpose: For distance vector protocols (RIP, IGRP, EIGRP), this command prevents routes selected by the access list from being advertised to a neighbor. OSPF is a link-state protocol and does not advertise routes to a neighbor but advertises a link-state database. The neighbor determines the routes from the information in the link-state database. Therefore, this command has no effect when used with OSPF.

Initial Cisco IOS Software Release: 10.0. The *interface-type* and *interface-number* parameters were added in 11.2.

7-4: distribute-list *access-list-number* out *interface-type interface-number*

Syntax Description:

- *access-list-number*—Standard IP access number used to determine which routes learned via OSPF will be prevented from being installed in the IP routing table. The range of access list numbers is 1–99 and 1300–2699.

- *interface-type*—Optional parameter, along with the *interface-number*, used to apply the distribute list to OSPF routes learned through a particular interface.
- *interface-number*—Number of the interface type.

Purpose: For distance vector protocols (RIP, IGRP, EIGRP), this command prevents routes selected by the access list from being advertised to a neighbor. OSPF is a link-state protocol and does not advertise routes to a neighbor but advertises a link-state database. The neighbor determines the routes from the information in the link-state database. Therefore, this command has no effect when used with OSPF.

Initial Cisco IOS Software Release: 10.0. The *interface-type* and *interface-number* parameters were added in 11.2.

7-5: distribute-list *access-list-number* out *routing-process*

Syntax Description:

- *access-list-number*—Standard IP access number used to determine which routes redistributed into OSPF will be prevented from being installed in the OSPF database. This has the effect of preventing the blocked redistributed routes from being advertised to OSPF neighbors. The range of access list numbers is 1–99 and 1300–2699.
- *routing-process*—The routing process that has been redistributed into OSPF (RIP, IGRP, EIGRP, OSPF, BGP, EGP, static, or connected).

Purpose: To prevent routes that were redistributed into OSPF from another routing process from being installed in the OSPF database. This command can be used to filter OSPF routes by using two OSPF processes and to redistribute the routes between the OSPF processes.

Initial Cisco IOS Software Release: 10.0

Configuration Example: Preventing Routes Redistributed into OSPF from Being Installed in the IP Routing Table

In Figure 7-3, Router B is receiving the EIGRP routes 10.1.1.4/30, 3.3.3.0/24, and 4.4.4.0/24 from Router C. Router B is redistributing EIGRP into OSPF, and these routes will be advertised to Router A as OSPF external type two routes. Start by configuring Routers A, B, and C as shown in the listing that follows the figure.

Figure 7-3 *A Distribute List/Access List Prevents Redistributed Routes from Being Installed in the OSPF Database*

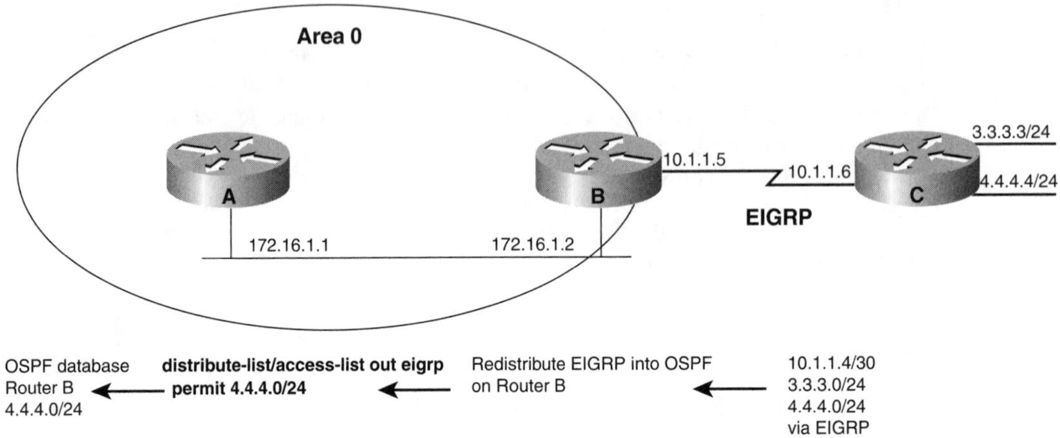


```
Router A

interface Loopback0
 ip address 1.1.1.1 255.255.255.255
!
interface Ethernet0/0
 ip address 172.16.1.1 255.255.255.0
!
router ospf 1
 network 172.16.1.0 0.0.0.255 area 0
```

```
Router B

interface Loopback0
 ip address 2.2.2.2 255.255.255.255
!
interface Ethernet0
 ip address 172.16.1.2 255.255.255.0
!
interface Serial1
 bandwidth 64
 ip address 10.1.1.5 255.255.255.252
 clockrate 64000
!
router eigrp 1
 network 10.0.0.0
!
router ospf 1
 redistribute eigrp 1 subnets
 network 2.2.2.2 0.0.0.0 area 1
```

```
 network 172.16.1.0 0.0.0.255 area 0
```

```
Router C

interface Loopback0
 ip address 3.3.3.3 255.255.255.0
!
interface Loopback1
 ip address 4.4.4.4 255.255.255.0
!
interface Serial0
 ip address 10.1.1.6 255.255.255.252
!
router eigrp 1
 network 3.0.0.0
 network 4.0.0.0
 network 10.0.0.0
 no auto-summary
```

Verify that Routers A and B have established a FULL OSPF neighbor relationship.

```
rtrA#show ip ospf neighbor

Neighbor ID     Pri   State           Dead Time   Address         Interface
2.2.2.2           1   FULL/BDR        00:00:30    172.16.1.2      Ethernet0/0

rtrB#show ip ospf neighbor

Neighbor ID     Pri   State           Dead Time   Address         Interface
1.1.1.1           1   FULL/DR         00:00:38    172.16.1.1      Ethernet0
```

Verify that Router B is receiving the routes 3.3.3.0/24 and 4.4.4.0/24 from Router C via EIGRP.

```
rtrB# show ip route
Codes: C - connected, S - static, I - IGRP, R - RIP, M - mobile, B - BGP
       D - EIGRP, EX - EIGRP external, O - OSPF, IA - OSPF inter area
       N1 - OSPF NSSA external type 1, N2 - OSPF NSSA external type 2
       E1 - OSPF external type 1, E2 - OSPF external type 2, E - EGP
       i - IS-IS, L1 - IS-IS level-1, L2 - IS-IS level-2, * - candidate default
       U - per-user static route, o - ODR

Gateway of last resort is not set

     2.0.0.0/32 is subnetted, 1 subnets
C       2.2.2.2 is directly connected, Loopback0
     3.0.0.0/24 is subnetted, 1 subnets
D       3.3.3.0 [90/40640000] via 10.1.1.6, 00:38:45, Serial1
     4.0.0.0/24 is subnetted, 1 subnets
```

continues

```
D       4.4.4.0 [90/40640000] via 10.1.1.6, 00:38:45, Serial1
     172.16.0.0/24 is subnetted, 1 subnets
C       172.16.1.0 is directly connected, Ethernet0
     10.0.0.0/30 is subnetted, 1 subnets
C       10.1.1.4 is directly connected, Serial1
```

Verify that Router A is receiving the routes 10.1.1.4/30, 3.3.3.0/24, and 4.4.4.0/24 from Router B as OSPF external type 2 routes.

```
rtrA#show ip route
Codes: C - connected, S - static, I - IGRP, R - RIP, M - mobile, B - BGP
       D - EIGRP, EX - EIGRP external, O - OSPF, IA - OSPF inter area
       N1 - OSPF NSSA external type 1, N2 - OSPF NSSA external type 2
       E1 - OSPF external type 1, E2 - OSPF external type 2, E - EGP
       i - IS-IS, L1 - IS-IS level-1, L2 - IS-IS level-2, ia - IS-IS inter area
       * - candidate default, U - per-user static route, o - ODR
       P - periodic downloaded static route

Gateway of last resort is not set

     1.0.0.0/32 is subnetted, 1 subnets
C       1.1.1.1 is directly connected, Loopback0
     2.0.0.0/32 is subnetted, 1 subnets
O IA    2.2.2.2 [110/11] via 172.16.1.2, 00:27:48, Ethernet0/0
     3.0.0.0/24 is subnetted, 1 subnets
O E2    3.3.3.0 [110/20] via 172.16.1.2, 00:05:41, Ethernet0/0
     4.0.0.0/24 is subnetted, 1 subnets
O E2    4.4.4.0 [110/20] via 172.16.1.2, 00:27:48, Ethernet0/0
     172.16.0.0/24 is subnetted, 1 subnets
C       172.16.1.0 is directly connected, Ethernet0/0
     10.0.0.0/30 is subnetted, 1 subnets
O E2    10.1.1.4 [110/20] via 172.16.1.2, 00:05:42, Ethernet0/0
```

For illustrative purposes, verify that these three routes are in the OSPF database on Router B.

```
rtrB#show ip ospf database external

       OSPF Router with ID (2.2.2.2) (Process ID 1)


                Type-5 AS External Link States

  LS age: 441
  Options: (No TOS-capability, DC)
  LS Type: AS External Link
  Link State ID: 3.3.3.0 (External Network Number )
  Advertising Router: 2.2.2.2
  LS Seq Number: 80000001
```

```
Checksum: 0x3F50
Length: 36
Network Mask: /24
      Metric Type: 2 (Larger than any link state path)
      TOS: 0
      Metric: 20
      Forward Address: 0.0.0.0
      External Route Tag: 0

LS age: 1788
Options: (No TOS-capability, DC)
LS Type: AS External Link
Link State ID: 4.4.4.0 (External Network Number )
Advertising Router: 2.2.2.2
LS Seq Number: 80000003
Checksum: 0x1773
Length: 36
Network Mask: /24
      Metric Type: 2 (Larger than any link state path)
      TOS: 0
      Metric: 20
      Forward Address: 0.0.0.0
      External Route Tag: 0

LS age: 459
Options: (No TOS-capability, DC)
LS Type: AS External Link
Link State ID: 10.1.1.4 (External Network Number )
Advertising Router: 2.2.2.2
LS Seq Number: 80000001
Checksum: 0xD7B3
Length: 36
Network Mask: /30
      Metric Type: 2 (Larger than any link state path)
      TOS: 0
      Metric: 20
      Forward Address: 0.0.0.0
      External Route Tag: 0
```

Modify the configuration on Router B to allow only the installation of EIGRP route 4.4.4.0/24 into the OSPF database.

```
Router B

router ospf 1
 redistribute eigrp 1 subnets
 network 2.2.2.2 0.0.0.0 area 1
 network 172.16.1.0 0.0.0.255 area 0
 distribute-list 1 out eigrp 1
!
access-list 1 permit 4.4.4.0 0.0.0.255
```

Verification

Verify that the EIGRP routes 10.1.1.4/30 and 3.3.3.0/24 have been blocked from entering the OSPF database on Router B.

```
rtrB#show ip ospf database external

       OSPF Router with ID (2.2.2.2) (Process ID 1)


                Type-5 AS External Link States

  LS age: 419
  Options: (No TOS-capability, DC)
  LS Type: AS External Link
  Link State ID: 4.4.4.0 (External Network Number )
  Advertising Router: 2.2.2.2
  LS Seq Number: 80000004
  Checksum: 0x1574
  Length: 36
  Network Mask: /24
        Metric Type: 2 (Larger than any link state path)
        TOS: 0
        Metric: 20
        Forward Address: 0.0.0.0
        External Route Tag: 0
```

Verify that Router A is receiving only one external type 2 route from Router B.

```
rtrA#show ip route
Codes: C - connected, S - static, I - IGRP, R - RIP, M - mobile, B - BGP
       D - EIGRP, EX - EIGRP external, O - OSPF, IA - OSPF inter area
       N1 - OSPF NSSA external type 1, N2 - OSPF NSSA external type 2
       E1 - OSPF external type 1, E2 - OSPF external type 2, E - EGP
       i - IS-IS, L1 - IS-IS level-1, L2 - IS-IS level-2, ia - IS-IS inter area
       * - candidate default, U - per-user static route, o - ODR
       P - periodic downloaded static route

Gateway of last resort is not set

     1.0.0.0/32 is subnetted, 1 subnets
C       1.1.1.1 is directly connected, Loopback0
     2.0.0.0/32 is subnetted, 1 subnets
O IA    2.2.2.2 [110/11] via 172.16.1.2, 00:38:45, Ethernet0/0
     4.0.0.0/24 is subnetted, 1 subnets
O E2    4.4.4.0 [110/20] via 172.16.1.2, 00:38:45, Ethernet0/0
     172.16.0.0/24 is subnetted, 1 subnets
C       172.16.1.0 is directly connected, Ethernet0/0
```

Troubleshooting

Step 1 Verify that there is a neighbor relationship between the OSPF routers by using the **show ip ospf neighbor** command.

Step 2 Verify that the **distribute-list** command is referencing the correct access list number and routing process.

Step 3 Verify the syntax of the access list.

Step 4 Verify that the intended routes are in the OSPF database using the command **show ip ospf database external**.

7-6: distribute-list *access-list-name* in

Syntax Description:

- *access-list-name*—Named IP access list that is used to determine which routes learned via OSPF will be prevented from being installed in the IP routing table.

Purpose: To prevent OSPF learned routes from being installed in the IP routing table. Even though an OSPF route may be prevented from being installed in the IP routing table, the route will still be in the OSPF database.

Initial Cisco IOS Software Release: 11.2

Configuration Example: Preventing OSPF Learned Routes from Being Installed in the IP Routing Table

In Figure 7-4, Router A is receiving the OSPF routes 2.2.2.2, 3.3.3.3, and 4.4.4.4 from Router B. Start by configuring Routers A and B as shown in the listing that follows the figure.

Figure 7-4 *A Distribute List/Named Access List Controls Which OSPF Routes Are Transferred from the OSPF Database Into the IP Routing Table*

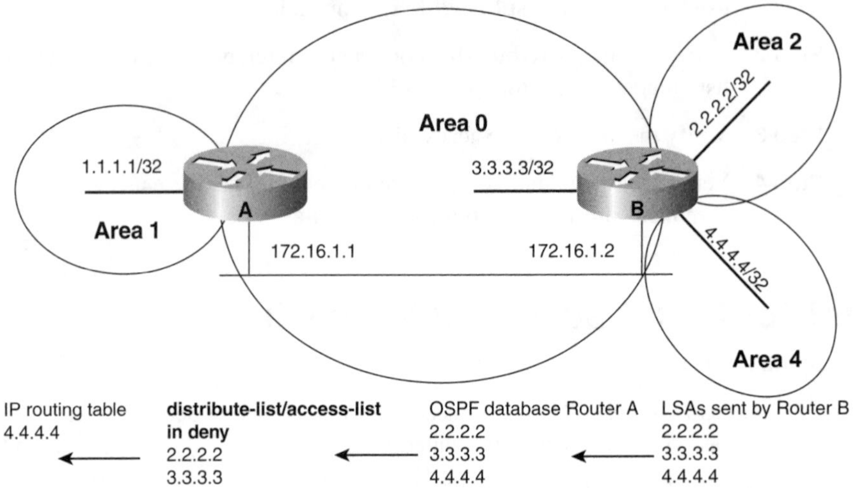


```
Router A

interface Loopback0
 ip address 1.1.1.1 255.255.255.255
!
interface Ethernet0/0
 ip address 172.16.1.1 255.255.255.0
!
router ospf 1
 network 1.1.1.1 0.0.0.0 area 1
 network 172.16.1.0 0.0.0.255 area 0
```

```
Router B

interface Loopback0
 ip address 2.2.2.2 255.255.255.255
!
interface Loopback1
 ip address 3.3.3.3 255.255.255.255
!
interface Loopback2
 ip address 4.4.4.4 255.255.255.255
!
interface Ethernet0
 ip address 172.16.1.2 255.255.255.0
!
router ospf 1
 router-id 2.2.2.2
 network 2.2.2.2 0.0.0.0 area 2
 network 3.3.3.3 0.0.0.0 area 0
 network 4.4.4.4 0.0.0.0 area 4
 network 172.16.1.2 0.0.0.0 area 0
```

Verify that Routers A and B have established a FULL OSPF neighbor relationship.

```
rtrA#show ip ospf neighbor

Neighbor ID     Pri   State           Dead Time   Address         Interface
2.2.2.2           1   FULL/BDR        00:00:30    172.16.1.2      Ethernet0/0
```

```
rtrB#show ip ospf neighbor

Neighbor ID     Pri   State           Dead Time   Address         Interface
1.1.1.1           1   FULL/DR         00:00:38    172.16.1.1      Ethernet0
```

Verify that Router A is receiving the routes 2.2.2.2, 3.3.3.3, and 4.4.4.4 from Router B.

```
rtrA#show ip route
Codes: C - connected, S - static, I - IGRP, R - RIP, M - mobile, B - BGP
       D - EIGRP, EX - EIGRP external, O - OSPF, IA - OSPF inter area
       N1 - OSPF NSSA external type 1, N2 - OSPF NSSA external type 2
       E1 - OSPF external type 1, E2 - OSPF external type 2, E - EGP
       i - IS-IS, L1 - IS-IS level-1, L2 - IS-IS level-2, ia - IS-IS inter area
       * - candidate default, U - per-user static route, o - ODR
       P - periodic downloaded static route

Gateway of last resort is not set

     1.0.0.0/32 is subnetted, 1 subnets
C       1.1.1.1 is directly connected, Loopback0
     2.0.0.0/32 is subnetted, 1 subnets
O IA    2.2.2.2 [110/11] via 172.16.1.2, 00:04:28, Ethernet0/0
     3.0.0.0/32 is subnetted, 1 subnets
O       3.3.3.3 [110/11] via 172.16.1.2, 00:04:28, Ethernet0/0
     4.0.0.0/32 is subnetted, 1 subnets
O IA    4.4.4.4 [110/11] via 172.16.1.2, 00:04:28, Ethernet0/0
     172.16.0.0/24 is subnetted, 1 subnets
C       172.16.1.0 is directly connected, Ethernet0/0
```

For illustrative purposes, verify that these three routes are in the OSPF database on Router A.

```
rtrA#show ip ospf database

            OSPF Router with ID (1.1.1.1) (Process ID 1)

                Router Link States (Area 0)

Link ID         ADV Router      Age         Seq#       Checksum Link count
1.1.1.1         1.1.1.1         493         0x800000A5 0x8F6F   1
2.2.2.2         2.2.2.2         489         0x80000030 0x7ECF   2
```

continues

```
                 Net Link States (Area 0)

Link ID          ADV Router       Age          Seq#        Checksum
172.16.1.1       1.1.1.1          496          0x80000001  0x6DFD

                 Summary Net Link States (Area 0)

Link ID          ADV Router       Age          Seq#        Checksum
1.1.1.1          1.1.1.1          714          0x80000033  0xE21F
2.2.2.2          2.2.2.2          487          0x80000049  0x6A79
4.4.4.4          2.2.2.2          490          0x80000001  0x9E85

                 Router Link States (Area 1)

Link ID          ADV Router       Age          Seq#        Checksum Link count
1.1.1.1          1.1.1.1          726          0x80000001  0xD351    1

                 Summary Net Link States (Area 1)

Link ID          ADV Router       Age          Seq#        Checksum
2.2.2.2          1.1.1.1          492          0x80000001  0x7DA8
3.3.3.3          1.1.1.1          492          0x80000001  0x4FD2
4.4.4.4          1.1.1.1          492          0x80000001  0x21FC
172.16.1.0       1.1.1.1          496          0x80000003  0x3B34
```

Modify the configuration on Router A to prevent the OSPF routes 2.2.2.2 and 3.3.3.3 from being installed in the IP routing table.

```
Router A

router ospf 1
 network 1.1.1.1 0.0.0.0 area 1
 network 172.16.1.0 0.0.0.255 area 0
 distribute-list filter-ospf in
!
ip access-list standard filter-ospf
 deny   2.2.2.0 0.0.0.255
 deny   3.3.3.0 0.0.0.255
 permit any
```

Verification

Verify that the OSPF routes 2.2.2.2 and 3.3.3.3 have been blocked from entering the IP routing table on Router A. They should be absent from the IP routing table.

```
rtrA#show ip route
Codes: C - connected, S - static, I - IGRP, R - RIP, M - mobile, B - BGP
       D - EIGRP, EX - EIGRP external, O - OSPF, IA - OSPF inter area
```

```
       N1 - OSPF NSSA external type 1, N2 - OSPF NSSA external type 2
       E1 - OSPF external type 1, E2 - OSPF external type 2, E - EGP
       i - IS-IS, L1 - IS-IS level-1, L2 - IS-IS level-2, ia - IS-IS inter area
       * - candidate default, U - per-user static route, o - ODR
       P - periodic downloaded static route

Gateway of last resort is not set

     1.0.0.0/32 is subnetted, 1 subnets
C       1.1.1.1 is directly connected, Loopback0
     4.0.0.0/32 is subnetted, 1 subnets
O IA    4.4.4.4 [110/11] via 172.16.1.2, 00:03:39, Ethernet0/0
     172.16.0.0/24 is subnetted, 1 subnets
C       172.16.1.0 is directly connected, Ethernet0/0
```

Verify that routes 2.2.2.2 and 3.3.3.3 are still in the OSPF database on Router A.

```
rtrA#show ip ospf database

            OSPF Router with ID (1.1.1.1) (Process ID 1)

                Router Link States (Area 0)

Link ID         ADV Router      Age         Seq#       Checksum Link count
1.1.1.1         1.1.1.1         951         0x800000A5 0x8F6F   1
2.2.2.2         2.2.2.2         947         0x80000030 0x7ECF   2

                Net Link States (Area 0)

Link ID         ADV Router      Age         Seq#       Checksum
172.16.1.1      1.1.1.1         954         0x80000001 0x6DFD

                Summary Net Link States (Area 0)

Link ID         ADV Router      Age         Seq#       Checksum
1.1.1.1         1.1.1.1         1172        0x80000033 0xE21F
2.2.2.2         2.2.2.2         945         0x80000049 0x6A79
4.4.4.4         2.2.2.2         948         0x80000001 0x9E85

                Router Link States (Area 1)

Link ID         ADV Router      Age         Seq#       Checksum Link count
1.1.1.1         1.1.1.1         1184        0x80000001 0xD351   1

                Summary Net Link States (Area 1)

Link ID         ADV Router      Age         Seq#       Checksum
3.3.3.3         1.1.1.1         946         0x80000001 0x4FD2
4.4.4.4         1.1.1.1         946         0x80000001 0x21FC
172.16.1.0      1.1.1.1         950         0x80000003 0x3B34
```

Troubleshooting

Step 1 Verify that there is a neighbor relationship between the OSPF routers by using the **show ip ospf neighbor** command.

Step 2 Verify that the **distribute-list** command is referencing the correct named access list.

Step 3 Verify the syntax of the named access list.

7-7: distribute-list *access-list-name* in *interface-type interface-number*

Syntax Description:

- *access-list-name*—Named IP access used to determine which routes learned via OSPF will be prevented from being installed in the IP routing table.
- *interface-type*—Optional parameter, along with the *interface-number*, used to apply the distribute list to OSPF routes learned through a particular interface.
- *interface-number*—Number of the interface type.

Purpose: To prevent OSPF routes learned over a specific interface from being installed in the IP routing table. Even though an OSPF route may be prevented from being installed in the IP routing table, the route will still be in the OSPF database. The route could be learned via another OSPF interface and would therefore appear in the IP routing table.

Initial Cisco IOS Software Release: 10.0. The *interface-type* and *interface-number* parameters were added in Release 11.2.

Configuration Example: Preventing Routes Learned via OSPF Over a Specific Interface from Being Installed in the IP Routing Table

In Figure 7-5, Router A is receiving the OSPF routes 2.2.2.2, 3.3.3.3, and 4.4.4.4 from Router B over two serial interfaces. Start by configuring routes A and B as shown in the listing that follows the figure.

Figure 7-5 *A Distribute List/Named Access List Is Used to Control Which OSPF Routes, Learned Over a Specific Interface, Are Transferred from the OSPF Database into the IP Routing Table*

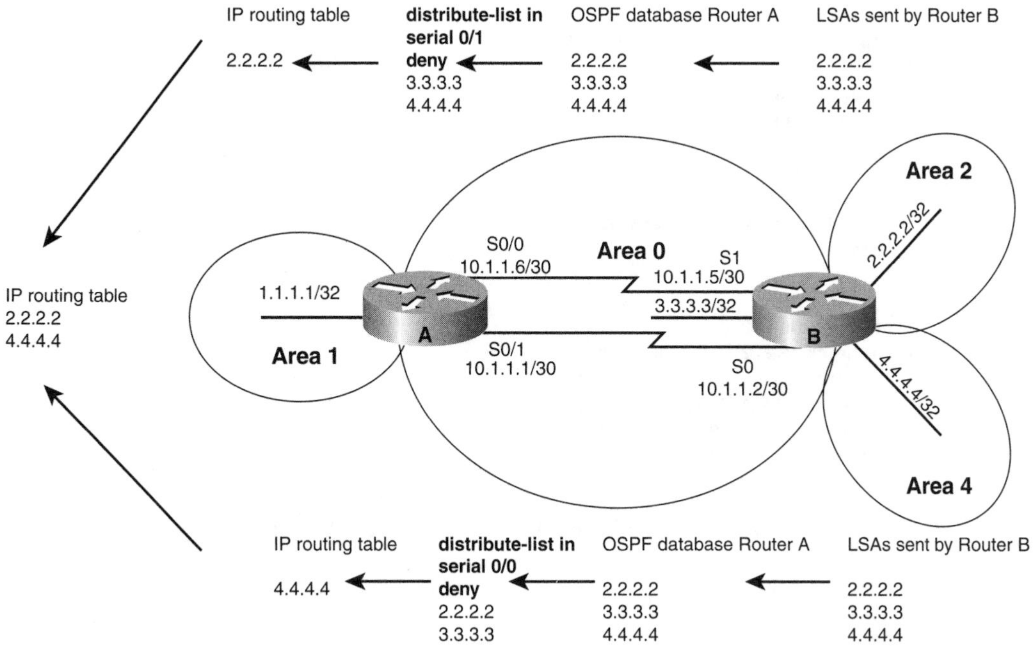


```
Router A

interface Loopback0
 ip address 1.1.1.1 255.255.255.255
!
interface Serial0/0
 ip address 10.1.1.6 255.255.255.252
 no ip mroute-cache
!
interface Serial0/1
 ip address 10.1.1.1 255.255.255.252
 clockrate 64000
!
router ospf 1
 network 1.1.1.1 0.0.0.0 area 1
 network 10.1.1.0 0.0.0.3 area 0
 network 10.1.1.4 0.0.0.3 area 0
```

```
Router B

interface Loopback0
 ip address 2.2.2.2 255.255.255.255
!
```

continues

```
interface Loopback1
 ip address 3.3.3.3 255.255.255.255
!
interface Loopback2
 ip address 4.4.4.4 255.255.255.255
!
interface Serial0
 ip address 10.1.1.2 255.255.255.252
!
interface Serial1
 bandwidth 64
 ip address 10.1.1.5 255.255.255.252
 clockrate 64000
!
router ospf 1
 router-id 2.2.2.2
 network 2.2.2.2 0.0.0.0 area 2
 network 3.3.3.3 0.0.0.0 area 0
 network 4.4.4.4 0.0.0.0 area 4
 network 10.1.1.0 0.0.0.3 area 0
 network 10.1.1.4 0.0.0.3 area 0
```

Verify that Routers A and B have established a FULL OSPF neighbor relationship.

```
rtrA#show ip ospf neighbor

Neighbor ID     Pri   State           Dead Time   Address         Interface
2.2.2.2           1   FULL/  -        00:00:34    10.1.1.5        Serial0/0
2.2.2.2           1   FULL/  -        00:00:38    10.1.1.2        Serial0/1

rtrB#show ip ospf neighbor

Neighbor ID     Pri   State           Dead Time   Address         Interface
1.1.1.1           1   FULL/  -        00:00:32    10.1.1.1        Serial0
1.1.1.1           1   FULL/  -        00:00:30    10.1.1.6        Serial1
```

Verify that Router A is receiving the routes 2.2.2.2, 3.3.3.3, and 4.4.4.4 from Router B.

```
rtrA#show ip route
Codes: C - connected, S - static, I - IGRP, R - RIP, M - mobile, B - BGP
       D - EIGRP, EX - EIGRP external, O - OSPF, IA - OSPF inter area
       N1 - OSPF NSSA external type 1, N2 - OSPF NSSA external type 2
       E1 - OSPF external type 1, E2 - OSPF external type 2, E - EGP
       i - IS-IS, L1 - IS-IS level-1, L2 - IS-IS level-2, ia - IS-IS inter area
       * - candidate default, U - per-user static route, o - ODR
       P - periodic downloaded static route

Gateway of last resort is not set

     1.0.0.0/32 is subnetted, 1 subnets
```

```
C       1.1.1.1 is directly connected, Loopback0
     2.0.0.0/32 is subnetted, 1 subnets
O IA    2.2.2.2 [110/65] via 10.1.1.5, 00:00:10, Serial0/0
                [110/65] via 10.1.1.2, 00:00:10, Serial0/1
     3.0.0.0/32 is subnetted, 1 subnets
O       3.3.3.3 [110/65] via 10.1.1.5, 00:00:10, Serial0/0
                [110/65] via 10.1.1.2, 00:00:10, Serial0/1
     4.0.0.0/32 is subnetted, 1 subnets
O IA    4.4.4.4 [110/65] via 10.1.1.5, 00:00:10, Serial0/0
                [110/65] via 10.1.1.2, 00:00:11, Serial0/1
     172.16.0.0/24 is subnetted, 1 subnets
C       172.16.1.0 is directly connected, Ethernet0/0
     10.0.0.0/30 is subnetted, 2 subnets
C       10.1.1.0 is directly connected, Serial0/1
C       10.1.1.4 is directly connected, Serial0/0
```

For illustrative purposes, verify that these three routes are in the OSPF database on Router A.

```
rtrA#show ip ospf database

             OSPF Router with ID (1.1.1.1) (Process ID 1)

                Router Link States (Area 0)


1.1.1.1         1.1.1.1         1423        0x800000C1 0xE80E   4
2.2.2.2         2.2.2.2         1451        0x80000050 0xA7E3   5

                Summary Net Link States (Area 0)

Link ID         ADV Router      Age         Seq#       Checksum
1.1.1.1         1.1.1.1         165         0x80000044 0xC030
2.2.2.2         2.2.2.2         707         0x80000057 0x4E87
4.4.4.4         2.2.2.2         707         0x8000000F 0x8293

                Router Link States (Area 1)

Link ID         ADV Router      Age         Seq#       Checksum Link count
1.1.1.1         1.1.1.1         1666        0x80000008 0xC558   1

                Summary Net Link States (Area 1)

Link ID         ADV Router      Age         Seq#       Checksum
2.2.2.2         1.1.1.1         1423        0x80000006 0x9159
3.3.3.3         1.1.1.1         1669        0x80000009 0x5D86
4.4.4.4         1.1.1.1         1669        0x80000009 0x2FB0
10.1.1.0        1.1.1.1         168         0x80000007 0x36B3
10.1.1.4        1.1.1.1         1425        0x80000008 0xCD8
```

Modify the configuration on Router A to prevent the OSPF routes 2.2.2.2 and 3.3.3.3, received over interface Serial 0/0, and the routes 3.3.3.3 and 4.4.4.4, received over Serial 0/1, from being installed in the IP routing table.

```
Router A

router ospf 1
 network 1.1.1.1 0.0.0.0 area 1
 network 172.16.1.0 0.0.0.255 area 0
 distribute-list filter-ospf1 in Serial0/0
 distribute-list filter-ospf2 in Serial0/1
!
ip access-list standard filter-ospf1
 deny   2.2.2.0 0.0.0.255
 deny   3.3.3.0 0.0.0.255
 permit any
ip access-list standard filter-ospf2
 deny   3.3.3.0 0.0.0.255
 deny   4.4.4.0 0.0.0.255
 permit any
```

Verification

Determine which routes have been prevented from reaching the IP routing table on Router A.

```
rtrA#show ip route
Codes: C - connected, S - static, I - IGRP, R - RIP, M - mobile, B - BGP
       D - EIGRP, EX - EIGRP external, O - OSPF, IA - OSPF inter area
       N1 - OSPF NSSA external type 1, N2 - OSPF NSSA external type 2
       E1 - OSPF external type 1, E2 - OSPF external type 2, E - EGP
       i - IS-IS, L1 - IS-IS level-1, L2 - IS-IS level-2, ia - IS-IS inter area
       * - candidate default, U - per-user static route, o - ODR
       P - periodic downloaded static route

Gateway of last resort is not set

     1.0.0.0/32 is subnetted, 1 subnets
C       1.1.1.1 is directly connected, Loopback0
     2.0.0.0/32 is subnetted, 1 subnets
O IA    2.2.2.2 [110/65] via 10.1.1.2, 00:01:15, Serial0/1
     4.0.0.0/32 is subnetted, 1 subnets
O IA    4.4.4.4 [110/65] via 10.1.1.5, 00:01:15, Serial0/0
     172.16.0.0/24 is subnetted, 1 subnets
C       172.16.1.0 is directly connected, Ethernet0/0
     10.0.0.0/30 is subnetted, 2 subnets
C       10.1.1.0 is directly connected, Serial0/1
C       10.1.1.4 is directly connected, Serial0/0
```

Named access list **filter-ospf1** denies networks 2.2.2.0 and 3.3.3.0. Named access list **filter-ospf2** denies networks 3.3.3.0 and 4.4.4.0. The only network that is filtered by both access lists is 3.3.3.0. Verify that routes 2.2.2.2, 3.3.3.3, and 4.4.4.4 are still in the OSPF database on Router A.

```
rtrA#show ip ospf database

            OSPF Router with ID (1.1.1.1) (Process ID 1)

                Router Link States (Area 0)

Link ID         ADV Router      Age         Seq#       Checksum Link count
1.1.1.1         1.1.1.1         1815        0x800000C1 0xE80E   4
2.2.2.2         2.2.2.2         1843        0x80000050 0xA7E3   5

                Summary Net Link States (Area 0)

Link ID         ADV Router      Age         Seq#       Checksum
1.1.1.1         1.1.1.1         557         0x80000044 0xC030
2.2.2.2         2.2.2.2         1099        0x80000057 0x4E87
4.4.4.4         2.2.2.2         1099        0x8000000F 0x8293

                Router Link States (Area 1)

Link ID         ADV Router      Age         Seq#       Checksum Link count
1.1.1.1         1.1.1.1         43          0x80000009 0xC359   1

                Summary Net Link States (Area 1)

Link ID         ADV Router      Age         Seq#       Checksum
2.2.2.2         1.1.1.1         1815        0x80000006 0x9159
3.3.3.3         1.1.1.1         45          0x8000000A 0x5B87
4.4.4.4         1.1.1.1         45          0x8000000A 0x2DB1
10.1.1.0        1.1.1.1         559         0x80000007 0x36B3
10.1.1.4        1.1.1.1         1816        0x80000008 0xCD8
```

Troubleshooting

Step 1 Verify that there is a neighbor relationship between the OSPF routers by using the **show ip ospf neighbor** command.

Step 2 Verify that the **distribute-list** command is referencing the correctly named access list and interface.

Step 3 Verify the syntax of the named access list.

7-8: distribute-list *access-list-name* out

Syntax Description:

- *access-list-name*—Standard named IP access list that determines which routes learned via OSPF will be prevented from being installed in the IP routing table.

Purpose: For distance vector protocols (RIP, IGRP, EIGRP) this command prevents routes selected by the named access list from being advertised to a neighbor. OSPF is a link-state protocol and does not advertise routes to a neighbor but advertises a link-state database. The neighbor determines the routes from the information in the link-state database. Therefore, this command has no effect when used with OSPF.

Initial Cisco IOS Software Release: 11.2

7-9: distribute-list *access-list-name* out *interface-type interface-number*

Syntax Description:

- *access-list-name*—Named IP access list that determines which routes learned via OSPF will be prevented from being installed in the IP routing table.
- *interface-type*—Optional parameter, along with the *interface-number*, used to apply the distribute list to OSPF routes learned through a particular interface.
- *interface-number*—Number of the *interface-type*.

Purpose: For distance vector protocols (RIP, IGRP, EIGRP) this command prevents routes selected by the named access list from being advertised to a neighbor. OSPF is a link-state protocol and does not advertise routes to a neighbor, but advertises a link-state database. The neighbor determines the routes from the information in the link-state database. Therefore, this command has no effect when used with OSPF.

Initial Cisco IOS Software Release: 11.2.

7-10: distribute-list *access-list-name* out *routing-process*

Syntax Description:

- *access-list-name:*—Standard IP access list name that determines which routes redistributed into OSPF will be prevented from being installed in the OSPF database. This has the effect of preventing the blocked redistributed routes from being advertised to OSPF neighbors.
- *routing-process*—The routing process that has been redistributed into OSPF (RIP, IGRP, EIGRP, OSPF, BGP, EGP, static, or connected).

Purpose: To prevent routes, redistributed into OSPF from another routing process, from being installed in the OSPF database.

Initial Cisco IOS Software Release: 11.2

Configuration Example: Preventing Routes Redistributed into OSPF from Being Installed in the OSPF Database

In Figure 7-6, Router B is receiving the EIGRP routes 10.1.1.4/30, 3.3.3.0/24, and 4.4.4.0/24 from Router C. Router B is redistributing EIGRP into OSPF and these routes will be advertised to Router A as OSPF external type 2 routes. Start by configuring Routers A, B, and C as shown in the listing that follows the figure.

Figure 7-6 *A Distribute List/Named Access List Prevents Redistributed Routes from Being Installed in the OSPF Database*

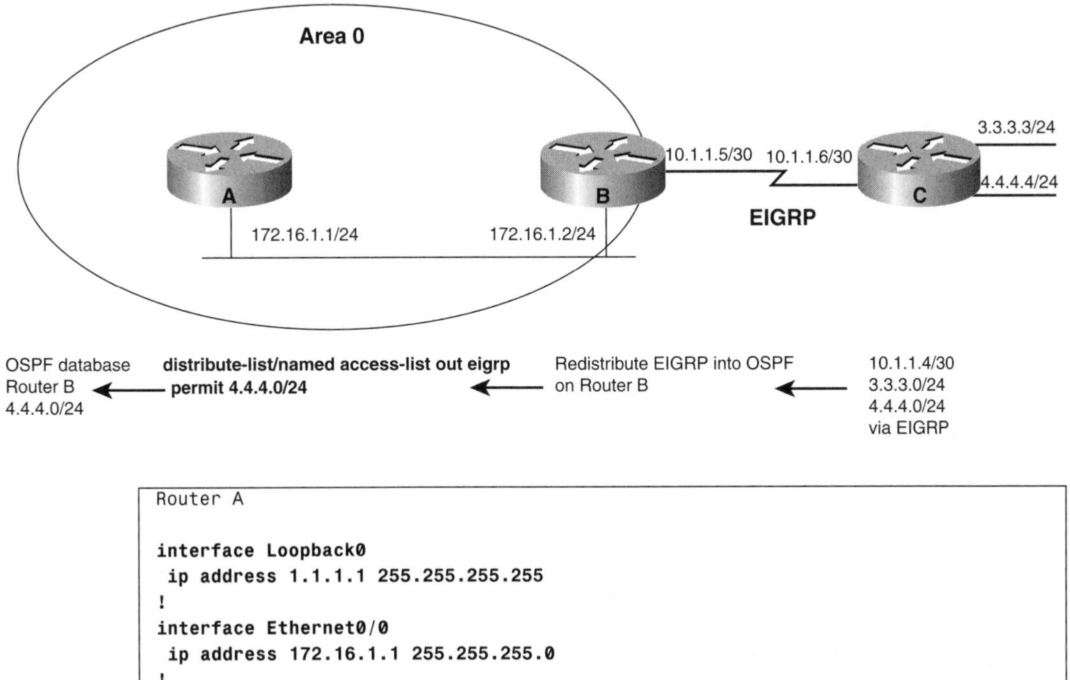


```
Router A

interface Loopback0
 ip address 1.1.1.1 255.255.255.255
!
interface Ethernet0/0
 ip address 172.16.1.1 255.255.255.0
!
router ospf 1
 network 172.16.1.0 0.0.0.255 area 0
```

```
Router B

interface Loopback0
 ip address 2.2.2.2 255.255.255.255
```

continues

```
!
interface Ethernet0
 ip address 172.16.1.2 255.255.255.0
!
interface Serial1
 bandwidth 64
 ip address 10.1.1.5 255.255.255.252
 clockrate 64000
!
router eigrp 1
 network 10.0.0.0
!
router ospf 1
 redistribute eigrp 1 subnets
 network 2.2.2.2 0.0.0.0 area 1
 network 172.16.1.0 0.0.0.255 area 0
```

```
Router C

interface Loopback0
 ip address 3.3.3.3 255.255.255.0
!
interface Loopback1
 ip address 4.4.4.4 255.255.255.0
!
interface Serial0
 ip address 10.1.1.6 255.255.255.252
!
router eigrp 1
 network 3.0.0.0
 network 4.0.0.0
 network 10.0.0.0
 no auto-summary
```

Verify that Routers A and B have established a FULL OSPF neighbor relationship.

```
rtrA#show ip ospf neighbor

Neighbor ID     Pri   State           Dead Time   Address         Interface
2.2.2.2           1   FULL/BDR        00:00:30    172.16.1.2      Ethernet0/0

rtrB#show ip ospf neighbor

Neighbor ID     Pri   State           Dead Time   Address         Interface
1.1.1.1           1   FULL/DR         00:00:38    172.16.1.1      Ethernet0
```

Verify that Router B is receiving routes 3.3.3.0/24 and 4.4.4.0/24 from Router C via EIGRP.

```
rtrB# show ip route
Codes: C - connected, S - static, I - IGRP, R - RIP, M - mobile, B - BGP
       D - EIGRP, EX - EIGRP external, O - OSPF, IA - OSPF inter area
       N1 - OSPF NSSA external type 1, N2 - OSPF NSSA external type 2
       E1 - OSPF external type 1, E2 - OSPF external type 2, E - EGP
       i - IS-IS, L1 - IS-IS level-1, L2 - IS-IS level-2, * - candidate default
       U - per-user static route, o - ODR

Gateway of last resort is not set

     2.0.0.0/32 is subnetted, 1 subnets
C       2.2.2.2 is directly connected, Loopback0
     3.0.0.0/24 is subnetted, 1 subnets
D       3.3.3.0 [90/40640000] via 10.1.1.6, 00:38:45, Serial1
     4.0.0.0/24 is subnetted, 1 subnets
D       4.4.4.0 [90/40640000] via 10.1.1.6, 00:38:45, Serial1
     172.16.0.0/24 is subnetted, 1 subnets
C       172.16.1.0 is directly connected, Ethernet0
     10.0.0.0/30 is subnetted, 1 subnets
C       10.1.1.4 is directly connected, Serial1
```

Verify that Router A is receiving routes 10.1.1.4/30, 3.3.3.0/24, and 4.4.4.0/24 from Router B as OSPF external type 2 routes.

```
rtrA#show ip route
Codes: C - connected, S - static, I - IGRP, R - RIP, M - mobile, B - BGP
       D - EIGRP, EX - EIGRP external, O - OSPF, IA - OSPF inter area
       N1 - OSPF NSSA external type 1, N2 - OSPF NSSA external type 2
       E1 - OSPF external type 1, E2 - OSPF external type 2, E - EGP
       i - IS-IS, L1 - IS-IS level-1, L2 - IS-IS level-2, ia - IS-IS inter area
       * - candidate default, U - per-user static route, o - ODR
       P - periodic downloaded static route

Gateway of last resort is not set

     1.0.0.0/32 is subnetted, 1 subnets
C       1.1.1.1 is directly connected, Loopback0
     2.0.0.0/32 is subnetted, 1 subnets
O IA    2.2.2.2 [110/11] via 172.16.1.2, 00:27:48, Ethernet0/0
     3.0.0.0/24 is subnetted, 1 subnets
O E2    3.3.3.0 [110/20] via 172.16.1.2, 00:05:41, Ethernet0/0
     4.0.0.0/24 is subnetted, 1 subnets
O E2    4.4.4.0 [110/20] via 172.16.1.2, 00:27:48, Ethernet0/0
     172.16.0.0/24 is subnetted, 1 subnets
C       172.16.1.0 is directly connected, Ethernet0/0
     10.0.0.0/30 is subnetted, 1 subnets
O E2    10.1.1.4 [110/20] via 172.16.1.2, 00:05:42, Ethernet0/0
```

For illustrative purposes, verify that these three routes are in the OSPF database on Router B.

```
rtrB#show ip ospf database external

       OSPF Router with ID (2.2.2.2) (Process ID 1)


                Type-5 AS External Link States

  LS age: 441
  Options: (No TOS-capability, DC)
  LS Type: AS External Link
  Link State ID: 3.3.3.0 (External Network Number )
  Advertising Router: 2.2.2.2
  LS Seq Number: 80000001
  Checksum: 0x3F50
  Length: 36
  Network Mask: /24
        Metric Type: 2 (Larger than any link state path)
        TOS: 0
        Metric: 20
        Forward Address: 0.0.0.0
        External Route Tag: 0

  LS age: 1788
  Options: (No TOS-capability, DC)
  LS Type: AS External Link
  Link State ID: 4.4.4.0 (External Network Number )
  Advertising Router: 2.2.2.2
  LS Seq Number: 80000003
  Checksum: 0x1773
  Length: 36
  Network Mask: /24
        Metric Type: 2 (Larger than any link state path)
        TOS: 0
        Metric: 20
        Forward Address: 0.0.0.0
        External Route Tag: 0

  LS age: 459
  Options: (No TOS-capability, DC)
  LS Type: AS External Link
  Link State ID: 10.1.1.4 (External Network Number )
  Advertising Router: 2.2.2.2
  LS Seq Number: 80000001
  Checksum: 0xD7B3
  Length: 36
  Network Mask: /30
        Metric Type: 2 (Larger than any link state path)
        TOS: 0
        Metric: 20
        Forward Address: 0.0.0.0
        External Route Tag: 0
```

Modify the configuration on Router B to allow only the installation of the EIGRP route 4.4.4.0/24 into the OSPF database using a named access list.

```
Router B

router ospf 1
 redistribute eigrp 1 subnets
 network 2.2.2.2 0.0.0.0 area 1
 network 172.16.1.0 0.0.0.255 area 0
 distribute-list filter-eigrp out eigrp 1
!
ip access-list standard filter-eigrp
 permit 4.4.4.0 0.0.0.255
```

Verification

Verify that the EIGRP routes 10.1.1.4/30 and 3.3.3.0/24 have been blocked from entering the OSPF database on Router B.

```
rtrB#show ip ospf database external

       OSPF Router with ID (2.2.2.2) (Process ID 1)


                Type-5 AS External Link States

  LS age: 419
  Options: (No TOS-capability, DC)
  LS Type: AS External Link
  Link State ID: 4.4.4.0 (External Network Number )
  Advertising Router: 2.2.2.2
  LS Seq Number: 80000004
  Checksum: 0x1574
  Length: 36
  Network Mask: /24
        Metric Type: 2 (Larger than any link state path)
        TOS: 0
        Metric: 20
        Forward Address: 0.0.0.0
        External Route Tag: 0
```

Verify that Router A is receiving only one external type 2 route from Router B.

```
rtrA#show ip route
Codes: C - connected, S - static, I - IGRP, R - RIP, M - mobile, B - BGP
       D - EIGRP, EX - EIGRP external, O - OSPF, IA - OSPF inter area
       N1 - OSPF NSSA external type 1, N2 - OSPF NSSA external type 2
       E1 - OSPF external type 1, E2 - OSPF external type 2, E - EGP
```

continues

```
       i - IS-IS, L1 - IS-IS level-1, L2 - IS-IS level-2, ia - IS-IS inter area
       * - candidate default, U - per-user static route, o - ODR
       P - periodic downloaded static route

Gateway of last resort is not set

     1.0.0.0/32 is subnetted, 1 subnets
C       1.1.1.1 is directly connected, Loopback0
     2.0.0.0/32 is subnetted, 1 subnets
O IA    2.2.2.2 [110/11] via 172.16.1.2, 00:38:45, Ethernet0/0
     4.0.0.0/24 is subnetted, 1 subnets
O E2    4.4.4.0 [110/20] via 172.16.1.2, 00:38:45, Ethernet0/0
     172.16.0.0/24 is subnetted, 1 subnets
C       172.16.1.0 is directly connected, Ethernet0/0
```

Troubleshooting

Step 1 Verify that there is a neighbor relationship between the OSPF routers using the **show ip ospf neighbor** command.

Step 2 Verify that the **distribute-list** command is referencing the correct access list name and routing process.

Step 3 Verify the syntax of the named access list.

Step 4 Verify that the intended routes are in the OSPF database using the command **show ip ospf database external**.

7-11: distribute-list prefix *prefix-list-name* in

Syntax Description:

- *prefix-list-name*—IP prefix list that determines which routes learned via OSPF will be prevented from being installed in the IP routing table.

Purpose: To prevent OSPF learned routes from being installed in the IP routing table. Even though an OSPF route may be prevented from being installed in the IP routing table, the route will still be in the OSPF database and advertised to OSPF neighbors. Therefore, the **distribute** command should be used with other routing protocols such as RIP, IGRP, EIGRP, and BGP.

Initial Cisco IOS Software Release: 12.0

Configuration Example: Preventing OSPF Learned Routes from Being Installed in the IP Routing Table

In Figure 7-7, Router A is receiving the OSPF routes 2.2.2.2, 3.3.3.3, and 4.4.4.4 from Router B. Start by configuring Routers A and B as shown in the listing that follows the figure.

Figure 7-7 *A Distribute List/Prefix List Controls Which OSPF Routes Are Transferred from the OSPF Database into the IP Routing Table*

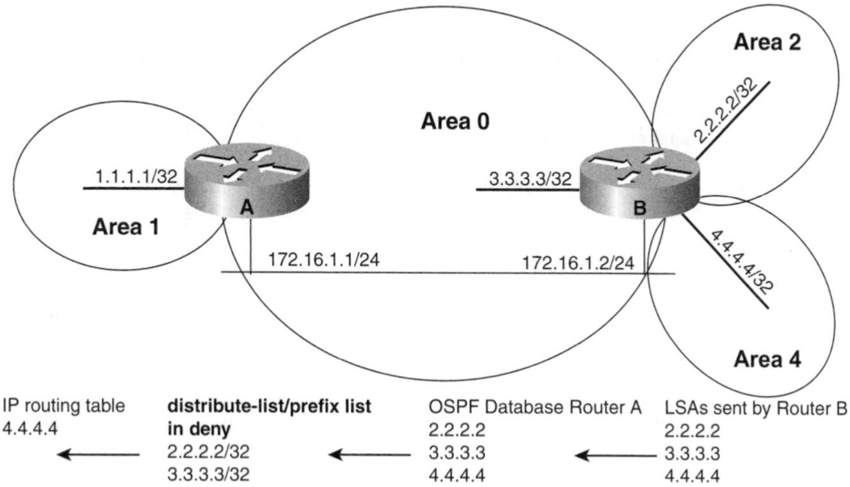


```
Router A

interface Loopback0
 ip address 1.1.1.1 255.255.255.255
!
interface Ethernet0/0
 ip address 172.16.1.1 255.255.255.0
!
router ospf 1
 network 1.1.1.1 0.0.0.0 area 1
 network 172.16.1.0 0.0.0.255 area 0
```

```
Router B

interface Loopback0
 ip address 2.2.2.2 255.255.255.255
!
interface Loopback1
 ip address 3.3.3.3 255.255.255.255
!
interface Loopback2
```

continues

```
 ip address 4.4.4.4 255.255.255.255
!
interface Ethernet0
 ip address 172.16.1.2 255.255.255.0
!
router ospf 1
 router-id 2.2.2.2
 network 2.2.2.2 0.0.0.0 area 2
 network 3.3.3.3 0.0.0.0 area 0
 network 4.4.4.4 0.0.0.0 area 4
 network 172.16.1.2 0.0.0.255 area 0
```

Verify that Routers A and B have established a FULL OSPF neighbor relationship.

```
rtrA#show ip ospf neighbor

Neighbor ID     Pri   State           Dead Time   Address         Interface
2.2.2.2           1   FULL/BDR        00:00:30    172.16.1.2      Ethernet0/0

rtrB#show ip ospf neighbor

Neighbor ID     Pri   State           Dead Time   Address         Interface
1.1.1.1           1   FULL/DR         00:00:38    172.16.1.1      Ethernet0
```

Verify that Router A is receiving routes 2.2.2.2, 3.3.3.3, and 4.4.4.4 from Router B.

```
rtrA#show ip route
Codes: C - connected, S - static, I - IGRP, R - RIP, M - mobile, B - BGP
       D - EIGRP, EX - EIGRP external, O - OSPF, IA - OSPF inter area
       N1 - OSPF NSSA external type 1, N2 - OSPF NSSA external type 2
       E1 - OSPF external type 1, E2 - OSPF external type 2, E - EGP
       i - IS-IS, L1 - IS-IS level-1, L2 - IS-IS level-2, ia - IS-IS inter area
       * - candidate default, U - per-user static route, o - ODR
       P - periodic downloaded static route

Gateway of last resort is not set

     1.0.0.0/32 is subnetted, 1 subnets
C       1.1.1.1 is directly connected, Loopback0
     2.0.0.0/32 is subnetted, 1 subnets
O IA    2.2.2.2 [110/11] via 172.16.1.2, 00:04:28, Ethernet0/0
     3.0.0.0/32 is subnetted, 1 subnets
O       3.3.3.3 [110/11] via 172.16.1.2, 00:04:28, Ethernet0/0
     4.0.0.0/32 is subnetted, 1 subnets
O IA    4.4.4.4 [110/11] via 172.16.1.2, 00:04:28, Ethernet0/0
     172.16.0.0/24 is subnetted, 1 subnets
C       172.16.1.0 is directly connected, Ethernet0/0
```

For illustrative purposes, verify that these three routes are in the OSPF database on Router A.

```
rtrA#show ip ospf database

            OSPF Router with ID (1.1.1.1) (Process ID 1)

                Router Link States (Area 0)

Link ID         ADV Router      Age         Seq#       Checksum Link count
1.1.1.1         1.1.1.1         493         0x800000A5 0x8F6F   1
2.2.2.2         2.2.2.2         489         0x80000030 0x7ECF   2

                Net Link States (Area 0)

Link ID         ADV Router      Age         Seq#       Checksum
172.16.1.1      1.1.1.1         496         0x80000001 0x6DFD

                Summary Net Link States (Area 0)

Link ID         ADV Router      Age         Seq#       Checksum
1.1.1.1         1.1.1.1         714         0x80000033 0xE21F
2.2.2.2         2.2.2.2         487         0x80000049 0x6A79
4.4.4.4         2.2.2.2         490         0x80000001 0x9E85

                Router Link States (Area 1)

Link ID         ADV Router      Age         Seq#       Checksum Link count
1.1.1.1         1.1.1.1         726         0x80000001 0xD351   1

                Summary Net Link States (Area 1)

Link ID         ADV Router      Age         Seq#       Checksum
2.2.2.2         1.1.1.1         492         0x80000001 0x7DA8
3.3.3.3         1.1.1.1         492         0x80000001 0x4FD2
4.4.4.4         1.1.1.1         492         0x80000001 0x21FC
172.16.1.0      1.1.1.1         496         0x80000003 0x3B34
```

Modify the configuration on Router A to prevent the OSPF routes 2.2.2.2 and 3.3.3.3 from being installed in the IP routing table. A 32-bit mask is needed in the prefix list because OSPF is advertising the loopback interfaces as host routes.

```
Router A

router ospf 1
 network 1.1.1.1 0.0.0.0 area 1
 network 172.16.1.0 0.0.0.255 area 0
 distribute-list prefix filter-ospf in
!
```

continues

```
ip prefix-list filter-ospf seq 5 deny 2.2.2.2/32
ip prefix-list filter-ospf seq 10 deny 3.3.3.3/32
ip prefix-list filter-ospf seq 15 permit 0.0.0.0/0
```

Verification

Verify that the OSPF routes 2.2.2.2 and 3.3.3.3 have been blocked from entering the IP routing table on Router A.

```
rtrA#show ip route
Codes: C - connected, S - static, I - IGRP, R - RIP, M - mobile, B - BGP
       D - EIGRP, EX - EIGRP external, O - OSPF, IA - OSPF inter area
       N1 - OSPF NSSA external type 1, N2 - OSPF NSSA external type 2
       E1 - OSPF external type 1, E2 - OSPF external type 2, E - EGP
       i - IS-IS, L1 - IS-IS level-1, L2 - IS-IS level-2, ia - IS-IS inter area
       * - candidate default, U - per-user static route, o - ODR
       P - periodic downloaded static route

Gateway of last resort is not set

     1.0.0.0/32 is subnetted, 1 subnets
C       1.1.1.1 is directly connected, Loopback0
     4.0.0.0/32 is subnetted, 1 subnets
O IA    4.4.4.4 [110/11] via 172.16.1.2, 00:03:39, Ethernet0/0
     172.16.0.0/24 is subnetted, 1 subnets
C       172.16.1.0 is directly connected, Ethernet0/0
```

Verify that routes 2.2.2.2 and 3.3.3.3 are still in the OSPF database on Router A.

```
rtrA#show ip ospf database

            OSPF Router with ID (1.1.1.1) (Process ID 1)

                Router Link States (Area 0)

Link ID         ADV Router      Age         Seq#       Checksum Link count
1.1.1.1         1.1.1.1         951         0x800000A5 0x8F6F   1
2.2.2.2         2.2.2.2         947         0x80000030 0x7ECF   2

                Net Link States (Area 0)

Link ID         ADV Router      Age         Seq#       Checksum
172.16.1.1      1.1.1.1         954         0x80000001 0x6DFD

                Summary Net Link States (Area 0)

Link ID         ADV Router      Age         Seq#       Checksum
1.1.1.1         1.1.1.1         1172        0x80000033 0xE21F
2.2.2.2         2.2.2.2         945         0x80000049 0x6A79
```

```
4.4.4.4         2.2.2.2         948         0x80000001 0x9E85

                Router Link States (Area 1)

Link ID         ADV Router      Age         Seq#       Checksum Link count
1.1.1.1         1.1.1.1         1184        0x80000001 0xD351   1

                Summary Net Link States (Area 1)

Link ID         ADV Router      Age         Seq#       Checksum
3.3.3.3         1.1.1.1         946         0x80000001 0x4FD2
4.4.4.4         1.1.1.1         946         0x80000001 0x21FC
172.16.1.0      1.1.1.1         950         0x80000003 0x3B34
```

Troubleshooting

Step 1 Verify that there is a neighbor relationship between the OSPF routers by using the **show ip ospf neighbor** command.

Step 2 Verify that the **distribute-list** command is referencing the correct IP prefix list.

Step 3 Verify the syntax of the prefix list.

7-12: distribute-list prefix *prefix-list-name* in *interface-type interface-number*

Syntax Description:

- *prefix-list-name*—Named IP prefix list that determines which routes learned via OSPF will be prevented from being installed in the IP routing table.
- *interface-type*—Optional parameter, along with the *interface-number*, used to apply the distribute list to OSPF routes learned through a particular interface.
- *interface-number*—Number of the *interface-type*.

Purpose: To prevent OSPF routes learned over a specific interface from being installed in the IP routing table. Even though an OSPF route may be prevented from being installed in the IP routing table, the route will still be in the OSPF database. The filtered routes may be learned via another OSPF interface and installed in the IP routing table.

Initial Cisco IOS Software Release: 10.0. The *interface-type* and *interface-number* parameters were added in Release 11.2.

Configuration Example: Preventing Routes Learned via OSPF Over a Specific Interface from Being Installed in the IP Routing Table

In Figure 7-8, Router A is receiving the OSPF routes 2.2.2.2, 3.3.3.3, and 4.4.4.4 from Router B over two serial interfaces. Start by configuring Routers A and B as shown in the listing that follows the figure.

Figure 7-8 *A Distribute List/Prefix List Controls Which OSPF Routes, Learned Over a Specific Interface, Are Transferred from the OSPF Database into the IP Routing Table*

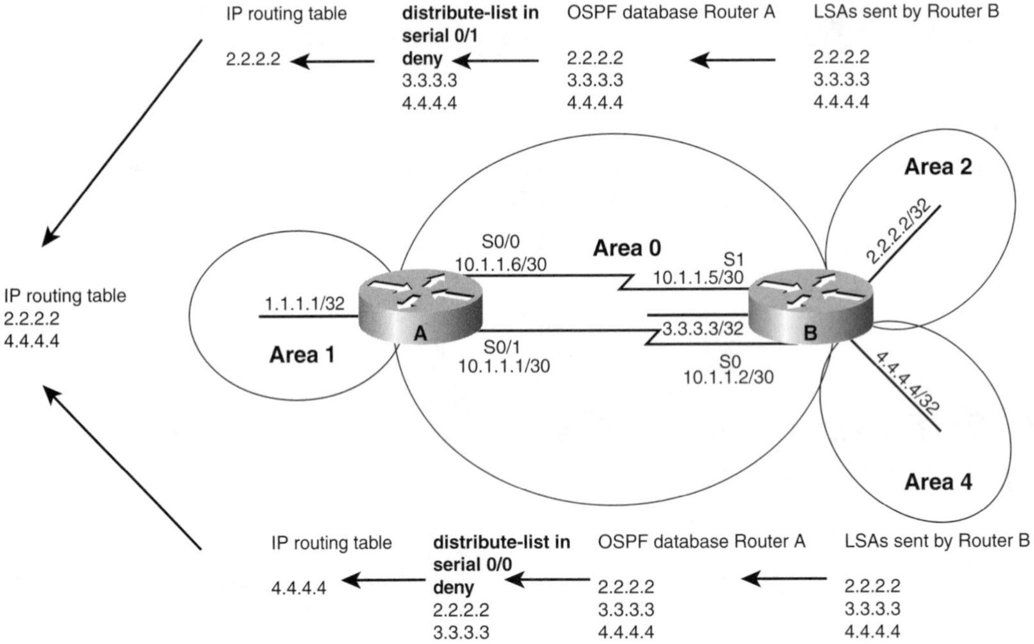


```
Router A

interface Loopback0
 ip address 1.1.1.1 255.255.255.255
!
interface Serial0/0
 ip address 10.1.1.6 255.255.255.252
 no ip mroute-cache
!
interface Serial0/1
 ip address 10.1.1.1 255.255.255.252
 clockrate 64000
!
router ospf 1
 network 1.1.1.1 0.0.0.0 area 1
```

```
 network 10.1.1.0 0.0.0.3 area 0
 network 10.1.1.4 0.0.0.3 area 0
```

```
Router B

interface Loopback0
 ip address 2.2.2.2 255.255.255.255
!
interface Loopback1
 ip address 3.3.3.3 255.255.255.255
!
interface Loopback2
 ip address 4.4.4.4 255.255.255.255
!
interface Serial0
 ip address 10.1.1.2 255.255.255.252
!
interface Serial1
 bandwidth 64
 ip address 10.1.1.5 255.255.255.252
 clockrate 64000
!
router ospf 1
 router-id 2.2.2.2
 network 2.2.2.2 0.0.0.0 area 2
 network 3.3.3.3 0.0.0.0 area 0
 network 4.4.4.4 0.0.0.0 area 4
 network 10.1.1.0 0.0.0.3 area 0
 network 10.1.1.4 0.0.0.3 area 0
```

Verify that Routers A and B have established a FULL OSPF neighbor relationship.

```
rtrA#show ip ospf neighbor

Neighbor ID     Pri   State           Dead Time   Address         Interface
2.2.2.2           1   FULL/  -        00:00:34    10.1.1.5        Serial0/0
2.2.2.2           1   FULL/  -        00:00:38    10.1.1.2        Serial0/1

rtrB#show ip ospf neighbor

Neighbor ID     Pri   State           Dead Time   Address         Interface
1.1.1.1           1   FULL/  -        00:00:32    10.1.1.1        Serial0
1.1.1.1           1   FULL/  -        00:00:30    10.1.1.6        Serial1
```

Verify that Router A is receiving routes 2.2.2.2, 3.3.3.3, and 4.4.4.4 from Router B.

```
rtrA#show ip route
Codes: C - connected, S - static, I - IGRP, R - RIP, M - mobile, B - BGP
       D - EIGRP, EX - EIGRP external, O - OSPF, IA - OSPF inter area
       N1 - OSPF NSSA external type 1, N2 - OSPF NSSA external type 2
       E1 - OSPF external type 1, E2 - OSPF external type 2, E - EGP
       i - IS-IS, L1 - IS-IS level-1, L2 - IS-IS level-2, ia - IS-IS inter area
       * - candidate default, U - per-user static route, o - ODR
       P - periodic downloaded static route

Gateway of last resort is not set

     1.0.0.0/32 is subnetted, 1 subnets
C       1.1.1.1 is directly connected, Loopback0
     2.0.0.0/32 is subnetted, 1 subnets
O IA    2.2.2.2 [110/65] via 10.1.1.5, 00:00:10, Serial0/0
                [110/65] via 10.1.1.2, 00:00:10, Serial0/1
     3.0.0.0/32 is subnetted, 1 subnets
O       3.3.3.3 [110/65] via 10.1.1.5, 00:00:10, Serial0/0
                [110/65] via 10.1.1.2, 00:00:10, Serial0/1
     4.0.0.0/32 is subnetted, 1 subnets
O IA    4.4.4.4 [110/65] via 10.1.1.5, 00:00:10, Serial0/0
                [110/65] via 10.1.1.2, 00:00:11, Serial0/1
     172.16.0.0/24 is subnetted, 1 subnets
C       172.16.1.0 is directly connected, Ethernet0/0
     10.0.0.0/30 is subnetted, 2 subnets
C       10.1.1.0 is directly connected, Serial0/1
C       10.1.1.4 is directly connected, Serial0/0
```

For illustrative purposes, verify that these three routes are in the OSPF database on Router A.

```
rtrA#show ip ospf database

            OSPF Router with ID (1.1.1.1) (Process ID 1)

                Router Link States (Area 0)


1.1.1.1         1.1.1.1         1423        0x800000C1 0xE80E   4
2.2.2.2         2.2.2.2         1451        0x80000050 0xA7E3   5

                Summary Net Link States (Area 0)

Link ID         ADV Router      Age         Seq#       Checksum
1.1.1.1         1.1.1.1         165         0x80000044 0xC030
2.2.2.2         2.2.2.2         707         0x80000057 0x4E87
4.4.4.4         2.2.2.2         707         0x8000000F 0x8293
```

```
                 Router Link States (Area 1)

Link ID          ADV Router       Age         Seq#         Checksum Link count
1.1.1.1          1.1.1.1          1666        0x80000008 0xC558   1

                 Summary Net Link States (Area 1)

Link ID          ADV Router       Age         Seq#         Checksum
2.2.2.2          1.1.1.1          1423        0x80000006 0x9159
3.3.3.3          1.1.1.1          1669        0x80000009 0x5D86
4.4.4.4          1.1.1.1          1669        0x80000009 0x2FB0
10.1.1.0         1.1.1.1          168         0x80000007 0x36B3
10.1.1.4         1.1.1.1          1425        0x80000008 0xCD8
```

Modify the configuration on Router A to prevent the OSPF routes 2.2.2.2 and 3.3.3.3, received over interface Serial 0/0, and the routes 3.3.3.3 and 4.4.4.4, received over Serial 0/1, from being installed in the IP routing table.

```
Router A

router ospf 1
 network 1.1.1.1 0.0.0.0 area 1
 network 172.16.1.0 0.0.0.255 area 0
 distribute-list prefix filter-ospf1 in Serial0/0
 distribute-list prefix filter-ospf2 in Serial0/1
!
ip prefix-list filter-ospf1 seq 5 deny 2.2.2.2/32
ip prefix-list filter-ospf1 seq 10 deny 3.3.3.3/32
ip prefix-list filter-ospf1 seq 15 permit 0.0.0.0/0
!
ip prefix-list filter-ospf2 seq 5 deny 3.3.3.3/32
ip prefix-list filter-ospf2 seq 10 deny 4.4.4.4/32
ip prefix-list filter-ospf2 seq 15 permit 0.0.0.0/0
```

Verification

Determine the routes that have been filtered from reaching the IP routing table on Router A.

```
rtrA#show ip route
Codes: C - connected, S - static, I - IGRP, R - RIP, M - mobile, B - BGP
       D - EIGRP, EX - EIGRP external, O - OSPF, IA - OSPF inter area
       N1 - OSPF NSSA external type 1, N2 - OSPF NSSA external type 2
       E1 - OSPF external type 1, E2 - OSPF external type 2, E - EGP
       i - IS-IS, L1 - IS-IS level-1, L2 - IS-IS level-2, ia - IS-IS inter area
       * - candidate default, U - per-user static route, o - ODR
       P - periodic downloaded static route

Gateway of last resort is not set
```

continues

```
     1.0.0.0/32 is subnetted, 1 subnets
C       1.1.1.1 is directly connected, Loopback0
     2.0.0.0/32 is subnetted, 1 subnets
O IA    2.2.2.2 [110/65] via 10.1.1.2, 00:01:15, Serial0/1
     4.0.0.0/32 is subnetted, 1 subnets
O IA    4.4.4.4 [110/65] via 10.1.1.5, 00:01:15, Serial0/0
     10.0.0.0/30 is subnetted, 2 subnets
C       10.1.1.0 is directly connected, Serial0/1
C       10.1.1.4 is directly connected, Serial0/0
```

ip prefix-list filter-ospf1 denies networks 2.2.2.2 and 3.3.3.3. **ip prefix-list filter-ospf2** denies networks 3.3.3.3 and 4.4.4.4. The only network that is denied by both prefix lists is 3.3.3.3. Verify that routes 2.2.2.2, 3.3.3.3, and 4.4.4.4 are still in the OSPF database on Router A.

```
rtrA#show ip ospf database

            OSPF Router with ID (1.1.1.1) (Process ID 1)

                Router Link States (Area 0)

Link ID         ADV Router      Age         Seq#       Checksum Link count
1.1.1.1         1.1.1.1         1815        0x800000C1 0xE80E   4
2.2.2.2         2.2.2.2         1843        0x80000050 0xA7E3   5

                Summary Net Link States (Area 0)

Link ID         ADV Router      Age         Seq#       Checksum
1.1.1.1         1.1.1.1         557         0x80000044 0xC030
2.2.2.2         2.2.2.2         1099        0x80000057 0x4E87
4.4.4.4         2.2.2.2         1099        0x8000000F 0x8293

                Router Link States (Area 1)

Link ID         ADV Router      Age         Seq#       Checksum Link count
1.1.1.1         1.1.1.1         43          0x80000009 0xC359   1

                Summary Net Link States (Area 1)

Link ID         ADV Router      Age         Seq#       Checksum
2.2.2.2         1.1.1.1         1815        0x80000006 0x9159
3.3.3.3         1.1.1.1         45          0x8000000A 0x5B87
4.4.4.4         1.1.1.1         45          0x8000000A 0x2DB1
10.1.1.0        1.1.1.1         559         0x80000007 0x36B3
10.1.1.4        1.1.1.1         1816        0x80000008 0xCD8
```

Troubleshooting

Step 1 Verify that there is a neighbor relationship between the OSPF routers by using the **show ip ospf neighbor** command.

Step 2 Verify that the **distribute-list** command is referencing the correct IP prefix list and interface.

Step 3 Verify the syntax of the prefix list.

7-13: distribute-list prefix *prefix-list-name* out

Syntax Description:

- *prefix-list-name*—Standard named IP prefix list that determines which routes learned via OSPF will be prevented from being installed in the IP routing table.

Purpose: For distance vector protocols (RIP, IGRP, EIGRP) this command prevents routes selected by the named prefix list from being advertised to a neighbor. OSPF is a link-state protocol and does not advertise routes to a neighbor but advertises a link-state database. The neighbor determines the routes from the information in the link-state database. Therefore, this command has no effect when used with OSPF.

Initial Cisco IOS Software Release: 11.2

7-14: distribute-list prefix *prefix-list-name* out *interface-type interface-number*

Syntax Description:

- *prefix-list-name*—Named IP prefix list that determines which routes learned via OSPF will be prevented from being installed in the IP routing table.
- *interface-type*—Optional parameter, along with the *interface-number*, used to apply the distribute list to OSPF routes learned through a particular interface.
- *interface-number*—Number of the *interface-type*.

Purpose: For distance vector protocols (RIP, IGRP, EIGRP) this command prevents routes selected by the named prefix list from being advertised to a neighbor. OSPF is a link-state protocol and does not advertise routes to a neighbor, but advertises a link-state database. The neighbor determines the routes from the information in the link-state database. Therefore, this command has no effect when used with OSPF.

Initial Cisco IOS Software Release: 12.0.

7-15: distribute-list prefix *prefix-list-name* out *routing-process*

Syntax Description:

- *prefix-list-name*—IP prefix list name that determines which routes redistributed into OSPF will be prevented from being installed in the OSPF database. This has the effect of preventing the blocked redistributed routes from being advertised to OSPF neighbors.
- *routing-process*—The routing process that has been redistributed into OSPF (RIP, IGRP, EIGRP, OSPF, BGP, EGP, static, or connected).

Purpose: To prevent routes that were redistributed into OSPF from another routing process from being installed in the OSPF database.

Initial Cisco IOS Software Release: 11.2

Configuration Example: Preventing Routes Redistributed into OSPF from Being Installed in the OSPF Database

In Figure 7-9, Router B is receiving the EIGRP routes 10.1.1.4/30, 3.3.3.0/24, and 4.4.4.0/24 from Router C. Router B is redistributing EIGRP into OSPF, and these routes will be advertised to Router A as OSPF external type 2 routes. Start by configuring Routers A, B, and C as shown in the listing that follows the figure.

Figure 7-9 *A Distribute List/Prefix List Prevents Redistributed Routes from Being Installed in the OSPF Database*

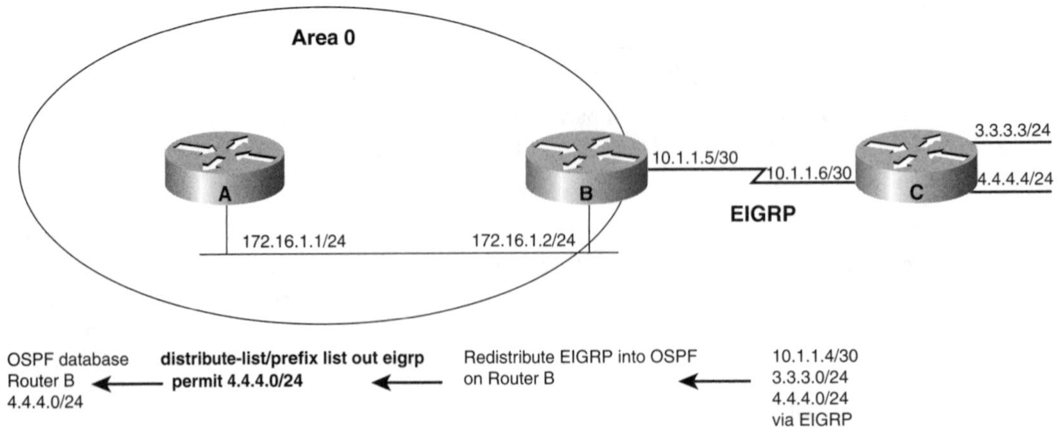

```
Router A

interface Loopback0
 ip address 1.1.1.1 255.255.255.255
!
interface Ethernet0/0
 ip address 172.16.1.1 255.255.255.0
!
router ospf 1
 network 172.16.1.0 0.0.0.255 area 0
```

```
Router B

interface Loopback0
 ip address 2.2.2.2 255.255.255.255
!
interface Ethernet0
 ip address 172.16.1.2 255.255.255.0
!
interface Serial1
 bandwidth 64
 ip address 10.1.1.5 255.255.255.252
 clockrate 64000
!
router eigrp 1
 network 10.0.0.0
!
router ospf 1
 redistribute eigrp 1 subnets
 network 2.2.2.2 0.0.0.0 area 1
 network 172.16.1.0 0.0.0.255 area 0
```

```
Router C

interface Loopback0
 ip address 3.3.3.3 255.255.255.0
!
interface Loopback1
 ip address 4.4.4.4 255.255.255.0
!
interface Serial0
 ip address 10.1.1.6 255.255.255.252
!
router eigrp 1
 network 3.0.0.0
 network 4.0.0.0
 network 10.0.0.0
 no auto-summary
```

Verify that Routers A and B have established a FULL OSPF neighbor relationship.

```
rtrA#show ip ospf neighbor

Neighbor ID     Pri   State           Dead Time   Address         Interface
2.2.2.2           1   FULL/BDR        00:00:30    172.16.1.2      Ethernet0/0
```

```
rtrB#show ip ospf neighbor

Neighbor ID     Pri   State           Dead Time   Address         Interface
1.1.1.1           1   FULL/DR         00:00:38    172.16.1.1      Ethernet0
```

Verify that Router B is receiving routes 3.3.3.0/24 and 4.4.4.0/24 from Router C via EIGRP.

```
rtrB# show ip route
Codes: C - connected, S - static, I - IGRP, R - RIP, M - mobile, B - BGP
       D - EIGRP, EX - EIGRP external, O - OSPF, IA - OSPF inter area
       N1 - OSPF NSSA external type 1, N2 - OSPF NSSA external type 2
       E1 - OSPF external type 1, E2 - OSPF external type 2, E - EGP
       i - IS-IS, L1 - IS-IS level-1, L2 - IS-IS level-2, * - candidate default
       U - per-user static route, o - ODR

Gateway of last resort is not set

     2.0.0.0/32 is subnetted, 1 subnets
C       2.2.2.2 is directly connected, Loopback0
     3.0.0.0/24 is subnetted, 1 subnets
D       3.3.3.0 [90/40640000] via 10.1.1.6, 00:38:45, Serial1
     4.0.0.0/24 is subnetted, 1 subnets
D       4.4.4.0 [90/40640000] via 10.1.1.6, 00:38:45, Serial1
     172.16.0.0/24 is subnetted, 1 subnets
C       172.16.1.0 is directly connected, Ethernet0
     10.0.0.0/30 is subnetted, 1 subnets
C       10.1.1.4 is directly connected, Serial1
```

Verify that Router A is receiving routes 10.1.1.4/30, 3.3.3.0/24, and 4.4.4.0/24 from Router B as OSPF external type 2 routes.

```
rtrA#show ip route
Codes: C - connected, S - static, I - IGRP, R - RIP, M - mobile, B - BGP
       D - EIGRP, EX - EIGRP external, O - OSPF, IA - OSPF inter area
       N1 - OSPF NSSA external type 1, N2 - OSPF NSSA external type 2
       E1 - OSPF external type 1, E2 - OSPF external type 2, E - EGP
       i - IS-IS, L1 - IS-IS level-1, L2 - IS-IS level-2, ia - IS-IS inter area
       * - candidate default, U - per-user static route, o - ODR
       P - periodic downloaded static route

Gateway of last resort is not set
```

```
     1.0.0.0/32 is subnetted, 1 subnets
C       1.1.1.1 is directly connected, Loopback0
     2.0.0.0/32 is subnetted, 1 subnets
O IA    2.2.2.2 [110/11] via 172.16.1.2, 00:27:48, Ethernet0/0
     3.0.0.0/24 is subnetted, 1 subnets
O E2    3.3.3.0 [110/20] via 172.16.1.2, 00:05:41, Ethernet0/0
     4.0.0.0/24 is subnetted, 1 subnets
O E2    4.4.4.0 [110/20] via 172.16.1.2, 00:27:48, Ethernet0/0
     172.16.0.0/24 is subnetted, 1 subnets
C       172.16.1.0 is directly connected, Ethernet0/0
     10.0.0.0/30 is subnetted, 1 subnets
O E2    10.1.1.4 [110/20] via 172.16.1.2, 00:05:42, Ethernet0/0
```

For illustrative purposes, verify that these three routes are in the OSPF database on Router B.

```
rtrB#show ip ospf database external

       OSPF Router with ID (2.2.2.2) (Process ID 1)


                Type-5 AS External Link States

  LS age: 441
  Options: (No TOS-capability, DC)
  LS Type: AS External Link
  Link State ID: 3.3.3.0 (External Network Number )
  Advertising Router: 2.2.2.2
  LS Seq Number: 80000001
  Checksum: 0x3F50
  Length: 36
  Network Mask: /24
        Metric Type: 2 (Larger than any link state path)
        TOS: 0
        Metric: 20
        Forward Address: 0.0.0.0
        External Route Tag: 0

  LS age: 1788
  Options: (No TOS-capability, DC)
  LS Type: AS External Link
  Link State ID: 4.4.4.0 (External Network Number )
  Advertising Router: 2.2.2.2
  LS Seq Number: 80000003
  Checksum: 0x1773
  Length: 36
  Network Mask: /24
        Metric Type: 2 (Larger than any link state path)
        TOS: 0
        Metric: 20
```

continues

```
        Forward Address: 0.0.0.0
        External Route Tag: 0

  LS age: 459
  Options: (No TOS-capability, DC)
  LS Type: AS External Link
  Link State ID: 10.1.1.4 (External Network Number )
  Advertising Router: 2.2.2.2
  LS Seq Number: 80000001
  Checksum: 0xD7B3
  Length: 36
  Network Mask: /30
        Metric Type: 2 (Larger than any link state path)
        TOS: 0
        Metric: 20
        Forward Address: 0.0.0.0
        External Route Tag: 0
```

Modify the configuration on Router B to allow only the installation of the EIGRP route 4.4.4.0/24 into the OSPF database using an IP prefix list.

```
Router B

router ospf 1
 redistribute eigrp 1 subnets
 network 2.2.2.2 0.0.0.0 area 1
 network 172.16.1.0 0.0.0.255 area 0
 distribute-list prefix filter-eigrp out eigrp 1
!
ip prefix-list filter-eigrp seq 5 permit 4.4.4.0/24
```

Verification

Verify that the EIGRP routes 10.1.1.4/30 and 3.3.3.0/24 have been blocked from entering the OSPF database on Router B.

```
rtrB#show ip ospf database external

       OSPF Router with ID (2.2.2.2) (Process ID 1)


                Type-5 AS External Link States

  LS age: 419
  Options: (No TOS-capability, DC)
  LS Type: AS External Link
  Link State ID: 4.4.4.0 (External Network Number )
  Advertising Router: 2.2.2.2
  LS Seq Number: 80000004
```

```
  Checksum: 0x1574
  Length: 36
  Network Mask: /24
        Metric Type: 2 (Larger than any link state path)
        TOS: 0
        Metric: 20
        Forward Address: 0.0.0.0
        External Route Tag: 0
```

Verify that Router A is receiving only one external type 2 route from Router B.

```
rtrA#show ip route
Codes: C - connected, S - static, I - IGRP, R - RIP, M - mobile, B - BGP
       D - EIGRP, EX - EIGRP external, O - OSPF, IA - OSPF inter area
       N1 - OSPF NSSA external type 1, N2 - OSPF NSSA external type 2
       E1 - OSPF external type 1, E2 - OSPF external type 2, E - EGP
       i - IS-IS, L1 - IS-IS level-1, L2 - IS-IS level-2, ia - IS-IS inter area
       * - candidate default, U - per-user static route, o - ODR
       P - periodic downloaded static route

Gateway of last resort is not set

     1.0.0.0/32 is subnetted, 1 subnets
C       1.1.1.1 is directly connected, Loopback0
     2.0.0.0/32 is subnetted, 1 subnets
O IA    2.2.2.2 [110/11] via 172.16.1.2, 00:38:45, Ethernet0/0
     4.0.0.0/24 is subnetted, 1 subnets
O E2    4.4.4.0 [110/20] via 172.16.1.2, 00:38:45, Ethernet0/0
     172.16.0.0/24 is subnetted, 1 subnets
C       172.16.1.0 is directly connected, Ethernet0/0
```

Troubleshooting

Step 1 Verify that there is a neighbor relationship between the OSPF routers by using the **show ip ospf neighbor** command.

Step 2 Verify that the **distribute-list** command is referencing the correct prefix list name and routing process.

Step 3 Verify the syntax of the prefix list.

Step 4 Verify that the intended routes are in the OSPF database by using the command **show ip ospf database external**.

CHAPTER 8

Handling of MOSPF LSAs

8-1: ignore lsa mospf

Syntax Description:

This command has no arguments.

Purpose: Cisco routers do not support Multicast OSPF (MOSPF). By default, if a type 6 MOSPF LSA is received, the router generates a syslog message. This command prevents the generation of a syslog message when a type 6 LSA is received.

Initial Cisco IOS Software Release: 11.1

CHAPTER 9

Logging OSPF Neighbor Changes

9-1: log-adjacency-changes

9-2: log adjacency-changes detail

Syntax Description:

This command has no arguments.

Purpose: To enable the logging of changes in an OSPF neighbor's status. If the UNIX syslog facility is enabled, messages can be sent to a UNIX host running the syslog daemon. If you are not using the UNIX syslog facility, then the status change messages are stored in the router's internal buffer. This command is an excellent tool for troubleshooting OSPF.

Initial Cisco IOS Software Release: 11.2. The **detail** keyword was added in 12.1.

Configuration Example 1: Enabling OSPF Neighbor Status-Change Logging to the Console

To enable the display of OSPF neighbor status-change events on the console, use the following configuration.

```
router ospf 1
 log-adjacency-changes
```

Verification

When the state of an OSPF neighbor changes, the events are displayed on the console. For example, if you execute the command **clear ip ospf process** on an OSPF neighbor, the following output should be displayed.

```
rtrA#clear ip ospf process
Reset ALL OSPF processes? [no]: y
rtrA#
00:52:14: %OSPF-5-ADJCHG: Process 1, Nbr 2.2.2.2 on Ethernet0/0 from FULL to DOW
N, Neighbor Down: Interface down or detached
00:52:23: %OSPF-5-ADJCHG: Process 1, Nbr 2.2.2.2 on Ethernet0/0 from LOADING to
FULL, Loading Done
```

If the keyword **detail** is used, then complete information regarding the neighbor status will be logged.

```
router ospf 1
 log-adjacency-changes detail

rtrA#clear ip ospf process
Reset ALL OSPF processes? [no]: yes
rtrA#
00:50:12: %OSPF-5-ADJCHG: Process 1, Nbr 2.2.2.2 on Ethernet0/0 from FULL to DOW
N, Neighbor Down: Interface down or detached
00:50:13: %OSPF-5-ADJCHG: Process 1, Nbr 2.2.2.2 on Ethernet0/0 from DOWN to INI
T, Received Hello
00:50:13: %OSPF-5-ADJCHG: Process 1, Nbr 2.2.2.2 on Ethernet0/0 from INIT to 2WA
Y, 2-Way Received
00:50:13: %OSPF-5-ADJCHG: Process 1, Nbr 2.2.2.2 on Ethernet0/0 from 2WAY to EXS
TART, AdjOK?
00:50:13: %OSPF-5-ADJCHG: Process 1, Nbr 2.2.2.2 on Ethernet0/0 from EXSTART to
EXCHANGE, Negotiation Done
00:50:13: %OSPF-5-ADJCHG: Process 1, Nbr 2.2.2.2 on Ethernet0/0 from EXCHANGE to
 LOADING, Exchange Done
00:50:13: %OSPF-5-ADJCHG: Process 1, Nbr 2.2.2.2 on Ethernet0/0 from LOADING to
FULL, Loading Done
```

Configuration Example 2: Enabling OSPF Neighbor Status-Change Logging to Memory

Use the following configuration to enable the logging of OSPF neighbor status-change events to memory.

```
logging buffered 4096 debugging
!
router ospf 1
 log-adjacency-changes detail
```

The parameters **4096** and **debugging** are default values and are supplied by the router when you use the command **logging buffered**. The default values vary by platform.

Verification

The **show logging** command displays the status of buffered logging. If logging is enabled, then the contents of the buffer will be displayed.

```
rtrA#show logging
Syslog logging: enabled (0 messages dropped, 0 messages rate-limited, 0 flushes,
 0 overruns)
    Console logging: level debugging, 67 messages logged
    Monitor logging: level debugging, 0 messages logged
    Buffer logging: level debugging, 8 messages logged
    Logging Exception size (4096 bytes)
    Trap logging: level informational, 71 message lines logged

Log Buffer (4096 bytes):

00:56:38: %OSPF-5-ADJCHG: Process 1, Nbr 2.2.2.2 on Ethernet0/0 from FULL to DOW
N, Neighbor Down: Interface down or detached
00:56:43: %OSPF-5-ADJCHG: Process 1, Nbr 2.2.2.2 on Ethernet0/0 from DOWN to INI
T, Received Hello
00:56:43: %OSPF-5-ADJCHG: Process 1, Nbr 2.2.2.2 on Ethernet0/0 from INIT to 2WA
Y, 2-Way Received
00:56:43: %OSPF-5-ADJCHG: Process 1, Nbr 2.2.2.2 on Ethernet0/0 from 2WAY to EXS
TART, AdjOK?
00:56:43: %OSPF-5-ADJCHG: Process 1, Nbr 2.2.2.2 on Ethernet0/0 from EXSTART to
EXCHANGE, Negotiation Done
00:56:43: %OSPF-5-ADJCHG: Process 1, Nbr 2.2.2.2 on Ethernet0/0 from EXCHANGE to
 LOADING, Exchange Done
00:56:43: %OSPF-5-ADJCHG: Process 1, Nbr 2.2.2.2 on Ethernet0/0 from LOADING to
FULL, Loading Done
```

Troubleshooting

Step 1 Verify that the OSPF neighbors have established a relationship.

Step 2 Verify that buffered logging is enabled using the **show logging** command.

CHAPTER 10

Multiple Path Configuration

10-1: maximum-paths *number-of-paths*

Syntax Description:

- *number-of-paths*—Determines the number of parallel equal-cost paths to the same destination that OSPF will install in the IP routing table. The range of values is 1 to 6. The default is 4 paths.

Purpose: To configure the number of equal-cost parallel paths that OSPF will install in the IP routing table.

Initial Cisco IOS Software Release: 11.2

Configuration Example: Setting the Maximum Number of Equal-Cost Paths That OSPF Will Install in the IP Routing Table

In Figure 10-1, Router A has two parallel equal-cost paths to the loopback network on Router B. By default, OSPF will install both paths in the IP routing table. Configure Routers A and B as shown in the following lines of code.

Figure 10-1 *OSPF Can Install Up to Six Parallel Equal-Cost Paths in the IP Routing Table*

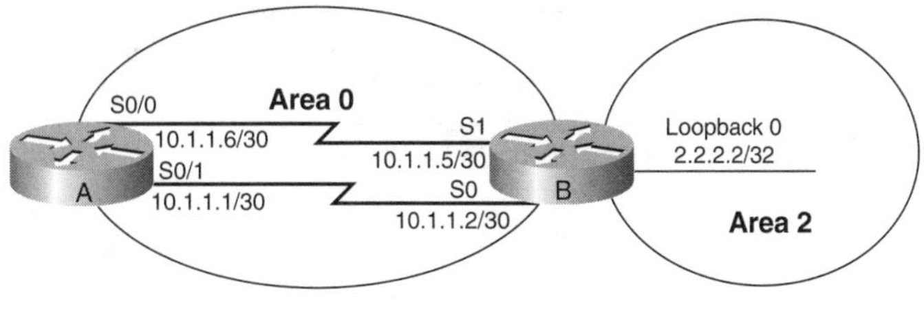

```
Router A
interface Serial0/0
 bandwidth 64
 ip address 10.1.1.6 255.255.255.252
!
interface Serial0/1
 bandwidth 64
 ip address 10.1.1.1 255.255.255.252
 clockrate 64000
!
router ospf 1
 network 10.1.1.0 0.0.0.3 area 0
 network 10.1.1.4 0.0.0.3 area 0
```

```
Router B
interface Loopback0
 ip address 2.2.2.2 255.255.255.255
!
interface Serial0
 bandwidth 64
 ip address 10.1.1.2 255.255.255.252
!
interface Serial1
 bandwidth 64
 ip address 10.1.1.5 255.255.255.252
!
router ospf 1
 network 10.1.1.0 0.0.0.3 area 0
 network 10.1.1.4 0.0.0.3 area 0
 network 2.2.2.2 0.0.0.0 area 2
```

Verify that OSPF on Router A has installed the two paths to network 2.2.2.2 on Router B.

```
rtrA#show ip route
Codes: C - connected, S - static, I - IGRP, R - RIP, M - mobile, B - BGP
       D - EIGRP, EX - EIGRP external, O - OSPF, IA - OSPF inter area
       N1 - OSPF NSSA external type 1, N2 - OSPF NSSA external type 2
       E1 - OSPF external type 1, E2 - OSPF external type 2, E - EGP
       i - IS-IS, L1 - IS-IS level-1, L2 - IS-IS level-2, ia - IS-IS inter area
       * - candidate default, U - per-user static route, o - ODR
       P - periodic downloaded static route

Gateway of last resort is not set

     1.0.0.0/32 is subnetted, 1 subnets
C       1.1.1.1 is directly connected, Loopback0
     2.0.0.0/32 is subnetted, 1 subnets
O IA    2.2.2.2 [110/1563] via 10.1.1.5, 00:00:36, Serial0/0
                [110/1563] via 10.1.1.2, 00:00:36, Serial0/1
     10.0.0.0/30 is subnetted, 2 subnets
C       10.1.1.0 is directly connected, Serial0/1
C       10.1.1.4 is directly connected, Serial0/0
```

To prove that the paths must have equal cost, change the bandwidth on Serial 0/1 on Router A to 63.

```
Router A
interface Serial0/0
 bandwidth 63
 ip address 10.1.1.6 255.255.255.252
```

The OSPF cost for Serial 0/0 is now 100,000,000/63,000 = 1587. The OSPF cost of Serial 0/1 is 100,000,000/64,000 = 1562. Display the routing table on Router A to determine the effect of changing the cost of interface Serial 0/0.

```
rtrA#show ip route
Codes: C - connected, S - static, I - IGRP, R - RIP, M - mobile, B - BGP
       D - EIGRP, EX - EIGRP external, O - OSPF, IA - OSPF inter area
       N1 - OSPF NSSA external type 1, N2 - OSPF NSSA external type 2
       E1 - OSPF external type 1, E2 - OSPF external type 2, E - EGP
       i - IS-IS, L1 - IS-IS level-1, L2 - IS-IS level-2, ia - IS-IS inter area
       * - candidate default, U - per-user static route, o - ODR
       P - periodic downloaded static route

Gateway of last resort is not set

     1.0.0.0/32 is subnetted, 1 subnets
C       1.1.1.1 is directly connected, Loopback0
     2.0.0.0/32 is subnetted, 1 subnets
O IA    2.2.2.2 [110/1563] via 10.1.1.2, 00:04:27, Serial0/1
     10.0.0.0/30 is subnetted, 2 subnets
C       10.1.1.0 is directly connected, Serial0/1
C       10.1.1.4 is directly connected, Serial0/0
```

The cost of the two paths to reach 2.2.2.2 on Router B is no longer equal, so OSPF will install the route with the lowest cost.

What happens if OSPF has more equal-cost paths to a destination than are allowed by the **maximum-paths** command? In Figure 10-1 there are two equal-cost paths to network 2.2.2.2 (if we reset the bandwidth on Serial 0/0 to 64). If we set the maximum paths variable to 1, which path will be installed in the IP routing table? Modify the configuration on Router A so Serial 0/0 has a bandwidth of 64 and the **maximum-paths** variable is set to 1.

```
Router A
interface Serial0/0
 bandwidth 64
 ip address 10.1.1.6 255.255.255.252
!
router ospf 1
 network 10.1.1.0 0.0.0.3 area 0
 network 10.1.1.4 0.0.0.3 area 0
 maximum-paths 1
```

Verification

Verify that OSPF has installed only one route to 2.2.2.2 on Router A.

```
rtrA#show ip route
Codes: C - connected, S - static, I - IGRP, R - RIP, M - mobile, B - BGP
       D - EIGRP, EX - EIGRP external, O - OSPF, IA - OSPF inter area
       N1 - OSPF NSSA external type 1, N2 - OSPF NSSA external type 2
       E1 - OSPF external type 1, E2 - OSPF external type 2, E - EGP
       i - IS-IS, L1 - IS-IS level-1, L2 - IS-IS level-2, ia - IS-IS inter area
       * - candidate default, U - per-user static route, o - ODR
       P - periodic downloaded static route

Gateway of last resort is not set

     1.0.0.0/32 is subnetted, 1 subnets
C       1.1.1.1 is directly connected, Loopback0
     2.0.0.0/32 is subnetted, 1 subnets
O IA    2.2.2.2 [110/1563] via 10.1.1.2, 00:02:00, Serial0/1
     10.0.0.0/30 is subnetted, 2 subnets
C       10.1.1.0 is directly connected, Serial0/1
C       10.1.1.4 is directly connected, Serial0/0
```

Troubleshooting

Nothing should go wrong with this command if configured correctly (famous last words?).

CHAPTER 11

OSPF neighbor Commands

11-1: neighbor *ip-address*

Syntax Description:

- *ip-address*—IP address of the OSPF neighbor. If a secondary address is used on the interface, then the primary address must be used with this command.

Purpose: To configure OSPF neighbors over a nonbroadcast multiaccess (NBMA) network such as Frame Relay or X.25.

Initial Cisco IOS Software Release: 10.0 (12.0 for multipoint networks)

Configuration Example 1: Using the neighbor Command to Enable OSPF on an NBMA

OSPF treats an NBMA network like any other broadcast network such as Ethernet. Because of this, OSPF thinks the network has broadcast capabilities even though it does not. This lack of a broadcast capability necessitates the use of the **neighbor** command to establish an OSPF neighbor. Prior to the introduction of the **ip ospf network** interface commands (see Sections 19-11 through 19-14) the **neighbor** command was used to configure OSPF neighbors over NBMA networks such as X.25 and Frame Relay. The **ip ospf network** interface commands have removed the necessity of using the **neighbor** command, but an understanding of the use of the **neighbor** command will reinforce the concepts covered in Sections 19-11 through 19-14. Figure 11-1 shows the topology that is used in this chapter to demonstrate the use of the OSPF **neighbor** command. A Cisco router has been configured as a Frame Relay switch in order to demonstrate the behavior of OSPF over an NBMA network. The configuration for the Frame Relay switch is shown in the listing that follows the figure. The four interfaces on the Frame Relay switch are fully meshed with the DLCIs shown in Figure 11-1.

Figure 11-1 *Fully Meshed Frame Relay Switch Used to Demonstrate the Use of the OSPF* **neighbor** *Command*

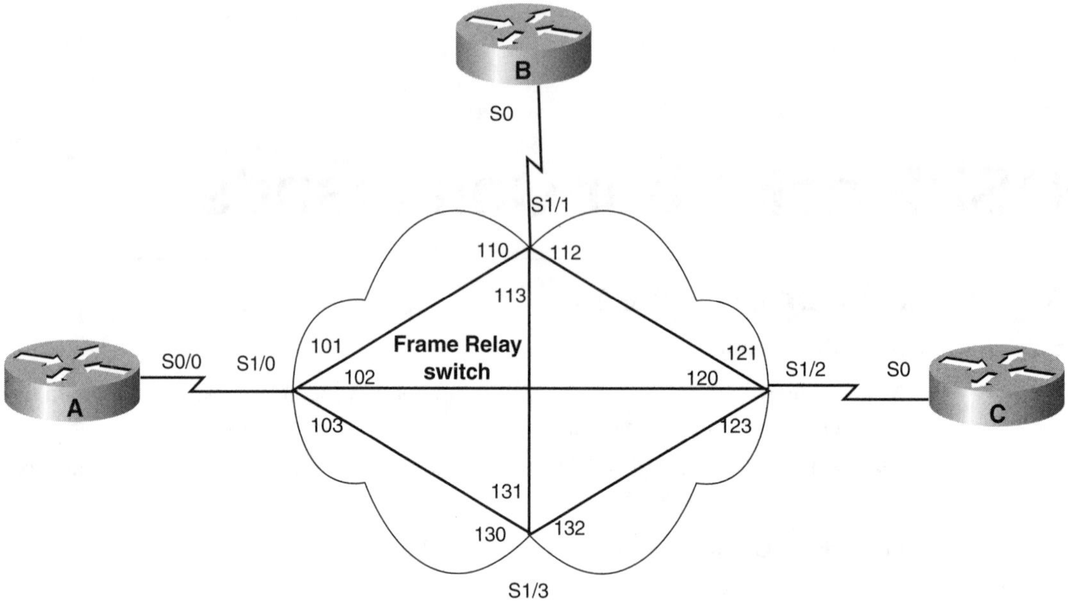


```
Frame Switch
hostname frame-relay
!
frame-relay switching
!
interface Serial1/0
 no ip address
 no ip directed-broadcast
 encapsulation frame-relay
 no ip mroute-cache
 no fair-queue
 clockrate 2015232
 frame-relay lmi-type ansi
 frame-relay intf-type dce
 frame-relay route 101 interface Serial1/1 110
 frame-relay route 102 interface Serial1/2 120
 frame-relay route 103 interface Serial1/3 130
!
```

```
interface Serial1/1
 no ip address
 no ip directed-broadcast
 encapsulation frame-relay
 clockrate 2015232
 frame-relay lmi-type ansi
 frame-relay intf-type dce
 frame-relay route 110 interface Serial1/0 101
 frame-relay route 112 interface Serial1/2 121
 frame-relay route 113 interface Serial1/3 131
!
interface Serial1/2
 no ip address
 no ip directed-broadcast
 encapsulation frame-relay
 clockrate 2015232
 frame-relay lmi-type ansi
 frame-relay intf-type dce
 frame-relay route 120 interface Serial1/0 102
 frame-relay route 121 interface Serial1/1 112
 frame-relay route 123 interface Serial1/3 132
!
interface Serial1/3
 no ip address
 no ip directed-broadcast
 encapsulation frame-relay
 clockrate 2015232
 frame-relay lmi-type ansi
 frame-relay intf-type dce
 frame-relay route 130 interface Serial1/0 103
 frame-relay route 131 interface Serial1/1 113
 frame-relay route 132 interface Serial1/2 123
```

For the first configuration example, an OSPF neighbor relationship will be established over Frame Relay between two OSPF routers as shown in Figure 11-2. The initial configurations for Routers A and B are shown in the listing that follows. The routers will learn the local DLCI numbers through inverse ARP so the DLCIs do not need to be explicitly configured.

Figure 11-2 *If the* **ip ospf network** *Command Is Not Used on an NBMA Network, then the OSPF* **neighbor** *Command Must Be Configured on One End of the Frame Relay Link*

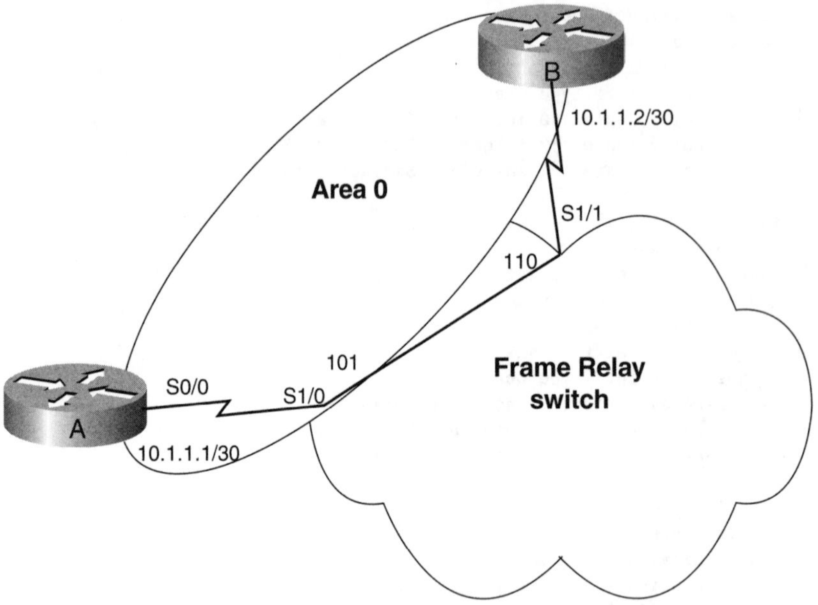


```
Router A
interface Loopback0
 ip address 1.1.1.1 255.255.255.255
!
interface Serial0/0
 ip address 10.1.1.1 255.255.255.252
 encapsulation frame-relay
 frame-relay lmi-type ansi
!
router ospf 1
 network 10.1.1.0 0.0.0.3 area 0
```

```
Router B
interface Loopback0
 ip address 2.2.2.2 255.255.255.255
!
interface Serial0
 ip address 10.1.1.2 255.255.255.252
 encapsulation frame-relay
 frame-relay lmi-type ansi
!
router ospf 1
 network 10.1.1.0 0.0.0.3 area 0
```

Verify that Routers A and B have IP connectivity by using the **ping** command.

```
rtrA#ping 10.1.1.2

Type escape sequence to abort.
Sending 5, 100-byte ICMP Echos to 10.1.1.2, timeout is 2 seconds:
!!!!!
Success rate is 100 percent (5/5), round-trip min/avg/max = 4/4/8 ms
```

List the Frame Relay DLCIs that the routers are using.

```
rtrB#show frame-relay map
Serial0 (up): ip 0.0.0.0 dlci 113(0x71,0x1C10)
              broadcast,
              CISCO, status defined, inactive
Serial0 (up): ip 0.0.0.0 dlci 112(0x70,0x1C00)
              broadcast,
              CISCO, status defined, inactive
Serial0 (up): ip 0.0.0.0 dlci 110(0x6E,0x18E0)
              broadcast,
              CISCO, status defined, active
Serial0 (up): ip 10.1.1.1 dlci 110(0x6E,0x18E0), dynamic,
              broadcast,, status defined, active
```

Because the Frame Relay switch is fully meshed, the routers are learning all the DLCIs for their particular interface via inverse ARP. Disable inverse ARP and map the appropriate IP address to its corresponding DLCI on Routers A and B.

```
Router A
interface Serial0/0
 ip address 10.1.1.1 255.255.255.252
 encapsulation frame-relay
 frame-relay map ip 10.1.1.2 101 broadcast
 no frame-relay inverse-arp
 frame-relay lmi-type ansi
```

```
Router B
interface Serial0
 ip address 10.1.1.2 255.255.255.252
 encapsulation frame-relay
 frame-relay map ip 10.1.1.1 110 broadcast
 no frame-relay inverse-arp
 frame-relay lmi-type ansi
```

Verify that Routers A and B are using the assigned DLCI.

```
rtrA#show frame-relay map
Serial0/0 (up): ip 10.1.1.2 dlci 101(0x65,0x1850), static,
              broadcast,
              CISCO, status defined, active
```

```
rtrB#show frame map
Serial0 (up): ip 10.1.1.1 dlci 110(0x6E,0x18E0), static,
              broadcast,
              CISCO, status defined, active
```

View the state of the OSPF neighbor relationship between Routers A and B.

```
rtrA#show ip ospf neighbor
<no output>
```

An OSPF neighbor relationship has not been established. The **neighbor** command can be used in order to establish OSPF neighbors over Frame Relay. Modify the configuration on Router A using the **neighbor** command.

```
Router A
router ospf 1
 network 10.1.1.0 0.0.0.3 area 0
 neighbor 10.1.1.2
```

Verification

Verify that an OSPF neighbor relationship has been established between Routers A and B.

```
rtrA#show ip ospf neighbor

Neighbor ID     Pri   State           Dead Time   Address         Interface
2.2.2.2           1   FULL/DR         00:01:53    10.1.1.2        Serial0/0
```

The neighbor relationship has been established even though the **neighbor** command was configured on only one end of the link. Why was a Designated Router (DR) elected? OSPF thinks that this point-to-point link is a broadcast network, and DRs are always elected on broadcast networks.

Configuration Example 2: Configuring OSPF Neighbors on a Hub and Spoke Topology with the Neighbors on the Same IP Subnet

In Figure 11-3, Routers A, B, and C are configured for a hub and spoke topology on a common IP subnet. For this topology, Router A *must* be elected as the DR because Router A has a direct connection to Router B and Router C. Routers B or C should never be elected as the DR. To prevent Routers B and C from becoming the DR on the Frame Relay subnet, set the OSPF priority to 0 on both of their interfaces. Configure Routers A, B, and C as shown in the listing that follows.

Figure 11-3 *In a Hub and Spoke Topology, the Hub Router Must Be Elected the OSPF DR if the Spokes Are on the Same IP Subnet*

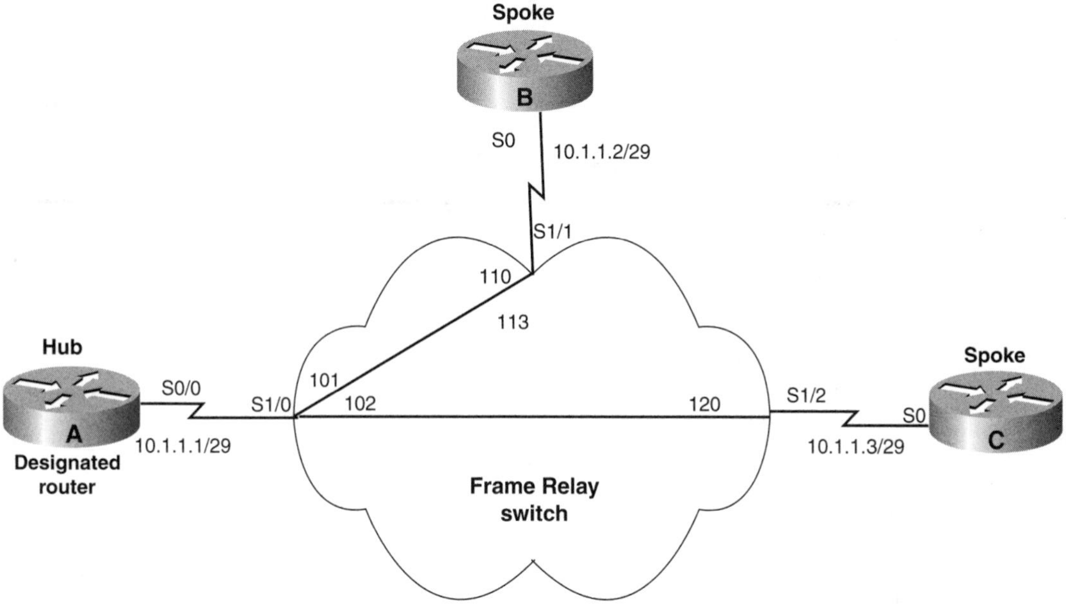


```
Router A
interface Loopback0
 ip address 1.1.1.1 255.255.255.255
!
interface Serial0/0
 ip address 10.1.1.1 255.255.255.248
 encapsulation frame-relay
 frame-relay map ip 10.1.1.2 101 broadcast
 frame-relay map ip 10.1.1.3 102 broadcast
 no frame-relay inverse-arp
 frame-relay lmi-type ansi
!
router ospf 1
```

continues

```
 network 1.1.1.1 0.0.0.0 area 1
 network 10.1.1.0 0.0.0.7 area 0
 neighbor 10.1.1.3
 neighbor 10.1.1.2
```

```
Router B
interface Loopback0
 ip address 2.2.2.2 255.255.255.255
!
interface Serial0
 ip address 10.1.1.2 255.255.255.248
 encapsulation frame-relay
 ip ospf priority 0
 frame-relay map ip 10.1.1.1 110 broadcast
 frame-relay map ip 10.1.1.3 110 broadcast
 no frame-relay inverse-arp
 frame-relay lmi-type ansi
!
router ospf 1
 network 2.2.2.2 0.0.0.0 area 2
 network 10.1.1.0 0.0.0.7 area 0
```

```
Router C
interface Loopback0
 ip address 3.3.3.3 255.255.255.255
!
interface Serial0
 ip address 10.1.1.3 255.255.255.248
 encapsulation frame-relay
 ip ospf priority 0
 frame-relay map ip 10.1.1.1 120 broadcast
 frame-relay map ip 10.1.1.2 120 broadcast
 no frame-relay inverse-arp
 frame-relay lmi-type ansi
!
router ospf 1
 network 3.3.3.3 0.0.0.0 area 0
 network 10.1.1.0 0.0.0.7 area 0
```

On Routers B and C, there are two **frame-relay map** statements. These are needed because Router B receives routes from Router C with a next hop of 10.1.1.3 and Router C receives routes from Router B with a next hop of 10.1.1.2. Because Routers B and C are not directly connected, the **frame-relay map** statements are required to direct traffic between Routers B and C to go through Router A.

Verification

Verify that Router A has an OSPF relationship with Routers B and C. Verify that all OSPF routes are being exchanged and are reachable.

```
rtrA#show ip ospf neighbor

Neighbor ID     Pri   State           Dead Time   Address         Interface
3.3.3.3           0   FULL/DROTHER    00:01:49    10.1.1.3        Serial0/0
2.2.2.2           0   FULL/DROTHER    00:01:58    10.1.1.2        Serial0/0
```

```
rtrB#show ip ospf neighbor

Neighbor ID     Pri   State           Dead Time   Address         Interface
1.1.1.1           1   FULL/DR         00:01:52    10.1.1.1        Serial0
```

```
rtrC#show ip ospf neighbor

Neighbor ID     Pri   State           Dead Time   Address         Interface
1.1.1.1           1   FULL/DR         00:01:32    10.1.1.1        Serial0
```

```
rtrA#show ip route
Codes: C - connected, S - static, I - IGRP, R - RIP, M - mobile, B - BGP
       D - EIGRP, EX - EIGRP external, O - OSPF, IA - OSPF inter area
       N1 - OSPF NSSA external type 1, N2 - OSPF NSSA external type 2
       E1 - OSPF external type 1, E2 - OSPF external type 2, E - EGP
       i - IS-IS, L1 - IS-IS level-1, L2 - IS-IS level-2, ia - IS-IS inter area
       * - candidate default, U - per-user static route, o - ODR
       P - periodic downloaded static route

Gateway of last resort is not set

     1.0.0.0/32 is subnetted, 1 subnets
C       1.1.1.1 is directly connected, Loopback0
     2.0.0.0/32 is subnetted, 1 subnets
O IA    2.2.2.2 [110/49] via 10.1.1.2, 00:20:27, Serial0/0
     3.0.0.0/32 is subnetted, 1 subnets
O       3.3.3.3 [110/49] via 10.1.1.3, 00:20:27, Serial0/0
10.0.0.0/29 is subnetted, 1 subnets
C       10.1.1.0 is directly connected, Serial0/0
```

```
rtrB#show ip route
Codes: C - connected, S - static, I - IGRP, R - RIP, M - mobile, B - BGP
       D - EIGRP, EX - EIGRP external, O - OSPF, IA - OSPF inter area
       N1 - OSPF NSSA external type 1, N2 - OSPF NSSA external type 2
       E1 - OSPF external type 1, E2 - OSPF external type 2, E - EGP
       i - IS-IS, L1 - IS-IS level-1, L2 - IS-IS level-2, * - candidate default
       U - per-user static route, o - ODR

Gateway of last resort is not set

     1.0.0.0/32 is subnetted, 1 subnets
O IA    1.1.1.1 [110/65] via 10.1.1.1, 00:21:19, Serial0
     2.0.0.0/32 is subnetted, 1 subnets
C       2.2.2.2 is directly connected, Loopback0
     3.0.0.0/32 is subnetted, 1 subnets
```

continues

```
O        3.3.3.3 [110/65] via 10.1.1.3, 00:21:20, Serial0
     172.16.0.0/24 is subnetted, 1 subnets
C       10.1.1.0 is directly connected, Serial0
```

```
rtrC#show ip route
Codes: C - connected, S - static, I - IGRP, R - RIP, M - mobile, B - BGP
       D - EIGRP, EX - EIGRP external, O - OSPF, IA - OSPF inter area
       N1 - OSPF NSSA external type 1, N2 - OSPF NSSA external type 2
       E1 - OSPF external type 1, E2 - OSPF external type 2, E - EGP
       i - IS-IS, L1 - IS-IS level-1, L2 - IS-IS level-2, * - candidate default
       U - per-user static route, o - ODR

Gateway of last resort is not set

     1.0.0.0/32 is subnetted, 1 subnets
O IA    1.1.1.1 [110/65] via 10.1.1.1, 00:22:18, Serial0
     2.0.0.0/32 is subnetted, 1 subnets
O IA    2.2.2.2 [110/65] via 10.1.1.2, 00:22:19, Serial0
     3.0.0.0/32 is subnetted, 1 subnets
C       3.3.3.3 is directly connected, Loopback0
     10.0.0.0/29 is subnetted, 1 subnets
C       10.1.1.0 is directly connected, Serial0
```

```
rtrA#ping 2.2.2.2

Type escape sequence to abort.
Sending 5, 100-byte ICMP Echos to 2.2.2.2, timeout is 2 seconds:
!!!!!
Success rate is 100 percent (5/5), round-trip min/avg/max = 4/4/8 ms


rtrA#ping 3.3.3.3

Type escape sequence to abort.
Sending 5, 100-byte ICMP Echos to 3.3.3.3, timeout is 2 seconds:
!!!!!
Success rate is 100 percent (5/5), round-trip min/avg/max = 4/4/8 ms
```

```
rtrB#ping 1.1.1.1

Type escape sequence to abort.
```

```
Sending 5, 100-byte ICMP Echos to 1.1.1.1, timeout is 2 seconds:
!!!!!
Success rate is 100 percent (5/5), round-trip min/avg/max = 4/4/8 ms

rtrB#ping 3.3.3.3

Type escape sequence to abort.
Sending 5, 100-byte ICMP Echos to 3.3.3.3, timeout is 2 seconds:
!!!!!
Success rate is 100 percent (5/5), round-trip min/avg/max = 8/8/8 ms

rtrC#ping 1.1.1.1

Type escape sequence to abort.
Sending 5, 100-byte ICMP Echos to 1.1.1.1, timeout is 2 seconds:
!!!!!
Success rate is 100 percent (5/5), round-trip min/avg/max = 4/4/8 ms


rtrC#ping 2.2.2.2

Type escape sequence to abort.
Sending 5, 100-byte ICMP Echos to 2.2.2.2, timeout is 2 seconds:
!!!!!
Success rate is 100 percent (5/5), round-trip min/avg/max = 8/9/12 ms
```

Configuration Example 3: Configuring OSPF Neighbors on a Hub and Spoke Topology with the Neighbors on Different IP Subnets

In Figure 11-4, the Frame Relay links between Routers A and B and Routers A and C are on different IP subnets. This topology requires the use of subinterfaces on the Serial 0/0 interface on Router A. Configure Routers A, B, and C as shown in the listing that follows the figure.

Figure 11-4 *In a Hub and Spoke Topology, Subinterfaces Are Required on the Hub Router if the Spokes Are in Different IP Subnets*

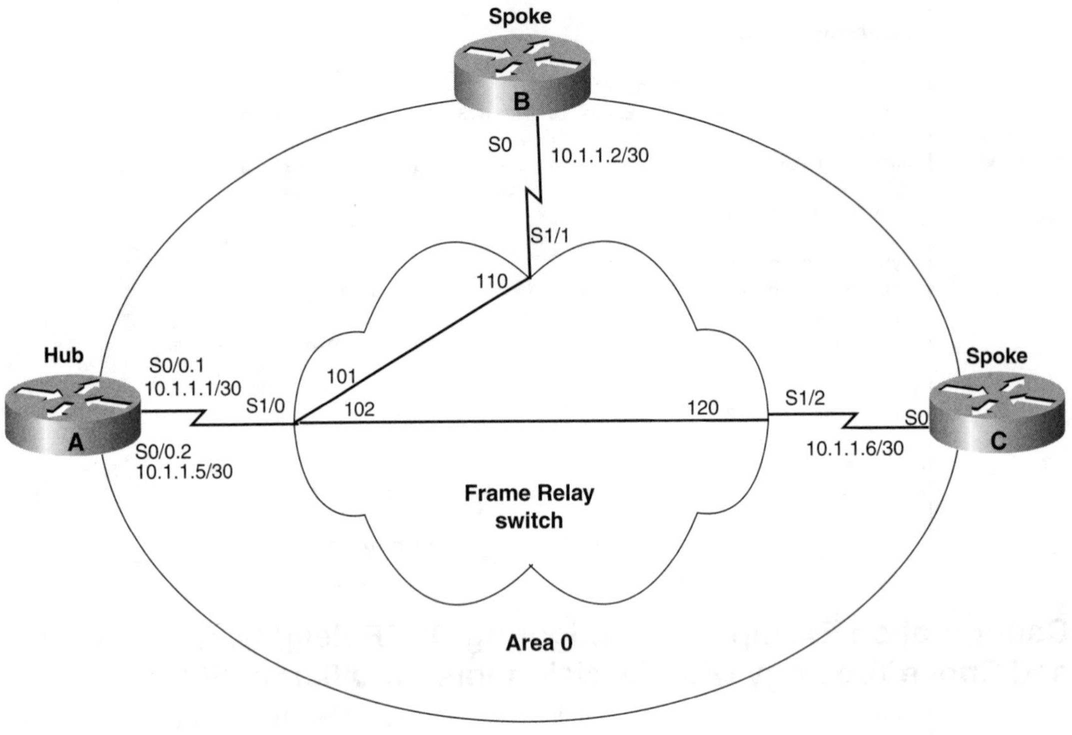


```
Router A
interface Loopback0
 ip address 1.1.1.1 255.255.255.255
!
interface Serial0/0
 no ip address
 encapsulation frame-relay
 frame-relay lmi-type ansi
!
interface Serial0/0.1 point-to-point
 ip address 10.1.1.1 255.255.255.252
 frame-relay interface-dlci 101
!
interface Serial0/0.2 point-to-point
 ip address 10.1.1.5 255.255.255.252
 frame-relay interface-dlci 102
!
router ospf 1
 network 1.1.1.1 0.0.0.0 area 1
```

```
 network 10.1.1.0 0.0.0.3 area 0
 network 10.1.1.4 0.0.0.3 area 0
```

```
Router B
interface Loopback0
 ip address 2.2.2.2 255.255.255.255
!

interface Serial0
 ip address 10.1.1.2 255.255.255.252
  encapsulation frame-relay
 frame-relay map ip 10.1.1.1 110 broadcast
 no frame-relay inverse-arp
 frame-relay lmi-type ansi
!
router ospf 1
 network 2.2.2.2 0.0.0.0 area 2
 network 10.1.1.0 0.0.0.3 area 0
 neighbor 10.1.1.1
```

```
Router C
interface Loopback0
 ip address 2.2.2.2 255.255.255.255
!
interface Ethernet0
 ip address 172.16.1.2 255.255.255.0
!
interface Serial0
 ip address 10.1.1.2 255.255.255.252
 encapsulation frame-relay
 frame-relay map ip 10.1.1.1 120 broadcast
 no frame-relay inverse-arp
 frame-relay lmi-type ansi
!
router ospf 1
 network 2.2.2.2 0.0.0.0 area 2
 network 10.1.1.0 0.0.0.3 area 0
 neighbor 10.1.1.1
```

Notice that the OSPF **neighbor** statements have been moved to Routers B and C. The **neighbor** statement cannot be used on a Frame Relay point-to-point subinterface. If you try to use this command on Router A, the router will notify you that this is unacceptable.

```
rtrA(config-router)#neighbor 10.1.1.2
OSPF: Neighbor command is allowed only on NBMA and point-to-multipoint networks
rtrA(config-router)#
```

Verification

Verify that Router A has formed an OSPF neighbor relationship with Routers B and C.

```
rtrA#show ip ospf neighbor
<no output>
```

Something is wrong. Enable OSPF debugging to see if you can determine the problem.

```
rtrA#debug ip ospf events
OSPF events debugging is on
rtrA#
00:16:18: OSPF: Rcv hello from 2.2.2.2 area 0 from Serial0/0.1 10.1.1.2
00:16:18: OSPF: Mismatched hello parameters from 10.1.1.2
00:16:52: OSPF: Rcv hello from 3.3.3.3 area 0 from Serial0/0.2 10.1.1.6
00:16:52: OSPF: Mismatched hello parameters from 10.1.1.6
00:16:52: Dead R 120 C 40, Hello R 30 C 10
```

If there is a mismatch of Hello parameters, then OSPF will not form a neighbor relationship. Inspect the Hello parameters on Router A and compare them to the Hello parameters on Routers B and C.

```
rtrA#show ip ospf interface s0/0.1
Serial0/0.1 is up, line protocol is up
  Internet Address 10.1.1.1/30, Area 0
  Process ID 1, Router ID 1.1.1.1, Network Type POINT_TO_POINT, Cost: 48
  Transmit Delay is 1 sec, State POINT_TO_POINT,
  Timer intervals configured, Hello 10, Dead 40, Wait 40, Retransmit 5
    Hello due in 00:00:18
  Neighbor Count is 1, Adjacent neighbor count is 1
    Adjacent with neighbor 2.2.2.2
  Suppress hello for 0 neighbor(s)
```

```
rtrB#show ip ospf interface s0
Serial0 is up, line protocol is up
  Internet Address 10.1.1.2/30, Area 0
  Process ID 1, Router ID 2.2.2.2, Network Type NON_BROADCAST, Cost: 64
  Transmit Delay is 1 sec, State DR, Priority 1
  Designated Router (ID) 2.2.2.2, Interface address 10.1.1.2
  Backup Designated router (ID) 1.1.1.1, Interface address 10.1.1.1
  Timer intervals configured, Hello 30, Dead 120, Wait 120, Retransmit 5
    Hello due in 00:00:04
  Neighbor Count is 1, Adjacent neighbor count is 1
    Adjacent with neighbor 1.1.1.1  (Backup Designated Router)
  Suppress hello for 0 neighbor(s)
```

Modify the configuration on Router A so that the Hello parameters match those being used on Routers B and C.

```
Router A
interface Serial0/0
 no ip address
 encapsulation frame-relay
 frame-relay lmi-type ansi
!
interface Serial0/0.1 point-to-point
 ip address 10.1.1.1 255.255.255.252
 ip ospf hello-interval 30
 frame-relay interface-dlci 101
!
interface Serial0/0.2 point-to-point
 ip address 10.1.1.5 255.255.255.252
 ip ospf hello-interval 30
 frame-relay interface-dlci 102
```

By default, the OSPF dead interval is four times the Hello interval, so the dead interval does not need to be reconfigured on Router A. When the Hello interval is set to 30, the dead interval will automatically be set to 120. Verify that Router A has established a FULL OSPF neighbor relationship with Routers B and C.

```
rtrA#show ip ospf neighbor

Neighbor ID     Pri   State           Dead Time   Address         Interface
2.2.2.2           1   FULL/  -        00:01:58    10.1.1.2        Serial0/0.1
3.3.3.3           0   FULL/  -        00:01:57    10.1.1.6        Serial0/0.2
```

Troubleshooting

Step 1 Verify IP connectivity over the NBMA network by pinging the other end of the link. If the ping is unsuccessful, there is a problem with the interface configuration. Check the interface for the correct encapsulation, lmi-type, IP address, and DLCI mapping.

Step 2 Verify that the **neighbor** command has been used on at least one end of the NBMA link.

Step 3 Verify that both ends of the link are using the same values for the Hello and dead intervals.

11-2: neighbor *ip-address* cost *cost*

Syntax Description:

- *ip-address*—IP address of the OSPF neighbor. If a secondary address is used on the interface, then the primary address must be used with this command.
- *cost*—The cost to reach the OSPF neighbor. The range of values is 1 to 65535.

Purpose: To configure the cost of an OSPF neighbor on a point-to-multipoint network.

Initial Cisco IOS Software Release: 11.3

Configuration Example: Modifying the Cost of an OSPF Neighbor on a Point-to-Multipoint Interface

The cost to reach an OSPF neighbor is, by default, the bandwidth of the network connecting the two neighbors divided into 100,000,000. In Figure 11-5, the bandwidth of the Frame Relay link is 2048 kbps. Therefore, the OSPF cost of the Frame Relay interfaces is 48 (100,000,000/2,048,000). The **cost** option of the **neighbor** command can be used to change the cost to reach the neighbor. The interface command **ip ospf cost** (see Section 19-3) can also be used to change this cost. The **neighbor cost** command can only be used on point-to-multipoint interfaces. The listing that follows the figure shows the configurations of the Frame Relay switch and Routers A and B.

Figure 11-5 *The Default Cost of an OSPF Interface Is 100,000,000/(Interface Bandwidth in bps). The* **neighbor cost** *Command Can Be Used to Modify the Interface Cost*

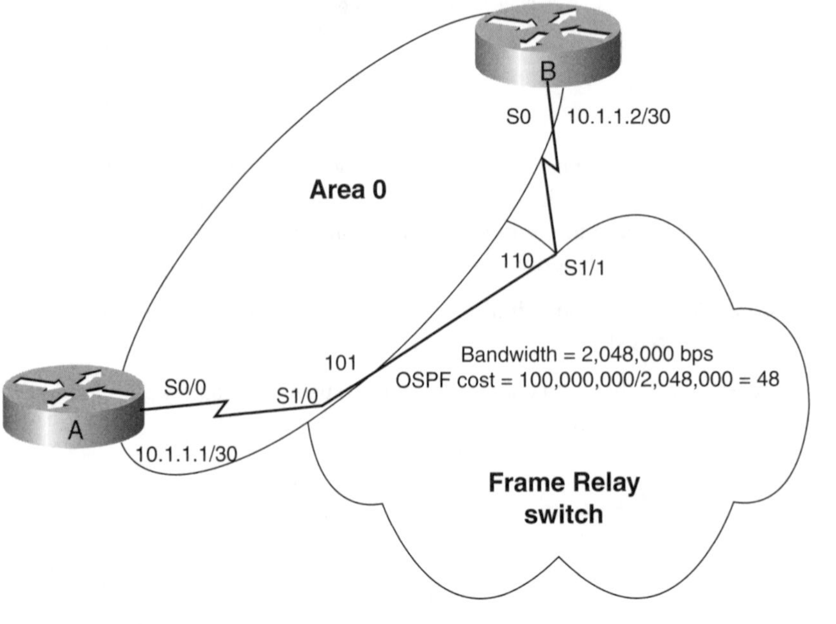

```
Frame Switch
hostname frame-relay
!
frame-relay switching
!
interface Serial1/0
 no ip address
 no ip directed-broadcast
 encapsulation frame-relay
 no ip mroute-cache
 no fair-queue
 clockrate 2015232
 frame-relay lmi-type ansi
 frame-relay intf-type dce
 frame-relay route 101 interface Serial1/1 110
 frame-relay route 102 interface Serial1/2 120
 frame-relay route 103 interface Serial1/3 130
!
interface Serial1/1
 no ip address
 no ip directed-broadcast
 encapsulation frame-relay
 clockrate 2015232
 frame-relay lmi-type ansi
 frame-relay intf-type dce
 frame-relay route 110 interface Serial1/0 101
 frame-relay route 112 interface Serial1/2 121
 frame-relay route 113 interface Serial1/3 131
```

```
Router A
interface Loopback0
 ip address 1.1.1.1 255.255.255.255
!
interface Serial0/0
 bandwidth 2048
 ip address 10.1.1.1 255.255.255.252
 encapsulation frame-relay
 ip ospf network point-to-multipoint
 frame-relay map ip 10.1.1.2 101 broadcast
 no frame-relay inverse-arp
 frame-relay lmi-type ansi
!
router ospf 1
 network 1.1.1.1 0.0.0.0 area 1
 network 10.1.1.0 0.0.0.3 area 0
```

```
Router B
interface Loopback0
 ip address 2.2.2.2 255.255.255.255
!
interface Serial0
 bandwidth 2048
```

continues

```
 ip address 10.1.1.2 255.255.255.252
 encapsulation frame-relay
 ip ospf network point-to-multipoint
 frame-relay map ip 10.1.1.1 110 broadcast
 no frame-relay inverse-arp
 frame-relay lmi-type ansi
!
router ospf 1
 network 2.2.2.2 0.0.0.0 area 2
 network 10.1.1.0 0.0.0.3 area 0
```

The interface command **ip ospf network point-to-multipoint** (see Section 19-15) is used because the **neighbor cost** command will work only on a point-to-multipoint interface. Display the IP routing table on Router B to see the cost of reaching the loopback network on Router A.

```
rtrB#show ip route
Codes: C - connected, S - static, I - IGRP, R - RIP, M - mobile, B - BGP
       D - EIGRP, EX - EIGRP external, O - OSPF, IA - OSPF inter area
       N1 - OSPF NSSA external type 1, N2 - OSPF NSSA external type 2
       E1 - OSPF external type 1, E2 - OSPF external type 2, E - EGP
       i - IS-IS, L1 - IS-IS level-1, L2 - IS-IS level-2, * - candidate default
       U - per-user static route, o - ODR

Gateway of last resort is not set

     1.0.0.0/32 is subnetted, 1 subnets
O IA    1.1.1.1 [110/49] via 10.1.1.1, 00:22:11, Serial0
     2.0.0.0/32 is subnetted, 1 subnets
C       2.2.2.2 is directly connected, Loopback0
     172.16.0.0/24 is subnetted, 1 subnets
C       172.16.1.0 is directly connected, Ethernet0
     10.0.0.0/8 is variably subnetted, 2 subnets, 2 masks
C       10.1.1.0/30 is directly connected, Serial0
O       10.1.1.1/32 [110/10] via 10.1.1.1, 00:22:11, Serial0
```

The cost is the sum of the cost of the loopback interface (1) and the cost of the Frame Relay link (48) for a total cost of 49. Modify the configuration on Router B to change the cost of the Frame Relay link to 10.

```
Router B
router ospf 1
 network 2.2.2.2 0.0.0.0 area 2
 network 10.1.1.0 0.0.0.3 area 0
 neighbor 10.1.1.1 cost 10
```

Verification

Verify that the cost of the Frame Relay interface, as seen by Router B, has changed to 10.

```
rtrB#show ip route
Codes: C - connected, S - static, I - IGRP, R - RIP, M - mobile, B - BGP
       D - EIGRP, EX - EIGRP external, O - OSPF, IA - OSPF inter area
       N1 - OSPF NSSA external type 1, N2 - OSPF NSSA external type 2
       E1 - OSPF external type 1, E2 - OSPF external type 2, E - EGP
       i - IS-IS, L1 - IS-IS level-1, L2 - IS-IS level-2, * - candidate default
       U - per-user static route, o - ODR

Gateway of last resort is not set

     1.0.0.0/32 is subnetted, 1 subnets
O IA    1.1.1.1 [110/11] via 10.1.1.1, 00:01:49, Serial0
     2.0.0.0/32 is subnetted, 1 subnets
C       2.2.2.2 is directly connected, Loopback0
     172.16.0.0/24 is subnetted, 1 subnets
C       172.16.1.0 is directly connected, Ethernet0
     10.0.0.0/8 is variably subnetted, 2 subnets, 2 masks
C       10.1.1.0/30 is directly connected, Serial0
O       10.1.1.1/32 [110/10] via 10.1.1.1, 00:01:49, Serial0
```

Troubleshooting

Step 1 Verify IP connectivity over the NBMA network by pinging the other end of the link. If the ping is unsuccessful, there is a problem with the interface configuration. Check the interface for the correct encapsulation, lmi-type, IP address, and DLCI mapping.

Step 2 Verify that the OSPF routers have established a FULL adjacency over the NBMA network.

Step 3 If the OSPF neighbors have a FULL adjacency, then the command **neighbor cost** should work. Remember that this command can be used only on a point-to-multipoint interface.

11-3: neighbor *ip-address* database-filter all out

Syntax Description:

- *ip-address*—IP address of the OSPF neighbor. If a secondary address is used on the interface, then the primary address must be used with this command because OSPF will only form an adjacency using the primary address.

Purpose: To prevent the flooding of link-state advertisements (LSAs) to the indicated neighbor. Many Internet service providers (ISPs) employ redundant links between OSPF neighbors. When an OSPF router receives an LSA, the LSA is flooded on all OSPF interfaces except for the interface on which the LSA was received. This command allows an ISP to choose between flooding overhead and flooding reliability. For example, if there are two links between OSPF neighbors, this command can be used to prevent the flooding of LSAs on one of the links. This command can be used only on a multipoint interface or an NBMA interface.

Initial Cisco IOS Software Release: 12.0

Configuration Example: Reducing the Flooding of LSAs on a Redundant OSPF Link

In Figure 11-6, there are two parallel links between Routers A and B. To reduce LSA flooding, overhead LSA flooding is prevented on link 2 using the **database-filter** option of the **neighbor** command. This reduction of LSA flooding can also be achieved by using the interface command **ip ospf database-filter all out** (see Section 19-4). Configure Routers A and B as shown in the listing that follows the figure. The point-to-multipoint network type is used on Router A's Serial 0/1 interface and Router B's Serial 0 interface so the database filter can be applied to the interface.

Figure 11-6 *Reducing LSA Flooding Overhead by Preventing LSA Flooding on One of the Parallel Links Using the* **neighbor database-filter all out** *Command*

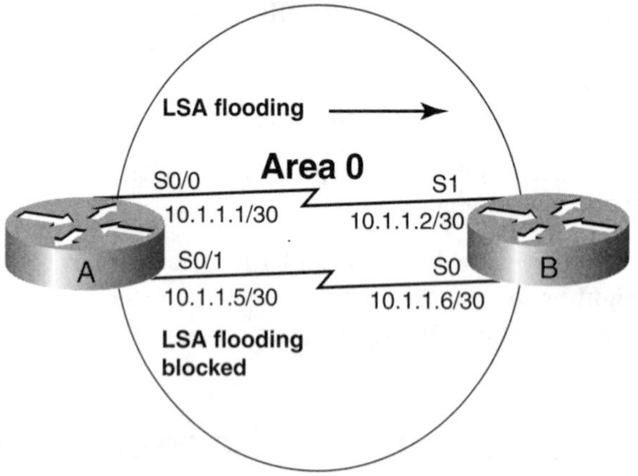


```
Router A
interface Loopback0
 ip address 1.1.1.1 255.255.255.255
!
interface Serial0/0
 bandwidth 64
 ip address 10.1.1.1 255.255.255.252
```

```
!
interface Serial0/1
 bandwidth 64
 ip address 10.1.1.5 255.255.255.252
 ip ospf network point-to-multipoint
 clockrate 64000
!
router ospf 1
 network 1.1.1.1 0.0.0.0 area 1
 network 10.1.1.0 0.0.0.3 area 0
 network 10.1.1.4 0.0.0.3 area 0
 neighbor 10.1.1.6 database-filter all out
```

```
Router B
interface Loopback0
 ip address 2.2.2.2 255.255.255.255
!
interface Serial0
ip address 10.1.1.6 255.255.255.252
 bandwidth 64
 ip ospf network point-to-multipoint
!
interface Serial1
 bandwidth 64
 ip address 10.1.1.2 255.255.255.252
 clockrate 64000
!
router ospf 1
 network 2.2.2.2 0.0.0.0 area 2
 network 10.1.1.0 0.0.0.3 area 0
 network 10.1.1.4 0.0.0.3 area 0
```

Verification

Verify that the database filter has been applied to interface Serial 0/1 on Router A.

```
rtrA#show ip ospf neighbor detail
 Neighbor 2.2.2.2, interface address 10.1.1.2
    In the area 0 via interface Serial0/0
    Neighbor priority is 1, State is FULL, 6 state changes
    DR is 0.0.0.0 BDR is 0.0.0.0
    Options 2
    Dead timer due in 00:00:33
 Neighbor 2.2.2.2, interface address 10.1.1.6
    In the area 0 via interface Serial0/1
    Neighbor priority is 1, State is FULL, 6 state changes
    Database-filter all out
    DR is 0.0.0.0 BDR is 0.0.0.0
    Options 2
    Dead timer due in 00:01:55
```

Troubleshooting

Step 1 The **database-filter all out** command can be applied only to a point-to-multipoint or NBMA interface.

Step 2 Verify that the OSPF routers have established a FULL adjacency.

Step 3 If the OSPF neighbors have a FULL adjacency, then the command **database-filter all out** should work.

11-4: neighbor *ip-address* poll-interval *interval*

Syntax Description:

- *ip-address*—IP address of the OSPF neighbor. If a secondary address is used on the interface, then the primary address must be used with this command because OSPF will only form an adjacency using the primary address.
- *interval*—Poll interval in seconds. The range of values is from 0–4,294,967,295.

Purpose: If a Hello packet has not been received from a neighbor during the dead interval, the neighbor is declared down. Hello packets will be sent to the neighbor at the rate specified by the poll interval when the neighbor is down. This option does not apply to point-to-multipoint interfaces.

Initial Cisco IOS Software Release: 10.0

Configuration Example: Setting the Poll Interval on an NBMA Network

In Figure 11-7, Routers A and B have formed an OSPF adjacency over the NBMA network. Hello packets will be sent by both routers periodically. The time between Hello packets is determined by the Hello interval. If Router A does not receive a Hello packet from Router B during a period of time determined by the dead interval, Router A will declare Router B down. Router A will continue to send Hello packets to Router B, but at a reduced rate. This reduced rate is the poll interval. The configuration for the routers in Figure 11-7 is shown in the listing that follows.

Figure 11-7 *When a Neighbor on an NBMA Network Is Declared Down, Hello Packets Will Be Sent at a Reduced Rate Determined by the Poll Interval*

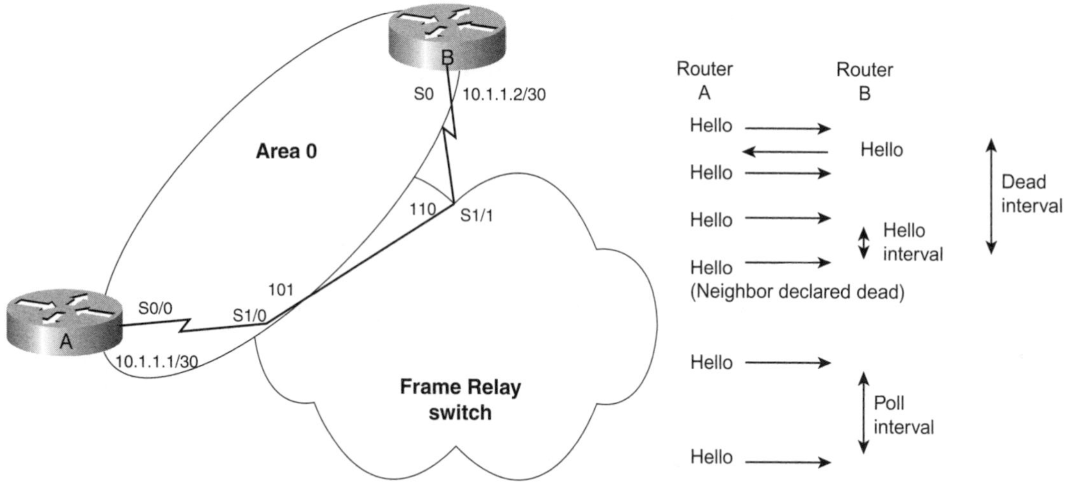


```
Router A
interface Loopback0
 ip address 1.1.1.1 255.255.255.255
!
interface Serial0/0
 bandwidth 64
 ip address 10.1.1.1 255.255.255.252
 encapsulation frame-relay
 frame-relay lmi-type ansi
!
router ospf 1
 network 1.1.1.1 0.0.0.0 area 1
 network 10.1.1.0 0.0.0.3 area 0
neighbor 10.1.1.2
```

```
Router B
interface Loopback0
 ip address 2.2.2.2 255.255.255.255
!
interface Serial0
 ip address 10.1.1.2 255.255.255.252
 no ip directed-broadcast
 encapsulation frame-relay
 no ip mroute-cache
 frame-relay lmi-type ansi
!
router ospf 1
 network 2.2.2.2 0.0.0.0 area 2
 network 10.1.1.0 0.0.0.3 area 0
```

The value of the poll interval can be viewed using the **show ip ospf neighbor detail** command.

```
rtrA#show ip ospf neighbor detail
 Neighbor 2.2.2.2, interface address 10.1.1.2
    In the area 0 via interface Serial0/0
    Neighbor priority is 1, State is FULL, 16 state changes
    DR is 10.1.1.2 BDR is 10.1.1.1
    Poll interval 60
    Options 2
    Dead timer due in 00:01:42
```

Modify the configuration on Router A to change the poll interval to 90.

```
router ospf 1
 network 1.1.1.1 0.0.0.0 area 1
 network 10.1.1.0 0.0.0.3 area 0
 neighbor 10.1.1.2 poll-interval 90
```

Verification

Verify that Router A is now using a poll interval of 90.

```
rtrA#show ip ospf neighbor detail

Neighbor 2.2.2.2, interface address 10.1.1.2
    In the area 0 via interface Serial0/0
    Neighbor priority is 0, State is FULL, 17 state changes
    DR is 10.1.1.2 BDR is 10.1.1.1
    Poll interval 90
    Options 2
    Dead timer due in 00:01:31
```

Troubleshooting

Step 1 The **poll-interval** option can be applied only to NBMA networks. This option is not allowed on a point-to-multipoint interface.

Step 2 Verify that the OSPF routers have established a FULL adjacency.

Step 3 If the OSPF neighbors have a FULL adjacency, the command **poll-interval** should work.

11-5: neighbor *ip-address* priority *priority*

Syntax Description:

- *ip-address*—IP address of the OSPF neighbor. If a secondary address is used on the interface, then the primary address must be used with this command because OSPF will only form an adjacency using the primary address.
- *priority*—The OSPF priority of the neighbor with the given IP address. The range of values is 0 to 255. The router with the lowest OSPF priority on a network will be elected the DR for the network. A priority of zero means that the router is not eligible to be elected the DR or Backup Designated Router (BDR). The default priority is 1.

Purpose: To influence the election of the DR. The router with the lowest non-zero priority will be elected the DR. In a hub and spoke topology, the hub router should be elected as the DR.

Initial Cisco IOS Software Release: 10.0

Configuration Example: Setting the Priority of an OSPF Neighbor

Configure the routers in Figure 11-8 as shown in the listing that follows.

Figure 11-8 *The Election of the DR Can Be Influenced by Using the* **priority** *Option with the* **neighbor** *Router Configuration Command*

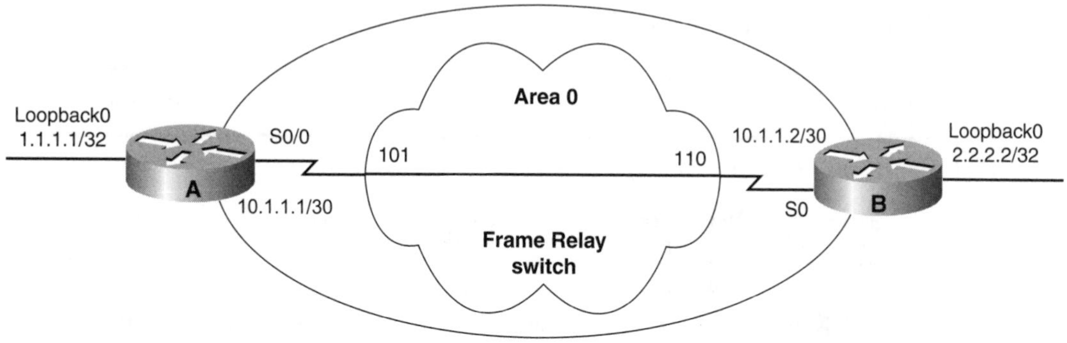


```
Router A
interface Loopback0
 ip address 1.1.1.1 255.255.255.255
!
interface Serial0/0
 bandwidth 64
 ip address 10.1.1.1 255.255.255.252
 encapsulation frame-relay
 frame-relay map ip 10.1.1.2 101 broadcast
 no frame-relay inverse-arp
```

continues

```
 frame-relay lmi-type ansi
!
router ospf 1
 network 1.1.1.1 0.0.0.0 area 1
 network 10.1.1.0 0.0.0.3 area 0
```

```
Router B
interface Loopback0
 ip address 2.2.2.2 255.255.255.255
!
interface Serial0
 ip address 10.1.1.2 255.255.255.252
 encapsulation frame-relay
 bandwidth 64
 frame-relay map ip 10.1.1.1 110 broadcast
 no frame-relay inverse-arp
 frame-relay lmi-type ansi
!
router ospf 1
 network 2.2.2.2 0.0.0.0 area 2
 network 10.1.1.0 0.0.0.3 area 0
 neighbor 10.1.1.1 priority 1
```

Examine the state of the OSPF neighbors to determine which router has been elected the DR.

```
rtrA#show ip ospf neighbor

Neighbor ID     Pri   State           Dead Time   Address         Interface
2.2.2.2           1   FULL/BDR        00:01:45    10.1.1.2        Serial0/0
```

```
rtrB#show ip ospf neighbor

Neighbor ID     Pri   State           Dead Time   Address         Interface
1.1.1.1           1   FULL/DR         00:01:37    10.1.1.1        Serial0
```

Router A is the DR because it has a lower OSPF router ID. Modify the configuration on Router B so that it will be elected the DR. This can be accomplished by either setting the priority to 0 or larger than 1 in the **neighbor** statement.

```
Router B
router ospf 1
 network 2.2.2.2 0.0.0.0 area 2
 network 10.1.1.0 0.0.0.3 area 0
 neighbor 10.1.1.1 priority 2
```

OSPF will not immediately elect a new DR. For stability reasons, OSPF will elect a new DR only if the current DR is down. Force the re-election of the DR by clearing the OSPF process on Router A.

```
rtrA#clear ip ospf process
Reset ALL OSPF processes? [no]: y
rtrA#
```

Verification

Verify that Router B has been elected as the DR.

```
rtrA#show ip ospf neighbor

Neighbor ID     Pri   State           Dead Time   Address         Interface
2.2.2.2           1   FULL/DR         00:01:45    10.1.1.2        Serial0/0
```

```
rtrB#show ip ospf neighbor

Neighbor ID     Pri   State           Dead Time   Address         Interface
1.1.1.1           1   FULL/BDR        00:01:44    10.1.1.1        Serial0
```

Troubleshooting

Step 1 The configured priority value will not take effect until the current DR is down and a new election takes place.

Step 2 Verify that the desired priority value has been used with the OSPF **neighbor** command.

CHAPTER 12

OSPF network Command

12-1: network *ip-address wild-card-mask* area *area-id*

Syntax Description:

- *ip-address*—The *ip-address* in conjunction with the *wild-card-mask* defines a block of IP addresses. An interface with an IP address that is contained within the defined block is configured to run OSPF in the indicated area.
- *wild-card-mask*—Inverse IP address mask used to determine a range of IP addresses.
- *area-id*—OSPF area ID. The value can be entered as a decimal number in the range of 0 to 4,294,967,295 or in IP address format in the range 0.0.0.0 to 255.255.255.255.

Purpose: The **network** command is used to define the interfaces that will run OSPF and the OSPF area of the interface. One or more interfaces can be selected with a single **network** command. If the IP address assigned to an interface is part of the address block the *ip-address/wild-card-mask* pair defines, the interface will be enabled for OSPF in the indicated area.

Initial Cisco IOS Software Release: 10.0

Configuration Example 1: Using a Host Address to Enable OSPF on an Interface

In Figure 12-1, host addresses are initially used to configure the interfaces to run OSPF. A host address consists of an IP address and a 32-bit mask in the form

A.B.C.D 0.0.0.0

This address/mask pair defines an IP address block that contains one address. Therefore, this form can be used to enable only one interface per **network** statement for OSPF.

Figure 12-1 *Network Used to Illustrate the Use of the OSPF* **network** *Command*

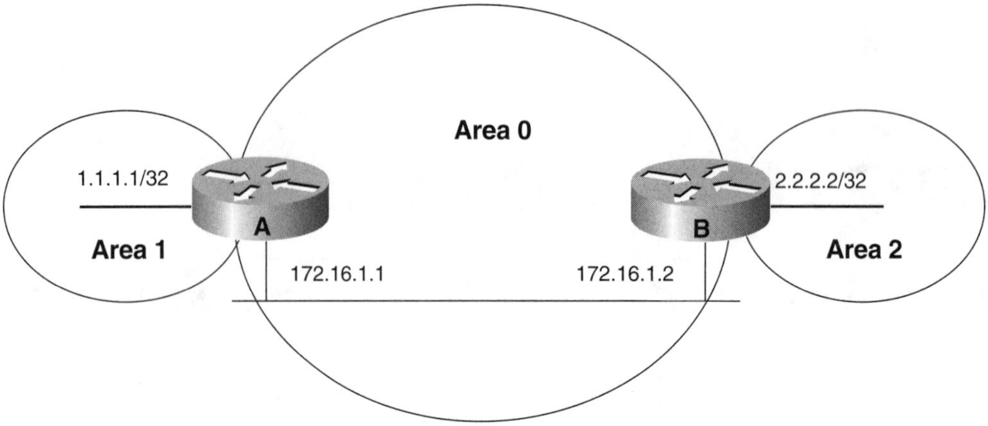


```
Router A
interface Loopback0
 ip address 1.1.1.1 255.255.255.255
!
interface Ethernet0/0
 ip address 172.16.1.1 255.255.255.0
!
router ospf 1
 network 1.1.1.1 0.0.0.0 area 1
 network 172.16.1.1 0.0.0.0 area 0
```

```
Router B
interface Loopback0
 ip address 2.2.2.2 255.255.255.255
!
interface Ethernet0
 ip address 172.16.1.2 255.255.255.0
!
router ospf 1
 network 2.2.2.2 0.0.0.0 area 2
 network 172.16.1.2 0.0.0.0 area 0
```

Verification

Verify that the proper interfaces have been configured for OSPF.

```
rtrA#show ip ospf interface
Ethernet0/0 is up, line protocol is up
  Internet Address 172.16.1.1/24, Area 0
  Process ID 1, Router ID 1.1.1.1, Network Type BROADCAST, Cost: 10
```

```
  Transmit Delay is 1 sec, State DR, Priority 1
  Designated Router (ID) 1.1.1.1, Interface address 172.16.1.1
  Backup Designated router (ID) 2.2.2.2, Interface address 172.16.1.2
  Timer intervals configured, Hello 10, Dead 40, Wait 40, Retransmit 5
    Hello due in 00:00:02
  Index 1/2, flood queue length 0
  Next 0x0(0)/0x0(0)
  Last flood scan length is 2, maximum is 2
  Last flood scan time is 0 msec, maximum is 0 msec
  Neighbor Count is 1, Adjacent neighbor count is 1
    Adjacent with neighbor 2.2.2.2  (Backup Designated Router)
  Suppress hello for 0 neighbor(s)
Loopback0 is up, line protocol is up
  Internet Address 1.1.1.1/32, Area 1
  Process ID 1, Router ID 1.1.1.1, Network Type LOOPBACK, Cost: 1
  Loopback interface is treated as a stub Host
```

```
rtrB#show ip ospf interface
Ethernet0 is up, line protocol is up
  Internet Address 172.16.1.2/24, Area 0
  Process ID 1, Router ID 2.2.2.2, Network Type BROADCAST, Cost: 10
  Transmit Delay is 1 sec, State BDR, Priority 1
  Designated Router (ID) 1.1.1.1, Interface address 172.16.1.1
  Backup Designated router (ID) 2.2.2.2, Interface address 172.16.1.2
  Timer intervals configured, Hello 10, Dead 40, Wait 40, Retransmit 5
    Hello due in 00:00:00
  Neighbor Count is 1, Adjacent neighbor count is 1
    Adjacent with neighbor 1.1.1.1  (Designated Router)
  Suppress hello for 0 neighbor(s)
Loopback0 is up, line protocol is up
  Internet Address 2.2.2.2/32, Area 2
  Process ID 1, Router ID 2.2.2.2, Network Type LOOPBACK, Cost: 1
  Loopback interface is treated as a stub Host
```

Configuration Example 2: Using the Same Network/Mask Pair in the OSPF network Statement That Is Used for the Interface

One problem that can arise when using a host address in the **network** statement is if the IP address of the interface changes. If you change the IP address of the Ethernet interface on Router A from 172.16.1.1 to 172.16.1.3, then the interface will no longer be enabled for OSPF. You need to delete the **network** statement containing the host route 172.16.1.1 and re-enter the **network** statement using the host route 172.16.1.3. If you change the IP address on the Ethernet interface on Router A, you should see the following output:

```
rtrA#conf t
Enter configuration commands, one per line.  End with CNTL/Z.
rtrA(config)#int e0/0
rtrA(config-if)#ip add 172.16.1.3 255.255.255.0
rtrA(config-if)#^Z
```

continues

```
rtrA#
05:23:52: %OSPF-5-ADJCHG: Process 1, Nbr 2.2.2.2 on Ethernet0/0 from FULL to DOW
N, Neighbor Down: Interface down or detached
```

You have broken the OSPF network and Routers A and B are no longer talking to OSPF. If you had used the same address (almost) and mask (reverse) that was assigned to the interface in the **network** command then this problem would have gone away.

```
Router A
router ospf 1
 network 1.1.1.1 0.0.0.0 area 1
 network 172.16.1.1 0.0.0.255 area 0
```

The new address/mask pair defines the IP address block 172.16.1.0–172.16.1.255. If any IP address in this range is used, the Ethernet interface will still be activated for OSPF.

Verification

Verify that OSPF is active on the Ethernet interface on Router A.

```
rtrA#show ip ospf interface ethernet 0/0
Ethernet0/0 is up, line protocol is up
  Internet Address 172.16.1.1/24, Area 0
  Process ID 1, Router ID 1.1.1.1, Network Type BROADCAST, Cost: 10
  Transmit Delay is 1 sec, State WAITING, Priority 1
  No designated router on this network
  No backup designated router on this network
  Timer intervals configured, Hello 10, Dead 40, Wait 40, Retransmit 5
    Hello due in 00:00:04
    Wait time before Designated router selection 00:00:34
  Index 1/2, flood queue length 0
  Next 0x0(0)/0x0(0)
  Last flood scan length is 1, maximum is 2
  Last flood scan time is 0 msec, maximum is 0 msec
  Neighbor Count is 0, Adjacent neighbor count is 0
  Suppress hello for 0 neighbor(s)
```

Changing the IP address on an active OSPF interface will cause OSPF to go inactive on the interface until the router determines that the new IP address falls within the range of one of the network commands. If it does, OSPF will be reactivated on the interface.

Configuration Example 3: Using a Shorter Mask to Enable OSPF on Multiple Interfaces

In Figure 12-2, the routers in Area 1 use IP addresses assigned from the IP address block 10.1.0.0/16, and the routers in Area 2 use the address block 10.2.0.0/16. For this case, only one **network** statement is needed on the routers in Areas 1 and 2 and two network statements are needed on the Area Border Routers (ABRs). Assume there are 20 routers in Area 1 and each router has five interfaces. If we use the methods from configuration example 1 or 2, we would need to configure five **network** statements per router. If an interface is added to a router, then a new OSPF **network** statement needs to be configured on that router. This would work well, but it could become administratively intensive. If one **network** statement is used, then no additional OSPF configuration would be necessary when a new interface is added to a router. The configurations for the routers are shown in the listing that follows the figure.

Figure 12-2 *If All Interfaces on a Router Have Been Assigned to a Common IP Address Block and OSPF Area, Then One* **network** *Statement Can Be Used To Enable the Interfaces for OSPF*

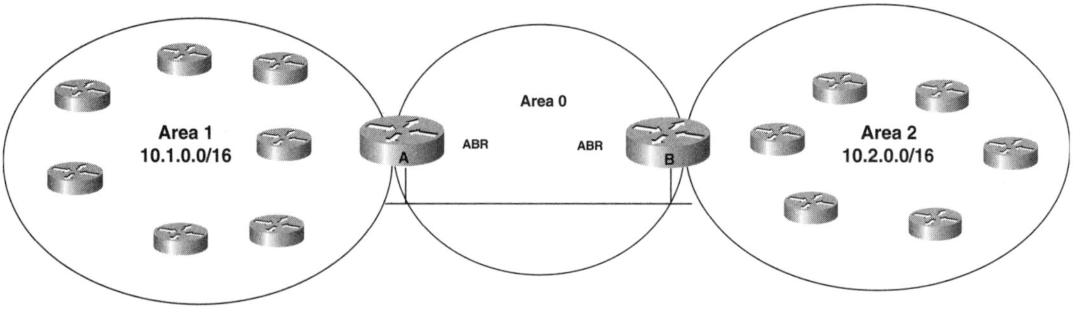


```
Router A
router ospf 1
 network 172.16.1.0 0.0.0.255 area 0
 network 10.1.0.0 0.0.255.255 area 1
```

```
Router B
router ospf 1
 network 172.16.1.0 0.0.0.255 area 0
 network 10.2.0.0 0.0.255.255 area 2
```

```
Area 1 Router
router ospf 1
 network 10.1.0.0 0.0.255.255 area 1
```

```
Area 2 Router
router ospf 1
 network 10.2.0.0 0.0.255.255 area 2
```

Troubleshooting

Step 1 Verify that there is a neighbor relationship between the OSPF routers by using the **show ip ospf** neighbors command.

Step 2 Verify that you are using the proper IP address/wild-card mask in the **network** statement.

Step 3 Use the **show ip ospf interface** command to verify that the interfaces are in the intended OSPF area.

CHAPTER 13

Passive OSPF Interfaces

13-1: passive-interface *interface-name interface-number*

Syntax Description:

- *interface-name*—Name of the interface.
- *interface-number*—Number of the interface.

Purpose: To prevent OSPF packets from being sent on the specified interface.

Initial Cisco IOS Software Release: 10.0

Configuration Example: Using a Passive Interface to Reduce Protocol Traffic

In Figure 13-1, Router B has a BGP neighbor relationship with Router C. The BGP routes learned by Router B from Router C are redistributed into OSPF. The network between Routers B and C needs to be advertised by OSPF to Router A so there is IP connectivity between Routers A and C. There is no need to send OSPF protocol packets to Router C. Therefore, the Serial 1 interface on Router B can be made passive under OSPF. The network between Routers B and C could also be advertised by redistributing connected routes on Router B. The redistributed networks would be advertised as OSPF external routes.

Figure 13-1 *OSPF Will Advertise the Network Assigned to an Interface if the Interface Is Included in One of the OSPF* **network** *Statements. If the Interface Does Not Have Any OSPF Neighbors, then the Interface Can Be Made Passive*

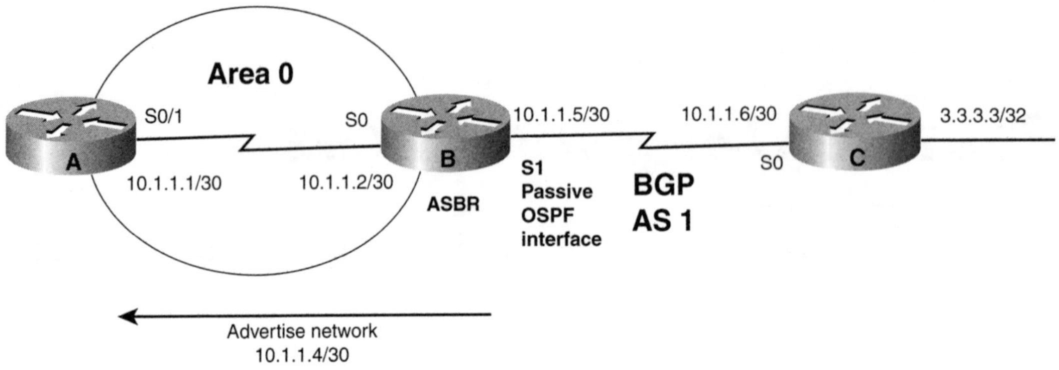


```
Router A
interface Loopback0
 ip address 1.1.1.1 255.255.255.255
!
interface Serial0/1
 bandwidth 64
 ip address 10.1.1.1 255.255.255.252
 clock rate 64000
!
router ospf 1
 network 1.1.1.1 0.0.0.0 area 1
 network 10.1.1.0 0.0.0.3 area 0
```

```
Router B
interface Loopback0
 ip address 2.2.2.2 255.255.255.255
!
interface Serial0
 ip address 10.1.1.2 255.255.255.252
!
interface Serial1
 ip address 10.1.1.5 255.255.255.252
 clock rate 64000
!
router ospf 1
 redistribute bgp 1 subnets
 passive-interface Serial1
 network 2.2.2.2 0.0.0.0 area 2
 network 10.1.1.0 0.0.0.3 area 0
```

```
 network 10.1.1.4 0.0.0.3 area 0
!
router bgp 1
 neighbor 10.1.1.6 remote-as 2
```

```
Router C
interface Loopback0
 ip address 3.3.3.3 255.255.255.255
!
interface Serial0
 ip address 10.1.1.6 255.255.255.252
!
router bgp 2
 network 3.3.3.3 mask 255.255.255.255
 neighbor 10.1.1.5 remote-as 1
!
ip route 0.0.0.0 0.0.0.0 Serial0
```

The OSPF configuration on Router B contains the following statement:

```
network 10.1.1.4 0.0.0.3 area 0
```

This statement enables OSPF on the Serial 1 interface on Router B and causes OSPF to advertise the network 10.1.1.4. OSPF protocol packets will be sent from the Serial 1 interface on Router B. Router C is not running OSPF, so there is no need to send protocol packets over this network. The **passive-interface** command prevents the OSPF packets from being sent while allowing the network to be advertised into OSPF. The redistribution of BGP into OSPF on Router B allows Router A to reach the 3.3.3.3 network on Router C. The static default route on Router C allows Router C to reach the 1.1.1.1 network on Router A.

Verification

Verify that the Serial 1 interface is a passive OSPF interface.

```
rtrB#show ip ospf interface serial 1
Serial1 is up, line protocol is up
  Internet Address 10.1.1.5/30, Area 0
  Process ID 1, Router ID 2.2.2.2, Network Type POINT_TO_POINT, Cost: 1562
  Transmit Delay is 1 sec, State POINT_TO_POINT,
  Timer intervals configured, Hello 10, Dead 40, Wait 40, Retransmit 5
    No Hellos (Passive interface)
  Neighbor Count is 0, Adjacent neighbor count is 0
  Suppress hello for 0 neighbor(s)
```

Verify that the 10.1.1.4 network is being advertised to Router A via OSPF.

```
rtrA#show ip route
Codes: C - connected, S - static, I - IGRP, R - RIP, M - mobile, B - BGP
       D - EIGRP, EX - EIGRP external, O - OSPF, IA - OSPF inter area
       N1 - OSPF NSSA external type 1, N2 - OSPF NSSA external type 2
       E1 - OSPF external type 1, E2 - OSPF external type 2, E - EGP
       i - IS-IS, L1 - IS-IS level-1, L2 - IS-IS level-2, * - candidate default
       U - per-user static route, o - ODR

Gateway of last resort is not set

     1.0.0.0/32 is subnetted, 1 subnets
C       1.1.1.1 is directly connected, Loopback0
     2.0.0.0/32 is subnetted, 1 subnets
O IA    2.2.2.2 [110/1563] via 10.1.1.2, 03:30:49, Serial0/1
     3.0.0.0/32 is subnetted, 1 subnets
O E2    3.3.3.3 [110/1] via 10.1.1.2, 03:30:49, Serial0/1
     172.16.0.0/24 is subnetted, 1 subnets
C       10.1.1.0 is directly connected, Serial0/1
O       10.1.1.4 [110/3124] via 10.1.1.2, 03:30:49, Serial0/1
```

Verify that Routers A and C can reach each other's attached networks.

```
rtrA#ping 3.3.3.3

Type escape sequence to abort.
Sending 5, 100-byte ICMP Echos to 3.3.3.3, timeout is 2 seconds:
!!!!!
Success rate is 100 percent (5/5), round-trip min/avg/max = 56/58/60 ms
```

```
rtrC#ping 1.1.1.1

Type escape sequence to abort.
Sending 5, 100-byte ICMP Echos to 1.1.1.1, timeout is 2 seconds:
!!!!!
Success rate is 100 percent (5/5), round-trip min/avg/max = 56/57/60 ms
```

Troubleshooting

Step 1 Verify that the intended interface has been made passive. A common mistake is to make the wrong OSPF interface passive.

13-2: passive-interface default

Syntax Description:

This form of the command has no arguments.

Purpose: To make all OSPF interfaces passive.

Initial Cisco IOS Software Release: 12.0

Configuration Example: Many Interfaces, Few Neighbors

In Figure 13-2, Router A has one OSPF neighbor and connections to five non-OSPF routers. Router A wants to advertise all connected networks to Router B via OSPF, but does not want to transmit OSPF traffic on the interfaces connecting to non-OSPF routers. In addition, Router A wants to advertise the connected networks as OSPF routes. This condition means that redistributing connected routes on Router A is not an option, because these routes would be advertised as external routes.

Figure 13-2 *All OSPF Interfaces Can Be Made Passive Using the Command* **passive-interface default**. *The* **no** *Form of the Command Can Then Be Used to Enable Selected Interfaces*

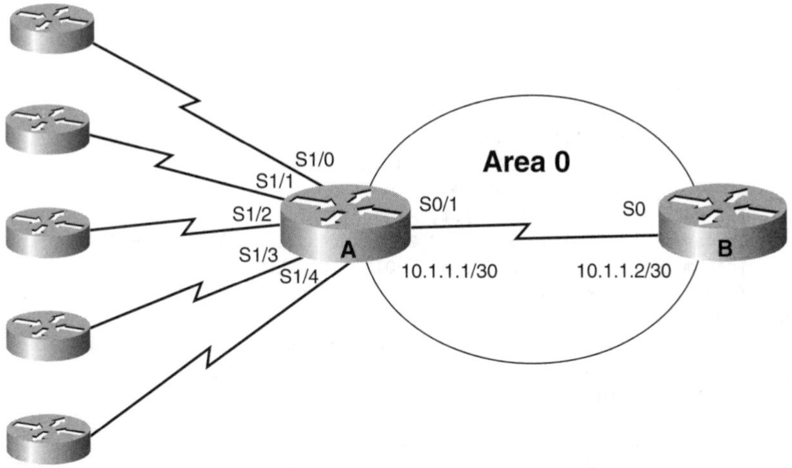

For the moment, assume that the **default** option is not available with the **passive-interface** command. The configuration for Router A would require five **passive-interface** commands.

```
Router A
router ospf 1
 passive-interface Serial1/0
 passive-interface Serial1/1
 passive-interface Serial1/2
```

continues

```
 passive-interface Serial1/3
 passive-interface Serial1/4
 network 10.1.0.0 0.0.255.255 area 0
```

The OSPF configuration for Router A is not very complicated. But assume that you have a core router with over 100 interfaces to non-OSPF routers. The configuration would become rather cumbersome. There would be over 100 **passive-interface** statements in the OSPF configuration. Therefore, the **default** option is an option of convenience. Start by using the command **passive-interface default** to make all OSPF interfaces passive. Then activate the interfaces that have OSPF neighbors, using the **no passive-interface** form of the command. The previous configuration would become

```
router ospf 1
 passive-interface default
 no passive-interface Serial0/1
 network 10.1.0.0 0.0.255.255 area 0
```

Verification

Verify that the Serial 1 interface is a passive OSPF interface.

```
rtrB#show ip ospf interface
Loopback0 is up, line protocol is up
  Internet Address 2.2.2.2/32, Area 2
  Process ID 1, Router ID 2.2.2.2, Network Type LOOPBACK, Cost: 1
  Loopback interface is treated as a stub Host
Serial0/1 is up, line protocol is up
  Internet Address 10.1.1.2/30, Area 0
  Process ID 1, Router ID 2.2.2.2, Network Type POINT_TO_POINT, Cost: 64
  Transmit Delay is 1 sec, State POINT_TO_POINT,
  Timer intervals configured, Hello 10, Dead 40, Wait 40, Retransmit 5
    Hello due in 00:00:02
  Neighbor Count is 1, Adjacent neighbor count is 1
    Adjacent with neighbor 1.1.1.1
  Suppress hello for 0 neighbor(s)
Serial1/0 is up, line protocol is up
  Internet Address 10.1.1.5/30, Area 0
  Process ID 1, Router ID 2.2.2.2, Network Type POINT_TO_POINT, Cost: 1562
  Transmit Delay is 1 sec, State POINT_TO_POINT,
  Timer intervals configured, Hello 10, Dead 40, Wait 40, Retransmit 5
    No Hellos (Passive interface)
  Neighbor Count is 0, Adjacent neighbor count is 0
  Suppress hello for 0 neighbor(s)
...
```

Troubleshooting

Step 1 When using the **default** option, make sure that interfaces with OSPF neighbors have been made active using the **no passive-interface** command.

CHAPTER 14

Route Redistribution

14-1: **redistribute** *routing-process process-id*

14-2: **redistribute** *routing-process process-id* **metric** *ospf-metric*

14-3: **redistribute** *routing-process process-id* **metric-type** *metric-type*

14-4: **redistribute** *routing-process process-id* **subnets**

14-5: **redistribute** *routing-process process-id* **tag** *tag-value*

Syntax Description:

- *routing-process*—Routing process to redistribute into OSPF. The routing process can be BGP, Connected, EGP, EIGRP, IGRP, ISIS, ISO-IGRP, Mobile, ODR, OSPF, RIP, or Static.
- *process-id*—The process ID of the routing process (if applicable).
- *ospf-metric*—The metric or cost to assign to the redistributed routes. If this option is not used, a default metric of 1 will be used for redistributed BGP routes and a default metric of 20 will be used for all other protocols. The range of values is 0–16,777,214.
- *metric-type*—Routes are redistributed into OSPF as either type 1 or type 2 routes. The default is type 2.
- *tag-value*—A 32-bit value that is attached to the redistributed routes. The route tag is not used by OSPF but can be referenced in a route map for making policy decisions. One possible use is to base the decision to redistribute a route based on the route tag

(see Section 14-6). The default tag value is 0. The range of values for the tag is 0–4,294,967,295.

Purpose: To redistribute routes learned from another routing process into OSPF. Redistributed routes become OSPF external type 2 routes by default. The default cost or metric of a redistributed route is 1 for BGP and 20 for all other protocols. This command will redistribute classful routes into OSPF only if the **subnets** keyword is not used. There are three general types of classful routes:

- A Class A address with an 8-bit subnet mask
- A Class B address with a 16-bit subnet mask
- A Class C address with a 24-bit subnet mask

Initial Cisco IOS Software Release: 10.0

Configuration Example 1: Redistributing Classful Routes into OSPF with the Default Type and Metric

In Figure 14-1, Router B is receiving six routes from Router C via EIGRP. Three of the EIGRP routes are classful (5.0.0.0/8, 145.5.0.0/16, 205.5.5.0/24) and three are classless (6.0.0.0/12, 146.6.0.0/20, 206.6.6.0/28). Before redistributing the EIGRP routes into OSPF on Router B, configure the routers as shown in the listing that follows.

Figure 14-1 *By Default, OSPF Will Redistribute Only Classful Routes*

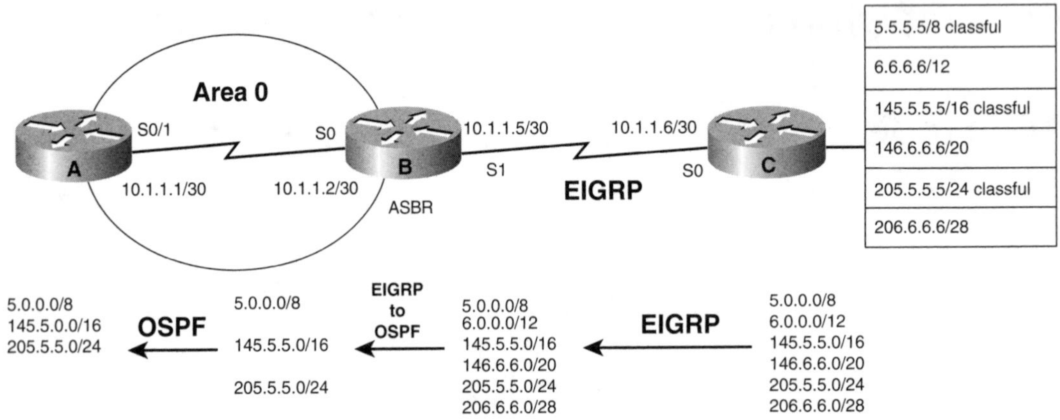


```
Router A
interface Loopback0
 ip address 1.1.1.1 255.255.255.255
!
```

```
interface Serial0/1
 ip address 10.1.1.1 255.255.255.252
 clockrate 64000
!
router ospf 1
 network 10.1.1.0 0.0.0.3 area 0
```

```
Router B
interface Loopback0
 ip address 2.2.2.2 255.255.255.255
!
interface Serial0
 ip address 10.1.1.2 255.255.255.252
!
interface Serial 1
 ip address 10.1.1.5 255.255.255.252
!
router eigrp 1
 network 10.0.0.0
!
router ospf 1
 network 10.1.1.0 0.0.0.3 area 0
```

```
Router C
interface Loopback0
 ip address 3.3.3.3 255.255.255.255
!
interface Loopback1
 ip address 5.5.5.5 255.0.0.0
!
interface Loopback2
 ip address 6.6.6.6 255.240.0.0
!
interface Loopback3
 ip address 145.5.5.5 255.255.0.0
!
interface Loopback4
 ip address 146.6.6.6 255.255.240.0
!
interface Loopback5
 ip address 205.5.5.5 255.255.255.0
!
interface Loopback6
 ip address 206.6.6.6 255.255.255.240
!
interface Serial0
 ip address 10.1.1.6 255.255.255.252
!
router eigrp 1
 network 5.0.0.0
 network 6.0.0.0
```

continues

```
network 10.0.0.0
network 145.5.0.0
network 146.6.0.0
network 205.5.5.0
network 206.6.6.0
no auto-summary
```

Verify that Routers A and B have established an OSPF neighbor relationship.

```
rtrA#show ip ospf neighbor

Neighbor ID     Pri   State           Dead Time   Address         Interface
2.2.2.2           1   FULL/  -        00:00:36    10.1.1.2        Serial0/1
```

Verify that Routers B and C have formed an EIGRP neighbor relationship.

```
rtrB#show ip eigrp neighbors
IP-EIGRP neighbors for process 1
H   Address                 Interface   Hold Uptime   SRTT   RTO  Q  Seq
                                        (sec)         (ms)       Cnt Num
0   10.1.1.6                Se1           11 00:25:42  308  2280  0  4
```

Verify that Router B is receiving the six EIGRP routes from Router C.

```
rtrB#show ip route
Codes: C - connected, S - static, I - IGRP, R - RIP, M - mobile, B - BGP
       D - EIGRP, EX - EIGRP external, O - OSPF, IA - OSPF inter area
       N1 - OSPF NSSA external type 1, N2 - OSPF NSSA external type 2
       E1 - OSPF external type 1, E2 - OSPF external type 2, E - EGP
       i - IS-IS, L1 - IS-IS level-1, L2 - IS-IS level-2, * - candidate default
       U - per-user static route, o - ODR

Gateway of last resort is not set

     2.0.0.0/32 is subnetted, 1 subnets
C       2.2.2.2 is directly connected, Loopback0
D    205.5.5.0/24 [90/40640000] via 10.1.1.6, 00:26:25, Serial1
     206.6.6.0/28 is subnetted, 1 subnets
D       206.6.6.0 [90/40640000] via 10.1.1.6, 00:26:25, Serial1
D    5.0.0.0/8 [90/40640000] via 10.1.1.6, 00:26:25, Serial1
     6.0.0.0/12 is subnetted, 1 subnets
D       6.0.0.0 [90/40640000] via 10.1.1.6, 00:26:25, Serial1
D    145.5.0.0/16 [90/40640000] via 10.1.1.6, 00:26:25, Serial1
     10.0.0.0/30 is subnetted, 2 subnets
C       10.1.1.0 is directly connected, Serial0
C       10.1.1.4 is directly connected, Serial1
     146.6.0.0/20 is subnetted, 1 subnets
D       146.6.0.0 [90/40640000] via 10.1.1.6, 00:26:27, Serial1
```

Modify the configuration on Router B to redistribute the classful EIGRP routes into OSPF.

```
router ospf 1
 redistribute eigrp 1
```

When the command **redistribute eigrp 1** is entered, the router will give you the following friendly reminder:

```
rtrB(config-router)#redistribute eigrp 1
% Only classful networks will be redistributed
```

Verification

Determine the routes that have been redistributed by examining the IP routing table on Router A.

```
rtrA#show ip route
Codes: C - connected, S - static, I - IGRP, R - RIP, M - mobile, B - BGP
       D - EIGRP, EX - EIGRP external, O - OSPF, IA - OSPF inter area
       N1 - OSPF NSSA external type 1, N2 - OSPF NSSA external type 2
       E1 - OSPF external type 1, E2 - OSPF external type 2, E - EGP
       i - IS-IS, L1 - IS-IS level-1, L2 - IS-IS level-2, ia - IS-IS inter area
       * - candidate default, U - per-user static route, o - ODR
       P - periodic downloaded static route

Gateway of last resort is not set

     1.0.0.0/32 is subnetted, 1 subnets
C       1.1.1.1 is directly connected, Loopback0
O E2 205.5.5.0/24 [110/20] via 10.1.1.2, 00:33:23, Serial0/1
O E2 5.0.0.0/8 [110/20] via 10.1.1.2, 00:33:23, Serial0/1
O E2 145.5.0.0/16 [110/20] via 10.1.1.2, 00:33:23, Serial0/1
     10.0.0.0/30 is subnetted, 1 subnets
C       10.1.1.0 is directly connected, Serial0/1
```

Only the EIGRP classful routes were redistributed into OSPF. As you can see in the routing table on Router A, EIGRP routes were redistributed as external type 2 with a cost or metric of 20. This information can also be found by inspecting the OSPF database on Router B.

```
rtrB#show ip ospf database external

       OSPF Router with ID (2.2.2.2) (Process ID 1)


                Type-5 AS External Link States
```

continues

```
LS age: 410
Options: (No TOS-capability, DC)
LS Type: AS External Link
Link State ID: 5.0.0.0 (External Network Number )
Advertising Router: 2.2.2.2
LS Seq Number: 80000004
Checksum: 0x642C
Length: 36
Network Mask: /8
      Metric Type: 2 (Larger than any link state path)
      TOS: 0
      Metric: 20
      Forward Address: 0.0.0.0
      External Route Tag: 0

LS age: 419
Options: (No TOS-capability, DC)
LS Type: AS External Link
Link State ID: 145.5.0.0 (External Network Number )
Advertising Router: 2.2.2.2
LS Seq Number: 80000004
Checksum: 0x5F9
Length: 36
Network Mask: /16
      Metric Type: 2 (Larger than any link state path)
      TOS: 0
      Metric: 20
      Forward Address: 0.0.0.0
      External Route Tag: 0

LS age: 435
Options: (No TOS-capability, DC)
LS Type: AS External Link
Link State ID: 205.5.5.0 (External Network Number )
Advertising Router: 2.2.2.2
LS Seq Number: 80000004
Checksum: 0xBEFE
Length: 36
Network Mask: /24
      Metric Type: 2 (Larger than any link state path)
      TOS: 0
      Metric: 20
      Forward Address: 0.0.0.0
      External Route Tag: 0
```

Configuration Example 2: Redistributing Classful Routes into OSPF with the Default Type and Specific Metric

In the first configuration example for Figure 14-1, the EIGRP routes were redistributed into OSPF with a default metric of 20. For this example, modify the configuration on Router B to change the metric of all the redistributed EIGRP routes to 66.

```
Router B
router ospf 1
 redistribute eigrp 1 metric 66
```

Verification

Verify that the new metric has been applied to the redistributed EIGRP routes. On Router A you can look at the IP routing table and on Router B you can inspect the OSPF database.

```
rtrA#show ip route
Codes: C - connected, S - static, I - IGRP, R - RIP, M - mobile, B - BGP
       D - EIGRP, EX - EIGRP external, O - OSPF, IA - OSPF inter area
       N1 - OSPF NSSA external type 1, N2 - OSPF NSSA external type 2
       E1 - OSPF external type 1, E2 - OSPF external type 2, E - EGP
       i - IS-IS, L1 - IS-IS level-1, L2 - IS-IS level-2, ia - IS-IS inter area
       * - candidate default, U - per-user static route, o - ODR
       P - periodic downloaded static route

Gateway of last resort is not set

     1.0.0.0/32 is subnetted, 1 subnets
C       1.1.1.1 is directly connected, Loopback0
O E2 205.5.5.0/24 [110/66] via 10.1.1.2, 00:00:16, Serial0/1
O E2 5.0.0.0/8 [110/66] via 10.1.1.2, 00:00:16, Serial0/1
O E2 145.5.0.0/16 [110/66] via 10.1.1.2, 00:00:16, Serial0/1
     10.0.0.0/30 is subnetted, 1 subnets
C       10.1.1.0 is directly connected, Serial0/1
```

Configuration Example 3: Redistributing Classful Routes into OSPF as Type 1 Routes Using a Specific Metric

Routes are redistributed in OSPF as either type 1 (E1) routes or type 2 (E2) routes, with type 2 being the default. A type 1 route has a metric that is the sum of the internal OSPF cost and the external redistributed cost. A type 2 route has a metric equal only to the redistributed cost, as shown in Figure 14-2. If routes are redistributed into OSPF as type 2 then every router in the OSPF domain will see the same cost to reach the external networks. If routes are redistributed into OSPF as type 1, then the cost to reach the external networks could vary from router to router.

Figure 14-2 *OSPF Routes Are Redistributed as Either Type 1 or Type 2 Routes*

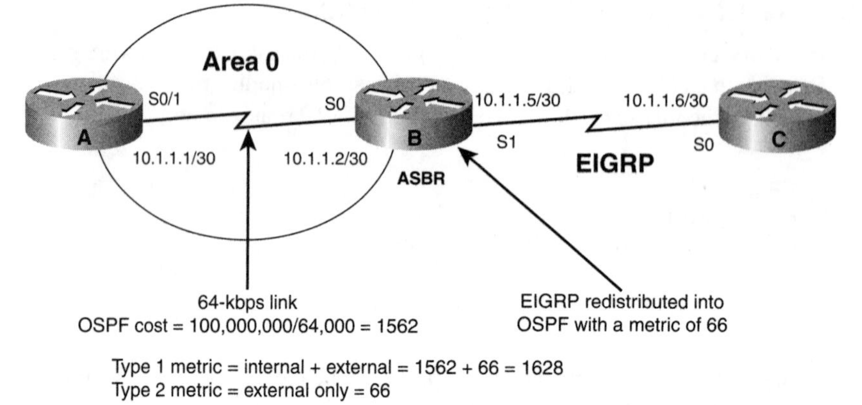

Modify the configuration on Router B so that the EIGRP routes are redistributed as type 1 routes.

```
Router B
router ospf 1
 redistribute eigrp 1 metric 66 metric-type 1
```

Verification

Verify that the EIGRP routes have been redistributed into OSPF as type 1 routes with a metric of 66.

```
rtrB#show ip ospf database external

       OSPF Router with ID (2.2.2.2) (Process ID 1)


                Type-5 AS External Link States

  LS age: 149
  Options: (No TOS-capability, DC)
  LS Type: AS External Link
  Link State ID: 5.0.0.0 (External Network Number )
  Advertising Router: 2.2.2.2
  LS Seq Number: 80000008
  Checksum: 0xA638
  Length: 36
  Network Mask: /8
        Metric Type: 1 (Comparable directly to link state metric)
        TOS: 0
```

```
        Metric: 66
        Forward Address: 0.0.0.0
        External Route Tag: 0

  LS age: 158
  Options: (No TOS-capability, DC)
  LS Type: AS External Link
  Link State ID: 145.5.0.0 (External Network Number )
  Advertising Router: 2.2.2.2
  LS Seq Number: 80000008
  Checksum: 0x4706
  Length: 36
  Network Mask: /16
        Metric Type: 1 (Comparable directly to link state metric)
        TOS: 0
        Metric: 66
        Forward Address: 0.0.0.0
        External Route Tag: 0

  LS age: 168
  Options: (No TOS-capability, DC)
  LS Type: AS External Link
  Link State ID: 205.5.5.0 (External Network Number )
  Advertising Router: 2.2.2.2
  LS Seq Number: 80000008
  Checksum: 0x10B
  Length: 36
  Network Mask: /24
        Metric Type: 1 (Comparable directly to link state metric)
        TOS: 0
        Metric: 66
        Forward Address: 0.0.0.0
        External Route Tag: 0
```

Verify that the cost of these routes as seen by Router A is the sum of the redistributed metric and the OSPF cost to reach Router B.

```
rtrA#show ip route
Codes: C - connected, S - static, I - IGRP, R - RIP, M - mobile, B - BGP
       D - EIGRP, EX - EIGRP external, O - OSPF, IA - OSPF inter area
       N1 - OSPF NSSA external type 1, N2 - OSPF NSSA external type 2
       E1 - OSPF external type 1, E2 - OSPF external type 2, E - EGP
       i - IS-IS, L1 - IS-IS level-1, L2 - IS-IS level-2, ia - IS-IS inter area
       * - candidate default, U - per-user static route, o - ODR
       P - periodic downloaded static route

Gateway of last resort is not set

     1.0.0.0/32 is subnetted, 1 subnets
C       1.1.1.1 is directly connected, Loopback0
O E1 205.5.5.0/24 [110/1628] via 10.1.1.2, 00:05:36, Serial0/1
```

continues

```
O E1 5.0.0.0/8 [110/1628] via 10.1.1.2, 00:05:36, Serial0/1
O E1 145.5.0.0/16 [110/1628] via 10.1.1.2, 00:05:36, Serial0/1
     10.0.0.0/30 is subnetted, 1 subnets
C       10.1.1.0 is directly connected, Serial0/1
```

Configuration Example 4: Redistributing Subnet Routes into OSPF as Type 1 Routes Using a Specific Metric

The previous configuration examples redistributed only the classful EIGRP routes into OSPF. Modify the configuration on Router B to redistribute all the EIGRP routes.

```
Router B
router ospf 1
 redistribute eigrp 1 metric 66 metric-type 1 subnets
```

Verification

Verify that the classless EIGRP routes have been redistributed into OSPF on Router B by inspecting the IP routing table on Router A.

```
rtrA#show ip route
Codes: C - connected, S - static, I - IGRP, R - RIP, M - mobile, B - BGP
       D - EIGRP, EX - EIGRP external, O - OSPF, IA - OSPF inter area
       N1 - OSPF NSSA external type 1, N2 - OSPF NSSA external type 2
       E1 - OSPF external type 1, E2 - OSPF external type 2, E - EGP
       i - IS-IS, L1 - IS-IS level-1, L2 - IS-IS level-2, ia - IS-IS inter area
       * - candidate default, U - per-user static route, o - ODR
       P - periodic downloaded static route

Gateway of last resort is not set

     1.0.0.0/32 is subnetted, 1 subnets
C       1.1.1.1 is directly connected, Loopback0
O E1 205.5.5.0/24 [110/1628] via 10.1.1.2, 00:22:36, Serial0/1
     206.6.6.0/28 is subnetted, 1 subnets
O E1    206.6.6.0 [110/1628] via 10.1.1.2, 00:02:37, Serial0/1
O E1 5.0.0.0/8 [110/1628] via 10.1.1.2, 00:22:36, Serial0/1
     6.0.0.0/12 is subnetted, 1 subnets
O E1    6.0.0.0 [110/1628] via 10.1.1.2, 00:02:37, Serial0/1
O E1 145.5.0.0/16 [110/1628] via 10.1.1.2, 00:22:37, Serial0/1
     10.0.0.0/30 is subnetted, 2 subnets
C       10.1.1.0 is directly connected, Serial0/1
O E1    10.1.1.4 [110/1628] via 10.1.1.2, 00:02:40, Serial0/1
     146.6.0.0/20 is subnetted, 1 subnets
O E1    146.6.0.0 [110/1628] via 10.1.1.2, 00:02:40, Serial0/1
```

Configuration Example 5: Redistributing Subnet Routes into OSPF as Type 1 Routes Using a Specific Metric and Route Tag

A route tag is a 32-bit value that is attached to the redistributed routes. Every route that is redistributed will be assigned the same route tag unless a route map is used (see Section 14-6). OSPF itself does not use the route tag, but you can use the tag value to implement policy decisions. For example, in Section 14-6, the tag value is used to determine which routes will be redistributed into OSPF based on their tag values. This example presents only the mechanics of assigning the tag. Modify the configuration on Router B to redistribute the EIGRP routes with a tag value of 555.

```
Router B
router ospf 1
 redistribute eigrp 1 metric 66 metric-type 1 subnets tag 555
```

Verification

The tag value can be verified by examining a particular route in the IP routing table on Router A.

```
rtrA#show ip route 5.0.0.0
Routing entry for 5.0.0.0/8
  Known via "ospf 1", distance 110, metric 1628
  Tag 555, type extern 1
  Last update from 10.1.1.2 on Serial0/1, 00:03:57 ago
  Routing Descriptor Blocks:
  * 10.1.1.2, from 2.2.2.2, 00:03:57 ago, via Serial0/1
      Route metric is 1628, traffic share count is 1
```

The tag value can also be verified by inspecting the external routes in the OSPF database on either Router A or B.

```
rtrA#show ip ospf database external 5.0.0.0

            OSPF Router with ID (1.1.1.1) (Process ID 1)

                Type-5 AS External Link States

  Routing Bit Set on this LSA
  LS age: 313
  Options: (No TOS-capability, DC)
  LS Type: AS External Link
  Link State ID: 5.0.0.0 (External Network Number )
  Advertising Router: 2.2.2.2
  LS Seq Number: 8000002A
  Checksum: 0x8D02
```

continues

```
  Length: 36
  Network Mask: /8
        Metric Type: 1 (Comparable directly to link state metric)
        TOS: 0
        Metric: 66
        Forward Address: 0.0.0.0
        External Route Tag: 555
```

```
rtrB#show ip ospf database external 145.5.0.0

       OSPF Router with ID (2.2.2.2) (Process ID 1)


                Type-5 AS External Link States

  LS age: 373
  Options: (No TOS-capability, DC)
  LS Type: AS External Link
  Link State ID: 145.5.0.0 (External Network Number )
  Advertising Router: 2.2.2.2
  LS Seq Number: 8000002A
  Checksum: 0x2ECF
  Length: 36
  Network Mask: /16
        Metric Type: 1 (Comparable directly to link state metric)
        TOS: 0
        Metric: 66
        Forward Address: 0.0.0.0
        External Route Tag: 555
```

Troubleshooting

Verify that there is a neighbor relationship between the OSPF routers by using the **show ip ospf** neighbors command.

Step 1 Verify that the **redistribute** command is referencing the correct routing process and process number (if applicable).

Step 2 Remember the defaults: metric = 20 (1 for BGP), metric type = 2, tag = 0.

To avoid problems associated with mutual redistribution, either use a distribute list (see Sections 7-5, 7-10, and 7-15) or a route map (see Section 14-6) to allow only routes that originated in the routing process domain.

For example, if on the same router, EIGRP is redistributed into OSPF and OSPF is redistributed into EIGRP, then OSPF routes will be redistributed back into OSPF from EIGRP and EIGRP routes will be redistributed back into EIGRP from OSPF. Use a route map or distribute list to prevent this from occurring.

14-6: redistribute *routing-process process-id* route-map *route-map-name*

Syntax Description:

- *routing-process*—Routing process to redistribute into OSPF. The routing process can be BGP, Connected, EGP, EIGRP, IGRP, ISIS, ISO-IGRP, Mobile, ODR, OSPF, RIP, or Static.
- *process-id*—The process ID of the routing process (if applicable).
- *route-map-name*—Name of the route map used to control which routes are redistributed or to set the parameters of the redistributed routes (metric, metric-type, or tag).

Purpose: To control the redistribution of routes learned from another routing process into OSPF. Redistributed routes become OSPF external type 2 routes by default. The default cost or metric of a redistributed route is 1 for BGP and 20 for all other protocols. This command will redistribute classful routes into OSPF only if the **subnets** keyword is not used. There are three general types of classful routes:

- A Class A address with an 8-bit mask
- A Class B address with a 16-bit mask
- A Class C address with a 24-bit mask

You can use the **subnets** keyword to redistribute all routes. You can also use the **metric**, **metric-type**, and **tag** keywords. These values can also be set in the route map as shown in the examples covered in this section.

Initial Cisco IOS Software Release: 10.0

Configuration Example 1: Controlling the Routes to Be Redistributed Based on IP Address

In Figure 14-3, Router B is receiving six routes from Router C via EIGRP. Three of the EIGRP routes are classful (5.0.0.0/8, 145.5.0.0/16, 205.5.5.0/24) and three are classless (6.0.0.0/12, 146.6.0.0/20, 206.6.6.0/28). For this example, only the classless routes will be redistributed. Before redistributing the EIGRP routes into OSPF on Router B, configure the routers as shown in the listing that follows.

Figure 14-3 *A Route Map Is Needed to Control Which Routes Are Redistributed into OSPF from EIGRP*

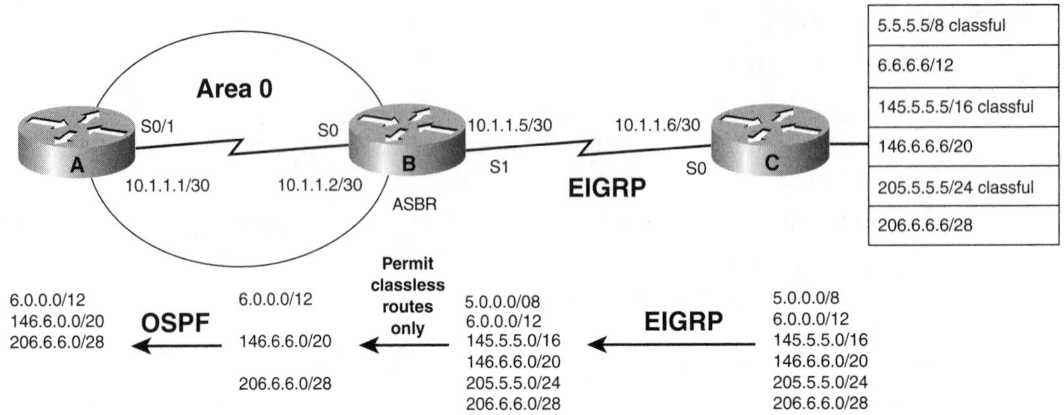

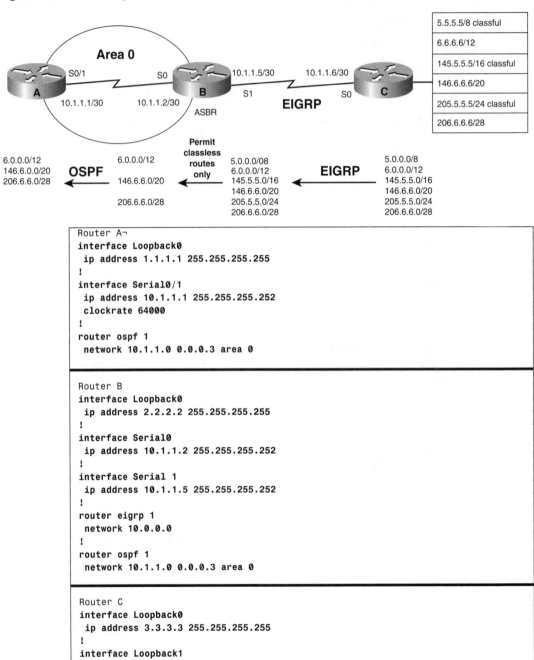

```
Router A¬
interface Loopback0
 ip address 1.1.1.1 255.255.255.255
!
interface Serial0/1
 ip address 10.1.1.1 255.255.255.252
 clockrate 64000
!
router ospf 1
 network 10.1.1.0 0.0.0.3 area 0
```

```
Router B
interface Loopback0
 ip address 2.2.2.2 255.255.255.255
!
interface Serial0
 ip address 10.1.1.2 255.255.255.252
!
interface Serial 1
 ip address 10.1.1.5 255.255.255.252
!
router eigrp 1
 network 10.0.0.0
!
router ospf 1
 network 10.1.1.0 0.0.0.3 area 0
```

```
Router C
interface Loopback0
 ip address 3.3.3.3 255.255.255.255
!
interface Loopback1
 ip address 5.5.5.5 255.0.0.0
```

```
!
interface Loopback2
 ip address 6.6.6.6 255.240.0.0
!
interface Loopback3
 ip address 145.5.5.5 255.255.0.0
!
interface Loopback4
 ip address 146.6.6.6 255.255.240.0
!
interface Loopback5
 ip address 205.5.5.5 255.255.255.0
!
interface Loopback6
 ip address 206.6.6.6 255.255.255.240
!
interface Serial0
 ip address 10.1.1.6 255.255.255.252
!
router eigrp 1
 network 5.0.0.0
 network 6.0.0.0
 network 10.0.0.0
 network 145.5.0.0
 network 146.6.0.0
 network 205.5.5.0
 network 206.6.6.0
 no auto-summary
```

Verify that Routers A and B have established an OSPF neighbor relationship.

```
rtrA#show ip ospf neighbor

Neighbor ID     Pri   State           Dead Time   Address         Interface
2.2.2.2           1   FULL/  -        00:00:36    10.1.1.2        Serial0/1
```

Verify that Routers B and C have formed an EIGRP neighbor relationship.

```
rtrB#show ip eigrp neighbors
IP-EIGRP neighbors for process 1
H   Address                 Interface   Hold Uptime   SRTT   RTO  Q  Seq
                                        (sec)         (ms)       Cnt Num
0   10.1.1.6                Se1           11 00:25:42  308  2280  0  4
```

Verify that Router B is receiving the six EIGRP routes from Router C.

```
rtrB#show ip route
Codes: C - connected, S - static, I - IGRP, R - RIP, M - mobile, B - BGP
       D - EIGRP, EX - EIGRP external, O - OSPF, IA - OSPF inter area
       N1 - OSPF NSSA external type 1, N2 - OSPF NSSA external type 2
       E1 - OSPF external type 1, E2 - OSPF external type 2, E - EGP
       i - IS-IS, L1 - IS-IS level-1, L2 - IS-IS level-2, * - candidate default
       U - per-user static route, o - ODR

Gateway of last resort is not set

     2.0.0.0/32 is subnetted, 1 subnets
C       2.2.2.2 is directly connected, Loopback0
D    205.5.5.0/24 [90/40640000] via 10.1.1.6, 00:26:25, Serial1
     206.6.6.0/28 is subnetted, 1 subnets
D       206.6.6.0 [90/40640000] via 10.1.1.6, 00:26:25, Serial1
D    5.0.0.0/8 [90/40640000] via 10.1.1.6, 00:26:25, Serial1
     6.0.0.0/12 is subnetted, 1 subnets
D       6.0.0.0 [90/40640000] via 10.1.1.6, 00:26:25, Serial1
D    145.5.0.0/16 [90/40640000] via 10.1.1.6, 00:26:25, Serial1
     10.0.0.0/30 is subnetted, 2 subnets
C       10.1.1.0 is directly connected, Serial0
C       10.1.1.4 is directly connected, Serial1
     146.6.0.0/20 is subnetted, 1 subnets
D       146.6.0.0 [90/40640000] via 10.1.1.6, 00:26:27, Serial1
```

Modify the configuration on Router B to redistribute only the classless EIGRP routes into OSPF.

```
Router B
router ospf 1
 redistribute eigrp 1 subnets route-map control-eigrp
!
access-list 1 permit 6.0.0.0 0.15.255.255
access-list 1 permit 146.6.0.0 0.0.15.255
access-list 1 permit 206.6.6.0 0.0.0.15
access-list 1 permit 10.1.1.4 0.0.0.3
route-map control-eigrp permit 10
 match ip address 1
```

Verification

Verify that only the classless EIGRP routes have been redistributed into OSPF.

```
rtrA#show ip route
Codes: C - connected, S - static, I - IGRP, R - RIP, M - mobile, B - BGP
       D - EIGRP, EX - EIGRP external, O - OSPF, IA - OSPF inter area
```

```
       N1 - OSPF NSSA external type 1, N2 - OSPF NSSA external type 2
       E1 - OSPF external type 1, E2 - OSPF external type 2, E - EGP
       i - IS-IS, L1 - IS-IS level-1, L2 - IS-IS level-2, ia - IS-IS inter area
       * - candidate default, U - per-user static route, o - ODR
       P - periodic downloaded static route

Gateway of last resort is not set

     1.0.0.0/32 is subnetted, 1 subnets
C       1.1.1.1 is directly connected, Loopback0
     206.6.6.0/28 is subnetted, 1 subnets
O E2    206.6.6.0 [110/20] via 10.1.1.2, 00:02:05, Serial0/1
     6.0.0.0/12 is subnetted, 1 subnets
O E2    6.0.0.0 [110/20] via 10.1.1.2, 00:02:05, Serial0/1
10.0.0.0/30 is subnetted, 1 subnets
C       10.1.1.0 is directly connected, Serial0/1
     146.6.0.0/20 is subnetted, 1 subnets
O E2    146.6.0.0 [110/20] via 10.1.1.2, 00:02:06, Serial0/1
O E2    10.1.1.4 [110/200] via 10.1.1.2, 00:02:06, Serial0/1
```

Configuration Example 2: Modifying the Metric of Redistributed Routes Using a Route Map

In the first configuration example for Figure 14-3, the EIGRP routes were redistributed into OSPF with a default metric of 20. For this example, modify the configuration on Router B to change the metric of the classful routes to 100 and the metric of the classless routes to 200.

```
Router B
router ospf 1
 redistribute eigrp 1 subnets route-map control-eigrp
!
access-list 1 permit 6.0.0.0 0.15.255.255
access-list 1 permit 146.6.0.0 0.0.15.255
access-list 1 permit 206.6.6.0 0.0.0.15
access-list 1 permit 10.1.1.4 0.0.0.3
route-map control-eigrp permit 10
 match ip address 1
 set metric 200
!
route-map control-eigrp permit 20
 set metric 100
```

Verification

Verify that the new metric has been applied to the redistributed EIGRP routes. On Router A you can look at the IP routing table and the OSPF database.

```
rtrA#show ip route
Codes: C - connected, S - static, I - IGRP, R - RIP, M - mobile, B - BGP
       D - EIGRP, EX - EIGRP external, O - OSPF, IA - OSPF inter area
       N1 - OSPF NSSA external type 1, N2 - OSPF NSSA external type 2
       E1 - OSPF external type 1, E2 - OSPF external type 2, E - EGP
       i - IS-IS, L1 - IS-IS level-1, L2 - IS-IS level-2, ia - IS-IS inter area
       * - candidate default, U - per-user static route, o - ODR
       P - periodic downloaded static route

Gateway of last resort is not set

     1.0.0.0/32 is subnetted, 1 subnets
C       1.1.1.1 is directly connected, Loopback0
O E2 205.5.5.0/24 [110/100] via 10.1.1.2, 00:01:53, Serial0/1
     206.6.6.0/28 is subnetted, 1 subnets
O E2    206.6.6.0 [110/200] via 10.1.1.2, 00:01:53, Serial0/1
O E2 5.0.0.0/8 [110/100] via 10.1.1.2, 00:01:53, Serial0/1
     6.0.0.0/12 is subnetted, 1 subnets
O E2    6.0.0.0 [110/200] via 10.1.1.2, 00:01:53, Serial0/1
     172.16.0.0/24 is subnetted, 1 subnets
C       172.16.1.0 is directly connected, Ethernet0/0
O E2 145.5.0.0/16 [110/100] via 10.1.1.2, 00:01:54, Serial0/1
     10.0.0.0/30 is subnetted, 2 subnets
C       10.1.1.0 is directly connected, Serial0/1
O E2    10.1.1.4 [110/200] via 10.1.1.2, 00:01:55, Serial0/1
     146.6.0.0/20 is subnetted, 1 subnets
O E2    146.6.0.0 [110/200] via 10.1.1.2, 00:01:55, Serial0/1

rtrA#show ip ospf database external 5.0.0.0

            OSPF Router with ID (1.1.1.1) (Process ID 1)

                Type-5 AS External Link States

  Routing Bit Set on this LSA
  LS age: 254
  Options: (No TOS-capability, DC)
  LS Type: AS External Link
  Link State ID: 5.0.0.0 (External Network Number )
  Advertising Router: 2.2.2.2
  LS Seq Number: 80000002
  Checksum: 0x8BB6
  Length: 36
  Network Mask: /8
        Metric Type: 2 (Larger than any link state path)
        TOS: 0
        Metric: 100
        Forward Address: 0.0.0.0
```

```
        External Route Tag: 0

rtrA#show ip ospf database external 206.6.6.0

            OSPF Router with ID (1.1.1.1) (Process ID 1)

                Type-5 AS External Link States

  Routing Bit Set on this LSA
  LS age: 297
  Options: (No TOS-capability, DC)
  LS Type: AS External Link
  Link State ID: 206.6.6.0 (External Network Number )
  Advertising Router: 2.2.2.2
  LS Seq Number: 80000003
  Checksum: 0x51C4
  Length: 36
  Network Mask: /28
        Metric Type: 2 (Larger than any link state path)
        TOS: 0
        Metric: 200
        Forward Address: 0.0.0.0
        External Route Tag: 0
```

Configuration Example 3: Modifying the Metric Type of Redistributed Routes Using a Route Map

In Figure 14-3, configuration example 1 for the **redistribute route-map** command, the EIGRP routes were redistributed into OSPF with a default metric type of 2. For this example, modify the configuration on Router B to change the metric type of the classful routes to type 1.

```
Router B
router ospf 1
 redistribute eigrp 1 subnets route-map control-eigrp
 network 10.1.1.0 0.0.0.3 area 0
!
access-list 1 permit 6.0.0.0 0.15.255.255
access-list 1 permit 146.6.0.0 0.0.15.255
access-list 1 permit 206.6.6.0 0.0.0.15
access-list 1 permit
route-map control-eigrp permit 10
 match ip address 1
 set metric 200
!
route-map control-eigrp permit 20
 set metric 100
 set metric-type type-1
```

Verification

Verify that the classful EIGRP routes have been redistributed into OSPF as metric type 1 routes.

```
rtrA#show ip route
Codes: C - connected, S - static, I - IGRP, R - RIP, M - mobile, B - BGP
       D - EIGRP, EX - EIGRP external, O - OSPF, IA - OSPF inter area
       N1 - OSPF NSSA external type 1, N2 - OSPF NSSA external type 2
       E1 - OSPF external type 1, E2 - OSPF external type 2, E - EGP
       i - IS-IS, L1 - IS-IS level-1, L2 - IS-IS level-2, ia - IS-IS inter area
       * - candidate default, U - per-user static route, o - ODR
       P - periodic downloaded static route

Gateway of last resort is not set

     1.0.0.0/32 is subnetted, 1 subnets
C       1.1.1.1 is directly connected, Loopback0
O E1 205.5.5.0/24 [110/1662] via 10.1.1.2, 00:01:38, Serial0/1
     206.6.6.0/28 is subnetted, 1 subnets
O E2    206.6.6.0 [110/200] via 10.1.1.2, 00:01:38, Serial0/1
O E1 5.0.0.0/8 [110/1662] via 10.1.1.2, 00:01:38, Serial0/1
     6.0.0.0/12 is subnetted, 1 subnets
O E2    6.0.0.0 [110/200] via 10.1.1.2, 00:01:38, Serial0/1
     172.16.0.0/24 is subnetted, 1 subnets
C       172.16.1.0 is directly connected, Ethernet0/0
O E1 145.5.0.0/16 [110/1662] via 10.1.1.2, 00:01:39, Serial0/1
     10.0.0.0/30 is subnetted, 2 subnets
C       10.1.1.0 is directly connected, Serial0/1
O E2    10.1.1.4 [110/200] via 10.1.1.2, 00:01:41, Serial0/1
     146.6.0.0/20 is subnetted, 1 subnets
O E2    146.6.0.0 [110/200] via 10.1.1.2, 00:01:41, Serial0/1
```

Configuration Example 4: Modifying the Tag Value of Redistributed Routes Using a Route Map

Modify the configuration on Router B (see Figure 14-3) to set the tag value for the classless routes to 1 and the classful routes to 2.

```
Router B
router ospf 1
 redistribute eigrp 1 subnets route-map control-eigrp
 network 10.1.1.0 0.0.0.3 area 0
!
access-list 1 permit 6.0.0.0 0.15.255.255
access-list 1 permit 146.6.0.0 0.0.15.255
access-list 1 permit 206.6.6.0 0.0.0.15
access-list 1 permit 10.1.1.4 0.0.0.3
route-map control-eigrp permit 10
```

```
 match ip address 1
 set metric 200
 set tag 1
!
route-map control-eigrp permit 20
 set metric 100
 set metric-type type-1
 set tag 2
```

Verification

Verify that the tags have been set on the redistributed EIGRP routes.

```
rtrB#show ip ospf database external 5.0.0.0

       OSPF Router with ID (2.2.2.2) (Process ID 1)


                Type-5 AS External Link States

  LS age: 164
  Options: (No TOS-capability, DC)
  LS Type: AS External Link
  Link State ID: 5.0.0.0 (External Network Number )
  Advertising Router: 2.2.2.2
  LS Seq Number: 80000007
  Checksum: 0x2299
  Length: 36
  Network Mask: /8
        Metric Type: 1 (Comparable directly to link state metric)
        TOS: 0
        Metric: 100
        Forward Address: 0.0.0.0
        External Route Tag: 2
```

```
rtrA#show ip route 206.6.6.0 255.255.255.240
Routing entry for 206.6.6.0/28
  Known via "ospf 1", distance 110, metric 200
  Tag 1, type extern 2, forward metric 1562
  Last update from 10.1.1.2 on Serial0/1, 00:04:40 ago
  Routing Descriptor Blocks:
  * 10.1.1.2, from 2.2.2.2, 00:04:40 ago, via Serial0/1
      Route metric is 200, traffic share count is 1
```

Configuration Example 5: Controlling Route Redistribution Based on Tag Values

In Figure 14-4, Router B is learning six routes via EIGRP. The EIGRP routes are redistributed into OSPF with the classful routes assigned a tag of 2 and the classless routes a tag of 1. Router A is redistributing the OSPF external routes into RIP-2. The policy is to redistribute only the classless routes into RIP-2. This can be accomplished using a route map and an IP access list. Because the external routes have been tagged, a route map can be used that redistributes only routes with a tag value equal to 1. Configure the routers as shown in the listing that follows the figure. Initially, all OSPF routes will be redistributed into RIP-2 on Router A.

Figure 14-4 *A Route Map Can Be Used to Control Route Redistribution Based on the Tag Value*

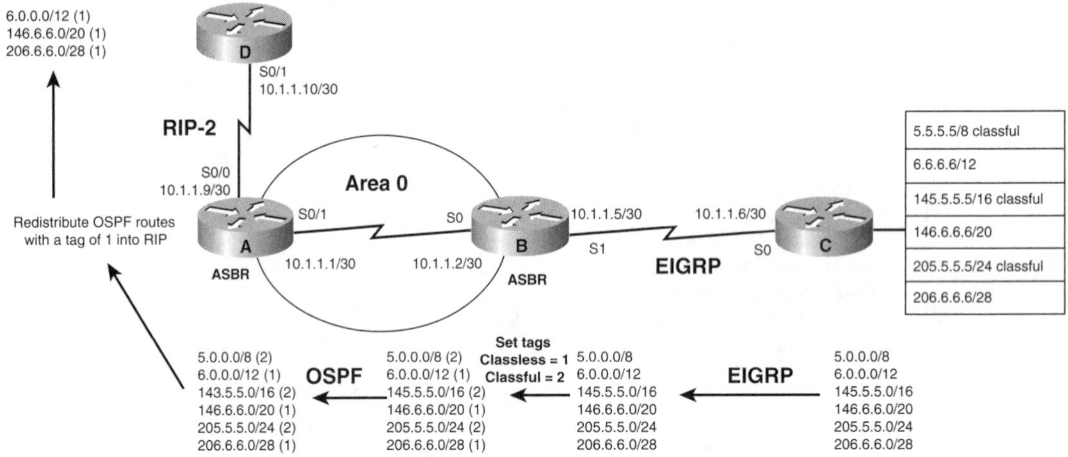


```
Router A
interface Loopback0
 ip address 1.1.1.1 255.255.255.255
!
interface Serial0/0
 bandwidth 64
 ip address 10.1.1.9 255.255.255.252
 no ip mroute-cache
!
interface Serial0/1
 bandwidth 64
 ip address 10.1.1.1 255.255.255.252
 clockrate 64000
!
router ospf 1
 network 10.1.1.0 0.0.0.3 area 0
```

```
!
router rip
 version 2
 redistribute ospf 1 metric 1
 passive-interface Serial0/1
 network 10.0.0.0
 no auto-summary
```

```
Router B
interface Loopback0
 ip address 2.2.2.2 255.255.255.255
!
interface Serial0
 bandwidth 64
 ip address 10.1.1.2 255.255.255.252
 no ip directed-broadcast
!
interface Serial1
 bandwidth 64
 ip address 10.1.1.5 255.255.255.252
 clockrate 64000
!
!
router eigrp 1
 network 10.0.0.0
!
router ospf 1
 redistribute eigrp 1 subnets route-map set-tags
 network 10.1.1.0 0.0.0.3 area 0
!
access-list 1 permit 6.0.0.0 0.15.255.255
access-list 1 permit 146.6.0.0 0.0.15.255
access-list 1 permit 206.6.6.0 0.0.0.15
access-list 1 permit 10.1.1.4 0.0.0.3
route-map set-tags permit 10
 match ip address 1
  set tag 1
!
route-map set-tags permit 20
 set tag 2
```

```
Router C
interface Loopback0
 ip address 3.3.3.3 255.255.255.255
!
interface Loopback1
 ip address 5.5.5.5 255.0.0.0
!
interface Loopback2
 ip address 6.6.6.6 255.240.0.0
!
interface Loopback3
```

continues

```
 ip address 145.5.5.5 255.255.0.0
!
interface Loopback4
 ip address 146.6.6.6 255.255.240.0
!
interface Loopback5
 ip address 205.5.5.5 255.255.255.0
!
interface Loopback6
 ip address 206.6.6.6 255.255.255.240
!
interface Serial0
 bandwidth 64
 ip address 10.1.1.6 255.255.255.252
 no ip directed-broadcast
!
router eigrp 1
 network 5.0.0.0
 network 6.0.0.0
 network 10.0.0.0
 network 145.5.0.0
 network 146.6.0.0
 network 205.5.5.0
 network 206.6.6.0
 no auto-summary
```

```
Router D
interface Serial0/1
 ip address 10.1.1.10 255.255.255.252
 clockrate 64000
!
router rip
 version 2
 network 10.0.0.0
```

Verify that Router D is receiving the redistributed OSPF routes from Router A.

```
rtrD#show ip route
Codes: C - connected, S - static, I - IGRP, R - RIP, M - mobile, B - BGP
       D - EIGRP, EX - EIGRP external, O - OSPF, IA - OSPF inter area
       N1 - OSPF NSSA external type 1, N2 - OSPF NSSA external type 2
       E1 - OSPF external type 1, E2 - OSPF external type 2, E - EGP
       i - IS-IS, L1 - IS-IS level-1, L2 - IS-IS level-2, * - candidate default
       U - per-user static route, o - ODR

Gateway of last resort is not set

R    205.5.5.0/24 [120/1] via 10.1.1.9, 00:00:01, Serial0/1
     206.6.6.0/28 is subnetted, 1 subnets
R       206.6.6.0 [120/1] via 10.1.1.9, 00:00:02, Serial0/1
R    5.0.0.0/8 [120/1] via 10.1.1.9, 00:00:02, Serial0/1
```

```
      6.0.0.0/12 is subnetted, 1 subnets
R        6.0.0.0 [120/1] via 10.1.1.9, 00:00:02, Serial0/1
      172.16.0.0/24 is subnetted, 1 subnets
R        172.16.1.0 [120/1] via 10.1.1.9, 00:00:02, Serial0/1
R     145.5.0.0/16 [120/1] via 10.1.1.9, 00:00:02, Serial0/1
      10.0.0.0/30 is subnetted, 3 subnets
C        10.1.1.8 is directly connected, Serial0/1
R        10.1.1.0 [120/1] via 10.1.1.9, 00:00:02, Serial0/1
R        10.1.1.4 [120/1] via 10.1.1.9, 00:00:02, Serial0/1
      146.6.0.0/20 is subnetted, 1 subnets
R        146.6.0.0 [120/1] via 10.1.1.9, 00:00:05, Serial0/1
```

Modify the configuration on Router A so that only OSPF routes with a tag value of 1 get redistributed into RIP.

```
Router A
router rip
 version 2
 redistribute ospf 1 metric 1 route-map check-tags
 passive-interface Serial0/1
 network 10.0.0.0
 no auto-summary
!
route-map check-tags permit 10
 match tag 1
```

Verification

Verify that the only OSPF routes redistributed into RIP on Router A are those routes with a tag value of 1.

```
rtrD#show ip route
Codes: C - connected, S - static, I - IGRP, R - RIP, M - mobile, B - BGP
       D - EIGRP, EX - EIGRP external, O - OSPF, IA - OSPF inter area
       N1 - OSPF NSSA external type 1, N2 - OSPF NSSA external type 2
       E1 - OSPF external type 1, E2 - OSPF external type 2, E - EGP
       i - IS-IS, L1 - IS-IS level-1, L2 - IS-IS level-2, * - candidate default
       U - per-user static route, o - ODR

Gateway of last resort is not set

      206.6.6.0/28 is subnetted, 1 subnets
R        206.6.6.0 [120/1] via 10.1.1.9, 00:00:01, Serial0/1
      6.0.0.0/12 is subnetted, 1 subnets
R        6.0.0.0 [120/1] via 10.1.1.9, 00:00:02, Serial0/1
      10.0.0.0/30 is subnetted, 3 subnets
C        10.1.1.8 is directly connected, Serial0/1
R        10.1.1.0 [120/1] via 10.1.1.9, 00:00:02, Serial0/1
```

continues

```
R        10.1.1.4 [120/1] via 10.1.1.9, 00:00:02, Serial0/1
      146.6.0.0/20 is subnetted, 1 subnets
R        146.6.0.0 [120/1] via 10.1.1.9, 00:00:02, Serial0/1
```

Troubleshooting

Step 1 Verify that the routes have been assigned the proper tags by using the command **show ip ospf database external** or the command **show ip route** *ip-address mask.*

Step 2 Verify that the **redistribute** command is referencing the correct routing process and process number (if applicable).

Step 3 Verify that the **redistribute** command is referencing the correct route map name.

Step 4 Verify the syntax and logic of the route map.

To avoid problems associated with mutual redistribution, use a distribute list (see Sections 7-5, 7-10, and 7-15) or a route map to allow only routes that have originated in the routing process domain. For example, if EIGRP is redistributed into OSPF and OSPF is redistributed into EIGRP on the same router, then OSPF routes will be redistributed back into OSPF from EIGRP and EIGRP routes will be redistributed back into EIGRP from OSPF. Using a route map or distribute list will prevent this from occurring.

CHAPTER 15

Controlling the OSPF Router ID

15-1: router-id *ip-address*

Syntax Description:

- *ip-address*—The IP address that is to be used as the OSPF router ID.

Purpose: To configure the OSPF router ID. The default OSPF router ID is the numerically highest IP address of any loopback interface that has been configured on the router. If no loopback interfaces have been configured, then the OSPF router ID is the numerically highest IP address of any active interface. The router ID is a component of every OSPF exchange, including Hello packets and link-state advertisements (LSAs). For multiaccess networks, the OSPF router ID is used in the election of the Designated Router (DR). It is desirable to have an OSPF router ID that does not change. If loopback interfaces are not configured on an OSPF router, then the command **router-id** should be used to establish a stable OSPF router ID

Initial Cisco IOS Software Release: 12.0(1)T

Configuration Example: OSPF Router ID Selection

In Figure 15-1, Routers A and B are OSPF neighbors. Router A has two physical interfaces configured, Ethernet 0/0 and Serial 0/1. Initially, interface Ethernet 0/0 is in the shutdown state, so OSPF will choose the router ID as the IP address assigned to Serial 0/1 because it is the only remaining active interface. Configure Routers A and B as shown in the listing that follows the figure.

Figure 15-1 *OSPF Router ID*

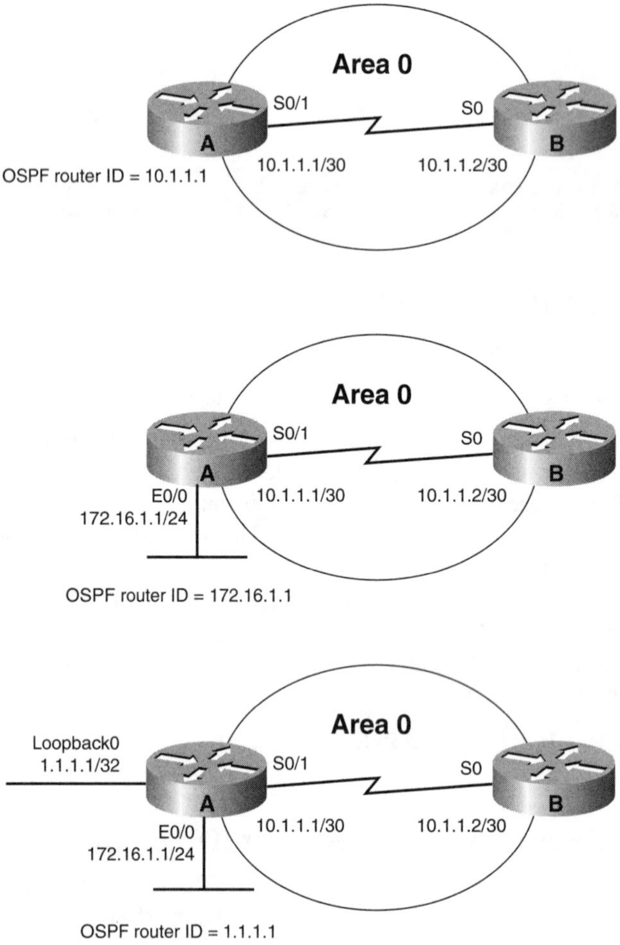


```
Router A
interface Ethernet0/0
 ip address 172.16.1.1 255.255.255.0
 shutdown
!
interface Serial0/1
 ip address 10.1.1.1 255.255.255.252
 clockrate 64000
!
router ospf 1
 network 10.1.1.0 0.0.0.3 area 0
```

```
Router B
interface Loopback0
 ip address 2.2.2.2 255.255.255.255
!
interface Serial0
 ip address 10.1.1.2 255.255.255.252
!
router ospf 1
 network 10.1.1.0 0.0.0.3 area 0
```

To determine the OSPF router ID of Router A, use the **show ip ospf** command on Router A or the **show ip ospf neighbor** command on Router B.

```
rtrA#show ip ospf
Routing Process "ospf 1" with ID 10.1.1.1 and Domain ID 0.0.0.1
 Supports only single TOS(TOS0) routes
 Supports opaque LSA
 SPF schedule delay 5 secs, Hold time between two SPFs 10 secs
 Minimum LSA interval 5 secs. Minimum LSA arrival 1 secs
 Number of external LSA 8. Checksum Sum 0x3BAD0
 Number of opaque AS LSA 0. Checksum Sum 0x0
 Number of DCbitless external and opaque AS LSA 0
 Number of DoNotAge external and opaque AS LSA 0
 Number of areas in this router is 1. 1 normal 0 stub 0 nssa
 External flood list length 0
    Area BACKBONE(0)
        Number of interfaces in this area is 1
        Area has no authentication
        SPF algorithm executed 2 times
        Area ranges are
        Number of LSA 3. Checksum Sum 0x23124
        Number of opaque link LSA 0. Checksum Sum 0x0
        Number of DCbitless LSA 0
        Number of indication LSA 0
        Number of DoNotAge LSA 0
        Flood list length 0
```

```
rtrB#show ip ospf neighbor

Neighbor ID     Pri   State           Dead Time   Address         Interface
10.1.1.1          1   FULL/  -        00:00:34    10.1.1.1        Serial0
```

Enable the Ethernet 0/0 interface on Router A and observe the effect on the OSPF router ID.

```
Router A
interface Ethernet0/0
 ip address 172.16.1.1 255.255.255.0
 no shutdown
```

Verify that interface E0/0 is up.

```
rtrA#show ip interface brief
Interface          IP-Address     OK? Method Status                Protocol
Ethernet0/0        172.16.1.1     YES NVRAM  up                          up

Serial0/0          unassigned     YES manual administratively down down

Ethernet0/1        unassigned     YES NVRAM  administratively down down

Serial0/1          10.1.1.1       YES NVRAM  up                          up
```

View the OSPF router ID on Router A.

```
rtrA#show ip ospf
 Routing Process "ospf 1" with ID 10.1.1.1 and Domain ID 0.0.0.1
 Supports only single TOS(TOS0) routes
 Supports opaque LSA
 SPF schedule delay 5 secs, Hold time between two SPFs 10 secs
 Minimum LSA interval 5 secs. Minimum LSA arrival 1 secs
 Number of external LSA 8. Checksum Sum 0x3AED6
 Number of opaque AS LSA 0. Checksum Sum 0x0
 Number of DCbitless external and opaque AS LSA 0
 Number of DoNotAge external and opaque AS LSA 0
 Number of areas in this router is 1. 1 normal 0 stub 0 nssa
 External flood list length 0
    Area BACKBONE(0)
        Number of interfaces in this area is 1
        Area has no authentication
        SPF algorithm executed 2 times
        Area ranges are
        Number of LSA 3. Checksum Sum 0x23124
        Number of opaque link LSA 0. Checksum Sum 0x0
        Number of DCbitless LSA 0
        Number of indication LSA 0
        Number of DoNotAge LSA 0
        Flood list length 0
```

The OSPF router ID has not changed, even though the IP address on Ethernet 0/0 is higher than the IP address on Serial 0/1. This is a stability feature of OSPF. The router ID will not change until you reload the router or remove the OSPF configuration and then reconfigure OSPF. Remove the OSPF process on Router A using the command **no router ospf 1** in configuration mode. Reconfigure the OSPF process on Router A using the previous listing. Has the OSPF router ID changed?

```
rtrA#show ip ospf
 Routing Process "ospf 1" with ID 172.16.1.1 and Domain ID 0.0.0.1
 Supports only single TOS(TOS0) routes
 Supports opaque LSA
 SPF schedule delay 5 secs, Hold time between two SPFs 10 secs
 Minimum LSA interval 5 secs. Minimum LSA arrival 1 secs
 Number of external LSA 8. Checksum Sum 0x3AED6
 Number of opaque AS LSA 0. Checksum Sum 0x0
 Number of DCbitless external and opaque AS LSA 0
 Number of DoNotAge external and opaque AS LSA 0
 Number of areas in this router is 1. 1 normal 0 stub 0 nssa
 External flood list length 0
    Area BACKBONE(0)
        Number of interfaces in this area is 1
        Area has no authentication
        SPF algorithm executed 1 times
        Area ranges are
        Number of LSA 4. Checksum Sum 0x27A6A
        Number of opaque link LSA 0. Checksum Sum 0x0
        Number of DCbitless LSA 0
        Number of indication LSA 0
        Number of DoNotAge LSA 0
        Flood list length 0
```

The OSPF router ID has changed. Now add a loopback interface on Router A with an IP address of 1.1.1.1/32. Even though this IP address is lower than the IP address assigned to Ethernet 0/0 and Serial 0/1, OSPF will use the loopback IP address as the router ID. Of course, OSPF will use the loopback address as the router ID only if the router is reloaded and the OSPF process is cleared or if the OSPF process is removed and then reconfigured. So remove and reconfigure the OSPF process on Router A and display the OSPF router ID.

```
Router A
interface Loopback0
 ip address 1.1.1.1 255.255.255.255
```

Now that the loopback interface has been added, remove and re-apply the OSPF configuration, clear the OSPF process, or simply save and reload the router.

```
rtrA#show ip ospf
 Routing Process "ospf 1" with ID 1.1.1.1 and Domain ID 0.0.0.1
 Supports only single TOS(TOS0) routes
 Supports opaque LSA
 SPF schedule delay 5 secs, Hold time between two SPFs 10 secs
 Minimum LSA interval 5 secs. Minimum LSA arrival 1 secs
```

continues

```
Number of external LSA 8. Checksum Sum 0x3AED6
Number of opaque AS LSA 0. Checksum Sum 0x0
Number of DCbitless external and opaque AS LSA 0
Number of DoNotAge external and opaque AS LSA 0
Number of areas in this router is 1. 1 normal 0 stub 0 nssa
External flood list length 0
   Area BACKBONE(0)
       Number of interfaces in this area is 1
       Area has no authentication
       SPF algorithm executed 2 times
       Area ranges are
       Number of LSA 4. Checksum Sum 0x1FF72
       Number of opaque link LSA 0. Checksum Sum 0x0
       Number of DCbitless LSA 0
       Number of indication LSA 0
       Number of DoNotAge LSA 0
       Flood list length 0
```

Finally, use the **router-id** command to change the OSPF router ID on Router A to 1.2.3.4.

```
Router A
router ospf 1
 router-id 1.2.3.4
 network 10.1.1.0 0.0.0.3 area 0
```

When the command **router-id** is entered, you should observe the router giving you some friendly advice:

```
rtrA(config-router)#router-id 1.2.3.4
Reload or use "clear ip ospf process" command, for this to take effect
```

Heed the router's advice and clear the OSPF process on Router A.

Verification

Verify that the OSPF process ID on Router A has been changed to 1.2.3.4.

```
rtrA#clear ip ospf process 1
rtrA#rtrA#show ip ospf
 Routing Process "ospf 1" with ID 1.2.3.4 and Domain ID 0.0.0.1
 Supports only single TOS(TOS0) routes
 Supports opaque LSA
 SPF schedule delay 5 secs, Hold time between two SPFs 10 secs
 Minimum LSA interval 5 secs. Minimum LSA arrival 1 secs
 Number of external LSA 16. Checksum Sum 0x75DAC
 Number of opaque AS LSA 0. Checksum Sum 0x0
```

```
Number of DCbitless external and opaque AS LSA 0
Number of DoNotAge external and opaque AS LSA 0
Number of areas in this router is 1. 1 normal 0 stub 0 nssa
External flood list length 0
   Area BACKBONE(0)
       Number of interfaces in this area is 1
       Area has no authentication
       SPF algorithm executed 4 times
       Area ranges are
       Number of LSA 7. Checksum Sum 0x3BFF9
       Number of opaque link LSA 0. Checksum Sum 0x0
       Number of DCbitless LSA 0
       Number of indication LSA 0
       Number of DoNotAge LSA 0
       Flood list length 0
```

Troubleshooting

Step 1 The only thing that can go wrong with this command is forgetting to clear the OSPF process using the EXEC command **clear ip ospf process**.

CHAPTER 16

Summarizing External Routes

16-1: summary-address *ip-address mask*

16-2: summary-address *ip-address mask* not-advertise

Syntax Description:

- *ip-address*—IP address of the summary route.
- *mask*—Subnet mask used to generate the summary.

Purpose: OSPF can summarize routes that have been redistributed into OSPF. The summary can be applied to routes redistributed from a dynamic routing protocol, static routes, and connected routes. The router performing the redistribution is called an Autonomous System Boundary Router (ASBR). The **summary-address** command can be used on an ASBR or an Area Border Router (ABR). When used on an ABR, only external OSPF routes can be summarized. Using the **not-advertise** keyword suppresses the advertisement of the summary route by the ASBR or ABR.

Initial Cisco IOS Software Release: 10.0

Configuration Example 1: Summarizing Routes Redistributed into OSPF

In Figure 16-1, Router B will summarize the four networks that are being redistributed into OSPF. For this example we will simulate four networks on Router B using loopback interfaces. These four networks will then be redistributed into OSPF. The router performing the redistribution is an ASBR.

Figure 16-1 *An ASBR Can Summarize Redistributed Routes into OSPF*

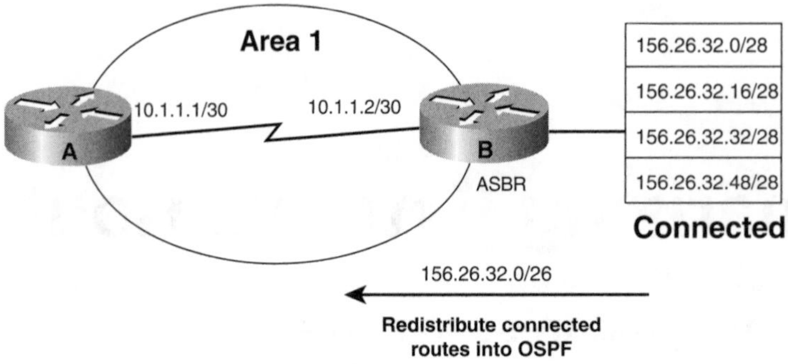


```
Router A
interface Loopback0
 ip address 1.1.1.1 255.255.255.255
!
interface Serial0/1
 ip address 10.1.1.1 255.255.255.252
 clockrate 64000
!
router ospf 1
 network 10.1.1.0 0.0.0.3 area 0
```

```
Router B
interface Loopback0
 ip address 2.2.2.2 255.255.255.255
!
interface Loopback1
 ip address 156.26.32.1 255.255.255.240
!
interface Loopback2
 ip address 156.26.32.17 255.255.255.240
 no ip directed-broadcast
!
interface Loopback3
 ip address 156.26.32.33 255.255.255.240
!
interface Loopback4
 ip address 156.26.32.49 255.255.255.240
!
interface Serial0
 ip address 10.1.1.2 255.255.255.252
 no ip directed-broadcast
!
router ospf 1
 network 10.1.1.0 0.0.0.3 area 0
 redistribute connected subnets
```

Before summarizing the routes, inspect the IP routing table on Router A to verify that the four networks are being advertised.

```
rtrA#show ip route
Codes: C - connected, S - static, I - IGRP, R - RIP, M - mobile, B - BGP
       D - EIGRP, EX - EIGRP external, O - OSPF, IA - OSPF inter area
       N1 - OSPF NSSA external type 1, N2 - OSPF NSSA external type 2
       E1 - OSPF external type 1, E2 - OSPF external type 2, E - EGP
       i - IS-IS, L1 - IS-IS level-1, L2 - IS-IS level-2, * - candidate default
       U - per-user static route, o - ODR

Gateway of last resort is not set

     1.0.0.0/32 is subnetted, 1 subnets
C       1.1.1.1 is directly connected, Loopback0
     2.0.0.0/32 is subnetted, 1 subnets
O E2    2.2.2.2 [110/20] via 10.1.1.2, 00:03:17, Serial0/1
     156.26.0.0/28 is subnetted, 4 subnets
O E2    156.26.32.32 [110/20] via 10.1.1.2, 00:03:17, Serial0/1
O E2    156.26.32.48 [110/20] via 10.1.1.2, 00:03:17, Serial0/1
O E2    156.26.32.0 [110/20] via 10.1.1.2, 00:02:52, Serial0/1
O E2    156.26.32.16 [110/20] via 10.1.1.2, 00:03:17, Serial0/1
     10.0.0.0/30 is subnetted, 1 subnets
C       10.1.1.0 is directly connected, Serial0/1
```

A 26-bit subnet mask is required to summarize the four loopback addresses being advertised by Router B. Modify the configuration on Router B in order to summarize the four loopback addresses.

```
Router B
router ospf 1
 summary-address 156.26.32.0 255.255.255.192
 network 10.1.1.0 0.0.0.3 area 0
```

Verification

Verify that the four loopback networks have been summarized by Router B by inspecting the IP routing table on Router A.

```
rtrA#show ip route
Codes: C - connected, S - static, I - IGRP, R - RIP, M - mobile, B - BGP
       D - EIGRP, EX - EIGRP external, O - OSPF, IA - OSPF inter area
       N1 - OSPF NSSA external type 1, N2 - OSPF NSSA external type 2
       E1 - OSPF external type 1, E2 - OSPF external type 2, E - EGP
       i - IS-IS, L1 - IS-IS level-1, L2 - IS-IS level-2, * - candidate default
       U - per-user static route, o - ODR
```

continues

```
Gateway of last resort is not set

     1.0.0.0/32 is subnetted, 1 subnets
C       1.1.1.1 is directly connected, Loopback0
     2.0.0.0/32 is subnetted, 1 subnets
O E2    2.2.2.2 [110/20] via 10.1.1.2, 00:05:36, Serial0/1
     156.26.0.0/26 is subnetted, 1 subnets
O E2    156.26.32.0 [110/20] via 10.1.1.2, 00:00:21, Serial0/1
     10.0.0.0/30 is subnetted, 2 subnets
C       10.1.1.0 is directly connected, Serial0/1
```

Troubleshooting

Step 1 Verify that there is a neighbor relationship between the OSPF routers by using the **show ip ospf neighbor** command.

Step 2 The **summary-address** command will only work on an OSPF ASBR.

Step 3 Verify that you are using the correct IP address and mask with the **summary-address** command.

16-3: summary-address *ip-address mask* tag *value*

Syntax Description:

- *ip-address*—IP address of the summary route.
- *mask*—Subnet mask used to generate the summary.
- *tag*—The summary route will be tagged with this value. The range of values is 0 to 4,294,967,295.

Purpose: OSPF can summarize routes that have been redistributed into OSPF. The summary can be applied to routes redistributed from a dynamic routing protocol, static, or connected routes. The router performing the redistribution is an ASBR. The **summary-address** command can only be used on an ASBR. Using the **not-advertise** keyword will suppress the advertisement of the summary route by the ASBR. Using a tag allows routing policies to be based on the tag value instead of the IP address.

Initial Cisco IOS Software Release: 10.0

Configuration Example 1: Attaching a Tag to Summarized Routes Created on an ASBR

In Figure 16-2, Router B will summarize the four networks that are being redistributed into OSPF into two summaries. Each summary will be given a different tag value. This example simulates four networks on Router B using loopback interfaces. These four networks will then be redistributed into OSPF. The router performing the redistribution is an ASBR.

Figure 16-2 *Tagging Redistributed Routes*

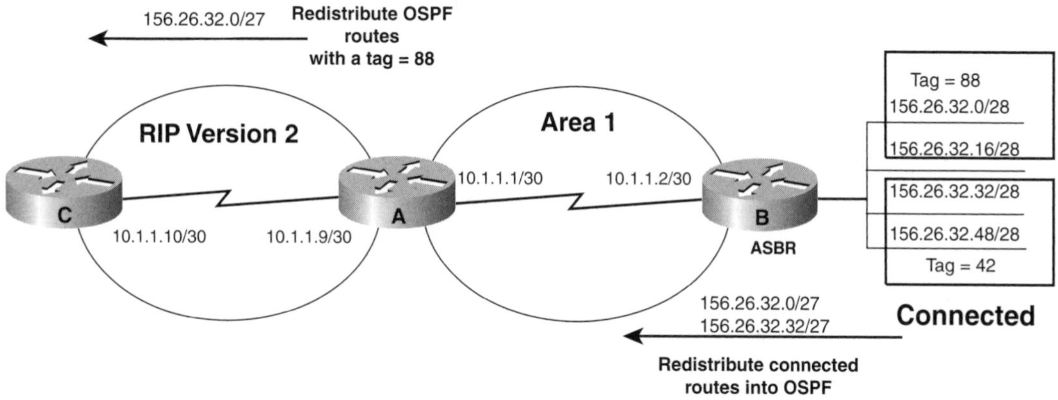


```
Router A
interface Loopback0
 ip address 1.1.1.1 255.255.255.255
!
interface Serial0/1
 ip address 10.1.1.1 255.255.255.252
 clockrate 64000
!
router ospf 1
 network 10.1.1.0 0.0.0.3 area 1
```

```
Router B
interface Loopback0
 ip address 2.2.2.2 255.255.255.255
!
interface Loopback1
 ip address 156.26.32.1 255.255.255.240
!
interface Loopback2
 ip address 156.26.32.17 255.255.255.240
 no ip directed-broadcast
!
interface Loopback3
 ip address 156.26.32.33 255.255.255.240
!
interface Loopback4
 ip address 156.26.32.49 255.255.255.240
!
interface Serial0
 ip address 10.1.1.2 255.255.255.252
 no ip directed-broadcast
!
router ospf 1
 network 10.1.1.0 0.0.0.3 area 1
 redistribute connected subnets
```

Before summarizing the routes, inspect the IP routing table on Router A to verify that the four networks are being advertised.

```
rtrA#show ip route
Codes: C - connected, S - static, I - IGRP, R - RIP, M - mobile, B - BGP
       D - EIGRP, EX - EIGRP external, O - OSPF, IA - OSPF inter area
       N1 - OSPF NSSA external type 1, N2 - OSPF NSSA external type 2
       E1 - OSPF external type 1, E2 - OSPF external type 2, E - EGP
       i - IS-IS, L1 - IS-IS level-1, L2 - IS-IS level-2, * - candidate default
       U - per-user static route, o - ODR

Gateway of last resort is not set

     1.0.0.0/32 is subnetted, 1 subnets
C       1.1.1.1 is directly connected, Loopback0
     2.0.0.0/32 is subnetted, 1 subnets
O E2    2.2.2.2 [110/20] via 10.1.1.2, 00:03:17, Serial0/1
     156.26.0.0/28 is subnetted, 4 subnets
O E2    156.26.32.32 [110/20] via 10.1.1.2, 00:03:17, Serial0/1
O E2    156.26.32.48 [110/20] via 10.1.1.2, 00:03:17, Serial0/1
O E2    156.26.32.0 [110/20] via 10.1.1.2, 00:02:52, Serial0/1
O E2    156.26.32.16 [110/20] via 10.1.1.2, 00:03:17, Serial0/1
     10.0.0.0/30 is subnetted, 1 subnets
C       10.1.1.0 is directly connected, Serial0/1
```

A 27-bit subnet mask will be used to summarize the four loopback addresses being advertised by Router B into two summaries. Modify the configuration on Router B in order to summarize the four loopback addresses into two summaries.

```
Router B
router ospf 1
 summary-address 156.26.32.0 255.255.255.224 tag 88
 summary-address 156.26.32.32 255.255.255.224 tag 42
 network 10.1.1.0 0.0.0.3 area 1
```

Verification

Verify that Router B has summarized the four loopback networks into two summaries by inspecting the IP routing table on Router A.

```
rtrA#show ip route
Codes: C - connected, S - static, I - IGRP, R - RIP, M - mobile, B - BGP
       D - EIGRP, EX - EIGRP external, O - OSPF, IA - OSPF inter area
       N1 - OSPF NSSA external type 1, N2 - OSPF NSSA external type 2
       E1 - OSPF external type 1, E2 - OSPF external type 2, E - EGP
       i - IS-IS, L1 - IS-IS level-1, L2 - IS-IS level-2, * - candidate default
       U - per-user static route, o - ODR
```

```
Gateway of last resort is not set

     1.0.0.0/32 is subnetted, 1 subnets
C       1.1.1.1 is directly connected, Loopback0
     2.0.0.0/32 is subnetted, 1 subnets
O E2    2.2.2.2 [110/20] via 10.1.1.2, 00:36:53, Serial0/1
     156.26.0.0/27 is subnetted, 2 subnets
O E2    156.26.32.32 [110/20] via 10.1.1.2, 00:01:04, Serial0/1
O E2    156.26.32.0 [110/20] via 10.1.1.2, 00:01:09, Serial0/1
     10.0.0.0/30 is subnetted, 1 subnets
C       10.1.1.0 is directly connected, Serial0/1
```

Verify that the summaries have been tagged with the proper values.

```
rtrA#show ip route 156.26.32.0
Routing entry for 156.26.32.0/27
  Known via "ospf 1", distance 110, metric 20
  Tag 88, type extern 2, forward metric 64
  Redistributing via ospf 1
  Last update from 10.1.1.2 on Serial0/1, 00:02:43 ago
  Routing Descriptor Blocks:
  * 10.1.1.2, from 2.2.2.2, 00:02:43 ago, via Serial0/1
      Route metric is 20, traffic share count is 1

rtrA#show ip route 156.26.32.32
Routing entry for 156.26.32.32/27
  Known via "ospf 1", distance 110, metric 20
  Tag 42, type extern 2, forward metric 64
  Redistributing via ospf 1
  Last update from 10.1.1.2 on Serial0/1, 00:02:46 ago
  Routing Descriptor Blocks:
  * 10.1.1.2, from 2.2.2.2, 00:02:46 ago, via Serial0/1
      Route metric is 20, traffic share count is 1
```

Configuration Example 2: Using the Tag Value to Control Route Redistribution

In Figure 16-2, Routers A and C are running RIP Version 2. Redistribute OSPF into RIP on Router A, but allow only those routes with a tag value of 88 to be redistributed. Add the configuration for Router C and modify the configuration for Router A as follows:

```
Router A
interface Serial0/0
 ip address 10.1.1.9 255.255.255.252
!
interface Serial0/1
 ip address 10.1.1.1 255.255.255.252
```

continues

```
 clockrate 64000
!
router ospf 1
 network 10.1.1.0 0.0.0.3 area 1
!
router rip
 version 2
 redistribute ospf 1 metric 1 route-map checktags
 passive-interface Serial0/1
 network 10.0.0.0
 no auto-summary
!
route-map checktags permit 10
 match tag 88
```

```
Router C
interface Serial1
 ip address 10.1.1.10 255.255.255.252
 clockrate 64000
!
router rip
 version 2
 network 10.0.0.0
```

Verification

Verify that the only routes that were redistributed into RIP on Router A are routes with a tag value of 88.

```
rtrC#show ip route
Codes: C - connected, S - static, I - IGRP, R - RIP, M - mobile, B - BGP
       D - EIGRP, EX - EIGRP external, O - OSPF, IA - OSPF inter area
       N1 - OSPF NSSA external type 1, N2 - OSPF NSSA external type 2
       E1 - OSPF external type 1, E2 - OSPF external type 2, E - EGP
       i - IS-IS, L1 - IS-IS level-1, L2 - IS-IS level-2, * - candidate default
       U - per-user static route, o - ODR

Gateway of last resort is not set

     156.26.0.0/27 is subnetted, 1 subnets
R       156.26.32.0 [120/1] via 10.1.1.9, 00:00:25, Serial1
     10.0.0.0/30 is subnetted, 2 subnets
C       10.1.1.8 is directly connected, Serial1
R       10.1.1.0 [120/1] via 10.1.1.9, 00:00:25, Serial1
```

Troubleshooting

Step 1 Verify that there is a neighbor relationship between the OSPF routers by using the **show ip ospf neighbor** command.

Step 2 The **summary-address** command will only work on an OSPF ASBR.

Step 3 Verify that you are using the correct IP address and mask with the **summary-address** command.

CHAPTER 17

OSPF Timers

17-1: timers lsa-group-pacing *seconds*

Syntax Description:

- *seconds*—The minimum time between sending groups of timer-expired link-state advertisements (LSAs). The range of values is 10 to 1800 seconds. The default time is 240 seconds.

Purpose: Each OSPF LSA has an age parameter indicating if it is still valid. When the age of an LSA is equal to the maximum age (1 hour), the LSA is discarded. In order to refresh LSAs, the originating router will send the LSAs every 30 minutes. This periodic refresh process prevents the LSAs from reaching the maximum age and therefore prevents the LSAs from being discarded. LSA refreshing occurs even if the LSA has not changed. In addition, a checksum is performed on all LSAs every 10 minutes. If an LSA is discarded, this means that the information it contained is no longer in the OSPF database. Routes based on the discarded LSA will be removed from the IP routing table.

Before the LSA group-pacing feature was available, refreshing was performed using a single timer. Another timer was used for the checksum and aging function. Every 30 minutes an OSPF router would scan the entire database and refresh every LSA that was originated by the router. This process was CPU intensive because every LSA, after being refreshed, would have identical age timers. After the LSA age timers were refreshed, the router would transmit the LSAs to neighboring OSPF routers. This resulted in periodically high network usage for large OSPF networks. LSA pacing was developed to solve the problem of periodic high CPU usage and network utilization.

Each LSA now has its own timers and LSAs are refreshed independently of other LSAs at random intervals. This paces the refreshing and transmitting of LSAs, which spreads out the CPU and network loads. For most situations the default pacing interval is sufficient. Decreasing the pacing interval may be of benefit for large OSPF networks.

Initial Cisco IOS Software Release: 11.3 (AA)

Configuration Example: Modifying the LSA Group Pacing

LSA group pacing can be modified with the **timers lsa-group-pacing** router configuration command as shown in the following listing.

```
Router A
router ospf 1
 log-adjacency-changes
 timers lsa-group-pacing 180
 network 1.1.1.1 0.0.0.0 area 1
 network 10.1.1.0 0.0.0.3 area 0
```

Verification

The LSA pacing interval can be verified with the **show ip ospf timer lsa-group** command.

```
rtrA#show ip ospf timer lsa-group

            OSPF Router with ID (1.1.1.1) (Process ID 1)

Group size 6, Head 0, Search Index 4, Interval 180 sec
Next update due in 00:00:22
Current time 134571
Index 0 Timestamp 134593
Index 1 Timestamp 134777
Index 2 Timestamp 134971
Index 3 Timestamp 135153
Index 4 Timestamp 135351
Index 5 Timestamp 135544
```

17-2: timers spf *delay interval*

Syntax Description:

- *delay*—The delay, in seconds, between when a topology change is received and the shortest path first (SPF) calculation begins. The range of values is 0 to 4,294,967,295 seconds. The default time is 5 seconds.
- *interval*—The interval, in seconds, between successive SPF calculations. The range of values is 0 to 4,294,967,295 seconds. The default time is 10 seconds.

Purpose: When a change in the OSPF topology occurs, the OSPF process will run an SPF calculation. The *delay* parameter of this command sets the delay time between receipt of an OSPF topology change and the start of the SPF calculation. The *interval* parameter is the wait time between two SPF calculations. If the SPF calculation is being executed frequently, there may be a flapping interface in the network, causing OSPF to send frequent topology changes.

Initial Cisco IOS Software Release: 10.3

Configuration Example: Modifying the LSA Group Pacing

The SPF timers can be modified with the **timers spf router** configuration command, as shown in the following listing.

```
Router A
router ospf 1
 log-adjacency-changes
 timers spf 8 16
 network 1.1.1.1 0.0.0.0 area 1
 network 10.1.1.0 0.0.0.3 area 0
```

Verification

The SPF timer values can be verified with the **show ip ospf** command.

```
rtrA#show ip ospf
 Routing Process "ospf 1" with ID 1.1.1.1 and Domain ID 0.0.0.1
 Supports only single TOS(TOS0) routes
 Supports opaque LSA
 It is an area border router
 SPF schedule delay 8 secs, Hold time between two SPFs 16 secs
 Minimum LSA interval 5 secs. Minimum LSA arrival 1 secs
 Number of external LSA 0. Checksum Sum 0x0
 Number of opaque AS LSA 0. Checksum Sum 0x0
 Number of DCbitless external and opaque AS LSA 0
 Number of DoNotAge external and opaque AS LSA 0
 Number of areas in this router is 2. 2 normal 0 stub 0 nssa
 External flood list length 0
    Area BACKBONE(0)
        Number of interfaces in this area is 1
        Area has no authentication
        SPF algorithm executed 24 times
        Area ranges are
        Number of LSA 16. Checksum Sum 0x8759C
        Number of opaque link LSA 0. Checksum Sum 0x0
        Number of DCbitless LSA 0
        Number of indication LSA 0
        Number of DoNotAge LSA 0
        Flood list length 0
    Area 1
        Number of interfaces in this area is 1
        Area has no authentication
        SPF algorithm executed 12 times
        Area ranges are
        Number of LSA 3. Checksum Sum 0x14E8B
        Number of opaque link LSA 0. Checksum Sum 0x0
        Number of DCbitless LSA 0
        Number of indication LSA 0
        Number of DoNotAge LSA 0
        Flood list length 0
```

CHAPTER 18

Traffic Sharing

18-1: traffic-share min across-interfaces

Syntax Description:

This command has no arguments.

Purpose: This command is used with IGRP and EIGRP to support unequal-cost load balancing. This command appears as an option under OSPF but the command does not apply to OSPF.

CHAPTER 19

Interface Configuration Commands

19-1: ip ospf authentication

19-2: ip ospf authentication authentication-key *password*

19-3: ip ospf authentication message-digest

Command 19-3 requires the use of command 19-11 (**ip ospf message-digest-key** *key-id* **md5** *password*).

19-4: ip ospf authentication null

Syntax Description:

- *key-id*—Key used to identify the password. Range of values is 1 to 255. Both ends of a link must use the same key and password.
- *password*—Password to be used for authentication in the selected area on the selected interface. The password is an alphanumeric string from 1 to 8 characters.

Purpose: In IOS versions before 12.0, if authentication was enabled for an OSPF area, then all interfaces in the area had to be configured with the same authentication type. This command allows the configuration of authentication on an interface that is different from the authentication type being used in the area.

Initial Cisco IOS Software Release: 12.0

Configuration Example 1: Simple Password Authentication on an OSPF Network

In Figure 19-1, the serial link in Area 0 is not using authentication, but simple password authentication is employed on the Ethernet network. Start by configuring Routers A and B as shown in the following listing.

Figure 19-1 *OSPF Authentication Can Be Configured on Individual Networks*

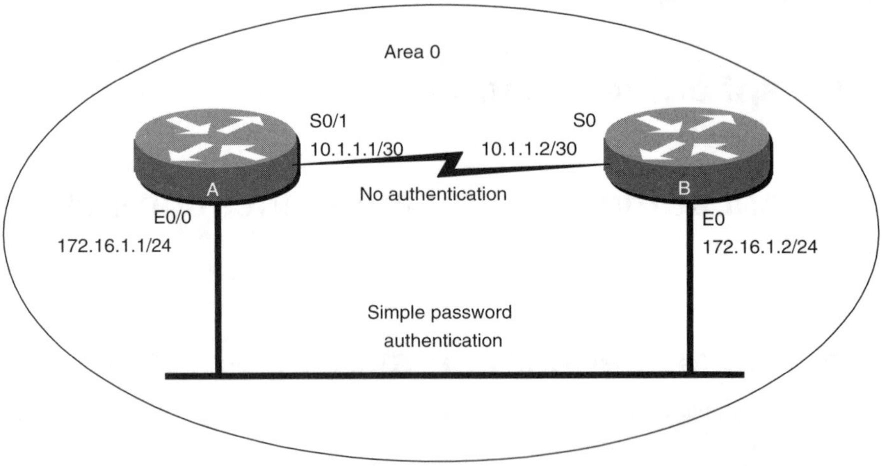


```
Router A
interface Loopback0
 ip address 1.1.1.1 255.255.255.255
!
interface Ethernet0/0
 ip address 172.16.1.1 255.255.255.0
!
interface Serial0/1
 ip address 10.1.1.1 255.255.255.252
 clockrate 64000
!
router ospf 1
 network 10.1.1.0 0.0.0.3 area 0
 network 172.16.1.0 0.0.0.255 area 0
 network 1.1.1.1 0.0.0.0 area 1
```

```
Router B
interface Loopback0
 ip address 2.2.2.2 255.255.255.255
!
interface Ethernet0
 ip address 172.16.1.2 255.255.255.0
!
```

```
interface Serial0
 ip address 10.1.1.2 255.255.255.252
!
router ospf 1
 network 10.1.1.0 0.0.0.3 area 0
 network 172.16.1.0 0.0.0.255 area 0
 network 2.2.2.2 0.0.0.0 area 2
```

Verify that Routers A and B have established a FULL OSPF neighbor relationship over the serial and Ethernet networks.

```
rtrA#show ip ospf neighbor

Neighbor ID     Pri   State           Dead Time   Address         Interface
2.2.2.2           1   FULL/BDR        00:00:32    172.16.1.2      Ethernet0/0
2.2.2.2           1   FULL/  -        00:00:35    10.1.1.2        Serial0/1
```

Verify that authentication is not being used in Area 0.

```
rtrA#show ip ospf
 Routing Process "ospf 1" with ID 1.1.1.1
 Supports only single TOS(TOS0) routes
 It is an area border router
 SPF schedule delay 5 secs, Hold time between two SPFs 10 secs
 Minimum LSA interval 5 secs. Minimum LSA arrival 1 secs
 Number of external LSA 0. Checksum Sum 0x0
 Number of DCbitless external LSA 0
 Number of DoNotAge external LSA 0
 Number of areas in this router is 2. 2 normal 0 stub 0 nssa
    Area BACKBONE(0)
        Number of interfaces in this area is 2
        Area has no authentication
        SPF algorithm executed 8 times
        Area ranges are
        Number of LSA 5. Checksum Sum 0x23C8C
        Number of DCbitless LSA 0
        Number of indication LSA 0
        Number of DoNotAge LSA 0
    Area 1
        Number of interfaces in this area is 1
        Area has no authentication
        SPF algorithm executed 5 times
        Area ranges are
        Number of LSA 4. Checksum Sum 0x22672
        Number of DCbitless LSA 0
        Number of indication LSA 0
        Number of DoNotAge LSA 0
```

Modify the configurations on Routers A and B so that simple password authentication is used on the Ethernet network. Use the clear-text password **laura**.

```
Router A
interface Ethernet0/0
 ip address 172.16.1.1 255.255.255.0
 ip ospf authentication
 ip ospf authentication-key laura
```

```
Router B
interface Ethernet0
 ip address 172.16.1.2 255.255.255.0
 ip ospf authentication
 ip ospf authentication-key laura
```

Verification

Verify that Routers A and B have a FULL OSPF neighbor relationship over both the serial and Ethernet networks.

```
rtrB#show ip ospf neighbor

Neighbor ID     Pri   State           Dead Time   Address         Interface
1.1.1.1           1   FULL/BDR        00:00:36    172.16.1.1      Ethernet0
1.1.1.1           1   FULL/  -        00:00:30    10.1.1.1        Serial0
```

Configuration Example 2: MD5 Authentication on an OSPF Network

Change the authentication type on the Ethernet network to MD5. Use the password **laura** and a key ID of **1**.

```
Router A
interface Ethernet0/0
 ip address 172.16.1.1 255.255.255.0
 ip ospf authentication message-digest
 ip ospf message-digest-key 1 md5 laura
```

```
Router B
interface Ethernet0
 ip address 172.16.1.2 255.255.255.0
 ip ospf authentication message-digest
 ip ospf message-digest-key 1 md5 laura
```

Verification

Verify that message digest authentication is being used on the Ethernet network.

```
rtrA#show ip ospf interface Ethernet0/0
Ethernet0/0 is up, line protocol is up
  Internet Address 172.16.1.1/24, Area 0
  Process ID 1, Router ID 1.1.1.1, Network Type BROADCAST, Cost: 10
  Transmit Delay is 1 sec, State BDR, Priority 1
  Designated Router (ID) 2.2.2.2, Interface address 172.16.1.2
  Backup Designated router (ID) 1.1.1.1, Interface address 172.16.1.1
  Timer intervals configured, Hello 10, Dead 40, Wait 40, Retransmit 5
    Hello due in 00:00:02
  Neighbor Count is 1, Adjacent neighbor count is 1
    Adjacent with neighbor 2.2.2.2  (Designated Router)
  Suppress hello for 0 neighbor(s)
  Message digest authentication enabled
    Youngest key id is 1
```

Also, verify that Routers A and B have established FULL OSPF neighbor relationships over the serial and Ethernet networks.

```
rtrA#show ip ospf neighbor

Neighbor ID     Pri   State           Dead Time   Address         Interface
2.2.2.2           1   FULL/DR         00:00:39    172.16.1.2      Ethernet0/0
2.2.2.2           1   FULL/  -        00:00:32    10.1.1.2        Serial0/1
```

Configuration Example 3: Changing Keys and Passwords

For additional security, you may choose to periodically change the key and password. With clear-text authentication, when you change passwords there will be a loss of OSPF connectivity from the time you change the password on one router's interface until you change the password on the remaining interfaces attached to the network. With MD5 authentication, you can configure a new key and password on an interface while leaving the old key and password in place. The old key and password will continue to be used until the new key and password are configured on the other interfaces attached to the network. Modify the key and password on the Ethernet network between Routers A and B. First add a new key and password to Router A in order to observe the behavior when the new key and password have been configured on only one interface.

```
Router A
interface Ethernet0/0
 ip address 172.16.1.1 255.255.255.0
 ip ospf authentication message-digest
 ip ospf message-digest-key 1 md5 laura
 ip ospf message-digest-key 2 md5 elvis
```

Examine the effect of adding a new key and password on only one interface.

```
rtrA#show ip ospf interface e0/0
Ethernet0/0 is up, line protocol is up
  Internet Address 172.16.1.1/24, Area 0
  Process ID 1, Router ID 1.1.1.1, Network Type BROADCAST, Cost: 10
  Transmit Delay is 1 sec, State BDR, Priority 1
  Designated Router (ID) 2.2.2.2, Interface address 172.16.1.2
  Backup Designated router (ID) 1.1.1.1, Interface address 172.16.1.1
  Timer intervals configured, Hello 10, Dead 40, Wait 40, Retransmit 5
    Hello due in 00:00:07
  Neighbor Count is 1, Adjacent neighbor count is 1
    Adjacent with neighbor 2.2.2.2  (Designated Router)
  Suppress hello for 0 neighbor(s)
  Message digest authentication enabled
    Youngest key id is 2
    Rollover in progress, 1 neighbor(s) using the old key(s):
      key id 1
```

Notice that both keys are being used for authentication. Configure the new key and password on Router B while leaving the old key and password in place.

```
Router B
interface Ethernet0/0
 ip address 172.16.1.2 255.255.255.0
 ip ospf authentication message-digest
 ip ospf message-digest-key 1 md5 laura
 ip ospf message-digest-key 2 md5 elvis
```

Verification

Verify that Router B is now using the new key and password.

```
rtrB#show ip ospf interface ethernet 0
Ethernet0 is up, line protocol is up
  Internet Address 172.16.1.2/24, Area 0
  Process ID 1, Router ID 2.2.2.2, Network Type BROADCAST, Cost: 10
  Transmit Delay is 1 sec, State DR, Priority 1
  Designated Router (ID) 2.2.2.2, Interface address 172.16.1.2
  Backup Designated router (ID) 1.1.1.1, Interface address 172.16.1.1
  Timer intervals configured, Hello 10, Dead 40, Wait 40, Retransmit 5
    Hello due in 00:00:05
  Neighbor Count is 1, Adjacent neighbor count is 1
    Adjacent with neighbor 1.1.1.1  (Backup Designated Router)
  Suppress hello for 0 neighbor(s)
  Message digest authentication enabled
    Youngest key id is 2
```

You can now remove the old key and password from Routers A and B.

```
Router A
interface Ethernet0/0
 no ip ospf message-digest-key 1
```

```
Router B
interface Ethernet0
 no ip ospf message-digest-key 1
```

Configuration Example 4: Null Authentication

Prior to Cisco IOS Software Release 12.0, if authentication was configured for an OSPF area then the same authentication type had to be enabled on all interfaces in the area. In Cisco IOS Software Release 12.0 and later, if authentication is not required on an interface, NULL authentication can be employed to override the authentication that has been configured for the area. Configure the routers in Figure 19-1 with simple password authentication in Area 0 and on the Ethernet network. Do not configure authentication on the serial link.

```
Router A
interface Loopback0
 ip address 1.1.1.1 255.255.255.255
!
interface Ethernet0/0
 ip address 172.16.1.1 255.255.255.0
 ip ospf authentication-key laura
!
interface Serial0/1
 ip address 10.1.1.1 255.255.255.252
 ip ospf authentication null
 clockrate 64000
!
router ospf 1
 area 0 authentication
 network 1.1.1.1 0.0.0.0 area 1
 network 10.1.1.0 0.0.0.3 area 0
 network 172.16.1.0 0.0.0.255 area 0
```

```
Router B
interface Loopback0
 ip address 2.2.2.2 255.255.255.255
!
interface Ethernet0
 ip add 172.16.1.2 255.255.255.0
 ip ospf authentication-key laura
!
```

continues

```
interface Serial0
 ip address 10.1.1.2 255.255.255.252
 ip ospf authentication null
!
router ospf 1
 area 0 authentication
 network 2.2.2.2 0.0.0.0 area 2
 network 10.1.1.0 0.0.0.3 area 0
 network 172.16.1.0 0.0.0.255 area 0
```

Verification

Verify that Routers A and B have formed FULL OSPF neighbor relationships over the Ethernet and serial networks.

```
rtrA#show ip ospf neighbor

Neighbor ID     Pri   State           Dead Time   Address         Interface
2.2.2.2           1   FULL/DR         00:00:31    172.16.1.2      Ethernet0/0
2.2.2.2           1   FULL/  -        00:00:35    10.1.1.2        Serial0/1
```

Troubleshooting

Step 1 If using simple password authentication, verify that the same password is being used on every interface attached to the network.

Step 2 If using MD5 authentication, verify that the same key and password are being used on every interface attached to the network.

Step 3 Mismatched keys and passwords can be found by enabling OSPF debugging. A sample session is shown in the following output where simple password authentication is used and the passwords assigned to the interfaces do not match.

```
rtrA#debug ip ospf adj
OSPF adjacency events debugging is on
rtrA#
00:47:55: OSPF: Rcv pkt from 172.16.1.2, Ethernet0/0 :
  Mismatch Authentication Key - Clear Text
00:47:55: OSPF: Rcv hello from 2.2.2.2 area 0 from Serial0/1 10.1.1.2
00:47:55: OSPF: End of hello processing
```

The following output is for message digest authentication when the keys match but the passwords do not.

```
rtrB#debug ip ospf adj
OSPF adjacency events debugging is on
rtrB#
00:51:37: OSPF: Rcv pkt from 10.1.1.1, Serial0 : Mismatch Authentication Key -
  Message Digest Key 1
```

The final **debug** output is for message digest authentication with a key mismatch. One interface has been configured with a key ID of 1 and the other interface has a key ID of 2.

```
rtrA#debug ip ospf adj
OSPF adjacency events debugging is on
rtrA#
00:53:31: OSPF: Send with youngest Key 1
00:53:36: OSPF: Rcv pkt from 10.1.1.2, Serial0/1 : Mismatch Authentication Key -
  No message digest key 2 on interface
00:53:41: OSPF: Send with youngest Key 1
```

19-5: ip ospf cost *cost*

Syntax Description:

- *cost*—OSPF metric to use for the interface. The range of values is 1 to 65535.

Purpose: By default OSPF calculates the cost of an interface by dividing the bandwidth of the interface into 100 million. Table 19-1 lists the costs for various interface types. Using the default value when your network has interfaces with a bandwidth greater than 100,000,000 bps is not recommended. OSPF will not be able to differentiate between a 100-Mbps interface and an interface with a bandwidth greater than 100 Mbps. The **ip ospf cost** command enables you to change the OSPF cost for an interface. The default reference value used to calculate the OSPF cost of an interface can be modified using the command **auto-cost reference-bandwidth** (see Section 3-1).

Table 19-1 *Default OSPF Cost for Selected Interfaces*

Interface Type	Interface Bandwidth in Bits per Second (bps)	OSPF Cost
Serial	56,000	1785
T1	1,544,000	64
Ethernet	10,000,000	10

continues

Table 19-1 *Default OSPF Cost for Selected Interfaces (Continued)*

Interface Type	Interface Bandwidth in Bits per Second (bps)	OSPF Cost
Fast Ethernet	100,000,000	1
Gigabit Ethernet	1,000,000,000	1
OC48	2,500,000,000	1

Initial Cisco IOS Software Release: 10.0

Configuration Example: Modifying the OSPF Cost of an Interface

In Figure 19-2, the Ethernet network has an OSPF cost of 10. Configure Routers A and B as shown and verify the OSPF cost of the interface.

Figure 19-2 *The Default Cost of an OSPF Interface Is 100,000,000 Divided by the Interface Bandwidth*

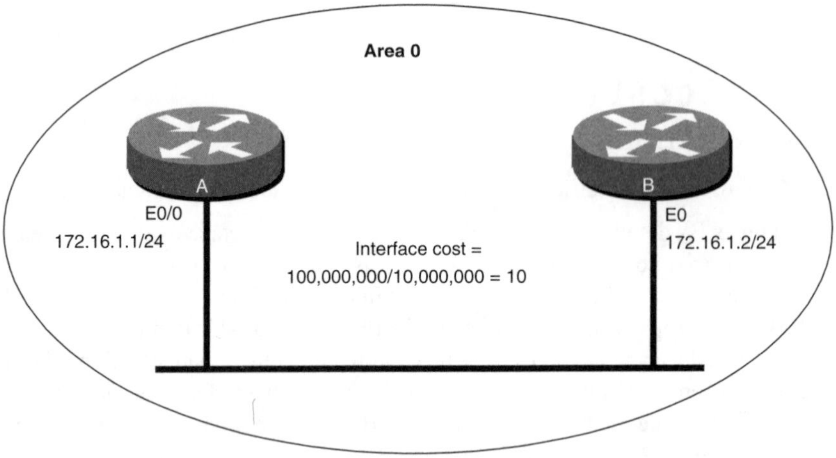


```
Router A
interface Loopback0
 ip address 1.1.1.1 255.255.255.255
!
interface Ethernet0/0
 ip address 172.16.1.1 255.255.255.0
!
router ospf 1
 network 172.16.1.0 0.0.0.255 area 0
 network 1.1.1.1 0.0.0.0 area 1
```

```
Router B
interface Loopback0
 ip address 2.2.2.2 255.255.255.255
!
interface Ethernet0
 ip address 172.16.1.2 255.255.255.0
!
router ospf 1
 network 172.16.1.0 0.0.0.255 area 0
 network 2.2.2.2 0.0.0.0 area 2
```

The OSPF cost of an interface can be found by using the **show ip ospf interface** command.

```
rtrA#show ip ospf interface Ethernet0/0
Ethernet0/0 is up, line protocol is up
  Internet Address 172.16.1.1/24, Area 0
  Process ID 1, Router ID 1.1.1.1, Network Type BROADCAST, Cost: 10
  Transmit Delay is 1 sec, State DR, Priority 1
  Designated Router (ID) 1.1.1.1, Interface address 172.16.1.1
  No backup designated router on this network
  Timer intervals configured, Hello 10, Dead 40, Wait 40, Retransmit 5
    Hello due in 00:00:06
  Neighbor Count is 0, Adjacent neighbor count is 0
  Suppress hello for 0 neighbor(s)
```

The cost to reach the loopback interface is the cost of the Ethernet interface plus the cost of the loopback interface, as shown here.

```
rtrA#show ip ospf interface loopback 0
Loopback0 is up, line protocol is up
  Internet Address 1.1.1.1/32, Area 1
  Process ID 1, Router ID 1.1.1.1, Network Type LOOPBACK, Cost: 1
  Loopback interface is treated as a stub Host

rtrA#show ip route
Codes: C - connected, S - static, I - IGRP, R - RIP, M - mobile, B - BGP
       D - EIGRP, EX - EIGRP external, O - OSPF, IA - OSPF inter area
       N1 - OSPF NSSA external type 1, N2 - OSPF NSSA external type 2
       E1 - OSPF external type 1, E2 - OSPF external type 2, E - EGP
       i - IS-IS, L1 - IS-IS level-1, L2 - IS-IS level-2, * - candidate default
       U - per-user static route, o - ODR

Gateway of last resort is not set

     1.0.0.0/32 is subnetted, 1 subnets
C       1.1.1.1 is directly connected, Loopback0
     2.0.0.0/32 is subnetted, 1 subnets
O IA    2.2.2.2 [110/11] via 172.16.1.2, 00:02:43, Ethernet0/0
```

continues

```
     172.16.0.0/24 is subnetted, 1 subnets
C       172.16.1.0 is directly connected, Ethernet0/0
     10.0.0.0/30 is subnetted, 1 subnets
C       10.1.1.0 is directly connected, Serial0/1
```

Modify the configuration on Routers A and B to change the cost of the Ethernet network to 100.

```
Router A
interface Ethernet0/0
 ip address 172.16.1.1 255.255.255.0
 ip ospf  cost 100
```

```
Router B
interface Ethernet0
 ip address 172.16.1.2 255.255.255.0
 ip ospf cost 100
```

Verification

Verify that the cost of the Ethernet interface is 100.

```
rtrA#show ip ospf interface ethernet 0/0
Ethernet0/0 is up, line protocol is up
  Internet Address 172.16.1.1/24, Area 0
  Process ID 1, Router ID 1.1.1.1, Network Type BROADCAST, Cost: 100
  Transmit Delay is 1 sec, State BDR, Priority 1
  Designated Router (ID) 2.2.2.2, Interface address 172.16.1.2
  Backup Designated router (ID) 1.1.1.1, Interface address 172.16.1.1
  Flush timer for old DR LSA due in 00:02:45
  Timer intervals configured, Hello 10, Dead 40, Wait 40, Retransmit 5
    Hello due in 00:00:09
  Neighbor Count is 1, Adjacent neighbor count is 1
    Adjacent with neighbor 2.2.2.2  (Designated Router)
  Suppress hello for 0 neighbor(s)
```

Verify that the cost to reach the loopback network is now 101 (100 + 1).

```
rtrA#show ip route
Codes: C - connected, S - static, I - IGRP, R - RIP, M - mobile, B - BGP
       D - EIGRP, EX - EIGRP external, O - OSPF, IA - OSPF inter area
       N1 - OSPF NSSA external type 1, N2 - OSPF NSSA external type 2
       E1 - OSPF external type 1, E2 - OSPF external type 2, E - EGP
       i - IS-IS, L1 - IS-IS level-1, L2 - IS-IS level-2, * - candidate default
       U - per-user static route, o - ODR
```

```
Gateway of last resort is not set

     1.0.0.0/32 is subnetted, 1 subnets
C       1.1.1.1 is directly connected, Loopback0
     2.0.0.0/32 is subnetted, 1 subnets
O IA    2.2.2.2 [110/101] via 172.16.1.2, 00:02:43, Ethernet0/0
     172.16.0.0/24 is subnetted, 1 subnets
C       172.16.1.0 is directly connected, Ethernet0/0
     10.0.0.0/30 is subnetted, 1 subnets
C       10.1.1.0 is directly connected, Serial0/1
```

Troubleshooting

Step 1 Verify that the correct cost has been used in the **ip ospf cost** interface command.

Step 2 For consistency, use the same cost for every interface attached to the same network.

19-6: ip ospf database-filter all out

Syntax Description:

This command has no arguments.

Purpose: To prevent the flooding of link-state advertisements (LSAs) on an interface. Many Internet service providers employ redundant links between OSPF neighbors. When an OSPF router receives an LSA, the LSA is flooded on all OSPF interfaces except for the interface on which the LSA was received. The **ip ospf database-filter all out** command enables an ISP to choose between flooding overhead and flooding reliability. For example, if there are two links between OSPF neighbors, this command can be used to prevent the flooding of LSAs on one of the links.

Initial Cisco IOS Software Release: 12.0

Configuration Example: Reducing the Flooding of LSAs on a Redundant OSPF Link

Figure 19-3 shows two parallel links between Routers A and B. To reduce the LSA flooding overhead, LSA flooding is prevented on link 2 using the **database-filter** option of the **ip ospf interface** command. This reduction of LSA flooding can also be achieved by using the router configuration command **neighbor ospf database-filter all out** (see Section 11-3). Configure Routers A and B as shown in the lines following the figure:

Figure 19-3 *LSA Flooding Overhead Can Be Reduced by Preventing LSA Flooding on One of the Parallel Links*

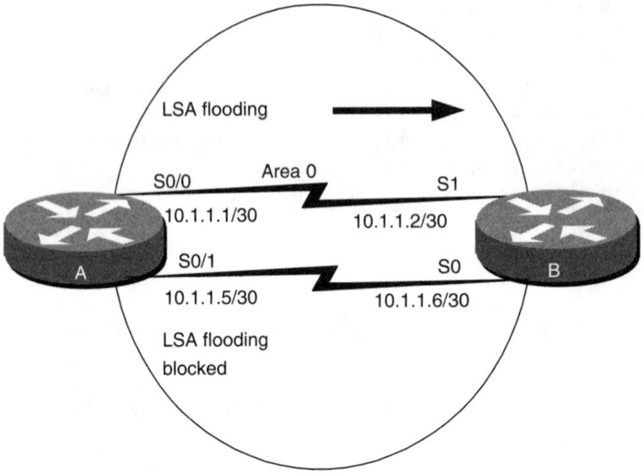


```
Router A
interface Loopback0
 ip address 1.1.1.1 255.255.255.255
!
interface Serial0/0
 bandwidth 64
 ip address 10.1.1.1 255.255.255.252
!
interface Serial0/1
 bandwidth 64
 ip address 10.1.1.5 255.255.255.252
 ip ospf database-filter all out
 clockrate 64000
!
router ospf 1
 network 1.1.1.1 0.0.0.0 area 1
 network 10.1.1.0 0.0.0.3 area 0
 network 10.1.1.4 0.0.0.3 area 0
```

```
Router B
interface Loopback0
 ip address 2.2.2.2 255.255.255.255
!
interface Serial0
ip address 10.1.1.6 255.255.255.252
 bandwidth 64
!
interface Serial1
 bandwidth 64
 ip address 10.1.1.2 255.255.255.252
 clockrate 64000
```

```
!
router ospf 1
 network 2.2.2.2 0.0.0.0 area 2
 network 10.1.1.0 0.0.0.3 area 0
 network 10.1.1.4 0.0.0.3 area 0
```

Verification

Verify that the database filter has been applied to interface Serial 0/1 on Router A.

```
rtrA#show ip ospf neighbor detail
 Neighbor 2.2.2.2, interface address 10.1.1.2
    In the area 0 via interface Serial0/0
    Neighbor priority is 1, State is FULL, 6 state changes
    DR is 0.0.0.0 BDR is 0.0.0.0
    Options 2
    Dead timer due in 00:00:33
 Neighbor 2.2.2.2, interface address 10.1.1.6
    In the area 0 via interface Serial0/1
    Neighbor priority is 1, State is FULL, 6 state changes
    Database-filter all out
    DR is 0.0.0.0 BDR is 0.0.0.0
    Options 2
    Dead timer due in 00:01:55
```

Troubleshooting

Step 1 If the OSPF neighbors have a FULL adjacency, then the interface command **ip ospf database-filter all out** should work.

19-7: ip ospf dead-interval *seconds*

Syntax Description:

- *seconds*—If Hello packets from a neighbor are not received during a period of time equal to the dead interval, the neighbor will be declared down. The range of values is 1–8192 seconds. The default value is four times the Hello interval.

Purpose: When an OSPF router receives a Hello packet from an OSPF neighbor, the receiving router assumes that the neighbor is active. The dead interval is used to determine when an OSPF neighbor has become inactive. If a Hello packet has not been received during the time set for the dead interval, then the neighbor will be declared down. By default, the dead interval is four times the Hello interval. The dead interval should always be greater than the Hello interval.

Initial Cisco IOS Software Release: 10.0

Configuration Example: Modifying the Interface Dead Interval

Configure the network in Figure 19-4 so you can observe the default timer values on an OSPF interface. You will then experiment with adjusting the values of the dead interval.

Figure 19-4 *The Dead Interval Must Be Configured with the Same Value on All Interfaces Attached to a Common Network*

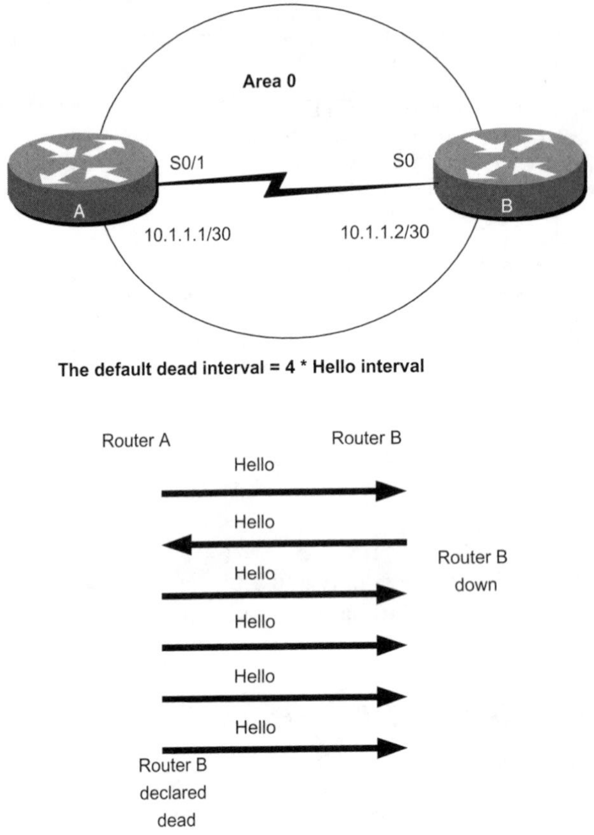


```
Router A
interface Loopback0
 ip address 1.1.1.1 255.255.255.255
!
interface Serial0/1
 ip address 10.1.1.1 255.255.255.252
 clockrate 64000
!
```

```
router ospf 1
 network 10.1.1.0 0.0.0.3 area 0
 network 1.1.1.1 0.0.0.0 area 1
```

```
Router B
interface Loopback0
 ip address 2.2.2.2 255.255.255.255
!
interface Serial0
 ip address 10.1.1.2 255.255.255.252
!
router ospf 1
 network 10.1.1.0 0.0.0.3 area 0
 network 2.2.2.2 0.0.0.0 area 2
```

Inspect the dead interval on the serial interface by using the command **show ip ospf interface**.

```
rtrA#show ip ospf interface serial 0/1
Serial0/1 is up, line protocol is up
  Internet Address 10.1.1.1/30, Area 0
  Process ID 1, Router ID 1.1.1.1, Network Type POINT_TO_POINT, Cost: 1562
  Transmit Delay is 1 sec, State POINT_TO_POINT,
  Timer intervals configured, Hello 10, Dead 40, Wait 40, Retransmit 5
    Hello due in 00:00:05
  Neighbor Count is 1, Adjacent neighbor count is 1
    Adjacent with neighbor 2.2.2.2
  Suppress hello for 0 neighbor(s)
```

Notice that the default Hello interval is 10 seconds and the default dead interval is 40 seconds. Modify the configuration on Router A to change the dead interval to 41 seconds while leaving the value for the dead interval on Router B set to the default of 40 seconds.

```
Router A
interface Serial0/1
 bandwidth 64
 ip address 10.1.1.1 255.255.255.252
 ip ospf dead-interval 41
 clockrate 64000
```

Verify that Routers A and B have formed an OSPF neighbor relationship.

```
rtrA#show ip ospf neighbor
(no output)
```

Because the dead interval on Router A does not match the dead interval on Router B, the routers will not form an OSPF neighbor relationship. OSPF neighbors must agree on the Hello and dead intervals and the authentication method used must be the same on both ends of a link. Enable OSPF debugging to verify the problem.

```
rtrA#debug ip ospf adj
OSPF adjacency events debugging is on
rtrA#
02:17:31: OSPF: Rcv hello from 2.2.2.2 area 0 from Serial0/1 10.1.1.2
02:17:31: OSPF: Mismatched hello parameters from 10.1.1.2
02:17:31: Dead R 40 C 41, Hello R 10 C 10
```

Modify the dead interval of the serial interface on Router B.

```
Router B
interface Serial0
 ip address 10.1.1.2 255.255.255.252
 ip ospf dead-interval 41
```

Verification

Verify that the dead interval on Router B matches the dead interval on Router A.

```
rtrB#show ip ospf interface serial 0
Serial0 is up, line protocol is up
  Internet Address 10.1.1.2/30, Area 0
  Process ID 1, Router ID 2.2.2.2, Network Type POINT_TO_POINT, Cost: 64
  Transmit Delay is 1 sec, State POINT_TO_POINT,
  Timer intervals configured, Hello 10, Dead 41, Wait 41, Retransmit 5
    Hello due in 00:00:04
  Neighbor Count is 1, Adjacent neighbor count is 1
    Adjacent with neighbor 1.1.1.1
  Suppress hello for 0 neighbor(s)
```

Verify that Routers A and B have established an OSPF neighbor relationship.

```
rtrA#show ip ospf neighbor

Neighbor ID     Pri   State           Dead Time   Address         Interface
2.2.2.2           1   FULL/  -        00:00:35    10.1.1.2        Serial0/1
```

Troubleshooting

Step 1 Verify that the same dead interval is being used on all interfaces attached to a common network.

Step 2 Verify that the dead interval is greater than the Hello interval.

19-8: ip ospf demand-circuit

Syntax Description:

This command has no arguments.

Purpose: On an OSPF demand circuit, periodic Hello messages are suppressed and periodic refreshes of LSAs do not flood the demand circuit. The **ip ospf demand-circuit** command allows the underlying data link layer to be closed when the topology is stable. In a point-to-multipoint topology, only the multipoint end must be configured with this command. This command is normally used on a tariff link such as ISDN. A tariff link is one that incurs a financial charge for every packet that is sent on the link. Configuring the link as a demand circuit will suppress periodic OSPF packets, reducing the line charges.

Initial Cisco IOS Software Release: 11.2

Configuration Example: Configuring a Point-to-Point Link as an OSPF Demand Circuit

Configure the serial network in Figure 19-5 as an OSPF demand circuit.

Figure 19-5 *Configuring a Link as an OSPF Demand Circuit Will Suppress Hello Packets and Periodic Refreshing of LSAs*

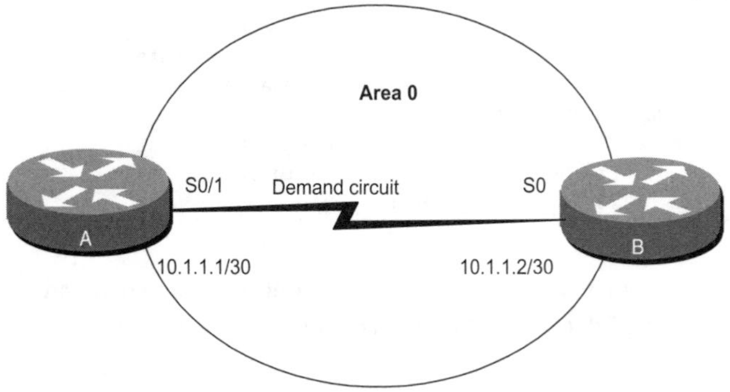

```
Router A
interface Loopback0
 ip address 1.1.1.1 255.255.255.255
!
interface Serial0/1
 ip address 10.1.1.1 255.255.255.252
 ip ospf demand-circuit
 clockrate 64000
!
router ospf 1
 network 10.1.1.0 0.0.0.3 area 0
 network 1.1.1.1 0.0.0.0 area 1
```

```
Router B
interface Loopback0
 ip address 2.2.2.2 255.255.255.255
!
interface Serial0
 ip address 10.1.1.2 255.255.255.252
!
router ospf 1
 network 10.1.1.0 0.0.0.3 area 0
 network 2.2.2.2 0.0.0.0 area 2
```

Verification

Verify that the serial interface has been configured as an OSPF demand circuit.

```
rtrA#show ip ospf interface serial 0/1
Serial0 is up, line protocol is up
  Internet Address 10.1.1.1/30, Area 0
  Process ID 1, Router ID 1.1.1.1, Network Type POINT_TO_POINT, Cost: 64
  Configured as demand circuit.
  Run as demand circuit.
  DoNotAge LSA allowed.  Transmit Delay is 1 sec, State POINT_TO_POINT,
  Timer intervals configured, Hello 10, Dead 40, Wait 41, Retransmit 5
    Hello due in 00:00:04
  Neighbor Count is 1, Adjacent neighbor count is 1
    Adjacent with neighbor 2.2.2.2  (Hello suppressed)
  Suppress hello for 1 neighbor(s)
```

Verify that the other end of the serial link is configured as a demand circuit even though the command **ip ospf demand-circuit** was not used on Router B.

```
rtrB#show ip ospf interface serial 0
Serial0 is up, line protocol is up
  Internet Address 10.1.1.2/30, Area 0
  Process ID 1, Router ID 2.2.2.2, Network Type POINT_TO_POINT, Cost: 64
```

```
  Configured as demand circuit.
  Run as demand circuit.
  DoNotAge LSA allowed.  Transmit Delay is 1 sec, State POINT_TO_POINT,
  Timer intervals configured, Hello 10, Dead 40, Wait 41, Retransmit 5
    Hello due in 00:00:04
  Neighbor Count is 1, Adjacent neighbor count is 1
    Adjacent with neighbor 1.1.1.1  (Hello suppressed)
  Suppress hello for 1 neighbor(s)
```

Verify that Routers A and B have established an OSPF neighbor relationship.

```
rtrA#show ip ospf neighbor

Neighbor ID     Pri   State           Dead Time   Address         Interface
2.2.2.2           1   FULL/  -        00:00:35    10.1.1.2        Serial0/1
```

Troubleshooting

Step 1 The **ip ospf demand-circuit** command will work if there are no errors in the configuration. Before using this command, ensure that the routers have established an OSPF neighbor relationship over the link that is to be configured as a demand circuit.

19-9: ip ospf flood-reduction

Syntax Description:

This command has no arguments.

Purpose: An OSPF LSA, by default, is refreshed every 30 minutes even if there has been no change to the LSA. If the LSAs are not changing, then this indicates a stable network topology. For large networks, the periodic flooding of LSAs in a stable network is unnecessary. The **ip ospf flood-reduction** interface command causes LSAs to be sent with the DoNotAge bit set, which has the effect of disabling the periodic refresh of LSAs. If there is a change in the network topology, the LSAs will be flooded regardless of whether or not this command is used. When flood reduction is enabled on an interface, the OSPF neighbor relationship on the interface will be reset.

Initial Cisco IOS Software Release: 12.1

Configuration Example: Configuring OSPF Flood Reduction on an Interface

Configure the routers in Figure 19-6 without using flood reduction in order to investigate the changes in the OSPF database once flood reduction is enabled.

Figure 19-6 *Network Used to Demonstrate the Changes in the OSPF Database when Flood Reduction Is Enabled*

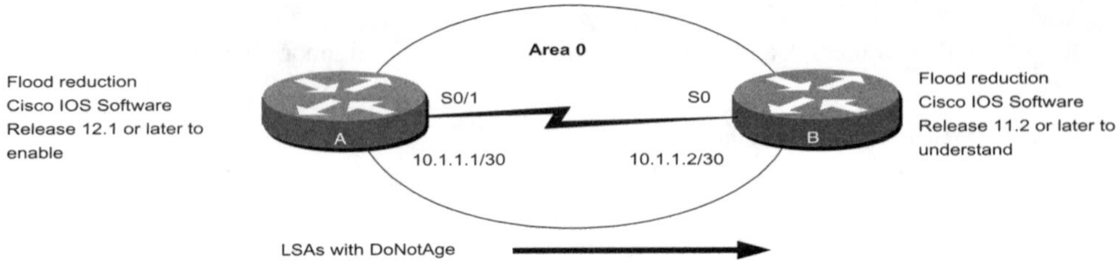


```
Router A
interface Loopback0
 ip address 1.1.1.1 255.255.255.255
!
interface Serial0/1
 ip address 10.1.1.1 255.255.255.252
 clockrate 64000
!
router ospf 1
 network 10.1.1.0 0.0.0.3 area 0
 network 1.1.1.1 0.0.0.0 area 1
```

```
Router B
interface Loopback0
 ip address 2.2.2.2 255.255.255.255
!
interface Serial0
 ip address 10.1.1.2 255.255.255.252
!
router ospf 1
 network 10.1.1.0 0.0.0.3 area 0
 network 2.2.2.2 0.0.0.0 area 2
```

Inspect the OSPF database on Router B for network 1.1.1.1.

```
rtrB#show ip ospf database router 1.1.1.1

       OSPF Router with ID (2.2.2.2) (Process ID 1)


                Router Link States (Area 0)
```

```
  Routing Bit Set on this LSA
  LS age: 113
  Options: (No TOS-capability, DC)
  LS Type: Router Links
  Link State ID: 1.1.1.1
  Advertising Router: 1.1.1.1
  LS Seq Number: 80000041
  Checksum: 0xDD9F
  Length: 48
  Area Border Router
   Number of Links: 2

    Link connected to: another Router (point-to-point)
     (Link ID) Neighboring Router ID: 2.2.2.2
     (Link Data) Router Interface address: 10.1.1.1
      Number of TOS metrics: 0
       TOS 0 Metrics: 1562

    Link connected to: a Stub Network
     (Link ID) Network/subnet number: 10.1.1.0
     (Link Data) Network Mask: 255.255.255.252
      Number of TOS metrics: 0
       TOS 0 Metrics: 1562
```

Modify the configuration on Router A to enable OSPF flood reduction on the serial interface.

```
Router A
interface Serial0/1
 bandwidth 64
 ip address 10.1.1.1 255.255.255.252
 ip ospf flood-reduction
 clockrate 64000
```

Verification

Verify that flood reduction is enabled on Router A by checking the OSPF database on Router B.

```
rtrB#show ip ospf database router 1.1.1.1

       OSPF Router with ID (2.2.2.2) (Process ID 1)


                Router Link States (Area 0)

  Routing Bit Set on this LSA
  LS age: 5 (DoNotAge)
```

continues

```
Options: (No TOS-capability, DC)
LS Type: Router Links
Link State ID: 1.1.1.1
Advertising Router: 1.1.1.1
LS Seq Number: 80000043
Checksum: 0xD9A1
Length: 48
Area Border Router
 Number of Links: 2

  Link connected to: another Router (point-to-point)
   (Link ID) Neighboring Router ID: 2.2.2.2
   (Link Data) Router Interface address: 10.1.1.1
    Number of TOS metrics: 0
     TOS 0 Metrics: 1562

  Link connected to: a Stub Network
   (Link ID) Network/subnet number: 10.1.1.0
   (Link Data) Network Mask: 255.255.255.252
    Number of TOS metrics: 0
     TOS 0 Metrics: 1562
```

Troubleshooting

Step 1 If there is an OSPF neighbor on an interface then the command **ip ospf flood-reduction** should work.

Step 2 The routers receiving the LSAs tagged as DoNotAge should be running Cisco IOS Software Release 11.2 or later.

19-10: ip ospf hello-interval *seconds*

Syntax Description:

- *seconds*—The time in seconds between sending Hello packets over a link. The range of values is 1–8192 seconds. The default value is 10 seconds (30 seconds on a nonbroadcast multiaccess [NBMA] network).

Purpose: OSPF Hello packets are used to initially establish the neighbor relationship. Once the neighbor relationship is established, the packets are used as a keepalive mechanism to determine if OSPF neighbors are active. The Hello interval should be less than the dead interval. All interfaces on a common network must have the same Hello interval or an OSPF neighbor relationship will not be established.

Initial Cisco IOS Software Release: 10.0

Configuration Example: Modifying the Interface Hello Interval

Configure the network in Figure 19-7 so you can observe the default timer values on an OSPF interface link. You will then experiment with adjusting the values of the Hello interval.

Figure 19-7 *The Hello Interval Must Be Configured with the Same Value on All Interfaces Attached to a Common Network*

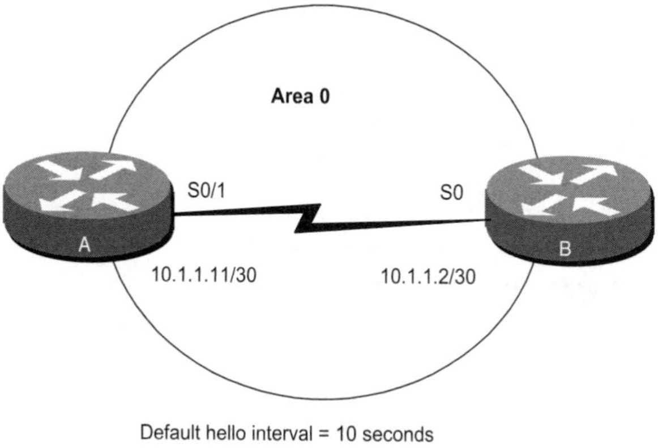


```
Router A
interface Loopback0
 ip address 1.1.1.1 255.255.255.255
!
interface Serial0/1
 ip address 10.1.1.1 255.255.255.252
 clockrate 64000
!
router ospf 1
 network 10.1.1.0 0.0.0.3 area 0
 network 1.1.1.1 0.0.0.0 area 1
```

```
Router B
interface Loopback0
 ip address 2.2.2.2 255.255.255.255
!
interface Serial0
 ip address 10.1.1.2 255.255.255.252
!
router ospf 1
 network 10.1.1.0 0.0.0.3 area 0
 network 2.2.2.2 0.0.0.0 area 2
```

View the timer values for the serial interface on Routers A and B.

```
rtrA#show ip ospf interface s0/1
Serial0/1 is up, line protocol is up
  Internet Address 10.1.1.1/30, Area 0
  Process ID 1, Router ID 1.1.1.1, Network Type POINT_TO_POINT, Cost: 1562
  Transmit Delay is 1 sec, State POINT_TO_POINT,
  Timer intervals configured, Hello 10, Dead 40, Wait 40, Retransmit 5
    Hello due in 00:00:09
  Index 1/2, flood queue length 0
  Next 0x0(0)/0x0(0)
  Last flood scan length is 1, maximum is 2
  Last flood scan time is 0 msec, maximum is 4 msec
  Neighbor Count is 1, Adjacent neighbor count is 1
    Adjacent with neighbor 2.2.2.2
  Suppress hello for 0 neighbor(s)
```

```
rtrB#show ip ospf interface serial 0
Serial0 is up, line protocol is up
  Internet Address 10.1.1.2/30, Area 0
  Process ID 1, Router ID 2.2.2.2, Network Type POINT_TO_POINT, Cost: 64
  Transmit Delay is 1 sec, State POINT_TO_POINT,
  Timer intervals configured, Hello 10, Dead 40, Wait 40, Retransmit 5
    Hello due in 00:00:09
  Neighbor Count is 1, Adjacent neighbor count is 1
    Adjacent with neighbor 1.1.1.1
  Suppress hello for 0 neighbor(s)
```

Notice that the default Hello interval is 10 seconds and the default dead interval is 40 seconds. Modify the configuration on Router A to change the Hello interval to 11 seconds while leaving the value for the Hello interval on Router B set to the default of 10 seconds.

```
Router A
interface Serial0/1
 bandwidth 64
 ip address 10.1.1.1 255.255.255.252
 ip ospf hello-interval 11
 clockrate 64000
```

Inspect the OSPF interface timers for serial 0/1 on Router A.

```
rtrA#show ip ospf interface serial 0/1
Serial0/1 is up, line protocol is up
  Internet Address 10.1.1.1/30, Area 0
  Process ID 1, Router ID 1.1.1.1, Network Type POINT_TO_POINT, Cost: 1562
  Transmit Delay is 1 sec, State POINT_TO_POINT,
  Timer intervals configured, Hello 11, Dead 44, Wait 44, Retransmit 5
```

```
    Hello due in 00:00:05
  Index 1/2, flood queue length 0
  Next 0x0(0)/0x0(0)
  Last flood scan length is 0, maximum is 2
  Last flood scan time is 0 msec, maximum is 4 msec
  Neighbor Count is 0, Adjacent neighbor count is 0
  Suppress hello for 0 neighbor(s)
```

The dead timer has been automatically set to four times the Hello interval.

Verify that Routers A and B have an OSPF neighbor relationship.

```
rtrA#show ip ospf neighbor
(no output)
```

Because the Hello interval time on Router A does not match the Hello interval on Router B, an OSPF neighbor relationship will not be established. This can be seen by enabling OSPF debugging on Router B.

```
rtrB#debug ip ospf adj
OSPF adjacency events debugging is on
rtrB#
17:03:20: OSPF: Rcv hello from 1.1.1.1 area 0 from Serial0 10.1.1.1
17:03:20: OSPF: Mismatched hello parameters from 10.1.1.1
17:03:20: Dead R 44 C 40, Hello R 11 C 10
```

Modify the Hello interval on Router B to match the Hello interval on Router A.

```
Router B
interface Serial0
 ip address 10.1.1.2 255.255.255.252
 ip ospf hello-interval 11
```

Verification

Verify that the Hello interval on Router A matches the Hello interval on Router B.

```
rtrB#show ip ospf interface serial 0
Serial0 is up, line protocol is up
  Internet Address 10.1.1.2/30, Area 0
  Process ID 1, Router ID 2.2.2.2, Network Type POINT_TO_POINT, Cost: 64
  Transmit Delay is 1 sec, State POINT_TO_POINT,
  Timer intervals configured, Hello 11, Dead 44, Wait 44, Retransmit 5
    Hello due in 00:00:07
```

continues

```
  Neighbor Count is 1, Adjacent neighbor count is 1
    Adjacent with neighbor 1.1.1.1
  Suppress hello for 0 neighbor(s)
```

Verify that the OSPF neighbor relationship has been re-established.

```
rtrB#show ip ospf neighbor

Neighbor ID     Pri   State           Dead Time   Address         Interface
1.1.1.1           1   FULL/  -        00:00:42    10.1.1.1        Serial0
```

Troubleshooting

Step 1 Verify that all interfaces attached to a common network are using the same value for the Hello interval.

19-11: ip ospf message-digest-key *key-id* md5 *password*

Syntax Description:

- *key-id*—Key used to identify the password. The range of values is 1 to 255. All interfaces attached to a common network must use the same key and password.
- *password*—Password to be used for authentication on the interface. The password is an alphanumeric string from 1 to 16 characters.

Purpose: If message digest authentication is enabled in Area 0 then all interfaces in the area need to be configured with the same authentication type. This command is used to configure message digest authentication on an OSPF interface. In Cisco IOS Software Release 12.0 and later, interface authentication can be configured independent of the authentication applied to an area (see Sections 19-1 to 19-4).

Initial Cisco IOS Software Release: 11.0

Configuration Example 1: Message Digest Authentication on an OSPF Interface

In Figure 19-8, message authentication has been enabled for Area 0. The serial interfaces in Area 0 are configured with message digest authentication using a key ID of **1** and a password of **cisco**.

Figure 19-8 *Prior to Cisco IOS Software Release 12.0, if Message Digest Authentication Is Enabled in an OSPF Area, Then Message Digest Authentication Must Be Enabled on All Interfaces in the Area*

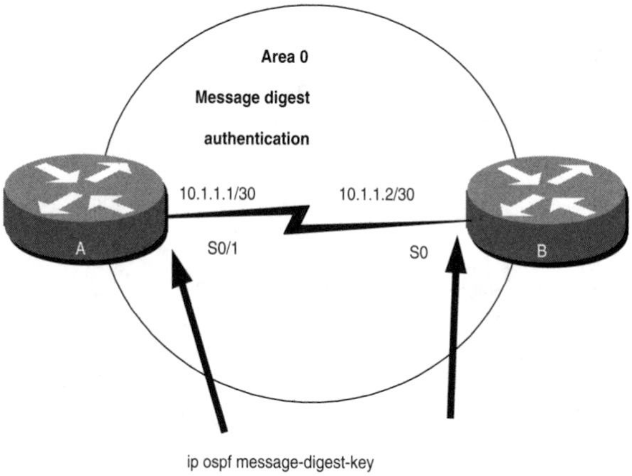


```
Router A
interface Loopback0
 ip address 1.1.1.1 255.255.255.255
!
interface Serial0/1
 ip address 10.1.1.1 255.255.255.252
 ip ospf message-digest-key 1 md5 cisco
 clockrate 64000
!
router ospf 1
 area 0 authentication-message digest
 network 10.1.1.0 0.0.0.3 area 0
 network 1.1.1.1 0.0.0.0 area 1
```

```
Router B
interface Loopback0
 ip address 2.2.2.2 255.255.255.255
!
interface Serial0
 ip address 10.1.1.2 255.255.255.252
 ip ospf message-digest-key 1 md5 cisco
!
router ospf 1
 area 0 authentication message-digest
 network 10.1.1.0 0.0.0.3 area 0
 network 2.2.2.2 0.0.0.0 area 2
```

Verification

Verify that authentication has been enabled for Area 0.

```
rtrA#show ip ospf
Routing Process "ospf 1" with ID 1.1.1.1 and Domain ID 0.0.0.1
 Supports only single TOS(TOS0) routes
 Supports opaque LSA
 It is an area border router
 SPF schedule delay 5 secs, Hold time between two SPFs 10 secs
 Minimum LSA interval 5 secs. Minimum LSA arrival 1 secs
 Number of external LSA 0. Checksum Sum 0x0
 Number of opaque AS LSA 0. Checksum Sum 0x0
 Number of DCbitless external and opaque AS LSA 0
 Number of DoNotAge external and opaque AS LSA 0
 Number of areas in this router is 2. 2 normal 0 stub 0 nssa
 External flood list length 0
    Area BACKBONE(0)
        Number of interfaces in this area is 1
        Area has message digest authentication
        SPF algorithm executed 41 times
        Area ranges are
        Number of LSA 8. Checksum Sum 0x404DC
        Number of opaque link LSA 0. Checksum Sum 0x0
        Number of DCbitless LSA 0
        Number of indication LSA 0
        Number of DoNotAge LSA 0
        Flood list length 0
    Area 1
        Number of interfaces in this area is 1
        Area has no authentication
        SPF algorithm executed 18 times
        Area ranges are
        Number of LSA 2. Checksum Sum 0x1A57A
        Number of opaque link LSA 0. Checksum Sum 0x0
        Number of DCbitless LSA 0
        Number of indication LSA 0
        Number of DoNotAge LSA 0
        Flood list length 0
```

```
rtrB#show ip ospf
Routing Process "ospf 1" with ID 2.2.2.2
 Supports only single TOS(TOS0) routes
 It is an area border router
 Summary Link update interval is 00:30:00 and the update due in 00:21:19
 SPF schedule delay 5 secs, Hold time between two SPFs 10 secs
 Number of DCbitless external LSA 0
 Number of DoNotAge external LSA 0
 Number of areas in this router is 2. 2 normal 0 stub 0 nssa
    Area BACKBONE(0)
        Number of interfaces in this area is 1
        Area has message digest authentication
```

```
        SPF algorithm executed 4 times
        Area ranges are
        Link State Update Interval is 00:30:00 and due in 00:21:19
        Link State Age Interval is 00:20:00 and due in 00:11:18
        Number of DCbitless LSA 0
        Number of indication LSA 0
        Number of DoNotAge LSA 0
    Area 2
        Number of interfaces in this area is 1
        Area has no authentication
        SPF algorithm executed 2 times
        Area ranges are
        Link State Update Interval is 00:30:00 and due in 00:21:16
        Link State Age Interval is 00:20:00 and due in 00:11:16
        Number of DCbitless LSA 0
        Number of indication LSA 0
        Number of DoNotAge LSA 0
```

Verify that message digest authentication is enabled on the serial interfaces.

```
rtrA#show ip ospf interface serial 0/1
Serial0/1 is up, line protocol is up
  Internet Address 10.1.1.1/30, Area 0
  Process ID 1, Router ID 1.1.1.1, Network Type POINT_TO_POINT, Cost: 1562
  Transmit Delay is 1 sec, State POINT_TO_POINT,
  Timer intervals configured, Hello 10, Dead 40, Wait 40, Retransmit 5
    Hello due in 00:00:02
  Index 1/2, flood queue length 0
  Next 0x0(0)/0x0(0)
  Last flood scan length is 1, maximum is 2
  Last flood scan time is 0 msec, maximum is 4 msec
  Neighbor Count is 1, Adjacent neighbor count is 1
    Adjacent with neighbor 2.2.2.2
  Suppress hello for 0 neighbor(s)
  Message digest authentication enabled
    Youngest key id is 1
```

```
rtrB#show ip ospf interface serial 0
Serial0 is up, line protocol is up
  Internet Address 10.1.1.2/30, Area 0
  Process ID 1, Router ID 2.2.2.2, Network Type POINT_TO_POINT, Cost: 64
  Transmit Delay is 1 sec, State POINT_TO_POINT,
  Timer intervals configured, Hello 10, Dead 40, Wait 40, Retransmit 5
    Hello due in 00:00:07
  Neighbor Count is 1, Adjacent neighbor count is 1
    Adjacent with neighbor 1.1.1.1
  Suppress hello for 0 neighbor(s)
  Message digest authentication enabled
    Youngest key id is 1
```

Verify that Routers A and B have established an OSPF neighbor relationship.

```
rtrA#show ip ospf neighbor

Neighbor ID     Pri   State           Dead Time   Address         Interface
2.2.2.2           1   FULL/  -        00:00:37    10.1.1.2        Serial0/1
```

Configuration Example 2: Changing Keys and Passwords

For additional security, you may choose to periodically change your key and password. With clear-text authentication, when you change passwords there will be a loss of OSPF connectivity from the time you change the password on one end interface until you change the password on the other interfaces in the area. With MD5 authentication, you can configure a new key and password on an OSPF interface while leaving the old key and password in place. The old key and password will continue to be used until the new key and password are configured on the other interface. Modify the key and password on the serial interfaces on Routers A and B. First, add a new key and password to Router A in order to observe the behavior when the new key and password have only been configured on one end of the serial network.

```
Router A
interface Serial0/1
 ip address 10.1.1.1 255.255.255.252
 ip ospf message-digest-key 1 md5 cisco
 ip ospf message-digest-key 2 md5 budman
 clockrate 64000
```

Examine the effect of adding a new key and password on only one end of the serial link.

```
rtrA#show ip ospf interface serial 0/1
Serial0/1 is up, line protocol is up
  Internet Address 10.1.1.1/30, Area 0
  Process ID 1, Router ID 1.1.1.1, Network Type POINT_TO_POINT, Cost: 1562
  Transmit Delay is 1 sec, State POINT_TO_POINT,
  Timer intervals configured, Hello 10, Dead 40, Wait 40, Retransmit 5
    Hello due in 00:00:04
  Index 1/2, flood queue length 0
  Next 0x0(0)/0x0(0)
  Last flood scan length is 1, maximum is 2
  Last flood scan time is 0 msec, maximum is 4 msec
  Neighbor Count is 1, Adjacent neighbor count is 1
    Adjacent with neighbor 2.2.2.2
  Suppress hello for 0 neighbor(s)
  Message digest authentication enabled
    Youngest key id is 2
    Rollover in progress, 1 neighbor(s) using the old key(s):
      key id 1
```

Notice that both keys are being used for authentication. Configure the new key and password on Router B while leaving the old key and password in place.

```
Router B
interface Serial0
 ip address 10.1.1.2 255.255.255.252
 ip ospf message-digest-key 1 md5 cisco
 ip ospf message-digest-key 2 md5 budman
```

Verification

Verify that Router B is now using the new key and password.

```
rtrB#show ip ospf interface serial 0
Serial0 is up, line protocol is up
  Internet Address 10.1.1.2/30, Area 0
  Process ID 1, Router ID 2.2.2.2, Network Type POINT_TO_POINT, Cost: 64
  Transmit Delay is 1 sec, State POINT_TO_POINT,
  Timer intervals configured, Hello 10, Dead 40, Wait 40, Retransmit 5
    Hello due in 00:00:00
  Neighbor Count is 1, Adjacent neighbor count is 1
    Adjacent with neighbor 1.1.1.1
  Suppress hello for 0 neighbor(s)
  Message digest authentication enabled
    Youngest key id is 2
```

You can now remove the old key and password from Routers A and B.

```
Router A
interface Serial0/1
 no ip ospf message-digest-key 1 md5 cisco
```

```
Router B
interface Serial0
 no ip ospf message-digest-key 1 md5 cisco
```

Troubleshooting

Step 1 Verify that the same key and password are being used on all interfaces attached to a common network.

19-12: ip ospf mtu-ignore

Syntax Description:

This command has no arguments.

Purpose: If there is a maximum transmission unit (MTU) mismatch between neighboring OSPF routers, then the routers will not form an OSPF adjacency.

Initial Cisco IOS Software Release: 12.0 (3)

Configuration Example: OSPF Adjacency and MTU Mismatch

In Figure 19-9, Routers A and B have an MTU of 1500 on their serial interfaces and Router C has an MTU of 1490. When Routers A and C reach the EXSTART state in the forming of the adjacency, they will attempt to exchange their OSPF database description packets. An OSPF router will ignore a database description packet if there is an MTU mismatch. When there is a mismatch, the database description packet will not be acknowledged and the sending router will continue to send the packets until they are acknowledged. The acknowledgement will never come and the routers will be stuck in the EXSTART state. To demonstrate this, Router C has been configured with an MTU of 1490 as shown in the following configurations.

Figure 19-9 *OSPF Will Not Form a Neighbor Relationship if There Is an MTU Mismatch Between the Interfaces Connecting the Routers*

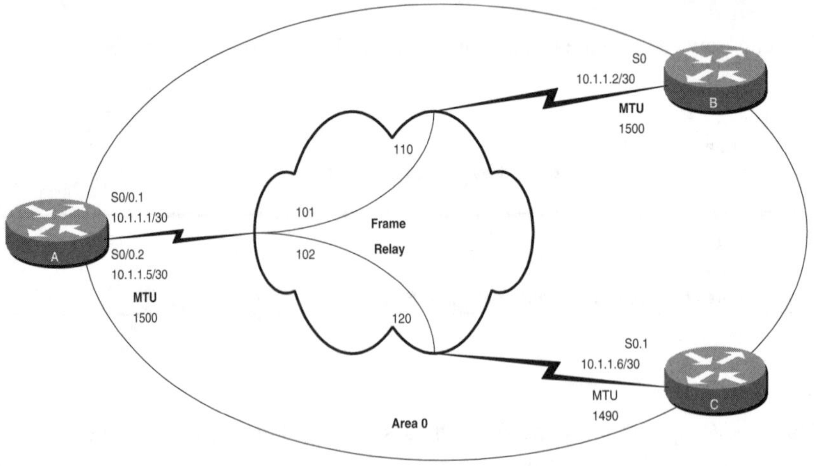

```
Router A
interface Loopback0
 ip address 1.1.1.1 255.255.255.255
!
interface Serial0/0
 bandwidth 64
 no ip address
 encapsulation frame-relay
 frame-relay lmi-type ansi
!
interface Serial0/0.1 point-to-point
 ip address 10.1.1.1 255.255.255.252
 frame-relay interface-dlci 101
!
interface Serial0/0.2 point-to-point
 ip address 10.1.1.5 255.255.255.252
 frame-relay interface-dlci 102
!
router ospf 1
 network 1.1.1.1 0.0.0.0 area 1
 network 10.1.1.0 0.0.0.3 area 0
 network 10.1.1.4 0.0.0.3 area 0
```

```
Router B
interface Loopback0
 ip address 2.2.2.2 255.255.255.255
!
interface Serial0
 ip address 10.1.1.2 255.255.255.252
 encapsulation frame-relay
 ip ospf network point-to-point
 no ip mroute-cache
 bandwidth 64
 frame-relay map ip 10.1.1.1 110 broadcast
 no frame-relay inverse-arp
 frame-relay lmi-type ansi
!
router ospf 1
 network 2.2.2.2 0.0.0.0 area 2
 network 10.1.1.0 0.0.0.3 area 0
```

```
Router C
interface Loopback0
 ip address 3.3.3.3 255.255.255.255
!
interface Serial0
 mtu 1490
 bandwidth 64
 no ip address
 encapsulation frame-relay
 no ip mroute-cache
!
```

continues

```
interface Serial0.1 point-to-point
 ip address 10.1.1.6 255.255.255.252
 frame-relay interface-dlci 120
!
router ospf 1
 network 3.3.3.3 0.0.0.0 area 3
 network 10.1.1.4 0.0.0.3 area 0
```

Enable OSPF debugging on Router A and then reset the OSPF process on Router A.

```
rtrA#debug ip ospf events
OSPF events debugging is on
rtrA#clear ip ospf process
Reset ALL OSPF processes? [no]: y
rtrA#
.
.
.
05:37:58: OSPF: Rcv DBD from 3.3.3.3 on Serial0/0.2 seq 0xF91 opt 0x2 flag 0x7 l
en 32  mtu 1490 state EXCHANGE
05:37:58: OSPF: Send DBD to 3.3.3.3 on Serial0/0.2 seq 0xF91 opt 0x42 flag 0x2 l
en 152
05:38:03: OSPF: Rcv hello from 3.3.3.3 area 0 from Serial0/0.2 10.1.1.6
05:38:03: OSPF: End of hello processing
05:38:03: OSPF: Rcv DBD from 3.3.3.3 on Serial0/0.2 seq 0xF91 opt 0x2 flag 0x7 l
en 32  mtu 1490 state EXCHANGE
05:38:03: OSPF: Send DBD to 3.3.3.3 on Serial0/0.2 seq 0xF91 opt 0x42 flag 0x2 l
en 152
.
.
.
```

You can see from the debug output on Router A that Routers A and C are stuck in the EXSTART state. This can also be seen by examining the OSPF neighbors as seen by Routers A and C.

```
rtrA#show ip ospf neighbor

Neighbor ID     Pri   State           Dead Time   Address         Interface
3.3.3.3           1   EXCHANGE/  -    00:00:35    10.1.1.6        Serial0/0.2
2.2.2.2           1   FULL/  -        00:00:38    10.1.1.2        Serial0/0.1
```

```
rtrC#show ip ospf neighbor

Neighbor ID     Pri   State           Dead Time   Address         Interface
1.1.1.1           1   EXSTART/  -     00:00:38    10.1.1.5        Serial0.1
```

This problem can be fixed by configuring the MTU to be the same on all of the serial interfaces. Cisco does not support the configuration of the MTU on Ethernet or Token Ring interfaces, so the only option is to use the **ip ospf mtu-ignore** interface command if a mismatch occurs on these network types. For this example, configure Routers A and C to ignore the MTU mismatch.

```
Router A
interface Serial0/0
 bandwidth 64
 no ip address
 encapsulation frame-relay
 frame-relay lmi-type ansi
!
interface Serial0/0.1 point-to-point
 ip address 10.1.1.1 255.255.255.252
 frame-relay interface-dlci 101
!
interface Serial0/0.2 point-to-point
 ip address 10.1.1.5 255.255.255.252
 ip ospf mtu-ignore
 frame-relay interface-dlci 102
```

```
Router C
interface Serial0
 mtu 1490
 bandwidth 64
 no ip address
 no ip directed-broadcast
 encapsulation frame-relay
!
interface Serial0.1 point-to-point
 ip address 10.1.1.6 255.255.255.252
 no ip directed-broadcast
 ip ospf mtu-ignore
 frame-relay interface-dlci 120
```

Verification

Verify that Routers A and C have formed an OSPF neighbor relationship.

```
rtrA#show ip ospf neighbor

Neighbor ID     Pri   State           Dead Time   Address         Interface
3.3.3.3           1   FULL/  -        00:00:36    10.1.1.6        Serial0/0.2
2.2.2.2           1   FULL/  -        00:00:36    10.1.1.2        Serial0/0.1
```

Troubleshooting

Step 1 Verify the IP address and netmask assignments used on the network interfaces.

Step 2 Verify that the proper DLCIs and IP addresses are used in the **frame relay map ip** statements. These can be checked using the **show frame-relay map** command, as shown here.

```
rtrA#show frame-relay map
Serial0/0 (up): ip 10.1.1.2 dlci 101(0x65,0x1850), static,
              broadcast,
              CISCO, status defined, active
Serial0/0 (up): ip 10.1.1.3 dlci 102(0x66,0x1860), static,
              broadcast,
              CISCO, status defined, active
```

Step 3 Before configuring OSPF, check IP connectivity by pinging the other end of the link.

Step 4 If you are mixing network types (multipoint and point-to-point) verify that the Hello intervals match on all routers.

Step 5 If there is an MTU mismatch, either modify the MTU on one end of the link to match the other end or use the **ip ospf mtu-ignore** interface command.

19-13: ip ospf network broadcast

Syntax Description:

This command has no arguments.

Purpose: Used to configure an NBMA network as a broadcast network.

Initial Cisco IOS Software Release: 10.0

Configuration Example 1: Fully-meshed OSPF Neighbors on an NBMA Network

OSPF views networks as being of one of three types:

- **A broadcast multiaccess network**—On a broadcast multiaccess network, all routers attached to the network have a direct communication link with all other routers on the network. Examples of a broadcast multiaccess network are Ethernet, Token Ring, and FDDI. When OSPF sends a protocol packet onto a broadcast multiaccess network, all OSPF routers on the network will receive the packet.
- **A point-to-point network**—On a point-to-point network, only two routers exist on the network, one at each end of the point-to-point link. Examples of a point-to-point network are High-Level Data Link Control (HDLC) and Point-to-Point Protocol (PPP).
- **An NBMA network**—Examples of an NBMA network are Frame Relay and X.25. On an NBMA network, all OSPF routers could possibly have connections to all other OSPF routers on the network, but all the connections are logical point-to-point links so an OSPF protocol packet sent on one link will not reach all OSPF neighbors. NBMA networks can be configured, from an OSPF point of view, as broadcast, point-to-point, or multipoint.

This example will investigate configuring Frame Relay as an OSPF broadcast network.

In Figure 19-10, three OSPF routers are fully meshed over a Frame Relay network. Every OSPF router has a connection to every other OSPF router. For this case, the Frame Relay network can be made to behave like a multiaccess network by configuring the network type as broadcast. As with all OSPF broadcast networks, a Designated Router (DR) and Backup Designated Router (BDR) will be elected for the network. Initially, the routers in Figure 19-10 are configured without specifying a network type in order to observe the OSPF behavior on an NBMA network.

Figure 19-10 *An NBMA Network Is Typically Configured as a Broadcast Network when the OSPF Routers Are Fully Meshed and the PVCs Are on the Same IP Subnet*

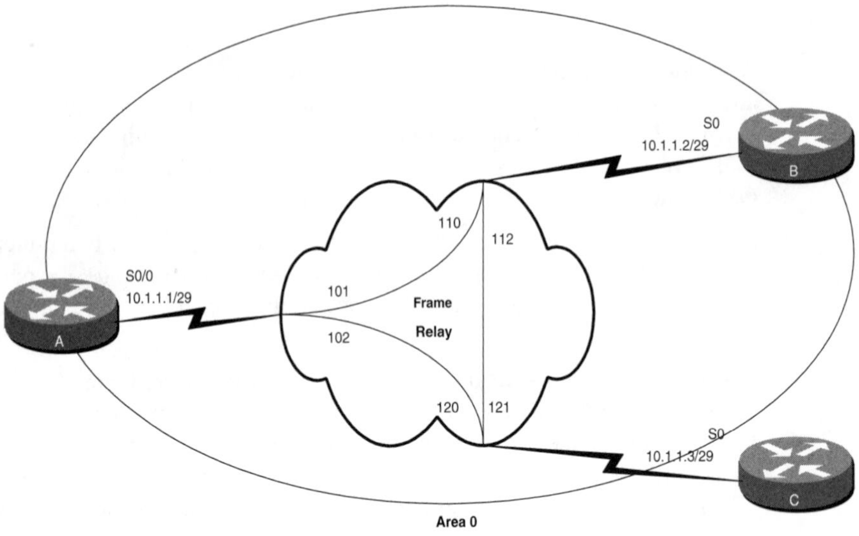


```
Router A
interface Loopback0
 ip address 1.1.1.1 255.255.255.255
!
interface Serial0/0
 bandwidth 64
 ip address 10.1.1.1 255.255.255.248
 encapsulation frame-relay
 frame-relay map ip 10.1.1.2 101 broadcast
 frame-relay map ip 10.1.1.3 102 broadcast
 no frame-relay inverse-arp
 frame-relay lmi-type ansi
!
router ospf 1
 network 1.1.1.1 0.0.0.0 area 1
 network 10.1.1.0 0.0.0.7 area 0
```

```
Router B
interface Loopback0
 ip address 2.2.2.2 255.255.255.255
!
interface Serial0
 ip address 10.1.1.2 255.255.255.248
 encapsulation frame-relay
 frame-relay map ip 10.1.1.1 110 broadcast
 frame-relay map ip 10.1.1.3 112 broadcast
 no frame-relay inverse-arp
```

```
 frame-relay lmi-type ansi
!
router ospf 1
 network 2.2.2.2 0.0.0.0 area 2
 network 10.1.1.0 0.0.0.7 area 0
```

```
Router C
interface Loopback0
 ip address 3.3.3.3 255.255.255.255
!

interface Serial0
 ip address 10.1.1.3 255.255.255.248
 encapsulation frame-relay
 frame-relay map ip 10.1.1.1 120 broadcast
 frame-relay map ip 10.1.1.2 121 broadcast
 no frame-relay inverse-arp
!
router ospf 1
 network 3.3.3.3 0.0.0.0 area 3
 network 10.1.1.0 0.0.0.7 area 0
```

Frame Relay inverse ARP is disabled on Routers A, B, and C and static **frame-relay map** statements are used to map remote IP addresses to the proper Frame Relay DLCI. This is not necessary for the operation of OSPF over Frame Relay but only prevents the routers from leaning DLCIs that are not used. Chapter 11 shows how the OSPF **neighbor** command is used to configure OSPF over an NBMA network. For this example, the OSPF interface command **ip ospf network broadcast** is used to have OSPF treat the Frame Relay network as a broadcast network. Without the **neighbor** command or the **ip ospf network broadcast** command, OSPF does not know how to treat the NBMA network so OSPF neighbor relationships will not be formed, as shown in the output of the **show ip ospf neighbor** command.

```
rtrA#show ip ospf neighbor
(no output)
```

OSPF is not sending any protocol packets to the NBMA network. Modify the configurations on Routers A, B, and C to configure the NBMA network as a broadcast network.

```
Router A
interface Serial0/0
 bandwidth 64
 ip address 10.1.1.1 255.255.255.248
 encapsulation frame-relay
 ip ospf network broadcast
```

continues

```
 frame-relay map ip 10.1.1.2 101 broadcast
 frame-relay map ip 10.1.1.3 102 broadcast
 no frame-relay inverse-arp
 frame-relay lmi-type ansi
```

```
Router B
interface Serial0
 ip address 10.1.1.2 255.255.255.248
 encapsulation frame-relay
 ip ospf network broadcast
 frame-relay map ip 10.1.1.1 110 broadcast
 frame-relay map ip 10.1.1.3 112 broadcast
 no frame-relay inverse-arp
 frame-relay lmi-type ansi
```

```
Router C
interface Serial0
 ip address 10.1.1.3 255.255.255.248
 encapsulation frame-relay
 ip ospf network broadcast
 frame-relay map ip 10.1.1.1 120 broadcast
 frame-relay map ip 10.1.1.2 121 broadcast
 no frame-relay inverse-arp
```

Verification

Verify that OSPF is treating the Frame Relay network as a broadcast network.

```
rtrA#show ip ospf interface serial 0/0
Serial0/0 is up, line protocol is up
  Internet Address 10.1.1.1/29, Area 0
  Process ID 1, Router ID 1.1.1.1, Network Type BROADCAST, Cost: 1562
  Transmit Delay is 1 sec, State DROTHER, Priority 1
  Designated Router (ID) 3.3.3.3, Interface address 10.1.1.3
  Backup Designated router (ID) 2.2.2.2, Interface address 10.1.1.2
  Timer intervals configured, Hello 10, Dead 40, Wait 40, Retransmit 5
    Hello due in 00:00:01
  Index 1/2, flood queue length 0
  Next 0x0(0)/0x0(0)
  Last flood scan length is 0, maximum is 2
  Last flood scan time is 0 msec, maximum is 0 msec
  Neighbor Count is 2, Adjacent neighbor count is 2
    Adjacent with neighbor 3.3.3.3  (Designated Router)
    Adjacent with neighbor 2.2.2.2  (Backup Designated Router)
  Suppress hello for 0 neighbor(s)
```

Verify that Routers A, B, and C have formed a FULL OSPF neighbor relationship.

```
rtrA#show ip ospf neighbor

Neighbor ID     Pri   State           Dead Time   Address         Interface
3.3.3.3           1   FULL/DR         00:00:35    10.1.1.3        Serial0/0
2.2.2.2           1   FULL/BDR        00:00:36    10.1.1.2        Serial0/0
```

Router C has been elected the DR and Router B has been elected the BDR. For a fully meshed configuration, the router selected as the DR is not important as long as all PVCs remain active and the full mesh is maintained. In the next example, the selection of the DR becomes an important issue if the routers are not fully meshed.

Configuration Example 2: Partially-meshed OSPF Neighbors on an NBMA Network

There is a scaling problem with a fully meshed broadcast network. The number of PVCs required grows exponentially with the number of routers in the mesh. The formula to determine the number of PVCs based on the number of routers (n) is given by this equation:

$$[(n)(n-1)]/2$$

Therefore, five routers require 10 PVCs and 10 routers require 45 PVCs. As you can see, this can become expensive not only in terms of cost but also in terms of management complexity. If you add one router to a 10-router mesh, then an additional 11 PVCs need to be purchased and configured. The number of PVCs can be reduced if a hub-and-spoke topology is used as shown in Figure 19-11. Router A is the hub router and Routers B and C are spoke routers. Spoke routers only have a connection or PVC to the hub router. A broadcast network can be used with a partial mesh, but there are a number of concerns that need to be addressed as will be pointed out in this example. Remove the PVC between Routers B and C (see Figure 19-10) to produce the topology in Figure 19-11.

Figure 19-11 *An NBMA Network Can Be Configured as a Broadcast Network Using a Partial Mesh Configuration. The Hub Router Should Always Be the DR*

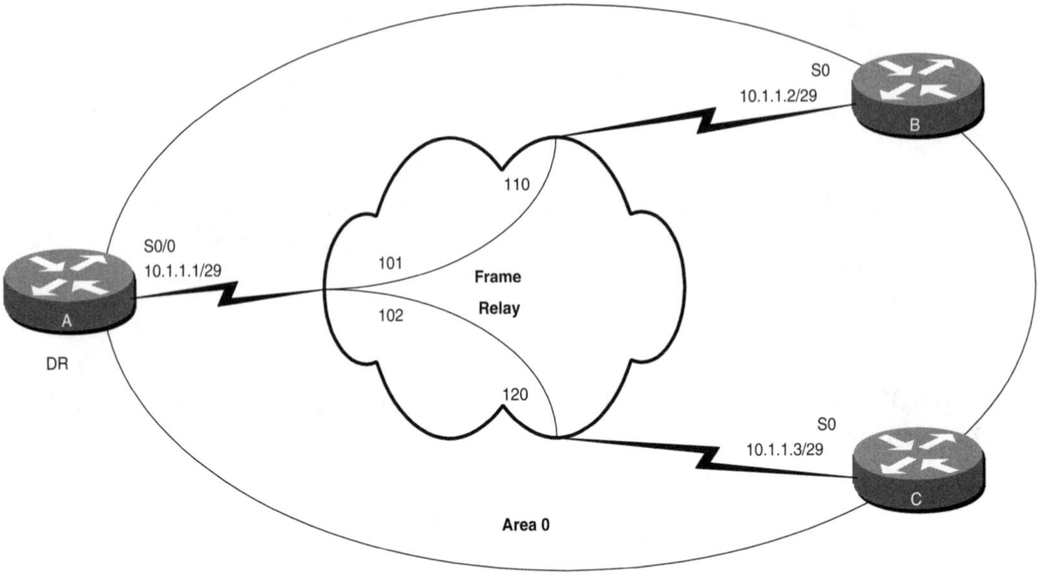


```
Router A
interface Loopback0
 ip address 1.1.1.1 255.255.255.255
!
interface Serial0/0
 bandwidth 64
 ip address 10.1.1.1 255.255.255.248
 encapsulation frame-relay
 ip ospf network broadcast
 frame-relay map ip 10.1.1.2 101 broadcast
 frame-relay map ip 10.1.1.3 102 broadcast
 no frame-relay inverse-arp
 frame-relay lmi-type ansi
!
router ospf 1
 network 1.1.1.1 0.0.0.0 area 1
 network 10.1.1.0 0.0.0.7 area 0
```

```
Router B
interface Loopback0
 ip address 2.2.2.2 255.255.255.255
!
interface Serial0
 ip address 10.1.1.2 255.255.255.248
 encapsulation frame-relay
ip ospf network broadcast
```

```
 frame-relay map ip 10.1.1.1 110 broadcast
 no frame-relay map ip 10.1.1.3 112 broadcast
 no frame-relay inverse-arp
 frame-relay lmi-type ansi
!
router ospf 1
 network 2.2.2.2 0.0.0.0 area 2
 network 10.1.1.0 0.0.0.7 area 0
```

```
Router C
interface Loopback0
 ip address 3.3.3.3 255.255.255.255
!

interface Serial0
 ip address 10.1.1.3 255.255.255.248
 encapsulation frame-relay
 ip ospf network broadcast
 frame-relay map ip 10.1.1.1 120 broadcast
 no frame-relay map ip 10.1.1.2 121 broadcast
 no frame-relay inverse-arp
!
router ospf 1
 network 3.3.3.3 0.0.0.0 area 3
 network 10.1.1.0 0.0.0.7 area 0
```

Use the command **clear ip ospf process** on Router A to reset OSPF. Check the status of the OSPF neighbors on Router A.

```
rtrA#show ip ospf neighbor

Neighbor ID     Pri   State           Dead Time   Address         Interface
3.3.3.3           1   FULL/DR         00:00:35    10.1.1.3        Serial0/0
2.2.2.2           1   FULL/DROTHER    00:00:34    10.1.1.2        Serial0/0
```

The first concern with a partial mesh broadcast network is the election of the DR. Router C was elected as the DR because it has the highest router ID. All routers on a broadcast network need to become adjacent with the DR. Router B cannot become adjacent with the DR because there is not a direct connection between Routers B and C. The solution is to ensure that the hub router, Router A, is elected as the DR. If Router A fails, then it does not make any difference if either Router B or C is the BDR because they will no longer have an IP path between them. Router A needs to be configured so it is always elected the DR. One way to accomplish this is to set the interface priority on Routers B and C to zero. Setting the OSPF priority to zero makes the router ineligible to become the DR on the network. The default interface priority is 1, so Router A will always be elected the DR.

Another way is to ensure that the router that you want to become DR has the highest OSPF router ID.

```
Router B
interface Serial0
 ip address 10.1.1.2 255.255.255.248
 encapsulation frame-relay
 ip ospf network broadcast
 ip ospf priority 0
 frame-relay map ip 10.1.1.1 110 broadcast
 no frame-relay inverse-arp
 frame-relay lmi-type ansi
```

```
Router C
interface Serial0
 ip address 10.1.1.3 255.255.255.248
 encapsulation frame-relay
 ip ospf network broadcast
 ip ospf priority 0
 frame-relay map ip 10.1.1.1 120 broadcast
 no frame-relay inverse-arp
```

Reset the OSPF process on Router A.

```
rtrA#clear ip ospf process
Reset ALL OSPF processes? [no]: y
```

Verify that Router A is now the DR and that neither router B nor C is the BDR.

```
rtrA#show ip ospf neighbor

Neighbor ID     Pri   State           Dead Time   Address         Interface
3.3.3.3           0   FULL/DROTHER    00:00:32    10.1.1.3        Serial0/0
2.2.2.2           0   FULL/DROTHER    00:00:32    10.1.1.2        Serial0/0
```

```
rtrB#show ip ospf neighbor

Neighbor ID     Pri   State           Dead Time   Address         Interface
1.1.1.1           1   FULL/DR         00:00:39    10.1.1.1        Serial0
```

```
rtrC#show ip ospf neighbor

Neighbor ID     Pri   State           Dead Time   Address         Interface
1.1.1.1           1   FULL/DR         00:00:35    10.1.1.1        Serial0
```

Each router is advertising its loopback network into OSPF. Check the routing tables on Routers A, B, and C to determine if the routes are being advertised to all routers.

```
rtrA#show ip route
Codes: C - connected, S - static, I - IGRP, R - RIP, M - mobile, B - BGP
       D - EIGRP, EX - EIGRP external, O - OSPF, IA - OSPF inter area
       N1 - OSPF NSSA external type 1, N2 - OSPF NSSA external type 2
       E1 - OSPF external type 1, E2 - OSPF external type 2, E - EGP
       i - IS-IS, L1 - IS-IS level-1, L2 - IS-IS level-2, ia - IS-IS inter area
       * - candidate default, U - per-user static route, o - ODR
       P - periodic downloaded static route

Gateway of last resort is not set

     1.0.0.0/32 is subnetted, 1 subnets
C       1.1.1.1 is directly connected, Loopback0
     2.0.0.0/32 is subnetted, 1 subnets
O IA    2.2.2.2 [110/1563] via 10.1.1.2, 00:01:06, Serial0/0
     3.0.0.0/32 is subnetted, 1 subnets
O IA    3.3.3.3 [110/1563] via 10.1.1.3, 00:01:06, Serial0/0
     10.0.0.0/29 is subnetted, 1 subnets
C       10.1.1.0 is directly connected, Serial0/0
```

```
rtrB#show ip route
Codes: C - connected, S - static, I - IGRP, R - RIP, M - mobile, B - BGP
       D - EIGRP, EX - EIGRP external, O - OSPF, IA - OSPF inter area
       N1 - OSPF NSSA external type 1, N2 - OSPF NSSA external type 2
       E1 - OSPF external type 1, E2 - OSPF external type 2, E - EGP
       i - IS-IS, L1 - IS-IS level-1, L2 - IS-IS level-2, * - candidate default
       U - per-user static route, o - ODR

Gateway of last resort is not set

     1.0.0.0/32 is subnetted, 1 subnets
O IA    1.1.1.1 [110/65] via 10.1.1.1, 00:03:23, Serial0
     2.0.0.0/32 is subnetted, 1 subnets
C       2.2.2.2 is directly connected, Loopback0
     3.0.0.0/32 is subnetted, 1 subnets
O IA    3.3.3.3 [110/65] via 10.1.1.3, 00:03:23, Serial0
C    169.254.0.0/16 is directly connected, Ethernet0
     10.0.0.0/29 is subnetted, 1 subnets
C       10.1.1.0 is directly connected, Serial0
```

```
rtrC#show ip route
Codes: C - connected, S - static, I - IGRP, R - RIP, M - mobile, B - BGP
       D - EIGRP, EX - EIGRP external, O - OSPF, IA - OSPF inter area
       N1 - OSPF NSSA external type 1, N2 - OSPF NSSA external type 2
       E1 - OSPF external type 1, E2 - OSPF external type 2, E - EGP
       i - IS-IS, L1 - IS-IS level-1, L2 - IS-IS level-2, * - candidate default
       U - per-user static route, o - ODR
```

continues

```
Gateway of last resort is not set

     1.0.0.0/32 is subnetted, 1 subnets
O IA    1.1.1.1 [110/65] via 10.1.1.1, 00:03:43, Serial0
     2.0.0.0/32 is subnetted, 1 subnets
O IA    2.2.2.2 [110/65] via 10.1.1.2, 00:03:44, Serial0
     3.0.0.0/32 is subnetted, 1 subnets
C       3.3.3.3 is directly connected, Loopback0
     10.0.0.0/29 is subnetted, 1 subnets
C       10.1.1.0 is directly connected, Serial0
```

The routes are being advertised, but can all routers reach them?

```
rtrA#ping 2.2.2.2

Type escape sequence to abort.
Sending 5, 100-byte ICMP Echos to 2.2.2.2, timeout is 2 seconds:
!!!!!
Success rate is 100 percent (5/5), round-trip min/avg/max = 4/5/8 ms

rtrA#ping 3.3.3.3

Type escape sequence to abort.
Sending 5, 100-byte ICMP Echos to 3.3.3.3, timeout is 2 seconds:
!!!!!
Success rate is 100 percent (5/5), round-trip min/avg/max = 4/5/8 ms
```

```
rtrB#ping 1.1.1.1

Type escape sequence to abort.
Sending 5, 100-byte ICMP Echos to 1.1.1.1, timeout is 2 seconds:
!!!!!
Success rate is 100 percent (5/5), round-trip min/avg/max = 4/6/8 ms

rtrB#ping 3.3.3.3

Type escape sequence to abort.
Sending 5, 100-byte ICMP Echos to 3.3.3.3, timeout is 2 seconds:
.....
Success rate is 0 percent (0/5)
```

```
rtrC#ping 1.1.1.1

Type escape sequence to abort.
Sending 5, 100-byte ICMP Echos to 1.1.1.1, timeout is 2 seconds:
!!!!!
Success rate is 100 percent (5/5), round-trip min/avg/max = 4/4/8 ms
```

```
rtrC#ping 2.2.2.2

Type escape sequence to abort.
Sending 5, 100-byte ICMP Echos to 2.2.2.2, timeout is 2 seconds:
.....
Success rate is 0 percent (0/5)
```

Router A can ping Routers B and C because they are directly connected. Router B can ping A but not C and Router C can ping A but not B. The problem is that Routers B and C think they are directly connected because they are on the same IP subnet and the network type is broadcast. This line was highlighted previously in the routing table on Router B.

```
O IA    3.3.3.3 [110/65] via 10.1.1.3, 00:03:23, Serial0
```

For Router B to reach network 3.3.3.3 on Router C, it must send the packet to 10.1.1.3. Router B is not directly connected to Router C so the packet must first be sent to Router A. This is accomplished by an additional **frame-relay map** statement on Routers B and C.

```
Router B
interface Serial0
 ip address 10.1.1.2 255.255.255.248
 encapsulation frame-relay
 ip ospf network broadcast
 ip ospf priority 0
 frame-relay map ip 10.1.1.1 110 broadcast
 frame-relay map ip 10.1.1.3 110 broadcast
 no frame-relay inverse-arp
 frame-relay lmi-type ansi
```

```
Router C
interface Serial0
 ip address 10.1.1.3 255.255.255.248
 encapsulation frame-relay
 ip ospf network broadcast
 ip ospf priority 0
 frame-relay map ip 10.1.1.1 120 broadcast
 frame-relay map ip 10.1.1.2 120 broadcast
 no frame-relay inverse-arp
```

Verification

Verify that all routers can ping the loopback interfaces on the other routers.

```
rtrA#ping 2.2.2.2

Type escape sequence to abort.
Sending 5, 100-byte ICMP Echos to 2.2.2.2, timeout is 2 seconds:
!!!!!
```

continues

```
Success rate is 100 percent (5/5), round-trip min/avg/max = 4/4/8 ms

rtrA#ping 3.3.3.3

Type escape sequence to abort.
Sending 5, 100-byte ICMP Echos to 3.3.3.3, timeout is 2 seconds:
!!!!!
Success rate is 100 percent (5/5), round-trip min/avg/max = 4/6/8 ms
```

```
rtrB#ping 1.1.1.1

Type escape sequence to abort.
Sending 5, 100-byte ICMP Echos to 1.1.1.1, timeout is 2 seconds:
!!!!!
Success rate is 100 percent (5/5), round-trip min/avg/max = 4/5/8 ms

rtrB#ping 3.3.3.3

Type escape sequence to abort.
Sending 5, 100-byte ICMP Echos to 3.3.3.3, timeout is 2 seconds:
!!!!!
Success rate is 100 percent (5/5), round-trip min/avg/max = 8/8/12 ms
```

```
rtrC#ping 1.1.1.1

Type escape sequence to abort.
Sending 5, 100-byte ICMP Echos to 1.1.1.1, timeout is 2 seconds:
!!!!!
Success rate is 100 percent (5/5), round-trip min/avg/max = 4/4/8 ms

rtrC#ping 2.2.2.2

Type escape sequence to abort.
Sending 5, 100-byte ICMP Echos to 2.2.2.2, timeout is 2 seconds:
!!!!!
Success rate is 100 percent (5/5), round-trip min/avg/max = 8/9/12 ms
```

Troubleshooting

Step 1 Verify the IP address and netmask assignments used on the NBMA network interfaces.

Step 2 Verify that the proper DLCIs and IP addresses are used in the **frame-relay map ip** statements. These can be checked using the **show frame-relay map** command, as shown here:

```
rtrA#show frame-relay map
Serial0/0 (up): ip 10.1.1.2 dlci 101(0x65,0x1850), static,
              broadcast,
```

```
              CISCO, status defined, active
Serial0/0 (up): ip 10.1.1.3 dlci 102(0x66,0x1860), static,
              broadcast,
              CISCO, status defined, active
```

Step 3 Before configuring OSPF, check IP connectivity by pinging the other end of each Frame Relay link.

Step 4 If using a partial mesh with a broadcast network, ensure that the hub router is elected DR.

Step 5 If using a partial mesh with a broadcast network, ensure that the spoke routers have been configured with a **frame relay map** command to each spoke through the hub router.

19-14: ip ospf network non-broadcast

Syntax Description:

This command has no arguments.

Purpose: OSPF sends Hello packets and other protocol packets as multicast. If the network does not support multicast or you want OSPF to communicate with neighbors using unicast, use this command. The **neighbor** command is required if the network is configured as non-broadcast. See Chapter 11 for configuration examples.

Initial Cisco IOS Software Release: 10.0

19-15: ip ospf network point-to-multipoint

19-16: ip ospf network point-to-multipoint non-broadcast

Syntax Description:

This command has no arguments.

Purpose: Used to configure an NBMA network as a multipoint network. OSPF uses multicast to send Hello and other protocol packets over a point-to-multipoint network. On some networks, such as ATM, the connections are dynamic and the Hello packets will be sent only over established connections. Therefore, the **non-broadcast** option needs to be used in conjunction with the **neighbor** command (see Chapter 11) if running OSPF over an ATM multipoint network.

Initial Cisco IOS Software Release: 10.3. The **non-broadcast** keyword was added in 11.3.

Configuration Example 1: Multipoint Hub with Point-to-Point Spokes

OSPF views networks as being of one of three types:

- **A broadcast multiaccess network**—On a broadcast multiaccess network, all routers attached to the network have a direct communication link with all other routers on the network. Examples of a broadcast multiaccess network are Ethernet, Token Ring, and FDDI. When OSPF sends a protocol packet onto a broadcast multiaccess network, all OSPF routers on the network will receive the packet.
- **A point-to-point network**—On a point-to-point network, only two routers exist on the network, one at each end of the point-to-point link. Examples of a point-to-point network are HDLC and PPP.
- **An NBMA network**—Examples of an NBMA network are Frame Relay and X.25. On an NBMA network, all OSPF routers could possibly have connections to all other OSPF routers on the network but all the connections are logical point-to-point links, so an OSPF protocol packet sent on one link will not reach all OSPF neighbors. NBMA networks can be configured, from an OSPF point of view, as broadcast, point-to-point, or multipoint.

This example investigates configuring Frame Relay as an OSPF multipoint network.

In Figure 19-12, three OSPF routers are partially meshed over a Frame Relay network. Router A is the hub and Routers B and C are spokes. The two PVCs are configured on the same IP subnet. Initially, the routers in Figure 19-12 are configured without specifying a network type in order to observe the OSPF behavior on an NBMA network.

Figure 19-12 *An OSPF Multipoint Network Is Used when There Is a Partial Mesh Between the Routers and the Routers Are on the Same IP Subnet*

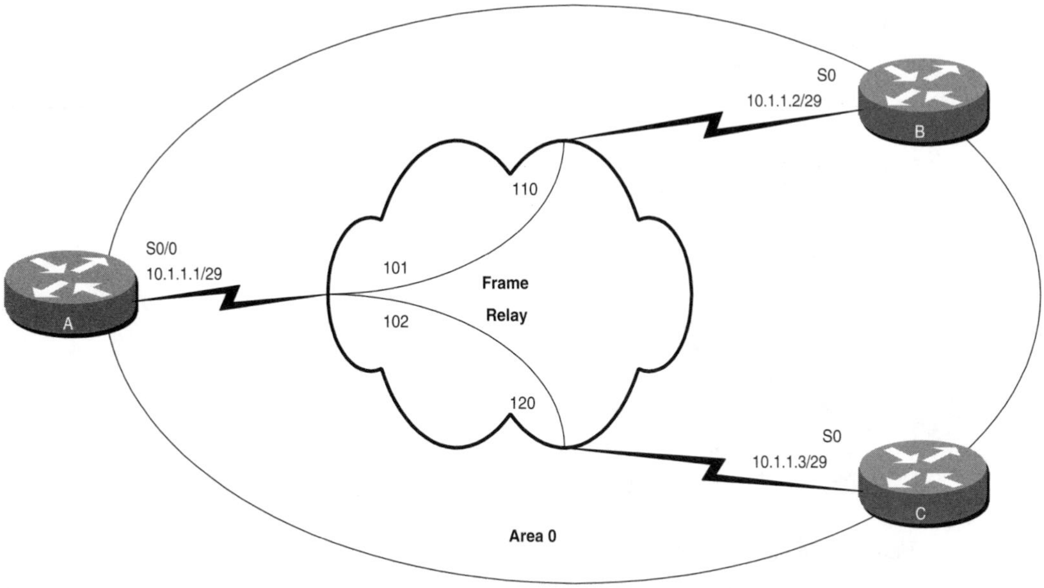


```
Router A
interface Loopback0
 ip address 1.1.1.1 255.255.255.255
!
interface Serial0/0
 bandwidth 64
 ip address 10.1.1.1 255.255.255.248
 encapsulation frame-relay
 frame-relay map ip 10.1.1.2 101 broadcast
 frame-relay map ip 10.1.1.3 102 broadcast
 no frame-relay inverse-arp
 frame-relay lmi-type ansi
!
router ospf 1
 network 1.1.1.1 0.0.0.0 area 1
 network 10.1.1.0 0.0.0.7 area 0
```

```
Router B
interface Loopback0
 ip address 2.2.2.2 255.255.255.255
!
interface Serial0
 ip address 10.1.1.2 255.255.255.248
 encapsulation frame-relay
 frame-relay map ip 10.1.1.1 110 broadcast
```

continues

```
 no frame-relay inverse-arp
 frame-relay lmi-type ansi
!
router ospf 1
 network 2.2.2.2 0.0.0.0 area 2
 network 10.1.1.0 0.0.0.7 area 0
```

```
Router C
interface Loopback0
 ip address 3.3.3.3 255.255.255.255
!

interface Serial0
 ip address 10.1.1.3 255.255.255.248
 encapsulation frame-relay
 frame-relay map ip 10.1.1.1 120 broadcast
 no frame-relay inverse-arp
!
router ospf 1
 network 3.3.3.3 0.0.0.0 area 3
 network 10.1.1.0 0.0.0.7 area 0
```

Frame Relay inverse ARP is disabled on Routers A, B, and C and static **frame-relay map** statements are used to map remote IP addresses to the proper Frame Relay DLCI. This is not necessary for the operation of OSPF over Frame Relay, but only prevents the routers from learning DLCIs that are not used. In Chapter 11, the OSPF **neighbor** command was used to configure OSPF over an NBMA network. For this example, the OSPF interface command **ip ospf network point-to-multipoint** forces OSPF to treat the Frame Relay network as a multipoint network. Without the **neighbor** command or the **ip ospf network** command, OSPF does not know how to treat the NBMA network, so OSPF neighbor relationships will not be formed. This is shown in the output of the **show ip ospf neighbor** command shown here.

```
rtrA#show ip ospf neighbor
(no output)
```

OSPF is not sending any protocol packets onto the NBMA network. Modify the configurations on Routers A, B, and C to configure the NBMA network as a multipoint network. For this example use the network type **point-to-multipoint** on Router A and **point-to-point** on Routers B and C.

```
Router A
interface Serial0/0
 bandwidth 64
 ip address 10.1.1.1 255.255.255.248
 encapsulation frame-relay
```

```
 ip ospf network point-to-multipoint
 frame-relay map ip 10.1.1.2 101 broadcast
 frame-relay map ip 10.1.1.3 102 broadcast
 no frame-relay inverse-arp
 frame-relay lmi-type ansi
```

```
Router B
interface Serial0
 bandwidth 64
 ip address 10.1.1.2 255.255.255.248
 encapsulation frame-relay
 ip ospf network point-to-point
 frame-relay map ip 10.1.1.1 110 broadcast
 no frame-relay inverse-arp
 frame-relay lmi-type ansi
```

```
Router C
interface Serial0
 bandwidth 64
 ip address 10.1.1.3 255.255.255.248
 encapsulation frame-relay
 ip ospf network  point-to-point
 frame-relay map ip 10.1.1.1 120 broadcast
 no frame-relay inverse-arp
```

Verification

Verify that OSPF is treating the Frame Relay network as a multipoint network on Router A and as a point-to-point network on Routers B and C.

```
rtrA#show ip ospf interface serial 0/0
Serial0/0 is up, line protocol is up
  Internet Address 10.1.1.1/29, Area 0
  Process ID 1, Router ID 1.1.1.1, Network Type POINT_TO_MULTIPOINT, Cost: 1562
  Transmit Delay is 1 sec, State POINT_TO_MULTIPOINT,
  Timer intervals configured, Hello 30, Dead 120, Wait 120, Retransmit 5
    Hello due in 00:00:16
  Index 1/2, flood queue length 0
  Next 0x0(0)/0x0(0)
  Last flood scan length is 1, maximum is 4
  Last flood scan time is 0 msec, maximum is 0 msec
  Neighbor Count is 2, Adjacent neighbor count is 2
    Adjacent with neighbor 3.3.3.3
    Adjacent with neighbor 2.2.2.2
  Suppress hello for 0 neighbor(s)
```

```
rtrB#show ip ospf interface serial 0
Serial0 is up, line protocol is up
  Internet Address 10.1.1.2/29, Area 0
```

continues

```
  Process ID 1, Router ID 2.2.2.2, Network Type POINT_TO_POINT, Cost: 1562
  Transmit Delay is 1 sec, State POINT_TO_POINT,
  Timer intervals configured, Hello 10, Dead 40, Wait 40, Retransmit 5
    Hello due in 00:00:18
  Neighbor Count is 1, Adjacent neighbor count is 1
    Adjacent with neighbor 1.1.1.1
  Suppress hello for 0 neighbor(s)
```

```
rtrC#show ip ospf interface serial 0
Serial0 is up, line protocol is up
  Internet Address 10.1.1.3/29, Area 0
  Process ID 1, Router ID 3.3.3.3, Network Type POINT_TO_POINT, Cost: 1562
  Transmit Delay is 1 sec, State POINT_TO_POINT,
  Timer intervals configured, Hello 10, Dead 40, Wait 40, Retransmit 5
    Hello due in 00:00:14
  Neighbor Count is 1, Adjacent neighbor count is 1
    Adjacent with neighbor 1.1.1.1
  Suppress hello for 0 neighbor(s)
```

Verify that Routers A, B, and C have formed an OSPF neighbor relationship.

```
rtrA#show ip ospf neighbor
(no neighbors)
```

Router A has not formed a neighbor relationship with either Router B or C. Enable OSPF debugging to determine the problem.

```
rtrA#debug ip ospf events
OSPF events debugging is on
rtrA#
23:42:12: OSPF: Rcv hello from 3.3.3.3 area 0 from Serial0/0 10.1.1.3
23:42:12: OSPF: Mismatched hello parameters from 10.1.1.3
23:42:12: OSPF: Dead R 40 C 120, Hello R 10 C 30
23:42:16: OSPF: Rcv hello from 2.2.2.2 area 0 from Serial0/0 10.1.1.2
23:42:16: OSPF: Mismatched hello parameters from 10.1.1.2
23:42:16: OSPF: Dead R 40 C 120, Hello R 10 C 30
```

There is a mismatch in the Hello parameters between Router A and Routers B and C. Router A is configured as a multipoint network and the Hello time is 30 seconds. Routers B and C are configured as point-to-point networks and the Hello time is 10 seconds. OSPF will not form an adjacency if the Hello intervals do not match. Change the Hello interval on Routers B and C to 30 seconds.

```
Router B
interface Serial0
 ip address 10.1.1.2 255.255.255.248
```

```
 encapsulation frame-relay
 ip ospf network point-to-point
 ip ospf hello-interval 30
 bandwidth 64
 frame-relay map ip 10.1.1.1 110 broadcast
 no frame-relay inverse-arp
 frame-relay lmi-type ansi
```

```
Router C
interface Serial0
 bandwidth 64
 ip address 10.1.1.3 255.255.255.248
 encapsulation frame-relay
 ip ospf network point-to-point
 ip ospf hello-interval 30
 no ip mroute-cache
 frame-relay map ip 10.1.1.1 120 broadcast
 no frame-relay inverse-arp
```

Verify that the OSPF neighbor relationships are established.

```
rtrA#show ip ospf neighbor

Neighbor ID     Pri   State           Dead Time   Address         Interface
3.3.3.3           1   FULL/  -        00:01:39    10.1.1.3        Serial0/0
2.2.2.2           1   FULL/  -        00:01:58    10.1.1.2        Serial0/0
```

Each router is advertising its loopback network into OSPF. Check the routing tables on Routers A, B, and C to determine if the routes are being advertised to all routers.

```
rtrA#show ip route
Codes: C - connected, S - static, I - IGRP, R - RIP, M - mobile, B - BGP
       D - EIGRP, EX - EIGRP external, O - OSPF, IA - OSPF inter area
       N1 - OSPF NSSA external type 1, N2 - OSPF NSSA external type 2
       E1 - OSPF external type 1, E2 - OSPF external type 2, E - EGP
       i - IS-IS, L1 - IS-IS level-1, L2 - IS-IS level-2, ia - IS-IS inter area
       * - candidate default, U - per-user static route, o - ODR
       P - periodic downloaded static route

Gateway of last resort is not set

     1.0.0.0/32 is subnetted, 1 subnets
C       1.1.1.1 is directly connected, Loopback0
     2.0.0.0/32 is subnetted, 1 subnets
O IA    2.2.2.2 [110/1563] via 10.1.1.2, 00:01:06, Serial0/0
     3.0.0.0/32 is subnetted, 1 subnets
O IA    3.3.3.3 [110/1563] via 10.1.1.3, 00:01:06, Serial0/0
```

continues

```
     10.0.0.0/29 is subnetted, 1 subnets
C       10.1.1.0 is directly connected, Serial0/0
```

```
rtrB#show ip route
Codes: C - connected, S - static, I - IGRP, R - RIP, M - mobile, B - BGP
       D - EIGRP, EX - EIGRP external, O - OSPF, IA - OSPF inter area
       N1 - OSPF NSSA external type 1, N2 - OSPF NSSA external type 2
       E1 - OSPF external type 1, E2 - OSPF external type 2, E - EGP
       i - IS-IS, L1 - IS-IS level-1, L2 - IS-IS level-2, * - candidate default
       U - per-user static route, o - ODR

Gateway of last resort is not set

     1.0.0.0/32 is subnetted, 1 subnets
O IA    1.1.1.1 [110/65] via 10.1.1.1, 00:03:23, Serial0
     2.0.0.0/32 is subnetted, 1 subnets
C       2.2.2.2 is directly connected, Loopback0
     3.0.0.0/32 is subnetted, 1 subnets
O IA    3.3.3.3 [110/65] via 10.1.1.1, 00:03:23, Serial0
C    169.254.0.0/16 is directly connected, Ethernet0
     10.0.0.0/29 is subnetted, 1 subnets
C       10.1.1.0 is directly connected, Serial0
```

```
rtrC#show ip route
Codes: C - connected, S - static, I - IGRP, R - RIP, M - mobile, B - BGP
       D - EIGRP, EX - EIGRP external, O - OSPF, IA - OSPF inter area
       N1 - OSPF NSSA external type 1, N2 - OSPF NSSA external type 2
       E1 - OSPF external type 1, E2 - OSPF external type 2, E - EGP
       i - IS-IS, L1 - IS-IS level-1, L2 - IS-IS level-2, * - candidate default
       U - per-user static route, o - ODR

Gateway of last resort is not set

     1.0.0.0/32 is subnetted, 1 subnets
O IA    1.1.1.1 [110/65] via 10.1.1.1, 00:03:43, Serial0
     2.0.0.0/32 is subnetted, 1 subnets
O IA    2.2.2.2 [110/65] via 10.1.1.1, 00:03:44, Serial0
     3.0.0.0/32 is subnetted, 1 subnets
C       3.3.3.3 is directly connected, Loopback0
     10.0.0.0/29 is subnetted, 1 subnets
C       10.1.1.0 is directly connected, Serial0
```

The routes are being advertised, but can all routers reach them?

```
rtrA#ping 2.2.2.2

Type escape sequence to abort.
Sending 5, 100-byte ICMP Echos to 2.2.2.2, timeout is 2 seconds:
!!!!!
Success rate is 100 percent (5/5), round-trip min/avg/max = 4/5/8 ms
```

```
rtrA#ping 3.3.3.3

Type escape sequence to abort.
Sending 5, 100-byte ICMP Echos to 3.3.3.3, timeout is 2 seconds:
!!!!!
Success rate is 100 percent (5/5), round-trip min/avg/max = 4/5/8 ms
```

```
rtrB#ping 1.1.1.1

Type escape sequence to abort.
Sending 5, 100-byte ICMP Echos to 1.1.1.1, timeout is 2 seconds:
!!!!!
Success rate is 100 percent (5/5), round-trip min/avg/max = 4/5/8 ms

rtrB#ping 3.3.3.3

Type escape sequence to abort.
Sending 5, 100-byte ICMP Echos to 3.3.3.3, timeout is 2 seconds:
!!!!!
Success rate is 100 percent (5/5), round-trip min/avg/max = 8/8/12 ms
```

```
rtrC#ping 1.1.1.1

Type escape sequence to abort.
Sending 5, 100-byte ICMP Echos to 1.1.1.1, timeout is 2 seconds:
!!!!!
Success rate is 100 percent (5/5), round-trip min/avg/max = 4/4/8 ms
rtrC#ping 2.2.2.2

Type escape sequence to abort.
Sending 5, 100-byte ICMP Echos to 2.2.2.2, timeout is 2 seconds:
!!!!!
Success rate is 100 percent (5/5), round-trip min/avg/max = 8/8/12 ms
```

Configuration Example 2: Partially Meshed Hub and Spoke Using a Multipoint Network

Change the network type on Routers B and C to **point-to-multipoint**. This will automatically set the Hello interval to 30 seconds.

```
Router B
interface Serial0
 ip address 10.1.1.2 255.255.255.248
 encapsulation frame-relay
 ip ospf network point-to-multipoint
 bandwidth 64
 frame-relay map ip 10.1.1.1 110 broadcast
```

continues

```
 no frame-relay inverse-arp
 frame-relay lmi-type ansi
```

```
Router C
interface Serial0
 bandwidth 64
 ip address 10.1.1.3 255.255.255.248
 encapsulation frame-relay
 ip ospf network point-to-multipoint
 frame-relay map ip 10.1.1.1 120 broadcast
 no frame-relay inverse-arp
```

Verification

Verify that all routers can ping the loopback interfaces on the other routers.

```
rtrA#ping 2.2.2.2

Type escape sequence to abort.
Sending 5, 100-byte ICMP Echos to 2.2.2.2, timeout is 2 seconds:
!!!!!
Success rate is 100 percent (5/5), round-trip min/avg/max = 4/4/8 ms

rtrA#ping 3.3.3.3

Type escape sequence to abort.
Sending 5, 100-byte ICMP Echos to 3.3.3.3, timeout is 2 seconds:
!!!!!
Success rate is 100 percent (5/5), round-trip min/avg/max = 4/6/8 ms
```

```
rtrB#ping 1.1.1.1

Type escape sequence to abort.
Sending 5, 100-byte ICMP Echos to 1.1.1.1, timeout is 2 seconds:
!!!!!
Success rate is 100 percent (5/5), round-trip min/avg/max = 4/5/8 ms

rtrB#ping 3.3.3.3

Type escape sequence to abort.
Sending 5, 100-byte ICMP Echos to 3.3.3.3, timeout is 2 seconds:
!!!!!
Success rate is 100 percent (5/5), round-trip min/avg/max = 8/8/12 ms
```

```
rtrC#ping 1.1.1.1

Type escape sequence to abort.
Sending 5, 100-byte ICMP Echos to 1.1.1.1, timeout is 2 seconds:
!!!!!
Success rate is 100 percent (5/5), round-trip min/avg/max = 4/4/8 ms
```

```
rtrC#ping 2.2.2.2

Type escape sequence to abort.
Sending 5, 100-byte ICMP Echos to 2.2.2.2, timeout is 2 seconds:
!!!!!
Success rate is 100 percent (5/5), round-trip min/avg/max = 8/9/12 ms
```

Troubleshooting

Step 1 Verify the IP address and netmask assignments used on the NBMA network interfaces.

Step 2 Verify that the proper DLCIs and IP addresses are used in the **frame-relay map ip** statements. These can be checked using the **show frame-relay map** command, as shown here.

```
rtrA#show frame-relay map
Serial0/0 (up): ip 10.1.1.2 dlci 101(0x65,0x1850), static,
              broadcast,
              CISCO, status defined, active
Serial0/0 (up): ip 10.1.1.3 dlci 102(0x66,0x1860), static,
              broadcast,
              CISCO, status defined, active
```

Step 3 Before configuring OSPF, check IP connectivity by pinging the other end of each Frame Relay link.

Step 4 If you are mixing network types (multipoint and point-to-point) verify that the Hello intervals match on all routers.

19-17: ip ospf network point-to-point

Syntax Description:

This command has no arguments.

Purpose: Used to configure an NBMA network as a point-to-point network.

Initial Cisco IOS Software Release: 10.0

Configuration Example: Point-to-Point Partially Meshed OSPF Neighbors

OSPF views networks as being of one of three types:

- **A broadcast multiaccess network**—On a broadcast multiaccess network, all routers attached to the network have a direct communication link with all other routers on the network. Examples of a broadcast multiaccess network are Ethernet, Token Ring, and FDDI. When OSPF sends a protocol packet onto a broadcast multiaccess network, all OSPF routers on the network will receive the packet.
- **A point-to-point network**—On a point-to-point network, only two routers exist on the network, one at each end of the point-to-point link. Examples of a point-to-point network are HDLC and PPP.
- **An NBMA network**—Examples of an NBMA network are Frame Relay and X.25. On an NBMA network, all OSPF routers could possibly have connections to all other OSPF routers on the network but all the connections are logical point-to-point links, so an OSPF protocol packet sent on one link will not reach all OSPF neighbors. NBMA networks can be configured, from an OSPF point of view, as broadcast, point-to-point, or multipoint.

This example investigates configuring Frame Relay as an OSPF point-to-point network.

In Figure 19-13, three OSPF routers are partially meshed over a Frame Relay network. Router A is the hub and routers B and C are spokes. The two PVCs are configured on different IP subnets; therefore, the hub router needs two logical interfaces, one for each IP subnet. Initially the routers in Figure 19-13 are configured without specifying a network type in order to observe the OSPF behavior on an NBMA network. Router C uses a subinterface and Router B uses a major interface to illustrate the configuration differences.

Figure 19-13 *A Point-to-Point NBMA Network*

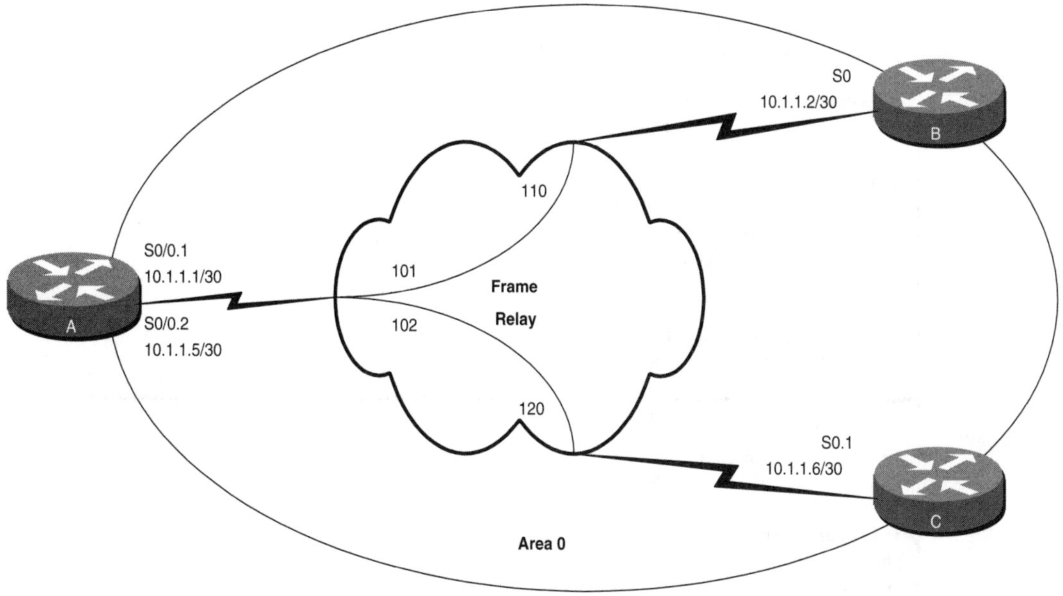


```
Router A
interface Loopback0
 ip address 1.1.1.1 255.255.255.255
interface Serial0/0
 bandwidth 64
 no ip address
 encapsulation frame-relay
 frame-relay lmi-type ansi
!
interface Serial0/0.1 point-to-point
 ip address 10.1.1.1 255.255.255.252
 frame-relay interface-dlci 101
!
interface Serial0/0.2 point-to-point
 ip address 10.1.1.5 255.255.255.252
 frame-relay interface-dlci 102
!
router ospf 1
 network 1.1.1.1 0.0.0.0 area 1
 network 10.1.1.0 0.0.0.3 area 0
 network 10.1.1.4 0.0.0.3 area 0
```

continues

```
Router B
interface Loopback0
 ip address 2.2.2.2 255.255.255.255
!
interface Serial0
 ip address 10.1.1.2 255.255.255.252
 encapsulation frame-relay
 bandwidth 64
 frame-relay map ip 10.1.1.1 110 broadcast
 no frame-relay inverse-arp
 frame-relay lmi-type ansi
!
router ospf 1
 network 2.2.2.2 0.0.0.0 area 2
 network 10.1.1.0 0.0.0.3 area 0
```

```
Router C
interface Loopback0
 ip address 3.3.3.3 255.255.255.255
!
interface Serial0
 bandwidth 64
 no ip address
 encapsulation frame-relay
 no frame-relay inverse-arp
!
interface Serial0.1 point-to-point
 ip address 10.1.1.6 255.255.255.252
 frame-relay interface-dlci 120
!
router ospf 1
 network 3.3.3.3 0.0.0.0 area 3
 network 10.1.1.4 0.0.0.3 area 0
```

Frame Relay inverse ARP has been disabled on Router B to prevent Router B from learning about DLCIs that are not being used. Subinterfaces are used on Routers A and C so Frame Relay inverse ARP is automatically disabled. Chapter 11 demonstrates how to use the OSPF **neighbor** command to configure OSPF over an NBMA network. For this example, the OSPF interface command **ip ospf network point-to-point** has not been used on any of the routers. Determine if any OSPF neighbor relationships have been formed with Router A.

```
rtrA#show ip ospf neighbor

Neighbor ID     Pri   State           Dead Time   Address         Interface
3.3.3.3           1   FULL/  -        00:00:38    10.1.1.6        Serial0/0.2
```

An OSPF neighbor relationship has been established between Routers A and C, but not Routers A and B. To understand why, you need to look at the OSPF network type that is being used on the Frame Relay interfaces.

```
rtrA#show ip ospf int s0/0.1
Serial0/0.1 is up, line protocol is up
  Internet Address 10.1.1.1/30, Area 0
  Process ID 1, Router ID 1.1.1.1, Network Type POINT_TO_POINT, Cost: 1562
  Transmit Delay is 1 sec, State POINT_TO_POINT,
  Timer intervals configured, Hello 10, Dead 40, Wait 40, Retransmit 5
    Hello due in 00:00:07
  Index 1/1, flood queue length 0
  Next 0x0(0)/0x0(0)
  Last flood scan length is 1, maximum is 6
  Last flood scan time is 0 msec, maximum is 0 msec
  Neighbor Count is 0, Adjacent neighbor count is 0
  Suppress hello for 0 neighbor(s)

rtrA#show ip ospf int s0/0.2
Serial0/0.2 is up, line protocol is up
  Internet Address 10.1.1.5/30, Area 0
  Process ID 1, Router ID 1.1.1.1, Network Type POINT_TO_POINT, Cost: 1562
  Transmit Delay is 1 sec, State POINT_TO_POINT,
  Timer intervals configured, Hello 10, Dead 40, Wait 40, Retransmit 5
    Hello due in 00:00:07
  Index 2/2, flood queue length 0
  Next 0x0(0)/0x0(0)
  Last flood scan length is 1, maximum is 2
  Last flood scan time is 0 msec, maximum is 0 msec
  Neighbor Count is 1, Adjacent neighbor count is 1
    Adjacent with neighbor 3.3.3.3
  Suppress hello for 0 neighbor(s)
```

```
rtrC#show ip ospf int s0.1
Serial0.1 is up, line protocol is up
  Internet Address 10.1.1.6/30, Area 0
  Process ID 1, Router ID 3.3.3.3, Network Type POINT_TO_POINT, Cost: 1562
  Transmit Delay is 1 sec, State POINT_TO_POINT,
  Timer intervals configured, Hello 10, Dead 40, Wait 40, Retransmit 5
    Hello due in 00:00:06
  Neighbor Count is 1, Adjacent neighbor count is 1
    Adjacent with neighbor 1.1.1.1
  Suppress hello for 0 neighbor(s)
```

When the subinterfaces were created on Routers A and C, the type was set to point-to-point; therefore, the interface command **ip ospf network point-to-point** is not needed. Router B is not using a subinterface and the default OSPF network type is nonbroadcast.

```
rtrB#show ip ospf interface serial 0
Serial0 is up, line protocol is up
  Internet Address 10.1.1.2/30, Area 0
  Process ID 1, Router ID 2.2.2.2, Network Type NON_BROADCAST, Cost: 1562
  Transmit Delay is 1 sec, State DR, Priority 1
  Designated Router (ID) 2.2.2.2, Interface address 10.1.1.2
  No backup designated router on this network
  Timer intervals configured, Hello 30, Dead 120, Wait 120, Retransmit 5
    Hello due in 00:00:16
  Neighbor Count is 0, Adjacent neighbor count is 0
  Suppress hello for 0 neighbor(s)
```

The **neighbor** command (Chapter 11) or the **ip ospf network point-to-point** command can be used on Router B to enable OSPF over the Frame Relay link. Modify Router B using the **ip ospf network** command.

```
Router B
interface Serial0
 ip address 10.1.1.2 255.255.255.252
 encapsulation frame-relay
 ip ospf network point-to-point
 bandwidth 64
 frame-relay map ip 10.1.1.1 110 broadcast
 no frame-relay inverse-arp
 frame-relay lmi-type ansi
```

Verification

Verify that OSPF is treating the Frame Relay network as a point-to-point network on Router B.

```
rtrB#show ip ospf interface serial 0
Serial0 is up, line protocol is up
  Internet Address 10.1.1.2/30, Area 0
  Process ID 1, Router ID 2.2.2.2, Network Type POINT_TO_POINT, Cost: 1562
  Transmit Delay is 1 sec, State POINT_TO_POINT,
  Timer intervals configured, Hello 10, Dead 40, Wait 40, Retransmit 5
    Hello due in 00:00:02
  Neighbor Count is 1, Adjacent neighbor count is 1
    Adjacent with neighbor 1.1.1.1
  Suppress hello for 0 neighbor(s)
```

Verify that the OSPF neighbor relationships are established.

```
rtrA#show ip ospf neighbor

Neighbor ID     Pri   State           Dead Time   Address         Interface
3.3.3.3           1   FULL/  -        00:00:31    10.1.1.6        Serial0/0.2
2.2.2.2           1   FULL/  -        00:00:36    10.1.1.2        Serial0/0.1
```

Each router is advertising its loopback network into OSPF. Check the routing tables on Routers A, B, and C to determine if the routes are being advertised to all routers.

```
rtrA#show ip route
Codes: C - connected, S - static, I - IGRP, R - RIP, M - mobile, B - BGP
       D - EIGRP, EX - EIGRP external, O - OSPF, IA - OSPF inter area
       N1 - OSPF NSSA external type 1, N2 - OSPF NSSA external type 2
       E1 - OSPF external type 1, E2 - OSPF external type 2, E - EGP
       i - IS-IS, L1 - IS-IS level-1, L2 - IS-IS level-2, ia - IS-IS inter area
       * - candidate default, U - per-user static route, o - ODR
       P - periodic downloaded static route

Gateway of last resort is not set

     1.0.0.0/32 is subnetted, 1 subnets
C       1.1.1.1 is directly connected, Loopback0
     2.0.0.0/32 is subnetted, 1 subnets
O IA    2.2.2.2 [110/1563] via 10.1.1.2, 00:45:57, Serial0/0.1
     3.0.0.0/32 is subnetted, 1 subnets
O IA    3.3.3.3 [110/1563] via 10.1.1.6, 00:45:57, Serial0/0.2
     10.0.0.0/30 is subnetted, 2 subnets
C       10.1.1.0 is directly connected, Serial0/0.1
C       10.1.1.4 is directly connected, Serial0/0.2
```

```
rtrB#show ip route
Codes: C - connected, S - static, I - IGRP, R - RIP, M - mobile, B - BGP
       D - EIGRP, EX - EIGRP external, O - OSPF, IA - OSPF inter area
       N1 - OSPF NSSA external type 1, N2 - OSPF NSSA external type 2
       E1 - OSPF external type 1, E2 - OSPF external type 2, E - EGP
       i - IS-IS, L1 - IS-IS level-1, L2 - IS-IS level-2, * - candidate default
       U - per-user static route, o - ODR

Gateway of last resort is not set

     1.0.0.0/32 is subnetted, 1 subnets
O IA    1.1.1.1 [110/1563] via 10.1.1.1, 00:46:46, Serial0
     2.0.0.0/32 is subnetted, 1 subnets
C       2.2.2.2 is directly connected, Loopback0
     3.0.0.0/32 is subnetted, 1 subnets
O IA    3.3.3.3 [110/3125] via 10.1.1.1, 00:46:46, Serial0
     10.0.0.0/30 is subnetted, 2 subnets
```

continues

```
C       10.1.1.0 is directly connected, Serial0
O       10.1.1.4 [110/3124] via 10.1.1.1, 00:46:46, Serial0
```

```
rtrC#show ip route
Codes: C - connected, S - static, I - IGRP, R - RIP, M - mobile, B - BGP
       D - EIGRP, EX - EIGRP external, O - OSPF, IA - OSPF inter area
       N1 - OSPF NSSA external type 1, N2 - OSPF NSSA external type 2
       E1 - OSPF external type 1, E2 - OSPF external type 2, E - EGP
       i - IS-IS, L1 - IS-IS level-1, L2 - IS-IS level-2, * - candidate default
       U - per-user static route, o - ODR

Gateway of last resort is not set

     1.0.0.0/32 is subnetted, 1 subnets
O IA    1.1.1.1 [110/1563] via 10.1.1.5, 00:47:13, Serial0.1
     2.0.0.0/32 is subnetted, 1 subnets
O IA    2.2.2.2 [110/3125] via 10.1.1.5, 00:47:13, Serial0.1
     3.0.0.0/32 is subnetted, 1 subnets
C       3.3.3.3 is directly connected, Loopback0
     10.0.0.0/30 is subnetted, 2 subnets
O       10.1.1.0 [110/3124] via 10.1.1.5, 00:47:14, Serial0.1
C       10.1.1.4 is directly connected, Serial0.1
```

Even though the routes are being advertised, they may not be reachable. Use the **ping** command to see if the routes can be reached.

```
rtrA#ping 2.2.2.2

Type escape sequence to abort.
Sending 5, 100-byte ICMP Echos to 2.2.2.2, timeout is 2 seconds:
!!!!!
Success rate is 100 percent (5/5), round-trip min/avg/max = 4/5/8 ms

rtrA#ping 3.3.3.3

Type escape sequence to abort.
Sending 5, 100-byte ICMP Echos to 3.3.3.3, timeout is 2 seconds:
!!!!!
Success rate is 100 percent (5/5), round-trip min/avg/max = 4/5/8 ms
```

```
rtrB#ping 1.1.1.1

Type escape sequence to abort.
Sending 5, 100-byte ICMP Echos to 1.1.1.1, timeout is 2 seconds:
!!!!!
Success rate is 100 percent (5/5), round-trip min/avg/max = 4/5/8 ms

rtrB#ping 3.3.3.3

Type escape sequence to abort.
```

```
Sending 5, 100-byte ICMP Echos to 3.3.3.3, timeout is 2 seconds:
!!!!!
Success rate is 100 percent (5/5), round-trip min/avg/max = 8/8/12 ms
```

```
rtrC#ping 1.1.1.1

Type escape sequence to abort.
Sending 5, 100-byte ICMP Echos to 1.1.1.1, timeout is 2 seconds:
!!!!!
Success rate is 100 percent (5/5), round-trip min/avg/max = 4/4/8 ms

rtrC#ping 2.2.2.2

Type escape sequence to abort.
Sending 5, 100-byte ICMP Echos to 2.2.2.2, timeout is 2 seconds:
!!!!!
Success rate is 100 percent (5/5), round-trip min/avg/max = 8/8/12 ms
```

Troubleshooting

Step 1 Verify the IP address and netmask assignments used on the NBMA network interfaces.

Step 2 Verify that the proper DLCIs and IP addresses are being used. These can be checked using the **show frame-relay map** command.

```
rtrA#show frame-relay map
Serial0/0.2 (up): point-to-point dlci, dlci 102(0x66,0x1860), broadcast
         status defined, active
Serial0/0.1 (up): point-to-point dlci, dlci 101(0x65,0x1850), broadcast
status defined, active
```

Step 3 Before configuring OSPF, check IP connectivity by pinging the other end of each Frame Relay link.

Step 4 If you are mixing network types (multipoint and point-to-point), verify that the Hello intervals match on all routers.

19-18: ip ospf priority *priority*

Syntax Description:

- *priority*—The OSPF priority value for the interface. The range of values is 0 to 255. The default value is 1.

Purpose: On a multiaccess network such as Ethernet, the router with the highest priority will be elected the DR. If all interface priorities are equal, then the router with the highest router ID will be elected the DR. The **ip ospf priority** command is used to influence the selection of the DR on a multiaccess network. If the priority is 0, then the router will not be elected the DR or BDR.

Initial Cisco IOS Software Release: 10.0

Configuration Example: Influencing the Election of the Designated Router

In Figure 19-14, Router B will be elected the DR on the Ethernet network because Router B has a higher router ID than Router A and their OSPF priorities on the Ethernet network are equal.

Figure 19-14 *Router B Is the DR on the Ethernet Network Because Its Router ID Is Higher than the Router ID for Router A*

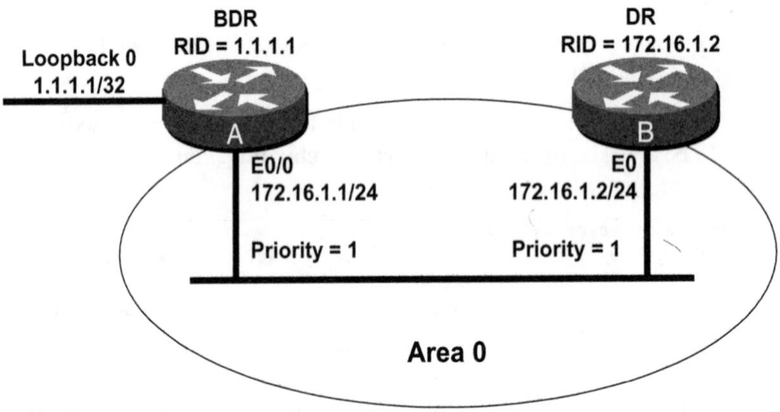


```
Router A
interface Loopback0
 ip address 1.1.1.1 255.255.255.255
!
interface Ethernet0/0
 ip address 172.16.1.1 255.255.255.0
!
router ospf 1
 network 1.1.1.1 0.0.0.0 area 1
 network 172.16.1.0 0.0.0.255 area 0
```

```
Router B
interface Ethernet0
```

```
 ip address 172.16.1.2 255.255.255.0
!
router ospf 1
 network 172.16.1.0 0.0.0.255 area 0
```

Verify that Routers A and B have formed an OSPF neighbor relationship.

```
rtrA#show ip ospf neighbor

Neighbor ID     Pri   State           Dead Time   Address         Interface
172.16.1.2        1   FULL/DR         00:00:36    172.16.1.2      Ethernet0/0
```

```
rtrB#show ip ospf neighbor

Neighbor ID     Pri   State           Dead Time   Address         Interface
1.1.1.1           1   FULL/BDR        00:00:39    172.16.1.1      Ethernet0
```

Router B has been elected the DR because it has a higher router ID and the OSPF priorities for Routers A and B are both 1.

```
rtrA#show ip ospf interface ethernet 0/0
Ethernet0/0 is up, line protocol is up
  Internet Address 172.16.1.1/24, Area 0
  Process ID 1, Router ID 1.1.1.1, Network Type BROADCAST, Cost: 10
  Transmit Delay is 1 sec, State BDR, Priority 1
  Designated Router (ID) 172.16.1.2, Interface address 172.16.1.2
  Backup Designated router (ID) 1.1.1.1, Interface address 172.16.1.1
  Timer intervals configured, Hello 10, Dead 40, Wait 40, Retransmit 5
    Hello due in 00:00:09
  Index 1/1, flood queue length 0
  Next 0x0(0)/0x0(0)
  Last flood scan length is 1, maximum is 3
  Last flood scan time is 0 msec, maximum is 0 msec
  Neighbor Count is 1, Adjacent neighbor count is 1
    Adjacent with neighbor 172.16.1.2  (Designated Router)
  Suppress hello for 0 neighbor(s)
```

Modify the OSPF priority for the Ethernet interface on Router B so the value is 2.

```
Router B
interface Ethernet0
 ip address 172.16.1.2 255.255.255.0
 ip ospf priority 2
```

Verification

Verify that the new priority has been configured on Router B.

```
rtrB#show ip ospf interface ethernet 0
Ethernet0 is up, line protocol is up
  Internet Address 172.16.1.2/24, Area 0
  Process ID 1, Router ID 172.16.1.2, Network Type BROADCAST, Cost: 10
  Transmit Delay is 1 sec, State DR, Priority 2
  Designated Router (ID) 1.1.1.1, Interface address 172.16.1.1
  Backup Designated router (ID) 172.16.1.2, Interface address 172.16.1.2
  Timer intervals configured, Hello 10, Dead 40, Wait 40, Retransmit 5
    Hello due in 00:00:02
  Neighbor Count is 1, Adjacent neighbor count is 1
    Adjacent with neighbor 1.1.1.1  (Designated Router)
  Suppress hello for 0 neighbor(s)
```

Router A is still the BDR. For stability, OSPF will not elect another router as DR unless the current DR goes down. Shut down the Ethernet interface on Router B and wait until the dead time has expired on Router A. After the dead time has expired on Router A, reenable the Ethernet interface on Router B. Verify that Router A is now the DR.

```
rtrA#show ip ospf neighbor

Neighbor ID     Pri   State           Dead Time   Address         Interface
172.16.1.2        2   FULL/BDR        00:00:39    172.16.1.2      Ethernet0/0
```

```
rtrB#show ip ospf neighbor

Neighbor ID     Pri   State           Dead Time   Address         Interface
1.1.1.1           1   FULL/DR         00:00:34    172.16.1.1      Ethernet0
```

Modify the priority on Router B so Router B is not eligible to be elected DRR or BDR.

```
Router B
interface Ethernet0
 ip address 172.16.1.2 255.255.255.0
 ip ospf priority 0
```

Shut down the Ethernet interface on Router B and wait for the dead time to expire. After the dead time has expired, reenable the Ethernet interface on Router B. Then check the status of the OSPF neighbor relationship.

```
rtrB#show ip ospf interface ethernet 0
Ethernet0 is up, line protocol is up
  Internet Address 172.16.1.2/24, Area 0
  Process ID 1, Router ID 172.16.1.2, Network Type BROADCAST, Cost: 10
  Transmit Delay is 1 sec, State DROTHER, Priority 0
  Designated Router (ID) 1.1.1.1, Interface address 172.16.1.1
  No backup designated router on this network
  Timer intervals configured, Hello 10, Dead 40, Wait 40, Retransmit 5
    Hello due in 00:00:09
  Neighbor Count is 1, Adjacent neighbor count is 1
    Adjacent with neighbor 1.1.1.1  (Designated Router)
  Suppress hello for 0 neighbor(s)
```

```
rtrA#show ip ospf neighbor

Neighbor ID     Pri   State           Dead Time   Address         Interface
172.16.1.2        0   FULL/DROTHER    00:00:31    172.16.1.2      Ethernet0/0
```

```
rtrB#show ip ospf neighbor

Neighbor ID     Pri   State           Dead Time   Address         Interface
1.1.1.1           1   FULL/DR         00:00:32    172.16.1.1      Ethernet0
```

Router B now has the status DROTHER because it cannot be the DR or BDR.

Troubleshooting

Step 1 Changing the priority value will not automatically cause OSPF to elect a new DR. If your design calls for a specific router to become the DR on a multiaccess network, configure the interface priority before enabling the OSPF process.

19-19: ip ospf retransmit-interval *seconds*

Syntax Description:

- *seconds*—The range of values is 1 to 8192 seconds. The default value is 5 seconds.

Purpose: When a router advertises an LSA over an interface, the LSA is added to a retransmission list for the interface. The LSA will be retransmitted until it is acknowledged. The number of seconds between the advertisements is called the retransmit interval.

Initial Cisco IOS Software Release: 10.0

Configuration Example: Modifying the Retransmit Interval

Configure the network in Figure 19-15 so you can observe the default timer values over the serial link. You will then experiment by adjusting the values of the retransmit interval.

Figure 19-15 *The Retransmit Interval Is the Time Between Resending Unacknowledged LSAs*

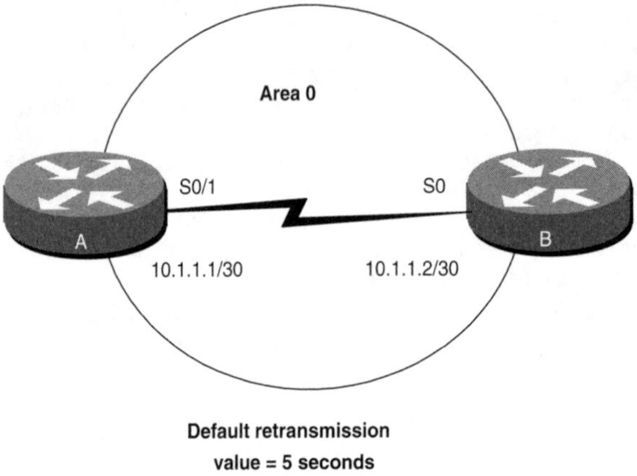


```
Router A
interface Loopback0
 ip address 1.1.1.1 255.255.255.255
!
interface Serial0/1
 bandwidth 64
 ip address 10.1.1.1 255.255.255.252
 clockrate 64000
!
router ospf 1
 network 1.1.1.1 0.0.0.0 area 1
 network 10.1.1.0 0.0.0.3 area 0
```

```
Router B
interface Loopback0
 ip address 2.2.2.2 255.255.255.255
!
interface Serial0
 ip address 10.1.1.2 255.255.255.252
 bandwidth 64
!
router ospf 1
 network 2.2.2.2 0.0.0.0 area 2
 network 10.1.1.0 0.0.0.3 area 0
```

Verify that Routers A and B have formed an OSPF neighbor relationship.

```
rtrA#show ip ospf neighbor

Neighbor ID     Pri   State           Dead Time   Address         Interface
2.2.2.2           1   FULL/  -        00:00:31    10.1.1.2        Serial0/1
```

Examine the default retransmission interval by inspecting the OSPF interface properties on Routers A and B.

```
rtrA#show ip ospf int serial 0/1
Serial0/1 is up, line protocol is up
  Internet Address 10.1.1.1/30, Area 0
  Process ID 1, Router ID 1.1.1.1, Network Type POINT_TO_POINT, Cost: 1562
  Transmit Delay is 1 sec, State POINT_TO_POINT,
  Timer intervals configured, Hello 10, Dead 40, Wait 40, Retransmit 5
    Hello due in 00:00:07
  Index 1/1, flood queue length 0
  Next 0x0(0)/0x0(0)
  Last flood scan length is 1, maximum is 1
  Last flood scan time is 0 msec, maximum is 0 msec
  Neighbor Count is 1, Adjacent neighbor count is 1
    Adjacent with neighbor 2.2.2.2
  Suspress hello for 0 neighbor(s)
```

```
rtrB#show ip ospf interface serial 0
Serial0 is up, line protocol is up
  Internet Address 10.1.1.2/30, Area 0
  Process ID 1, Router ID 2.2.2.2, Network Type POINT_TO_POINT, Cost: 1562
  Transmit Delay is 1 sec, State POINT_TO_POINT,
  Timer intervals configured, Hello 10, Dead 40, Wait 40, Retransmit 5
    Hello due in 00:00:05
  Neighbor Count is 1, Adjacent neighbor count is 1
    Adjacent with neighbor 1.1.1.1
  Suppress hello for 0 neighbor(s)
```

Change the retransmission interval on Router A to 10 seconds.

```
Router A
interface Serial0/1
 bandwidth 64
 ip address 10.1.1.1 255.255.255.252
 ip ospf retransmit-interval 10
 clockrate 64000
```

Unlike the Hello interval (discussed in Section 19-10) and the dead interval (discussed in Section 19-7), the retransmit interval does not have to be the same on every interface attached to a common network.

Verification

Verify that the new retransmit interval has been configured on Router A.

```
rtrA#show ip ospf interface serial 0/1
Serial0/1 is up, line protocol is up
  Internet Address 10.1.1.1/30, Area 0
  Process ID 1, Router ID 1.1.1.1, Network Type POINT_TO_POINT, Cost: 1562
  Transmit Delay is 1 sec, State POINT_TO_POINT,
  Timer intervals configured, Hello 10, Dead 40, Wait 40, Retransmit 10
    Hello due in 00:00:04
  Index 1/1, flood queue length 0
  Next 0x0(0)/0x0(0)
  Last flood scan length is 1, maximum is 1
  Last flood scan time is 0 msec, maximum is 0 msec
  Neighbor Count is 1, Adjacent neighbor count is 1
    Adjacent with neighbor 2.2.2.2
  Suppress hello for 0 neighbor(s)
```

Verify that Routers A and B have an OSPF neighbor relationship.

```
rtrA#show ip ospf neighbor

Neighbor ID     Pri   State           Dead Time   Address         Interface
2.2.2.2           1   FULL/  -        00:00:37    10.1.1.2        Serial0/1
```

Troubleshooting

Step 1 Verify that there is a neighbor relationship between the OSPF routers by using the **show ip ospf neighbor** command.

Step 2 Verify that the desired retransmit interval has been configured by using the command **show ip ospf interface**.

19-20: ip ospf transmit-delay *seconds*

Syntax Description:

- *seconds*—The range of values is 1 to 8192 seconds. The default value is 1 second.

Purpose: When an LSA is created, the router sets the LS age field to 0. The transmit delay value is added to the age field of the LSA. This initial value represents the time delay of propagating the LSA over the interface.

Initial Cisco IOS Software Release: 10.0

Configuration Example: Modifying the Transmit Delay Value for an OSPF Interface

Configure the network in Figure 19-16 and set the transmit delay value on Router A to 2 seconds.

Figure 19-16 *Transmit Delay Represents the LSA Propagation Delay Over an OSPF Interface*

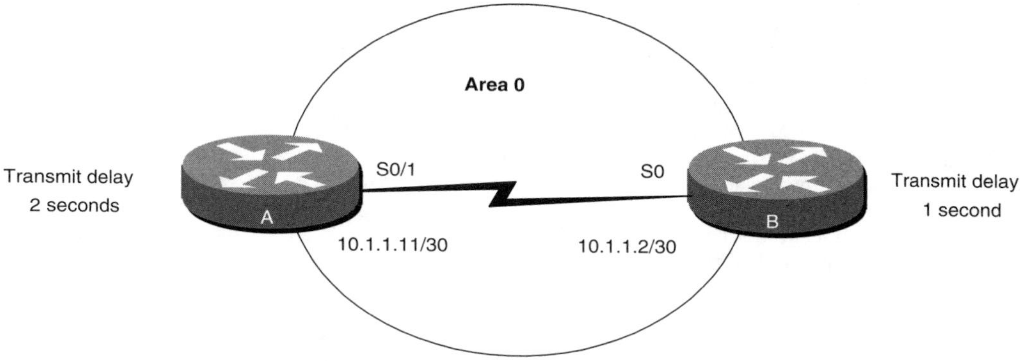


```
Router A
interface Loopback0
 ip address 1.1.1.1 255.255.255.255
!
interface Serial0/1
 bandwidth 64
 ip address 10.1.1.1 255.255.255.252
 ip ospf transmit-delay 2
 clockrate 64000
!
router ospf 1
 network 1.1.1.1 0.0.0.0 area 1
 network 10.1.1.0 0.0.0.3 area 0
```

```
Router B
interface Loopback0
 ip address 2.2.2.2 255.255.255.255
!
interface Serial0
 ip address 10.1.1.2 255.255.255.252
```

continues

```
 bandwidth 64
!
router ospf 1
 network 2.2.2.2 0.0.0.0 area 2
 network 10.1.1.0 0.0.0.3 area 0
```

Verification

Verify that the transmit delay value has been modified, that the OSPF neighbor relationship is active, and that all OSPF routes are being exchanged.

```
rtrA#show ip ospf interface serial 0/1
Serial0/1 is up, line protocol is up
  Internet Address 10.1.1.1/30, Area 0
  Process ID 1, Router ID 1.1.1.1, Network Type POINT_TO_POINT, Cost: 1562
  Transmit Delay is 2 sec, State POINT_TO_POINT,
  Timer intervals configured, Hello 10, Dead 40, Wait 40, Retransmit 5
    Hello due in 00:00:00
  Index 1/1, flood queue length 0
  Next 0x0(0)/0x0(0)
  Last flood scan length is 2, maximum is 2
  Last flood scan time is 0 msec, maximum is 0 msec
  Neighbor Count is 1, Adjacent neighbor count is 1
    Adjacent with neighbor 2.2.2.2
  Suppress hello for 0 neighbor(s)

rtrA#show ip ospf neighbor

Neighbor ID     Pri   State           Dead Time   Address         Interface
2.2.2.2           1   FULL/  -        00:00:36    10.1.1.2        Serial0/1
rtrA#show ip route
Codes: C - connected, S - static, I - IGRP, R - RIP, M - mobile, B - BGP
       D - EIGRP, EX - EIGRP external, O - OSPF, IA - OSPF inter area
       N1 - OSPF NSSA external type 1, N2 - OSPF NSSA external type 2
       E1 - OSPF external type 1, E2 - OSPF external type 2, E - EGP
       i - IS-IS, L1 - IS-IS level-1, L2 - IS-IS level-2, ia - IS-IS inter area
       * - candidate default, U - per-user static route, o - ODR
       P - periodic downloaded static route

Gateway of last resort is not set

     1.0.0.0/32 is subnetted, 1 subnets
C       1.1.1.1 is directly connected, Loopback0
     2.0.0.0/32 is subnetted, 1 subnets
O IA    2.2.2.2 [110/1563] via 10.1.1.2, 00:40:39, Serial0/1
     10.0.0.0/30 is subnetted, 1 subnets
C       10.1.1.0 is directly connected, Serial0/1
```

Troubleshooting

Step 1 Verify that there is a neighbor relationship between the OSPF routers by using the **show ip ospf neighbor** command.

Step 2 Verify that the desired transmit delay value has been configured by using the OSPF interface command **ip ospf transmit-delay**.

CHAPTER 20

show Commands

20-1: show ip ospf

20-2: show ip ospf *process-id*

Syntax Description:

- *process-id*—The OSPF process ID. The range of values is 1 to 4,294,967,295.

Purpose: To display information and parameters for one or more OSPF processes. The output of this command can be filtered, using regular expressions, by one of the following forms:

```
show ip ospf | begin regular-expression
show ip ospf | exclude regular-expression
show ip ospf | include regular-expression
```

Cisco IOS Software Initial Release: 10.0

Example: Displaying OSPF Process Information

The following is a representative output from the **show ip ospf** EXEC command.

```
r2#show ip ospf
Routing Process "ospf 1" with ID 2.2.2.2
Supports only single TOS(TOS0) routes
Supports opaque LSA
It is an area border router
SPF schedule delay 5 secs, Hold time between two SPFs 10 secs
Minimum LSA interval 5 secs. Minimum LSA arrival 1 secs
Number of external LSA 1. Checksum Sum 0xAB1F
Number of opaque AS LSA 0. Checksum Sum 0x0
Number of DCbitless external and opaque AS LSA 0
Number of DoNotAge external and opaque AS LSA 0
Number of areas in this router is 4. 4 normal 0 stub 0 nssa
External flood list length 0
```

continues

```
Area BACKBONE(0)
    Number of interfaces in this area is 3
    Area has no authentication
    SPF algorithm executed 19 times
    Area ranges are
    Number of LSA 15. Checksum Sum 0x7A630
    Number of opaque link LSA 0. Checksum Sum 0x0
    Number of DCbitless LSA 0
    Number of indication LSA 0
    Number of DoNotAge LSA 5
    Flood list length 0
Area 1
    Number of interfaces in this area is 1
    Area has no authentication
    SPF algorithm executed 10 times
    Area ranges are
    Number of LSA 22. Checksum Sum 0xD15F3
    Number of opaque link LSA 0. Checksum Sum 0x0
    Number of DCbitless LSA 0
    Number of indication LSA 0
    Number of DoNotAge LSA 0
    Flood list length 0
Area 2
    Number of interfaces in this area is 1
    Area has no authentication
    SPF algorithm executed 2 times
    Area ranges are
    Number of LSA 12. Checksum Sum 0x7AB94
    Number of opaque link LSA 0. Checksum Sum 0x0
    Number of DCbitless LSA 0
    Number of indication LSA 0
    Number of DoNotAge LSA 0
    Flood list length 0
Area 9
    Number of interfaces in this area is 2
    Area has no authentication
    SPF algorithm executed 3 times
    Area ranges are
       8.8.8.0/27 Active(1) Advertise
    Number of LSA 12. Checksum Sum 0x6FB7C
    Number of opaque link LSA 0. Checksum Sum 0x0
    Number of DCbitless LSA 0
    Number of indication LSA 0
    Number of DoNotAge LSA 0
    Flood list length 0
```

Table 20-1 provides an explanation for the significant lines in the preceding output.

Table 20-1 *Significant Output from* **show ip ospf**

Line	Content Description
`Routing Process "ospf 1" with ID 2.2.2.2`	The local OSPF process ID and OSPF router ID.
`It is an area border router`	OSPF router type. Possible types are Area Border Router (ABR), Autonomous System Border Router (ASBR), or internal.
`SPF schedule delay 5 secs, Hold time between two SPFs 10 secs`	The hold time between Shortest Path First (SPF) calculations is 10 seconds. If there is a flapping interface or a duplicate IP address in the OSPF domain, an SPF calculation will be triggered every time the router receives an update. If the number of SPF calculations (see lines 16, 27, 38, and 49) is incrementing every 10 seconds, then there is probably a flapping interface or a misconfiguration somewhere in the OSPF domain.
`Number of areas in this router is 4. 4 normal 0 stub 0 nssa`	Number and types of OSPF areas configured on the local router.

`Area BACKBONE(0)`
`Area 1`
`Area 2`
`Area 9`
	Indicates the start of the output containing information for a specific OSPF area.

`Number of interfaces in this area is 3`	Number of interfaces, either physical or loopback, that have been configured to run OSPF. The **network** command determines the interfaces that will be active.
`Area has no authentication`	Type of authentication configured for the area.
`SPF algorithm executed 19 times`	Number of times the SPF calculation has been run.

`Area ranges are`
`or`
`Area ranges are`
`    8.8.8.0/27 Active(1) Advertise`
	Indicates if OSPF routes are being summarized using the **area range** command.

20-3: show ip ospf border-routers

20-4: show ip ospf *process-id* border-routers

Syntax Description:

- *process-id*—The OSPF process ID. Range of values is 1 to 4,294,967,295.

Purpose: To display the OSPF routing table entries to ABRs and ASBRs. The output of this command can be filtered, using regular expressions, by one of the following forms:

```
show ip ospf border-routers | begin regular-expression
show ip ospf border-routers | exclude regular-expression
show ip ospf border-routers | include regular-expression
```

Initial Cisco IOS Software Release: 10.0

Example: Displaying OSPF Border Router Information

The following is a representative output from the **show ip ospf border-routers** EXEC command.

```
r6#show ip ospf border-routers

OSPF Process 1 internal Routing Table

Codes: i - Intra-area route, I - Inter-area route

I 4.4.4.4 [122] via 10.1.1.18, Serial0/1, ASBR, Area 7, SPF 5
i 1.1.1.1 [48] via 10.1.1.18, Serial0/1, ABR, Area 7, SPF 5
```

Table 20-2 provides an explanation for the highlighted line in the preceding output.

Table 20-2 *Significant Output from the* **show ip ospf border-routers** Command

Field	Description
`I`	Indicates the type of route to the ABR or ASBR. Possible values are I for an inter-area route and i for an intra-area route.
`4.4.4.4`	Indicates the router ID of the ABR or ASBR.
`[122]`	Indicates the OSPF cost of the route to the ABR or ASBR.
`via 10.1.1.18`	Indicates the next hop toward the ABR or ASBR.
`Serial0/1`	Indicates the interface used to reach the next hop.
`ASBR`	Indicates the border router type (ABR or ASBR).
`Area 7`	Indicates the area from which the route to the border router was learned.
`SPF 5`	The number of the SPF calculations that calculated this route.

20-5: show ip ospf database

20-6: show ip ospf *process-id* database

20-7: show ip ospf database adv-router *router-id*

20-8: show ip ospf *process-id* database adv-router *router-id*

20-9: show ip ospf database asbr-summary

20-10: show ip ospf *process-id* database asbr-summary

20-11: show ip ospf database asbr-summary *asbr-id*

20-12: show ip ospf *process-id* database asbr-summary *asbr-id*

20-13: show ip ospf database database-summary

20-14: show ip ospf *process-id* database database-summary

20-15: show ip ospf database external

20-16: show ip ospf *process-id* database external

20-17: show ip ospf database network

20-18: show ip ospf *process-id* database network

20-19: show ip ospf database nssa-external

20-20: show ip ospf *process-id* database nssa-external

20-21: show ip ospf database router

20-22: show ip ospf *process-id* database router

20-23: show ip ospf database self-originate

20-24: show ip ospf *process-id* database self-originate

20-25: show ip ospf database summary

20-26: show ip ospf *process-id* database summary

Syntax Description:

- *process-id*—The OSPF process ID. The range of values is 1 to 4,294,967,295.
- *router-id*—The OSPF router ID of the advertising router.
- *asbr-id*—The OSPF router ID of the ASBR.

Purpose: To display information contained in the OSPF database. An OSPF process ID can be used if more than one OSPF process is active, using the form **show ip ospf** *process-id* **database**. The output of this command can be filtered, using regular expressions, by one of the following forms:

```
show ip ospf database | begin regular-expression
show ip ospf database | exclude regular-expression
show ip ospf database | include regular-expression
```

Initial Cisco IOS Software Release: 10.0. The **database-summary** option was added in Release 11.0 and the **adv-router** and **self-originate** options were added in Release 12.0.

Example 1: Displaying OSPF Database Information from a Specific OSPF Router

The following is a representative output from the **show ip ospf database adv-router** EXEC command.

```
r6#show ip ospf database adv-router 1.1.1.1

            OSPF Router with ID (6.6.6.6) (Process ID 1)

                Router Link States (Area 7)

Link ID         ADV Router      Age         Seq#       Checksum Link count
1.1.1.1         1.1.1.1         431         0x80000012 0x2714   2

                Summary Net Link States (Area 7)

Link ID         ADV Router      Age         Seq#       Checksum
1.1.1.1         1.1.1.1         431         0x80000010 0x29FB
2.2.2.2         1.1.1.1         431         0x80000010 0x7D63
4.4.4.4         1.1.1.1         431         0x80000010 0x8549
8.8.8.0         1.1.1.1         431         0x80000003 0x18E4
10.1.1.0        1.1.1.1         431         0x80000010 0x24BC
10.1.1.4        1.1.1.1         431         0x80000010 0x3785
10.1.1.12       1.1.1.1         431         0x80000010 0xF1A8
172.16.1.0      1.1.1.1         1198        0x80000013 0x213
172.16.2.0      1.1.1.1         431         0x80000010 0x9888

                Summary ASB Link States (Area 7)

Link ID         ADV Router      Age         Seq#       Checksum
4.4.4.4         1.1.1.1         431         0x80000010 0x6D61
```

Table 20-3 provides an explanation for the highlighted line in the preceding output.

Table 20-3 *Significant Output from the* **show ip ospf database adv-router** Command

Field	Description
10.1.1.12	Indicates the route advertised by the advertising router.
1.1.1.1	Indicates the OSPF router ID of the advertising router.
431	Indicates the age of the LSA for this route.
0x80000010	Indicates the LSA sequence number used to detect old or duplicate LSAs.
0xF1A8	Indicates the LSA checksum.

Example 2: Displaying OSPF Database Information from an OSPF ASBR Router

The following is representative output from the **show ip ospf database asbr-summary** EXEC command.

```
r6#show ip ospf database asbr-summary

            OSPF Router with ID (6.6.6.6) (Process ID 1)

                Summary ASB Link States (Area 7)

  Routing Bit Set on this LSA
  LS age: 1124
  Options: (No TOS-capability, DC, Upward)
  LS Type: Summary Links(AS Boundary Router)
  Link State ID: 4.4.4.4 (AS Boundary Router address)
  Advertising Router: 1.1.1.1
  LS Seq Number: 80000010
  Checksum: 0x6D61
  Length: 28
  Network Mask: /0
        TOS: 0  Metric: 74
```

Table 20-4 provides an explanation for the highlighted lines in the preceding output.

Table 20-4 *Significant Output from the* **show ip ospf database asbr-summary** Command

Field	Description
`Link State ID: 4.4.4.4 (AS Boundary Router address)`	OSPF router ID of the ASBR.
`Advertising Router: 1.1.1.1`	OSPF router ID of the router advertising the LSA.

20-27: show ip ospf flood-list

20-28: show ip ospf *process-id* flood-list

20-29: show ip ospf flood-list *int-name int-number*

20-30: show ip ospf *process-id* flood-list *int-name int-number*

Syntax Description:

- *process-id*—The OSPF process ID. The range of values is 1 to 4,294,967,295.
- *int-name*—Interface name.
- *int-number*—Interface number.

Purpose: To display LSAs that are queued for flooding. An OSPF process ID can be used if more than one OSPF process is active using the form **show ip ospf** *process-id* **flood-list**. The output of this command can be filtered, using regular expressions, by one of the following forms:

```
show ip ospf flood-list | begin regular-expression
show ip ospf flood-list | exclude regular-expression
show ip ospf flood-list | include regular-expression
```

Initial Cisco IOS Software Release: 12.0 (1)T

Example: Displaying All OSPF Floodlist Information

The following is a representative output from the **show ip ospf flood-list** EXEC command.

```
r4#show ip ospf flood-list

            OSPF Router with ID (4.4.4.4) (Process ID 1)

 Interface Serial0/0, Queue length 0

 Interface Ethernet1/0, Queue length 0

 Interface Ethernet0/0, Queue length 0

 Interface Loopback0, Queue length 0
```

20-31: show ip ospf interface

20-32: show ip ospf *process-id* interface

20-33: show ip ospf interface *int-name int-number*

20-34: show ip ospf *process-id* interface *int-name int-number*

Syntax Description:

- *process-id*—The OSPF process ID. The range of values is 1 to 4,294,967,295.
- *int-name*—Interface name.
- *int-number*—Interface number.

Purpose: To display information regarding OSPF-enabled interfaces. An OSPF process ID can be used if more than one OSPF process is active using the form **show ip ospf** *process-id* **interface**. The output of this command can be filtered, using regular expressions, by one of the following forms:

```
show ip ospf interface | begin regular-expression
show ip ospf interface | exclude regular-expression
show ip ospf interface | include regular-expression
```

Initial Cisco IOS Software Release: 10.0

Example 1: Displaying Information for an OSPF-Enabled Interface

The following is a representative output from the **show ip ospf interface** EXEC command. This command can be used to verify that an interface is enabled for OSPF, verify that the interface is in the proper OSPF area, and inspect the OSPF parameters that have been configured such as priority, Hello interval, and dead interval.

```
r4#show ip ospf 1 interface ethernet 1/0
Ethernet1/0 is up, line protocol is up
  Internet Address 172.16.2.2/24, Area 0
  Process ID 1, Router ID 4.4.4.4, Network Type BROADCAST, Cost: 10
  Transmit Delay is 1 sec, State DR, Priority 1
  Designated Router (ID) 4.4.4.4, Interface address 172.16.2.2
  Backup Designated router (ID) 2.2.2.2, Interface address 172.16.2.1
  Timer intervals configured, Hello 10, Dead 40, Wait 40, Retransmit 5
    Hello due in 00:00:08
  Index 2/2, flood queue length 0
  Next 0x0(0)/0x0(0)
  Last flood scan length is 3, maximum is 3
  Last flood scan time is 0 msec, maximum is 0 msec
```

```
  Neighbor Count is 1, Adjacent neighbor count is 1
    Adjacent with neighbor 2.2.2.2  (Backup Designated Router)
  Suppress hello for 0 neighbor(s)
```

Table 20-5 provides an explanation for the significant lines in the preceding output.

Table 20-5 *Significant Output from* **show ip ospf interface**

Line	Content Description
`Ethernet1/0 is up, line protocol is up`	Link and protocol status.
`Internet Address 172.16.2.2/24, Area 0`	Interface IP address, prefix length, and assigned OSPF area.
`Process ID 1, Router ID 4.4.4.4, Network Type BROADCAST, Cost: 10`	OSPF process ID and local OSPF router ID. OSPF network type and link cost.
`Transmit Delay is 1 sec, State DR, Priority 1`	This router is the DR for the Ethernet network and has an OSPF priority of 1.
`Backup Designated router (ID) 2.2.2.2, Interface address 172.16.2.1`	Router ID and IP address of the BDR for this network.
`Timer intervals configured, Hello 10, Dead 40, Wait 40, Retransmit 5`	OSPF timer values for this interface.
`Neighbor Count is 1, Adjacent neighbor count is 1 Adjacent with neighbor 2.2.2.2 (Backup Designated Router)`	There is one neighbor on this interface and that neighbor is the BDR.

Example 2: Displaying OSPF Timer Information for an OSPF-enabled Interface

The following example demonstrates how to use a regular expression to limit the amount of information displayed by the **show ip ospf interface** command. A regular expression will be used to display only information regarding the OSPF timer values for a specific OSPF interface.

```
r4#show ip ospf interface ethernet 1/0 | include Timer
  Timer intervals configured, Hello 10, Dead 40, Wait 40, Retransmit 5
```

20-35: show ip ospf neighbor

20-36: show ip ospf *process-id* neighbor

20-37: show ip ospf neighbor *neighbor-id*

20-38: show ip ospf *process-id* neighbor *neighbor-id*

20-39: show ip ospf neighbor *int-name int-number*

20-40: show ip ospf *process-id* neighbor *int-name int-number*

20-41: show ip ospf neighbor detail

20-42: show ip ospf *process-id* neighbor detail

20-43: show ip ospf neighbor detail *neighbor-id*

20-44: show ip ospf *process-id* neighbor detail *neighbor-id*

20-45: show ip ospf neighbor *int-name int-number*

20-46: show ip ospf *process-id* neighbor *int-name int-number*

Syntax Description:

- *neighbor-id*—OSPF router ID.
- *int-name*—Interface name.
- *int-number*—Interface number.

Purpose: To display information regarding OSPF-enabled interfaces. An OSPF process ID can be used if more than one OSPF process is active using the form **show ip ospf** *process-id* **neighbor**. The output of this command can be filtered, using regular expressions, by one of the following forms:

```
show ip ospf neighbor | begin regular-expression
show ip ospf neighbor | exclude regular-expression
show ip ospf neighbor | include regular-expression
```

Initial Cisco IOS Software Release: 10.0

Example 1: Displaying Information for All OSPF Neighbors

The following is a representative output from the **show ip ospf neighbor** EXEC command.

```
r2#show ip ospf neighbor

Neighbor ID     Pri   State           Dead Time   Address         Interface
4.4.4.4           1   FULL/DR         00:00:35    172.16.2.2      Ethernet0/0
3.3.3.3           1   FULL/  -        00:00:38    10.1.1.6        Serial0/1
1.1.1.1           1   FULL/  -        00:00:38    10.1.1.1        Serial0/0
```

A regular expression can be used to display information about a specific neighbor.

```
r2#show ip ospf neighbor | include 4.4.4.4

4.4.4.4           1   FULL/DR         00:00:35    172.16.2.2      Ethernet0/0
```

Example 2: Displaying Detailed Information for a Specific OSPF Neighbor

```
r2#show ip ospf neighbor detail 1.1.1.1
 Neighbor 1.1.1.1, interface address 10.1.1.1
    In the area 1 via interface Serial0/0
    Neighbor priority is 1, State is FULL, 12 state changes
    DR is 0.0.0.0 BDR is 0.0.0.0
    Options is 0x2
    Dead timer due in 00:00:38
    Neighbor is up for 4d02h
    Index 1/1, retransmission queue length 0, number of retransmission 1
```

```
        First 0x0(0)/0x0(0) Next 0x0(0)/0x0(0)
        Last retransmission scan length is 1, maximum is 1
        Last retransmission scan time is 0 msec, maximum is 0 msec
```

Table 20-6 provides an explanation for the significant lines in the preceding output.

Table 20-6 *Significant Output from* **show ip ospf neighbor detail**

Line	Content Description
`Neighbor 1.1.1.1, interface address 10.1.1.1`	Neighbor's router ID and address on this network.
`In the area 1 via interface Serial0/0`	The neighbor is in Area 1 and reachable via interface Serial0/0.
`Neighbor priority is 1, State is FULL, 12 state changes`	The neighbor's OSPF priority, the state of the neighbor relationship, and number of state changes for the neighbor relationship.
`DR is 0.0.0.0 BDR is 0.0.0.0`	This is a serial link, so there is no DR or BDR.
`Options is 0x2`	0x00 indicates that the area is a stub area. 0x2 indicates that the area is not a stub area.

20-47: show ip ospf request-list

20-48: show ip ospf *process-id* request-list

20-49: show ip ospf request-list *neighbor-id*

20-50: show ip ospf *process-id* request-list *neighbor-id*

20-51: show ip ospf request-list *int-name int-number*

20-52: show ip ospf *process-id* request-list *int-name int-number*

Syntax Description:

- *process-id*—The OSPF process ID. The range of values is 1 to 4,294,967,295.
- *neighbor-id*—Neighbor's OSPF router ID.
- *int-name*—Interface name.
- *int-number*—Interface number.

Purpose: To display all link-state information requested by a router. An OSPF process ID can be used if more than one OSPF process is active using the form **show ip ospf** *process-id* **request-list**. The output of this command can be filtered, using regular expressions, by one of the following forms:

```
show ip ospf request-list | begin regular-expression
show ip ospf request-list | exclude regular-expression
show ip ospf request-list | include regular-expression
```

Initial Cisco IOS Software Release: 10.2

Example: Displaying Request List Information for a Particular OSPF Neighbor

The following is a representative output from the **show ip ospf request-list** EXEC command.

```
r2#show ip ospf request-list 3.3.3.3

            OSPF Router with ID (2.2.2.2) (Process ID 1)

 Neighbor 3.3.3.3, interface Serial0/1 address 10.1.1.6

 Type  LS ID           ADV RTR         Seq NO      Age     Checksum
    1  3.3.3.3         3.3.3.3         0x8000020C  9        0x6572
```

20-53: show ip ospf retransmission-list

20-54: show ip ospf *process-id* retransmission-list

20-55: show ip ospf retransmission *neighbor-id*

20-56: show ip ospf *process-id* retransmission *neighbor-id*

20-57: show ip ospf retransmission *int-name int-number*

20-58: show ip ospf *process-id* retransmission *int-name int-number*

Syntax Description:

- *process-id*—The OSPF process ID. The range of values is 1 to 4,294,967,295.
- *neighbor-id*—Neighbor's OSPF router ID.
- *int-name*—Interface name.
- *int-number*—Interface number.

Purpose: To display a list of LSAs waiting to be re-sent. An OSPF process ID can be used if more than one OSPF process is active using the form **show ip ospf** *process-id* **retransmission-list**. The output of this command can be filtered, using regular expressions, by one of the following forms:

```
show ip ospf retransmission-list | begin regular-expression
show ip ospf retransmission-list | exclude regular-expression
show ip ospf retransmission-list | include regular-expression
```

Initial Cisco IOS Software Release: 10.2

Example: Displaying the List of LSAs Waiting to Be Re-sent on a Particular Interface

The following is a representative output from the **show ip ospf retransmission-list** EXEC command.

```
r2#show ip ospf retransmission-list serial 0/0

           OSPF Router with ID (2.2.2.2) (Process ID 1)

 Neighbor 1.1.1.1, interface Serial0/0 address 10.1.1.1
Link state retransmission due in 2969 msec, Queue length 2

  Type  LS ID           ADV RTR          Seq NO       Age     Checksum
     1  2.2.2.2         2.2.2.2          0x80000219   0        0xB123
```

20-59: show ip ospf summary-address

20-60: show ip ospf *process-id* summary-address

Syntax Description:

- *process-id*—The OSPF process ID. The range of values is 1 to 4,294,967,295.

Purpose: To display a list of summary addresses that have been configured on the router. An OSPF process ID can be used if more than one OSPF process is active using the form **show ip ospf** *process-id* **summary-address**. The output of this command can be filtered, using regular expressions, by one of the following forms:

```
show ip ospf summary-address | begin regular-expression
show ip ospf summary-address | exclude regular-expression
show ip ospf summary-address | include regular-expression
```

Initial Cisco IOS Software Release: 10.0

Example: Displaying the List of Summary Addresses Configured on a Router

The following is a representative output from the **show ip ospf summary-address** EXEC command.

```
r4#show ip ospf summary-address
```

```
OSPF Process 1, Summary-address

169.254.0.0/255.254.0.0 Metric 10, Type 2, Tag 0
```

20-61: show ip ospf virtual-links

20-62: show ip ospf *process-id* virtual-links

Syntax Description:

- *process-id*—The OSPF process ID. The range of values is 1 to 4,294,967,295.

Purpose: To display the status and information regarding any virtual links that have been configured on the router. An OSPF process ID can be used if more than one OSPF process is active using the form **show ip ospf** *process-id* **virtual-links**. The output of this command can be filtered, using regular expressions, by one of the following forms:

```
show ip ospf virtual-links | begin regular-expression
show ip ospf virtual-links | exclude regular-expression
show ip ospf virtual-links | include regular-expression
```

Initial Cisco IOS Software Release: 10.0

Example: Displaying the Status of All Virtual Links Configured on the Local Router

The following is a representative output from the **show ip ospf virtual-links** EXEC command.

```
r1#show ip ospf virtual-links
Virtual Link OSPF_VL0 to router 2.2.2.2 is up
  Run as demand circuit
  DoNotAge LSA allowed.
  Transit area 1, via interface Serial0/0, Cost of using 64
  Transmit Delay is 1 sec, State POINT_TO_POINT,
  Timer intervals configured, Hello 10, Dead 40, Wait 40, Retransmit 5
    Hello due in 00:00:01
    Adjacency State FULL (Hello suppressed)
```

CHAPTER 21

debug Commands

21-1: debug ip ospf adj

Syntax Description:

This command has no arguments.

Purpose: To display information regarding the formation of an OSPF neighbor relationship. If an OSPF neighbor relationship is not being formed between two routers, this command can be used to determine the problem.

Example 1: Displaying the Successful Formation of an OSPF Adjacency

The following is representative output from the **debug ip ospf adj** EXEC command for a successful configuration. The EXEC command **clear ip ospf process** is used to clear the existing adjacency.

```
r6#debug ip ospf adj
OSPF adjacency events debugging is on
r6#clear ip ospf process
Reset ALL OSPF processes? [no]: yes
r6#
6w3d: OSPF: Interface Loopback0 going Down
6w3d: OSPF: 6.6.6.6 address 6.6.6.6 on Loopback0 is dead, state DOWN
6w3d: OSPF: Interface Serial0/1 going Down
6w3d: OSPF: 6.6.6.6 address 10.1.1.17 on Serial0/1 is dead, state DOWN
6w3d: OSPF: 1.1.1.1 address 10.1.1.18 on Serial0/1 is dead, state DOWN
6w3d: %OSPF-5-ADJCHG: Process 1, Nbr 1.1.1.1 on Serial0/1 from FULL to DOWN,
Neighbor Down: Interface down or detached
6w3d: OSPF: Interface Loopback0 going Up
6w3d: OSPF: Interface Serial0/1 going Up
6w3d: OSPF: Build router LSA for area 7, router ID 6.6.6.6, seq 0x80000001
6w3d: OSPF: 2 Way Communication to 1.1.1.1 on Serial0/1, state 2WAY
6w3d: OSPF: Send DBD to 1.1.1.1 on Serial0/1 seq 0x12F4 opt 0x42 flag 0x7 len 32

6w3d: OSPF: Rcv DBD from 1.1.1.1 on Serial0/1 seq 0x2071 opt 0x2 flag 0x7 len 32
  mtu 1500 state EXSTART
6w3d: OSPF: First DBD and we are not SLAVE
```

continues

```
6w3d: OSPF: Rcv DBD from 1.1.1.1 on Serial0/1 seq 0x12F4 opt 0x2 flag 0x2 len 27
2  mtu 1500 state EXSTART
6w3d: OSPF: NBR Negotiation Done. We are the MASTER
6w3d: OSPF: Send DBD to 1.1.1.1 on Serial0/1 seq 0x12F5 opt 0x42 flag 0x3 len 52

6w3d: OSPF: Database request to 1.1.1.1
6w3d: OSPF: sent LS REQ packet to 10.1.1.18, length 144
6w3d: OSPF: Rcv DBD from 1.1.1.1 on Serial0/1 seq 0x12F5 opt 0x2 flag 0x0 len 32
  mtu 1500 state EXCHANGE
6w3d: OSPF: Send DBD to 1.1.1.1 on Serial0/1 seq 0x12F6 opt 0x42 flag 0x1 len 32

6w3d: OSPF: Rcv DBD from 1.1.1.1 on Serial0/1 seq 0x12F6 opt 0x2 flag 0x0 len 32
  mtu 1500 state EXCHANGE
6w3d: OSPF: Exchange Done with 1.1.1.1 on Serial0/1
6w3d: OSPF: Synchronized with 1.1.1.1 on Serial0/1, state FULL
6w3d: %OSPF-5-ADJCHG: Process 1, Nbr 1.1.1.1 on Serial0/1 from LOADING to FULL,
Loading Done
```

Example 2: Displaying the Attempted Formation of an OSPF Adjacency when There Is an Area Mismatch

The following is representative output from the **debug ip ospf adj** EXEC command when one end of a serial link has been configured in the wrong OSPF area. The EXEC command **clear ip ospf process** is used to clear the existing adjacency.

```
r6#debug ip ospf adj
OSPF adjacency events debugging is on
r6#clear ip ospf process
Reset ALL OSPF processes? [no]: yes
r6#
6w3d: OSPF: Interface Loopback0 going Down
6w3d: OSPF: 6.6.6.6 address 6.6.6.6 on Loopback0 is dead, state DOWN
6w3d: OSPF: Interface Serial0/1 going Down
6w3d: OSPF: 6.6.6.6 address 10.1.1.17 on Serial0/1 is dead, state DOWN
6w3d: OSPF: Interface Loopback0 going Up
6w3d: OSPF: Interface Serial0/1 going Up
6w3d: OSPF: Build router LSA for area 7, router ID 6.6.6.6, seq 0x80000001
6w3d: OSPF: Build router LSA for area 17, router ID 6.6.6.6, seq 0x80000001
6w3d: OSPF: Rcv pkt from 10.1.1.18, Serial0/1, area 0.0.0.17
      mismatch area 0.0.0.7 in the header
```

21-2: debug ip ospf events

Syntax Description:

This command has no arguments.

Purpose: To display information regarding OSPF events such as the forming of adjacencies, Hello packets, LSA flooding, Designated Router (DR) selection, and shortest path first (SPF) calculations. If an OSPF neighbor relationship is not being formed between two routers, then this command can be used to determine the problem.

Example 1: Displaying the Successful Formation of an OSPF Adjacency

The following is representative output from the **debug ip ospf events** EXEC command for a successful configuration. The EXEC command **clear ip ospf process** is used to clear the existing adjacency.

```
r6#debug ip ospf events
OSPF events debugging is on
r6#clear ip ospf process
Reset ALL OSPF processes? [no]: yes
r6#
6w4d: OSPF: Rcv hello from 1.1.1.1 area 7 from Serial0/1 10.1.1.18
6w4d: OSPF: 2 Way Communication to 1.1.1.1 on Serial0/1, state 2WAY
6w4d: OSPF: Send DBD to 1.1.1.1 on Serial0/1 seq 0x22BC opt 0x42 flag 0x7 len 32

6w4d: OSPF: End of hello processing
6w4d: OSPF: Rcv DBD from 1.1.1.1 on Serial0/1 seq 0x1D6E opt 0x2 flag 0x7 len 32
  mtu 1500 state EXSTART
6w4d: OSPF: First DBD and we are not SLAVE
6w4d: OSPF: Rcv DBD from 1.1.1.1 on Serial0/1 seq 0x22BC opt 0x2 flag 0x2 len 27
2  mtu 1500 state EXSTART
6w4d: OSPF: NBR Negotiation Done. We are the MASTER
6w4d: OSPF: Send DBD to 1.1.1.1 on Serial0/1 seq 0x22BD opt 0x42 flag 0x3 len 52

6w4d: OSPF: Database request to 1.1.1.1
6w4d: OSPF: sent LS REQ packet to 10.1.1.18, length 144
6w4d: OSPF: Rcv DBD from 1.1.1.1 on Serial0/1 seq 0x22BD opt 0x2 flag 0x0 len 32
  mtu 1500 state EXCHANGE
6w4d: OSPF: Send DBD to 1.1.1.1 on Serial0/1 seq 0x22BE opt 0x42 flag 0x1 len 32

6w4d: OSPF: Rcv DBD from 1.1.1.1 on Serial0/1 seq 0x22BE opt 0x2 flag 0x0 len 32
  mtu 1500 state EXCHANGE
6w4d: OSPF: Exchange Done with 1.1.1.1 on Serial0/1
6w4d: OSPF: Synchronized with 1.1.1.1 on Serial0/1, state FULL
6w4d: %OSPF-5-ADJCHG: Process 1, Nbr 1.1.1.1 on Serial0/1 from LOADING to FULL,
Loading Done
```

Example 2: Debugging an OSPF Adjacency Problem

The following is representative output from the **debug ip ospf events** EXEC command when there is a mismatch in the dead interval.

```
r6#debug ip ospf events
OSPF events debugging is onr6#
6w4d: OSPF: Rcv hello from 1.1.1.1 area 7 from Serial0/1 10.1.1.18
6w4d: OSPF: Mismatched hello parameters from 10.1.1.18
6w4d: OSPF: Dead R 40 C 123, Hello R 10 C 10
```

R is the received dead interval time and **C** is the dead interval time configured on the local router.

21-3: debug ip ospf flood

21-4: debug ip ospf flood *ip-access-list-number*

Syntax Description:

- *ip-access-list-number*—Number of the IP access list used to filter the output of the **flood** command. Valid ranges are 1 to 99 and 1300 to 1999.

Purpose: To enable the display of events generated by the OSPF flooding protocol. The **debug ip ospf flood** command generates information about flooding, which includes the sending and receiving of update and acknowledgement packets.

Example 1: Displaying All Output from the OSPF Flooding Protocol

Debugging the OSPF flooding protocol will generate an enormous amount of information on its operation, as shown in the following output.

```
r6#debug ip ospf flood
OSPF flooding debugging is on
r6#clear ip ospf process
Reset ALL OSPF processes? [no]: yes
r6#
6w4d: Inc retrans unit nbr count index 1 (0/1) to 1/1
6w4d: Set Nbr 1.1.1.1 1 first flood info from 0 (0) to 623AA2D8 (300)
6w4d: Init Nbr 1.1.1.1 1 next flood info to 623AA2D8
6w4d: OSPF: Add Type 1 LSA ID 6.6.6.6 Adv rtr 6.6.6.6 Seq 80000125 to Serial0/1
1.1.1.1 retransmission list
6w4d: OSPF: Start Serial0/1 1.1.1.1 retrans timer
6w4d: Set idb next flood info from 0 (0) to 623AA2D8 (300)
```

```
6w4d: OSPF: Add Type 1 LSA ID 6.6.6.6 Adv rtr 6.6.6.6 Seq 80000125 to Serial0/1
flood list
6w4d: OSPF: Start Serial0/1 pacing timer
6w4d: OSPF: Flooding update on Serial0/1 to 224.0.0.5 Area 7
6w4d: OSPF: Send Type 1, LSID 6.6.6.6, Adv rtr 6.6.6.6, age 3600, seq 0x80000125
 (0)
6w4d: Create retrans unit 0x623B71A8/0x623C5DE8 1 (0/1) 1
6w4d: OSPF: Set nbr 1 (0/1) retrans to 4560 count to 1
6w4d: Set idb next flood info from 623AA2D8 (300) to 0 (0)
6w4d: OSPF: Remove Type 1 LSA ID 6.6.6.6 Adv rtr 6.6.6.6 Seq 80000125 from
Serial0/1 flood list
6w4d: OSPF: Stop Serial0/1 flood timer
6w4d: %OSPF-5-ADJCHG: Process 1, Nbr 1.1.1.1 on Serial0/1 from FULL to DOWN,
Neighbor Down: Interface down or detached
6w4d: Dec retrans unit nbr count index 1 (0/1) to 0/0
6w4d: Free nbr retrans unit 0x623B71A8/0x623C5DE8 0 total 0. Also Free nbr
retrans block
6w4d: Set Nbr 1.1.1.1 1 first flood info from 623AA2D8 (300) to 0 (0)
6w4d: Adjust Nbr 1.1.1.1 1 next flood info to 0
6w4d: OSPF: Remove Type 1 LSA ID 6.6.6.6 Adv rtr 6.6.6.6 Seq 80000125 from 1.1.1
.1 retransmission list
6w4d: OSPF: Stop nbr 1.1.1.1 retransmission timer
6w4d: OSPF: Build router LSA for area 7, router ID 6.6.6.6, seq 0x80000001
6w4d: OSPF: received update from 1.1.1.1, Serial0/1
6w4d: OSPF: Rcv Update Type 1, LSID 1.1.1.1, Adv rtr 1.1.1.1, age 5, seq 0x80000
130
6w4d: OSPF: Rcv Update Type 3, LSID 172.16.2.0, Adv rtr 1.1.1.1, age 107, seq 0x
80000001
6w4d:       Mask /24
6w4d: OSPF: Rcv Update Type 3, LSID 172.16.1.0, Adv rtr 1.1.1.1, age 107, seq 0x
80000001
6w4d:       Mask /24
6w4d: OSPF: Rcv Update Type 3, LSID 10.1.1.12, Adv rtr 1.1.1.1, age 107, seq 0x8
0000001
6w4d:       Mask /30
6w4d: OSPF: Rcv Update Type 3, LSID 10.1.1.4, Adv rtr 1.1.1.1, age 107, seq 0x80
000001
6w4d:       Mask /30
6w4d: OSPF: Rcv Update Type 3, LSID 10.1.1.0, Adv rtr 1.1.1.1, age 353, seq 0x80
000110
6w4d:       Mask /30
6w4d: OSPF: Rcv Update Type 3, LSID 8.8.8.0, Adv rtr 1.1.1.1, age 107, seq 0x800
00001
6w4d:       Mask /27
6w4d: OSPF: Rcv Update Type 3, LSID 4.4.4.4, Adv rtr 1.1.1.1, age 107, seq 0x800
00001
6w4d:       Mask /32
6w4d: OSPF: Rcv Update Type 3, LSID 2.2.2.2, Adv rtr 1.1.1.1, age 107, seq 0x800
00001
6w4d:       Mask /32
6w4d: OSPF: Rcv Update Type 3, LSID 1.1.1.1, Adv rtr 1.1.1.1, age 353, seq 0x800
00110
6w4d:       Mask /32
```

continues

```
6w4d: OSPF: Rcv Update Type 4, LSID 4.4.4.4, Adv rtr 1.1.1.1, age 107, seq 0x800
00001
6w4d:       Mask /0
6w4d: OSPF: Rcv Update Type 5, LSID 169.254.0.0, Adv rtr 4.4.4.4, age 989, seq 0
x80000090
6w4d:       Mask /15
6w4d: %OSPF-5-ADJCHG: Process 1, Nbr 1.1.1.1 on Serial0/1 from LOADING to FULL,
Loading Done
… (many more pages of output!!!)
```

Example 2: Selective Display of OSPF Protocol Debugging Output

For this example, only flooding protocol information for LSAs with an ID of 172.16.1.0/24 will be displayed.

```
access-list 1 permit 172.16.1.0 0.0.0.255

r6#debug ip ospf flood 1
OSPF flooding debugging is on for access list 1
r6#clear ip ospf process
Reset ALL OSPF processes? [no]: yes
r6#
6w4d: Inc retrans unit nbr count index 1 (0/1) to 1/1
6w4d: Set Nbr 1.1.1.1 1 first flood info from 0 (0) to 623AA408 (303)
6w4d: Init Nbr 1.1.1.1 1 next flood info to 623AA408
6w4d: OSPF: Start Serial0/1 1.1.1.1 retrans timer
6w4d: Set idb next flood info from 0 (0) to 623AA408 (303)
6w4d: OSPF: Start Serial0/1 pacing timer
6w4d: Create retrans unit 0x623B71A8/0x623C5DE8 1 (0/1) 1
6w4d: OSPF: Set nbr 1 (0/1) retrans to 4504 count to 1
6w4d: Set idb next flood info from 623AA408 (303) to 0 (0)
6w4d: OSPF: Stop Serial0/1 flood timer
6w4d: %OSPF-5-ADJCHG: Process 1, Nbr 1.1.1.1 on Serial0/1 from FULL to DOWN,
Neighbor Down: Interface down or detached
6w4d: Dec retrans unit nbr count index 1 (0/1) to 0/0
6w4d: Free nbr retrans unit 0x623B71A8/0x623C5DE8 0 total 0. Also Free nbr
retrans block
6w4d: Set Nbr 1.1.1.1 1 first flood info from 623AA408 (303) to 0 (0)
6w4d: Adjust Nbr 1.1.1.1 1 next flood info to 0
6w4d: OSPF: Stop nbr 1.1.1.1 retransmission timer
6w4d: OSPF: Build router LSA for area 7, router ID 6.6.6.6, seq 0x80000001
6w4d: OSPF: received update from 1.1.1.1, Serial0/1
6w4d: OSPF: Rcv Update Type 3, LSID 172.16.1.0, Adv rtr 1.1.1.1, age 287, seq 0x
80000001
6w4d:       Mask /24
6w4d: %OSPF-5-ADJCHG: Process 1, Nbr 1.1.1.1 on Serial0/1 from LOADING to FULL,
Loading Done
6w4d: Inc retrans unit nbr count index 1 (0/1) to 1/1
6w4d: Set Nbr 1.1.1.1 1 first flood info from 0 (0) to 623AA324 (304)
6w4d: Init Nbr 1.1.1.1 1 next flood info to 623AA324
6w4d: OSPF: Start Serial0/1 1.1.1.1 retrans timer
```

```
6w4d: Set idb next flood info from 0 (0) to 623AA324 (304)
6w4d: OSPF: Start Serial0/1 pacing timer
6w4d: OSPF: Build router LSA for area 7, router ID 6.6.6.6, seq 0x80000002
6w4d: Create retrans unit 0x623B71A8/0x623C5DE8 1 (0/1) 1
6w4d: OSPF: Set nbr 1 (0/1) retrans to 4568 count to 1
6w4d: Set idb next flood info from 623AA324 (304) to 0 (0)
6w4d: OSPF: Stop Serial0/1 flood timer
6w4d: Update router LSA 6.6.6.6 6.6.6.6 1 80000126
6w4d: OSPF: Rate limit LSA generation for 6.6.6.6 6.6.6.6 1
6w4d: OSPF: Sending delayed ACK on Serial0/1
6w4d: OSPF: Ack Type 3, LSID 172.16.1.0, Adv rtr 1.1.1.1, age 287, seq 0x8000000
1
6w4d: OSPF: Set nbr 1 (0/1) retrans to 4960 count to 2
6w4d: Set Nbr 1.1.1.1 1 next flood info from 623AA324 (304) to 623AA324 (304)
6w4d: Dec retrans unit nbr count index 1 (0/1) to 0/0
6w4d: Free nbr retrans unit 0x623B71A8/0x623C5DE8 0 total 0. Also Free nbr
retrans block
ns block
6w4d: Adjust Nbr 1.1.1.1 1 next flood info to 0
6w4d: OSPF: Stop nbr 1.1.1.1 retransmission timer
6w4d: Inc retrans unit nbr count index 1 (0/1) to 1/1
6w4d: Set Nbr 1.1.1.1 1 first flood info from 0 (0) to 623AA324 (305)
6w4d: Init Nbr 1.1.1.1 1 next flood info to 623AA324
6w4d: OSPF: Start Serial0/1 1.1.1.1 retrans timer
6w4d: Set idb next flood info from 0 (0) to 623AA324 (305)
6w4d: OSPF: Start Serial0/1 pacing timer
6w4d: OSPF: Build router LSA for area 7, router ID 6.6.6.6, seq 0x80000127
6w4d: Create retrans unit 0x623B71A8/0x623C5DE8 1 (0/1) 1
6w4d: OSPF: Set nbr 1 (0/1) retrans to 4576 count to 1
6w4d: Set idb next flood info from 623AA324 (305) to 0 (0)
6w4d: OSPF: Stop Serial0/1 flood timer
6w4d: OSPF: Set nbr 1 (0/1) retrans to 4596 count to 2
6w4d: Set Nbr 1.1.1.1 1 next flood info from 623AA324 (305) to 623AA324 (305)
6w4d: Dec retrans unit nbr count index 1 (0/1) to 0/0
6w4d: Free nbr retrans unit 0x623B71A8/0x623C5DE8 0 total 0. Also Free nbr retra
ns block
6w4d: Set Nbr 1.1.1.1 1 first flood info from 623AA324 (305) to 0 (0)
6w4d: Adjust Nbr 1.1.1.1 1 next flood info to 0
6w4d: OSPF: Stop nbr 1.1.1.1 retransmission timer
```

21-5: debug ip ospf lsa-generation

21-6: debug ip ospf lsa-generation *ip-access-list-number*

Syntax Description:

- *ip-access-list-number*—Number of the IP access list used to filter the output of the **flood** command. Valid ranges are 1 to 99 and 1300 to 1999.

Purpose: To display information regarding the generation and flooding of summary LSAs.

Example: Displaying the Successful Formation of an OSPF Adjacency

The following is representative output from the **debug ip ospf lsa-generation** EXEC command on a router that is redistributing EIGRP routes into OSPF.

```
r4#debug ip ospf lsa-generation
OSPF summary lsa generation debugging is on
r4#clear ip ospf process
Reset ALL OSPF processes? [no]: yes
r4#
6w4d: %OSPF-5-ADJCHG: Process 1, Nbr 2.2.2.2 on Ethernet1/0 from FULL to DOWN,
Neighbor Down: Interface down or detached
6w4d: %OSPF-5-ADJCHG: Process 1, Nbr 3.3.3.3 on Ethernet0/0 from FULL to DOWN,
Neighbor Down: Interface down or detached
6w4d: OSPF: Start redist-scanning
6w4d: OSPF: Scan the RIB for both redistribution and translation
6w4d: OSPF: net 169.254.0.0 up, new metric decreases: old 16777215, new 10
6w4d: OSPF: Generate external LSA 169.254.0.0, mask 255.254.0.0, type 5, age 0,
metric 10, tag 0, metric-type 2, seq 0x80000001
6w4d: OSPF: generate external LSA for summary 169.254.0.0 255.254.0.0, metric 10

6w4d: OSPF: End scanning, Elapsed time 4ms
6w4d: %OSPF-5-ADJCHG: Process 1, Nbr 3.3.3.3 on Ethernet0/0 from LOADING to FULL
, Loading Done
6w4d: OSPF: Generate external LSA 169.254.0.0, mask 255.254.0.0, type 5, age 0,
metric 10, tag 0, metric-type 2, seq 0x80000091
6w4d: %OSPF-5-ADJCHG: Process 1, Nbr 2.2.2.2 on Ethernet1/0 from LOADING to FULL
, Loading Done
```

21-7: debug ip ospf packet

Syntax Description:

This command has no arguments.

Purpose: To display OSPF packet information.

Example: Displaying OSPF Packet Information

The following is representative output from the **debug ip ospf packet** EXEC command.

```
r6#debug ip ospf packet
OSPF packet debugging is on
r6#
6w4d: OSPF: rcv. v:2 t:1 l:48 rid:1.1.1.1
      aid:0.0.0.7 chk:0 aut:2 keyid:8 seq:0xC from Serial0/1
```

Table 21-1 provides a description for the highlighted lines of output as follows:

Table 21-1 *Explanation for* **debug ip ospf packet** *Output*

Field	What It Represents
v:	OSPF version
t:	Packet type: 1 – Hello 2 – Database Description 3 – Link-State Request 4 – Link-State Update 5 – Link-State Acknowledgement
l:	Packet length in bytes
rid:	OSPF router ID
aid:	OSPF area ID
aut:	Authentication used: 0 – None 1 – Simple password 2 – MD5
keyid:	MD5 authentication key
seq:	Sequence number
From	Interface that received the packet

21-8: debug ip ospf retransmission

Syntax Description:

The command has no parameters.

Purpose: To display OSPF LSA retransmission events. The link-state retransmission list is a list of LSAs that have been flooded but not acknowledged by an OSPF neighbor. The unacknowledged LSAs will be retransmitted at intervals until they are acknowledged, or until the adjacency with the neighbor is removed.

21-9: debug ip ospf spf

21-10: debug ip ospf spf external

21-11: debug ip ospf spf external *access-list-number*

21-12: debug ip ospf spf inter

21-13: debug ip ospf spf inter *access-list-number*

21-14: debug ip ospf spf intra

21-15: debug ip ospf spf intra *access-list-number*

Syntax Description:

- *ip-access-list-number*—Number of the IP access list used to filter the output of the **debug ip ospf spf** command. Valid ranges are 1 to 99 and 1300 to 1999.

Purpose: To display OSPF shortest path first (SPF) calculations.

Example: Displaying SPF Output for External OSPF Routes

The following is representative output from the **debug ip ospf spf external** EXEC command.

```
r4#debug ip ospf spf external
OSPF spf external events debugging is on
r6#
6w4d: OSPF: Started Building Type 5 External Routes
6w4d: OSPF: Start processing Type 5 External LSA 169.254.0.0, mask 255.254.0.0,
adv 4.4.4.4, age 39, seq 0x80000095, metric 10, metric-type 2
6w4d: OSPF: Did not find route to ASBR 4.4.4.4
6w4d: OSPF: ex_delete_old_routes
6w4d: OSPF: Started Building Type 7 External Routes
6w4d: OSPF: ex_delete_old_routes
6w4d: OSPF: Started Building Type 5 External Routes
6w4d: OSPF: Start processing Type 5 External LSA 169.254.0.0, mask 255.254.0.0,
adv 4.4.4.4, age 49, seq 0x80000095, metric 10, metric-type 2
6w4d:     Add better path to LSA ID 169.254.0.0, gateway 10.1.1.18, dist 10
6w4d:     Add path: next-hop 10.1.1.18, interface Serial0/1
6w4d:     Add External Route to 169.254.0.0. Metric: 10, Next Hop: 10.1.1.18
6w4d: OSPF: insert route list LS ID 169.254.0.0, type 5, adv rtr 4.4.4.4
6w4d: OSPF: ex_delete_old_routes
6w4d: OSPF: Started Building Type 7 External Routes
6w4d: OSPF: ex_delete_old_routes
```

CHAPTER 22

clear Commands

22-1: clear ip ospf counters

22-2: clear ip ospf *process-id* counters

22-3: clear ip ospf *process-id* counters neighbor

22-4: clear ip ospf *process-id* counters neighbor *int-name int-number*

Syntax Description:

- *process-id*—The OSPF process ID. The range of values is from 1 to 4,294,967,295.
- *int-name*—Interface name.
- *int-number*—Interface number.

Purpose: To reset neighbor state transition counters.

Initial Cisco IOS Software Release: 11.1

Example: Viewing and Clearing OSPF Neighbor State Transition Counters

The **show ip ospf neighbor detail** command is used to display the neighbor state transition counter.

```
r4#show ip ospf neighbor detail
 Neighbor 2.2.2.2, interface address 172.16.2.1
    In the area 0 via interface Ethernet1/0
    Neighbor priority is 1, State is FULL, 6 state changes
    DR is 172.16.2.2 BDR is 172.16.2.1
```

continues

```
    Options is 0x42
    Dead timer due in 00:00:38
    Neighbor is up for 01:06:06
    Index 2/2, retransmission queue length 0, number of retransmission 1
    First 0x0(0)/0x0(0) Next 0x0(0)/0x0(0)
    Last retransmission scan length is 1, maximum is 1
    Last retransmission scan time is 0 msec, maximum is 0 msec
```

The **clear ip ospf counters** command will reset the state transition counter to 0.

```
r4#clear ip ospf counters
r4#show ip ospf neighbor detail
 Neighbor 2.2.2.2, interface address 172.16.2.1
    In the area 0 via interface Ethernet1/0
    Neighbor priority is 1, State is FULL, 0 state changes
    DR is 172.16.2.2 BDR is 172.16.2.1
    Options is 0x42
    Dead timer due in 00:00:33
    Neighbor is up for 01:11:01
    Index 2/2, retransmission queue length 0, number of retransmission 1
    First 0x0(0)/0x0(0) Next 0x0(0)/0x0(0)
    Last retransmission scan length is 1, maximum is 1
    Last retransmission scan time is 0 msec, maximum is 0 msec
```

22-5: clear ip ospf process

22-6: clear ip ospf *process-id* process

Syntax Description:

- *process-id*—The OSPF process ID. The range of values is from 1 to 4,294,967,295.

Purpose: To reset and restart all OSPF processes or a specific OSPF process on the local router. Be aware that routes learned via OSPF will be cleared until the OSPF routing process re-establishes adjacencies with neighbor routers.

Initial Cisco IOS Software Release: 11.1

22-7: clear ip ospf redistribution

22-8: clear ip ospf *process-id* redistribition

Syntax Description:

- *process-id*—The OSPF process ID. The range of values is from 1 to 4,294,967,295.

Purpose: To clear routes that have been redistributed into OSPF.

Initial Cisco IOS Software Release: 11.1

INDEX

A

B

C

D

E

F

G

H

I-J

K

L

M

N

O

P-Q

R

S

T

U

V

W-Z

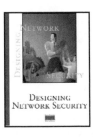

Cisco Press Solutions

EIGRP Network Design Solutions

Ivan Pepelnjak, CCIE

1-57870-165-1 • **Available Now**

EIGRP Network Design Solutions uses case studies and real-world configuration examples to help you gain an in-depth understanding of the issues involved in designing, deploying, and managing EIGRP-based networks. This book details proper designs that can be used to build large and scalable EIGRP-based networks and documents possible ways each EIGRP feature can be used in network design, implmentation, troubleshooting, and monitoring.

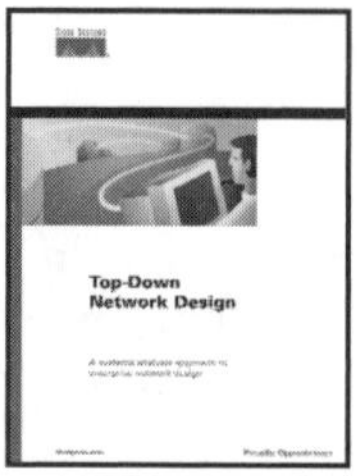

Top-Down Network Design

Priscilla Oppenheimer

1-57870-069-8 • **Available Now**

Building reliable, secure, and manageable networks is every network professional's goal. This practical guide teaches you a systematic method for network design that can be applied to campus LANs, remote-access networks, WAN links, and large-scale internetworks. Learn how to analyze business and technical requirements, examine traffic flow and Quality of Service requirements, and select protocols and technologies based on performance goals.

Cisco IOS Releases: The Complete Reference

Mack M. Coulibaly

1-57870-179-1 • **Available Now**

Cisco IOS Releases: The Complete Reference is the first comprehensive guide to the more than three dozen types of Cisco IOS releases being used today on enterprise and service provider networks. It details the release process and its numbering and naming conventions, as well as when, where, and how to use the various releases. A complete map of Cisco IOS software releases and their relationships to one another, in addition to insights into decoding information contained within the software, make this book an indispensable resource for any network professional.

Cisco Press

Committed to being your long-term learning resource while you grow as a Cisco Networking Professional

Help Cisco Press **stay connected** to the issues and challenges you face on a daily basis by registering your product and filling out our brief survey. Complete and mail this form, or better yet ...

Register online and enter to win a FREE book!

Jump to **www.ciscopress.com/register** and register your product online. Each complete entry will be eligible for our monthly drawing to win a FREE book of the winner's choice from the Cisco Press library.

May we contact you via e-mail with information about **new releases, special promotions**, and **customer benefits**?

❒ Yes ❒ No

E-mail address ____________________

Name ____________________

Address ____________________

City ____________________ State/Province ____________________

Country ____________________ Zip/Post code ____________________

Where did you buy this product?

❒ Bookstore ❒ Computer store/Electronics store ❒ Direct from Cisco Systems
❒ Online retailer ❒ Direct from Cisco Press ❒ Office supply store
❒ Mail order ❒ Class/Seminar ❒ Discount store
❒ Other ____________________

When did you buy this product? __________ **Month** __________ **Year**

What price did you pay for this product?

❒ Full retail price ❒ Discounted price ❒ Gift

Was this purchase reimbursed as a company expense?

❒ Yes ❒ No

How did you learn about this product?

❒ Friend ❒ Store personnel ❒ In-store ad ❒ cisco.com
❒ Cisco Press catalog ❒ Postcard in the mail ❒ Saw it on the shelf ❒ ciscopress.com
❒ Other catalog ❒ Magazine ad ❒ Article or review
❒ School ❒ Professional organization ❒ Used other products
❒ Other ____________________

What will this product be used for?

❒ Business use ❒ School/Education
❒ Certification training ❒ Professional development/Career growth
❒ Other ____________________

How many years have you been employed in a computer-related industry?

❒ less than 2 years ❒ 2–5 years ❒ more than 5 years

Have you purchased a Cisco Press product before?

❒ Yes ❒ No

CISCO SYSTEMS

Cisco Press

ciscopress.com

How many computer technology books do you own?

- ❒ 1
- ❒ 2–7
- ❒ more than 7

Which best describes your job function? (check all that apply)

- ❒ Corporate Management
- ❒ Network Design
- ❒ Marketing/Sales
- ❒ Professor/Teacher
- ❒ Systems Engineering
- ❒ Network Support
- ❒ Consultant
- ❒ Other ______________________
- ❒ IS Management
- ❒ Webmaster
- ❒ Student
- ❒ Cisco Networking Academy Program Instuctor

Do you hold any computer certifications? (check all that apply)

- ❒ MCSE
- ❒ CCNP
- ❒ CCNA
- ❒ CCDP
- ❒ CCDA
- ❒ CCIE
- ❒ Other ______________

Are you currently pursuing a certification? (check all that apply)

- ❒ MCSE
- ❒ CCNP
- ❒ CCNA
- ❒ CCDP
- ❒ CCDA
- ❒ CCIE
- ❒ Other ______________

On what topics would you like to see more coverage?

____

____

Do you have any additional comments or suggestions?

____

____

Thank you for completing this survey and registration. Please fold here, seal, and mail to Cisco Press.

Cisco OSPF Command and Configuration Handbook (1-58705-071-4)

Cisco Press
201 West 103rd Street
Indianapolis, IN 46290
ciscopress.com

Place
Stamp
Here

Cisco Press
Customer Registration—CP0500227
P.O. Box #781046
Indianapolis, IN 46278-8046